THE ETHICS CHALLENGE IN PUBLIC SERVICE

A Problem-Solving Guide

SECOND EDITION

Carol W. Lewis
Stuart C. Gilman

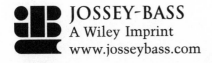

JOSSEY-BASS
A Wiley Imprint
www.josseybass.com

Published by Jossey-Bass
A Wiley Imprint
989 Market Street, San Francisco, CA 94103-1741   www.josseybass.com

Jossey-Bass books and products are available through most bookstores. To contact Jossey-Bass directly call our Customer Care Department within the U.S. at 800-956-7739, outside the U.S. at 317-572-3986 or fax 317-572-4002.

Jossey-Bass also publishes its books in a variety of electronic formats. Some content that appears in print may not be available in electronic books.

Library of Congress Cataloging-in-Publication Data
Lewis, Carol W. (Carol Weiss), 1946-
  The ethics challenge in public service : a problem-solving guide / by Carol W. Lewis, Stuart C. Gilman.—2nd ed.
    p. cm.
  Includes bibliographical references and index.
  ISBN 0-7879-6756-4 (alk. paper)
  1. Civil service ethics—United States. I. Gilman, Stuart. II. Title.
  JK468.E7L49 2005
  172'.2'0973—dc22
                     2004028269

Printed in the United States of America
SECOND EDITION
HB Printing   10 9 8 7 6 5 4 3 2

CONTENTS

PART ONE: ETHICAL RESPONSIBILITIES OF PUBLIC MANAGERS   19

EXHIBITS, TABLES, AND FIGURES

Exhibits

Tables

Figures

To our colleagues and students

PREFACE

Why write a second edition of *The Ethics Challenge in Public Service?* In his *Metamorphoses*, Ovid tells us that *"omnia mutantu"* (everything changes). Much has changed since this book's initial publication. Then why not just write a completely new book? Our historical perspective also reminds us that *plus ça change, plus c'est la même chose* (the more things change, the more they stay the same). So we opted for writing an update and taking a broader look across time and around the profession and the globe. The breadth of the undertaking, the pace and volume of change, and the value we place on intellectual exchange explain why we decided to collaborate in this effort.

This book's subject is managing in—not moralizing about—today's public service. It is written for professional managers in public agencies, where unprecedented demands for ethical judgment and decisive action resound at increasingly higher decibel levels.

Yet there is something about ethics that triggers nostalgia. It seems that people are not what they were. Except for classical music (the golden oldies of rock), ethics is the only subject we know of that sets off a yearning for the old days in young and old, public servants and private citizens alike.

Some argue that World War II was a watershed; after that war, moral decay set in. Others single out the political activists and hippies of the 1960s—beaded and bearded youths who pointed disrespectfully at their parents and political leaders and today symbolize intergenerational conflict, lack of self-discipline, and rejection of community standards. Still others cite the baby boomers—grown into yuppies by the 1980s—who drove Ivan Boesky's ethic "Greed is good" to its limits and faxed us new national symbols of greed and corruption. Then the century turns, and we discover low ethics in high places: scandals rock boardrooms, bedrooms, Wall Street, and Sunbelt freeways. Along Washington's Beltway, defense procurement attracts procurers, and federal programs fall to the fixers.

Common wisdom has it that a pervasive disillusionment and loss of confidence touch political, economic, and even religious leaders and institutions on America's Main Street. Bill Moyers (1988, pp. 81–82) captured the perceived change by quoting two well-known sports ethics. The 1920s coached, "It is not that you won or lost but how you played the game." By the 1960s, the coaching outlook had become "Winning isn't everything. It's the only thing."

Is behavior today better or worse? Is there more corruption in government and society generally? Is moral character—that ingrained sense of right and wrong—a thing of the past? There really is no evidence either way, except through anecdotes, media images, and public opinion polls. More important (and the reason these questions are not confronted with evidence and argument in this book) is that the answers are intellectually interesting but practically irrelevant to managers in public service. First, we have no choice but to depend on the moral character of public managers and employees. Our whole system is built on the premise that they have good character. Second, to work at all, public managers must work with what is here now. Nostalgia contributes nothing to daily operations; it solves no ethical problems on the job.

We would argue that public service attracts a special breed and that the majority of the many millions of practicing and aspiring public managers and employees are well intentioned and do bring good moral character to public service. It is the job itself—the ambiguous, complex, pressured world of public service—that presents special problems for ethical people who want to do the right thing. The job is a site that reinforces moral character and engages adults in a dialogue about ethics where it counts. And count it does, for supervisors, subordinates, colleagues, citizens, taxpayers, people around the world, and generations to come.

Our Approach to the Challenge

Given our purpose of promoting ethical practice and assisting ethical managers in making ethical decisions, we opt for a managerial perspective. *The Ethics Challenge in Public Service* is designed for managers and is meant to be a shortcut through a mass of information and alternatives. We chose issues according to our assessment of their current and future managerial impact rather than academic coinage or strictly philosophical import.

Our method is, first, to link good character with the special values and principles that distinguish public from personal ethics. The spirit of informed individual judgment pervades our arguments, and the same rationalist approach obligates us to provide readers with some explanations of inclusions, omissions, emphases, and biases. We assume the following:

- Public ethics is different from personal ethics.
- The dominant values and guiding principles are different.
- The burdens are heavier.

Second, we provide practical tools and techniques for resolving workaday dilemmas at the individual and agency levels. Third, our purpose is to help ethical managers structure the work environment so that it fosters ethical behavior and eases the transition of good intentions into meaningful action in the agency.

The cases included here illustrate problems or are test runs in applied problem solving. They allow readers to practice in private (and at no public cost) until, following Aristotle, ethics becomes a habit. The cases exercise the two-step by requiring: (1) informed, systematic reasoning and (2) followed by action. The open-ended questions encourage analysis, and other questions force decision making. Some resolutions depend on empathy and imagination. Cases work best when readers alter decision premises and circumstances to double-check ethical judgments or reconcile different philosophical perspectives. The cases, like the book, are driven by democratic processes, for which accommodation is the vehicle and tolerance the grease.

Overview of the Contents

This book offers some tools and techniques that professional public managers can use to meet the demands for making ethical judgments and taking decisive action on the job. In sum, what counts? What is at stake? How can managers ensure ethical survival and professional success? Veterans and rookies alike may wonder now and then, Are both possible? The answer here is an emphatic *yes*. We argue that ethics and genuine success march together.

The Ethics Challenge in Public Service examines these questions in terms of managerial realities and their ethical dimensions, which together shape the book's structure. The Introduction offers readers a look at ethical issues encountered on the job and in the profession. In Part One, public service ethics is rooted in moral character and anchored in ethical values and principle. Chapter One distinguishes public service ethics from personal morality and shows how contending values and many cross-pressures translate into a personally demanding, ambiguous, complex context for everyday decision making. One of public service's special ethical claims on the manager is to implement and comply with the law; an elementary decision-making model given in Chapter Two helps decision makers act on legal obligations without devaluing other considerations. The obligation of serving the public interest entails empathy, as well as respect, for future generations and spawns the public service standards regarding conflict of interest, impartiality, and the appearance of impropriety under public scrutiny (Chapter Three). Combined with the idea of individual responsibility, these obligations are converted, in Chapter Four, into general guides to action for managers who work in an organizational context: individual responsibility for decisions and behavior, for what is done and how, and for professional competence. The obligations and action guides are the ethical underpinnings for doing public service.

The earlier chapters expose the problems, conflicts, and claims shouldered by the public manager. Now the task, in Part Two, is to provide tools for reconciling and sorting them ethically. In these chapters, we discuss individual managers who make ethical decisions and live with the consequences. Ethical reasoning is grounded in commonsense and different philosophical perspectives that lead to varying outlooks on what is important in particular decisions; experience and political tradition advise impartiality and open-mindedness over ethical extremism (Chapter Five). Using a decision-making model that allows for contending viewpoints and values, managers gear up for fact finding, accommodating, and making selective trade-offs that lead to the informed, principled choices managers must make (Chapter Six). The obligation to avoid doing harm is reconciled with collective action and selective action. Practical tools and techniques for resolving workaday dilemmas help answer questions about *what* counts (obligations and responsibilities in Chapter Six) and *who* counts (stakeholders in Chapter Seven). Ethical managers are counted as well, and principled discrimination in responding to ethical offenses equips managers to discount trivialities and survive professionally, with integrity intact (Chapter Seven).

Moving from the individual to the organization, Part Three looks at ethics in the agency. Ethics codes and ethics systems—their functions, development, and management—in all their variety, are benchmarks for the current record and forecasts of things to come (Chapter Eight). What can professional public managers learn from the global movement in public service ethics? Chapter Nine offers a glance at colleagues in other administrative settings so that we may better understand and appreciate our own. A look around at the global context is an efficient way to push back boundaries and a useful way to trigger the moral imagination. In Chapter Ten, the supervisory function—a central managerial responsibility—turns the spotlight on organizational interaction. In a host of ways, including modeling, the manager shapes ethical conduct and the ethical organization. Supervising employee time is an ongoing stress point and demands special care. Workforce diversity, alternate recruitment channels, mixed administrative settings, and collaborative relationships, illustrated by the procurement function, are among the current challenges (Chapter Ten). Chapter Ten argues that routine agency operations set the organization's ethical tone, and these operations can be structured to support and promote ethical action.

Throughout, *The Ethics Challenge in Public Service* pays special attention to what lies ahead on the manager's agenda; with an eye on the future, the Afterword draws together the book's major themes.

January 2005

Carol W. Lewis
Storrs, Connecticut

Stuart C. Gilman
Manassas, Virginia

ACKNOWLEDGMENTS

Now to the customary IOUs, which are heartfelt. A fitting start is to acknowledge the many individual and institutional contributors to the first edition. Foremost among these are the University of Connecticut, the American Society for Public Administration (ASPA), Bayard L. Catron, professor emeritus at George Washington University, and the many practitioners, professors, and students who contributed in so many ways.

The University of Connecticut and the Ethics Resource Center (ERC) supported the second edition with words and resources, and we are grateful for both. The University of Connecticut's Roper Center and its staff provided guidance and survey data; many practitioners in numerous forums, as well as students in academic settings, willingly provided feedback on cases and exercises. Brian Baird, a doctoral student in engineering at the University of Connecticut and research assistant in the Connecticut Center for Economic Analysis, deserves a special salute for his graphics work. As a graduate student in the master's of public administration program at the University of Connecticut, Jason Guilietti enthusiastically assisted with research. The ERC staff's support is much appreciated.

An overview of practices and purposes cannot be written in glorious isolation, off in an ivory tower that is reputedly unaffected by deferred maintenance or other realities. Our deep appreciation is extended to individual managers and academics throughout the country and abroad who responded generously to requests or volunteered assistance. Government offices on many continents, state and local ethics commissions, public interest groups, professional associations, private research groups, consulting firms, and individual authors responded to requests for information or research materials. By their very nature, citations note only those contributions ultimately incorporated, but broad assistance nourished the project.

By combining kindness with criticism, the colleagues, friends, and family who read parts of the draft manuscript confirm what we have long suspected: public service is part diplomacy. Bayard L. Catron, Morton J. Tenzer, James R. Heichelbech, George H. Frederickson, Richard Vengroff, Robert Bifulco, Elizabeth Keller, Charles Fox, Alexis Halley, and others offered perceptive comments and valuable suggestions.

It is standard practice among authors who draw on so many resources, contributors, and talents to close with a disclaimer on behalf of others and to take the responsibility for errors, omissions, and choices solely on themselves. Doing so is easy here, simply because it is not a formality but a statement of fact. And with a subject such as ethics, which is open to nuance, bias, opinion, and contention, there are not so many facts that such an important one should be discounted.

THE AUTHORS

Carol W. Lewis is professor of political science at the University of Connecticut, where she teaches ethics, public budgeting, and public administration. A Phi Beta Kappa graduate of Cornell, she received her B.A. (1967) degree in government. Her M.A. (1970) and Ph.D. (1975) degrees in politics are from Princeton University. Lewis's teaching and research interests include public budgeting and financial management and ethics in public service.

Lewis has taught in colleges and universities in four states, lectured to scholars and practitioners nationally and internationally, and conducted training programs for public managers in many locales. As consultant or project member, she has worked with the World Bank, International Institute of Administrative Sciences, the U.S. National Academy of Public Administration, cross-national projects with the U.S. Department of Housing and Urban Development, and government agencies at all levels.

Lewis has designed and delivered ethics programs for numerous government agencies, public interest organizations, and professional associations. Examples include the Brookings Institution, Council of State Governments, Connecticut General Assembly, International Personnel Management Association, Government Finance Officers Association, National Association of State Training and Development Directors (regional and state), and other associations in her home and other states.

Writing for professional managers, Lewis has published in *Public Manager,* the Council on Governmental Ethics Laws' *Guardian,* the Government Finance Officers Association's *Government Finance Review,* and the International City Management

Association's *Municipal Year Book* and *Public Management*. Her popular publications on ethics include articles in the *Hartford Courant*. Her numerous scholarly articles have appeared in *Public Administration Review, Urban Affairs Quarterly, Municipal Finance Journal, Publius,* and other journals. She is coeditor of several books and handbooks for practitioners and the author of *Scruples & Scandals: A Handbook on Public Service Ethics for State and Local Government Officials and Employees in Connecticut* (1986).

As a state employee, elected union representative, consultant, trainer, writer, professor, and former public official in elective office, Lewis confronts many issues addressed in this book firsthand.

Stuart C. Gilman is an independent consultant in Washington, D.C. He is a 1970 graduate of the University of New Orleans and received his M.A. in 1971 and Ph.D. in 1974 in political science from Miami University. He completed postdoctoral work at the Center for Advanced Study in the Behavioral Sciences at Stanford University, the University of Virginia, and the Senior Managers in Government Program at Harvard University. Gilman taught at Eastern Kentucky University, the University of Richmond, and Saint Louis University. Subsequently, he served as Professor of Ethics and Public Policy at the Federal Executive Institute in Charlottesville, Virginia. He also held adjunct professorships at Georgetown University and George Washington University.

Appointed the first associate director for education at the U.S. Office of Government Ethics in 1988, Gilman subsequently served as director of strategic development for the U.S. Treasury's inspector general for tax and as president of the Ethics Resource Center. He has been an ethics consultant for state governments and federal agencies and for large corporations and nonprofit organizations, as well as multinational organizations such as the World Bank. Gilman has been an ethics consultant for governments as diverse as Egypt, Japan, South Africa, Argentina, and Romania, New Zealand, and the Philippines.

Gilman is a recipient of many awards, including the OGE Director's Award for exemplary work in international anticorruption efforts, and awards for excellence and individual accomplishment from the President's Council on Integrity and Efficiency.

Gilman has coauthored several books and monographs and contributed to many journals, including *Public Integrity, The ANNALS, Public Administration Review, Government, Law and Public Policy, The Public Manager,* the *Journal of Public Inquiry, Ethikos,* and *Practising Manager* (Australia).

As an ethics practitioner, Gilman has worked with individuals confronting a variety of ethical dilemmas and problems, from line procurement officials to cabinet secretaries and from prime ministers to local judges and prosecutors. Experienced as he is in the trenches, he understands how important ethics is to public administrators.

The Ethics Challenge in Public Service

INTRODUCTION

Ethics in Public Service

Ethics and genuine professional success go together in the enterprise called *public service*. How? Why? The answers stem from the links between ethics and professionalism in a democracy. So, we begin here by examining the meaning of *ethics* and *professionalism*—a few definitions mean we talk the same language. Then we take a hard look at public service's track record on these matters. (See Resource A for a chronology of major developments in ethics; Resource B offers readers Internet resources.)

Next, we lay out our own approach to the future by drawing on professional public service's tradition, experience, and current agenda. Our approach blends two standard ones: (1) using compliance measures and (2) depending on individual integrity in decision making. We recommend combining the two into a *fusion approach* (see the compilation of our decision-making tools in Resource C), based on the idea that public service and public employees will both be better served when management chooses the best of both approaches and uses them to move forward with all deliberate speed.

Now, we set the stage for action with some hard questions from real workaday experience:

- Scuttlebutt has it that the new facility in the state-sponsored industrial park is structurally unsound. Maria, the town's building inspector, mulls over doing and saying nothing because it's not her job and the town's tax base certainly could use a boost; besides, she could be wrong.

- Learning that an HIV-positive client refuses to tell or protect the partner and being torn in different directions by law, confidentiality, public safety, and compassion, Bill considers quitting or just settling for a serious case of burnout.
- Your coworker's personal troubles are affecting his work performance. You understand that his irritability and unreliability are temporary, stemming from a messy divorce. Staying late to help finish his monthly reports, you feel your resentment build, and you wonder whether covering for him is good for the agency and fair to you.
- A town ordinance forbids more than four unrelated people to share common living quarters. Verifying a neighbor's complaint on a site visit, you discover a somewhat unorthodox domestic setup by otherwise law-abiding adults. Their lifestyle appears to offend the neighbor. After years in the health department, you know ordinances like these have not stood up in court. Do you start eviction proceedings?

What is the right thing to do? What makes a problem your responsibility, a resolution your obligation? What does the difference between helping someone and not hurting someone mean on the job? What is the right thing to do when the rules push one way and reason or compassion another?

And here is another dilemma:

- The legislature is giving your agency its "fair share": an across-the-board budget cut. Because you have seen to it that your agency is very efficient, it is hard to absorb a cut like this. As the current fiscal year draws to a close, you confirm that there are unexpended funds in an appropriation account. You remember how your first boss ran up the postage meter to buy some slack at the end of the fiscal year.

Where do loyalties lie? When good management is penalized, should a responsible manager circumvent shortsighted economies to protect the agency, its mission, its employees, and service recipients? If an action is legal, does that make it ethical?

About 15 percent of the U.S. civilian labor force works for the government. Of these 21.5 million workers, 23 percent are employed by state and 64 percent by local governments. According to the U.S. Bureau of Labor Statistics, about 56 percent (7.7 million) of all local government employees and 46 percent (2.3 million) of all state government employees work in elementary, secondary, and higher education. The economic downturns in the late 1980s and early 2000s hurt government budgets and public programs, including education, across the country.

An earlier fiscal crisis offers a partial glimpse of the impact of budget cutting. A senior human resource manager in New York City's education headquarters describes her most painful memory. In the city's fiscal crisis of the mid-1970s, her division ranked teachers by seniority in their licensed subject, prepared layoff letters, and listened to pleas and objections. Among the sixteen thousand laid off, there had to be personal tragedies and disrupted lives. The manager said, "I would not have the emotional stamina to live through that again" (Berger, 1990, p. B2).

If pain is not a good-bad meter, how do you know that what you are doing is right? "What am I doing, keeping my job and firing operational employees? What is the agency's purpose, after all?" What is the difference between what is right and what is easy? How do you cope when the job requires dirty work? How do you survive budget-crunch pressures?

The exercise in Exhibit I.1 speaks to the moral content and moral challenge in these types of decisions, and illustrates the power that professional public managers exercise over people's lives.

Public service, which is crucial to society's smooth functioning, sometimes calls for watchful if not downright adversarial relations. Government regulators keep an eye on public land, airwaves, health, safety, and more. Contract compliance officers in the U.S. Department of Defense (DOD) oversee hundreds of billions of dollars each year. Policy analysts connect the dots between legislation and implementation. However, public service often comes up short on rewards when whistle-blowers sound alarms about waste, fraud, and abuse in government agencies. They may even find their complaints in limbo, as relatively small staffs are swamped by rising workloads. At the U.S. Office of Special Counsel, disclosures increased by almost 50 percent after October 1991, to 555 filings in fiscal 2002. But disclosures don't necessarily result in action. "It's like calling 911 and being put on hold." "Hundreds of federal employees risk their careers to blow the whistle, only to find that no one is home to hear it" (Branigan, 2003, p. A4). Some face threats to their career or even their life (Egan, 1990, p. A20). The U.S. Department of Health and Human Services' chief actuary for Medicare costs reported in 2004 that "administration officials threatened to fire him last year if he disclosed to Congress that he believed the prescription drug legislation favored by the White House would prove far more expensive than lawmakers had been told." He said "he nearly resigned in protest because he thought the top Medicare administrator, and perhaps White House officials, were acting against the public interest by withholding information about how much changes to the program would cost" (Goldstein, 2004, p. A1).

If threats and supervisors' approval are no barometers, how do you know you are right? Who is the client and who are the stakeholders? Why buck the system? How do you decide whether to blow the whistle or keep quiet? How do you know what is in the public interest?

Relentless pressures and the need for quick decisions are routine in public service. Because the choices truly matter for everyone, including the public manager, this book examines dilemmas like these and offers some resolutions.

EXHIBIT I.1. CUTBACKS AND PRIORITIES.

Cutback . . . retrenchment . . . downsizing . . . this technical jargon actually translates into withholding help—someone or something is going to lose help or get less.
The challenge is to choose in a way that is (1) ethically principled, (2) legal, (3) politically accountable, (4) publicly and personally defensible, (5) professionally credible
and conforming to best practices, and (6) fiscally and managerially prudent.

Problem. An unexpected drop in state revenue dictates taking immediate steps to
avoid a deficit. In a strategy session, legislative leadership develops guidelines and
asks you, a professional analyst in the nonpartisan office, to use them to rank several programs and recommend cuts.

Priorities. (Priorities are adapted from a letter of December 4, 1990, from Connecticut Office of Policy and Management's Secretary-designate Wm. J. Cibes, Jr., to
agency heads.) These are leadership's priorities for evaluating programs.

    A. Essential to preserve life in long or short term
    B. Provide for health and safety
    C. Avoid significant future harm
    D. Prevent more costly services in future
    E. Contribute to state's fiscal health or revenues
    F. Maintain or enhance quality of life
    G. Obsolete, duplicative, ineffective (alternatives are available or better)

Step #1. Evaluate policies using priorities A to G.
Step #2. Rank policies from critical (5) to worthy (3) to good target for cut (1).

    A-G   1–5 (Letters and numbers may be used more than once.)
    ____ ____ 1. Disaster relief (food, water) for victims' immediate use
    ____ ____ 2. Support for water quality inspection teams
    ____ ____ 3. Computer link to speed processing of vendor and third-party pay-
                    ments (and avoid charges for late payment)
    ____ ____ 4. Funding ambulance and rescue services at subsidized charge to
                    user
    ____ ____ 5. Scheduled pay increases for government employees
    ____ ____ 6. Computer security to protect confidentiality of personal records
                    (client, employee)
    ____ ____ 7. Serving general obligation bonds
    ____ ____ 8. Upkeep of parks and recreational areas

1. Assume funding is zero or 100 percent. Select two programs to be cut (from
   among the programs you ranked "1" or "2").

        # ____   # ____

        Reason for choice: Reason for choice:

2. Are you willing to defend these choices publicly?

3. Is something important missing? What else should we think about?

The Problem
In one form or another, the problem described in the exercise is probably familiar to most public service practitioners. In this example, the task is to recommend immediate steps to counter an impending budget shortfall, and targeting programs to eliminate amounts to withdrawing or denying help. Although individuals opposing certain steps mistakenly or cynically may confuse not helping with purposefully doing harm, it is in fact a very different matter. Avoiding doing harm is the customary minimum ethical duty. But it is also true that someone or something is going to lose help or get less of it. The first option illustrates how moral responsibility often is seen as especially forceful and urgent in matters of life and death or acute, immediate need. Disaster relief therefore may be assigned an "A" or "B" and ranked a "5," meaning that many decision makers will not tolerate this option.

Budgetary measures and fiscal policies through which scarce resources are allocated and costs distributed carry significant moral content. They pronounce the moral judgments that are very much a part of the answer to the classic question posed by V. O. Key, Jr.: "On what basis shall it be decided to allocate X dollars to Activity A instead of activity B?" (Key, 1940). While Key opted for an efficiency criterion, decision makers working through this exercise may find themselves thinking about the people who would be affected, and how. Can they survive the cut? Are we breaking a law or a promise?

Ethical Analysis of Options
The options laid out here speak to ethical issues and claims. The third option of the computer link illustrates how economy so often crowds out efficiency when moral imperatives come into play. Similar reasoning may affect the eighth item, which also carries a substantial future price tag. The third and eighth options, neither involving urgent human harm, were routinely the majority choices in numerous programs conducted by the authors with several thousand practitioners in federal, state, and local government and nonprofit organizations.

The eighth and second options raise questions of stewardship—for whom is the professional administrator a fiduciary? Should anyone speak for the voiceless, future stakeholders? Yet, doesn't this stance dilute immediate democratic responsiveness and accountability? If someone should act as steward, then who? The eighth option also stands for the familiar choice of deferred maintenance, perhaps made relatively palatable by the arguable proposition that current damage can be undone and the harm is temporary at worst.

The fifth option illustrates two main lines of ethical thought—one based on duty and principles, the other grounded in results or consequences. Because denying the salary increase is not itself life-threatening, it may be preferred by decision makers who value consequences; others, more influenced by principles, may reject the fifth option because of the implied broken promise. (The promise-breaking suggests why like choices may trigger a sense of betrayal and moral outrage.)

The seventh choice evokes another promise—implicitly or explicitly sworn—to comply with the law when acting in one's official capacity. Legal compliance, with constitutional obligations at its core, affects both procedural and substantive responsibilities (Rohr, 1989, and Rosenbloom, 1992). Long-term bonded indebtedness represents a legally binding commitment but also prompts consideration of intergenerational equity and higher future costs.

The sixth option points to the concern with information integrity and confidentiality. Considerations of privacy and confidentiality are especially productive sources of ethical dilemmas (and prohibitions) today because of accelerating technological capacity, but also and more fundamentally because they stand as a first line of defense against using people as objects, or instrumentally. For example,

Chicago's ethics ordinance (Chapter 2, 156–070 of municipal code) specifically addresses the issue of confidential information.

> No current or former official or employee shall use or disclose, other than in the performance of his official duties and responsibilities, or as may be required by law, confidential information gained in the course of or by reason of his position or employment. For purposes of this section, "confidential information" means any information that may not be obtained pursuant to the Illinois Freedom of Information Act, as amended.

Reprinted by permission of Marcel Dekker. C. W. Lewis, "Ethics in Public Service." In J. Rabin, R. Munzenrider, and S. M. Bartell (eds.), *Principles and Practices of Public Administration.* New York: Marcell Dekker, 2003b.

Working Definitions

Public sector managers routinely do their jobs, solve problems, and even work some miracles. And they practice ethics besides. Personal, professional, and public expectations converge to challenge managers who voice and resolve both routine and emergency ethical problems. Ethical action is another part of the job.

Only a few definitions are needed so that we can begin a meaningful, practical dialogue. First, *ethics* involves thinking systematically about morals and conduct and making moral choices about right and wrong (making moral judgments) when faced with ethical dilemmas. *Moral choice* and *moral judgment* are explored in Exhibit I.2.

What makes ethics so important to public service is that it goes beyond thought and talk to performance and action. As a guideline for action, ethics draws on what is right and important, or "abstract standards that persist over time and that identify what is right and proper" (Boling and Dempsey, 1981, p. 14). Rooted in the idea of responsibility, ethics implies the willingness to accept the consequences of one's actions. Ethics also refers to principles of action that implement or promote moral values.

Moral character means having appropriate ethical values and is associated with attributes such as honesty and fidelity. Character is a sort of internal gyroscope that helps a person distinguish right from wrong and inhibits wrongdoing. Bringing their moral character to the job, ethical managers do a two-step: (1) they use informed, systematic reasoning and (2) follow it by action.

In sum, the subject of ethics is action based on judgments of right and wrong. Three questions summarize the subject's pragmatic underpinnings: (1) What counts in public service? (2) What is at stake? and (3) How can managers ensure professional success and ethical survival? Finer distinctions and elegant terminology are available for conceptual clarification, but they threaten to bury the subject in semantics, killing interest, along with utility, for practical managers who are more concerned with deeds than definitions.

EXHIBIT I.2. WOULD I? SHOULD I?

Begin by reading the four scenarios, and answer each with a *yes* or *no* on the chart below. Please be spontaneous, go with your gut feel, and be candid. Then answer the two questions below the table.

1. Driving a government vehicle on the most direct route to a late-morning meeting in another town, you pass within a block of a store holding a personal package for you. For efficiency's sake, do you stop by to pick it up?

2. An irresponsible and disagreeable employee is looking for a job in the private sector. To get rid of this person, do you agree to provide a positive reference?

3. Substantiated charges come to light that the likely appointee to the assistant commissioner position (who has public support and political backing) was denied visitation rights because of child abuse a few years ago. Do you advise your new chief to go ahead with the appointment?

4. Through personal business channels, you are privy to information that is not publicly known about a parcel of land your agency is considering for a development program. The information would save the state a material sum now and big headaches later. Because the public interest is at stake, along with your professional standing, do you privately tip off the commissioner?

		Would I do this?	Should I do this?	Would others do this?*
Write *yes* or *no* for each scenario	1. Do personal errand			
	2. Write reference			
	3. Recommend appointment			
	4. Tip off			

*If you think some would, then write in yes. If you don't think this happens now and again, then write in no.

1. Are your responses the same across each row?

    This enterprise demonstrates *moral choice*—the *would-should* divide, the heart of good moral character to which most of us are exposed as children. The *mama test* (what mama would have said) clarifies simple choices between right and wrong.

    But adults must make *moral judgments* when they find themselves between the rock and the hard place of incongruent duties and conflicting claims—the stuff of ethical dilemmas. Unfamiliar situations, organizational and technological impersonality, and professional and public power intensify pressures.

    This exercise illustrates that decision making turns on several factors:
    - Ethical, legal, and pragmatic considerations
    - Others' likely motive
    - One's own concern (seriousness of the ethical issue or offense)
    - Price tag: considerations of career, cost, convenience, competence, commitment, and courage.

2. Does the last column have more *yes* responses than the other columns?

Discussion

As you work through the cases, you may notice that the problems get tougher and more complicated, until the later cases propel you between that rock and a hard place of incongruent claims and competing ethical ideas.

The first case speaks to the experience that for many government employees, using a government vehicle (because of rules on gifts and travel reimbursements) triggers impatience, annoyance, or even outrage over petty controls. But it is not an *ethical* dilemma. It is a relatively simple choice between right versus wrong, virtue versus vice. In fact, many statutes and ordinances restrict the use of public resources and expressly prohibit the use of government cars for personal use. Here we are talking price tag that may surface as courage, or career, or cost considerations. Here it is personal convenience. Perhaps because it *is* relatively trivial—not earth-shattering, not arousing human urgency—it's been known to happen—probably *is* happening somewhere at this moment. Apparently using a cost-to-benefit-to-risk ratio precisely the opposite of a scoundrel's, even ethical people may slip into compromise over seemingly trivial matters.

The first question asks, "Are your responses the same across each row?" Usually, the answer is no. The "Would I?–Should I?" divide captures the heart of good moral character to which most of us are exposed as children, when we learn fundamental ethical perspectives. Because there's probably very little anyone can tell you about these choices that you don't already know, the *mama test* of disclosure is useful for simple moral choices.

How about writing a less-than-candid reference in the second case? Do you think it's ever done? This case is about evasion, lack of candor, perhaps even deception. It is different from the personal errand because it serves the organization rather than the individual. Some people may try to justify it for that very reason. Writing that reference may be useful, may be pragmatic, but it opposes ethical values such as telling the truth and taking responsibility.

Life in public service is not always so clear-cut and raises the need for ethical judgment when facing ethical dilemmas that involve morally unacceptable options or trade-offs. Four factors sum up the difference between childhood moral lessons and the adult world: ambiguity, uncertainty, complexity, and responsibility. As a result, the would-should choice turns on ethical, legal, and practical concerns, attributed motivation, the weight of the ethical issues or offenses, and the price tag. (For Plato's classic example, see "Moral Dilemma," 2001).

The third and fourth cases shove you squarely into that sometimes perplexing adult world. The appointment case illustrates the special responsibilities associated with public service, and how the need for public confidence and trust quickly blurs the line between public and private lives as one becomes professionally more successful, more powerful, and more visible. In the appointment case, vulnerability takes on a human face and vies with moral repugnance. This is a tough call, and well-intentioned people of moral character may disagree.

The last case presents a painful dilemma in which the decision maker struggles with competing obligations: professionalism faces off against the public interest. What's the right thing to do in this fourth case? Confusion? Complexity? Precisely. Wrong versus wrong, right versus right, nuance, and judgment are what dilemmas are all about. When it comes to dilemmas, information is especially productive because (1) accountability is so important in a democracy and relies on the honored virtue of truth telling, and (2) because information is a pivotal resource in modern governance. The case suggests that the price tag for either silence or disclosure may be quite high. Although ethical decision makers may disagree on what is the right thing to do, the tip-off tactic is offensive because it annuls personal responsibility and voids accountability.

Now take a look at the second question. Does your last column have more *yes* responses than other columns? The "Would Others?" column translates into the conventional view of ethics as the other person's problem. People typically express a belief that their own ethical standards are higher than other people's, so we readily anticipate unethical behavior by others. The danger is that, in a search for an excuse for our own unethical conduct, we may slip over the would-should divide and argue "everybody is doing it" or self-defense. Because responsibility is fundamental to ethics, this is an ethically bankrupt argument.

The Scope of Public Service

Public service is *doing* and for that reason is better defined by its public mission—what the manager is doing—than by legal statutes or other formal criteria. For our purposes, *public service* refers to agencies and activities *tending toward* the public side of the continuum shown in Figure I.1. In actuality, there is no clear division between public and private.

Embracing more than government service alone, public service includes quasi-governmental agencies and the many nonprofit organizations devoted to community services and to the public interest (and often publicly funded, at least in part). The many mixed activities and joint operations, such as public-private partnerships and contractual relationships, turn on working with government and are also oriented toward public service. In the United States, the nonprofit or independent sector encompasses all organizations that the IRS classifies as 501(c)(3) and 501(c)(4). "This includes charitable nonprofit organizations; private, family, operating, community, and corporate foundations; and organizations whose primary purpose is advocacy. We call these the organizations of the independent sector" (INDEPENDENT SECTOR, 2004). Almost 6 percent of U.S. organizations are nonprofits. They account for more than 9 percent of paid employees in the United States and more than two-thirds of a trillion dollars in annual revenue. Institutionally dominant, health services represent almost one-half of all U.S. nonprofits (INDEPENDENT SECTOR, 2002).

As a practical matter, there is no autonomous, isolated agency or activity that does not respond to, interact with, or affect those all along the continuum between the public and private sectors. Consider, for example, the following: taxation and corporate decisions; business location and land-use regulation; immigration, government hiring, and the labor pool; Social Security payments and consumer demand; and private producers and government procurement. Most activities, most institutions, and most resources fall between the polar extremes of purely governmental and purely private.

FIGURE I.1. THE PUBLIC-PRIVATE CONTINUUM.

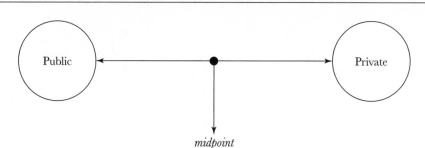

Use four criteria to position an agency on the continuum:
1. Formal source and nature of authority and accountability
2. Source of funding, including taxes, subsidy, marketplace
3. Function, mission, goal, purpose
4. IRS tax status

The first three criteria are of theoretical significance; the fourth is of practical importance.

Because public service is broader than government service, it may be useful to take a moment to think over the status of your agency. Where is your agency on the continuum? Are you a public manager? Should public service standards and obligations apply to you?

A Special Calling

Given their action orientation, savvy public managers logically ask what the point of all the noise about public service ethics really is. Ideally, the point is to promote ethical practice and support ethical practitioners in public service and, through that, in the larger society. Many people (that includes us) unashamedly believe that this purpose underlies most public managers' choice of profession. Rational managers certainly are not in public service solely or even primarily for the money; other inducements also draw them to the office.

That most public managers work to make a positive difference is a central tenet of public service lore. Their goal is to have an impact on more than their own pocketbook. This attitude toward their work recalls President Kennedy's famous line in his 1961 inaugural address: "And so, my fellow Americans, ask not what your country can do for you—ask what you can do for your country." For great and small matters, "May I help you?" could be the public service mantra. The motive of wanting to make a difference means that optimism underlies action and progress is a premier purpose. The hard part about working for the best, however, is knowing what "the best" is and then doing it. This is what ethics is all about.

Disabling or Empowering

Although belief in progress is a public service attribute, it does *not* cast public managers in the role of Don Quixote, tilting at imaginary windmills. It does *not* demand that managers butt futilely against a brick wall. It pays, then, to begin by assessing the situation, that is, finding out what managers actually face.

The profession is animated by the dual potential of ethics to either disable or empower managers. The concern with ethics has the potential for disabling managers if it is used as a coercive control device, an exploitative tool, a subtle motivational gimmick, or a public relations scheme. Alternatively, the concern with ethics can empower managers by promoting ethical practices, supporting ethical managers, and reinforcing accountability.

For many managers (and for us), the first set of possibilities cries out "Stop!" The second signals a careful "Go!" Either way, ethics is "the new political symbol to change controls over the bureaucracy," as Vera Vogelsang-Coombs, a state-manager-turned-academic in the mid-West, remarked in August of 1990. Ethics is more accurately seen as a renewal rather than a radical departure from traditional practice. In its early years, professional public administration in the United States had a strongly moralistic dimension that had developed partly in revulsion against the partisan spoils system's blatant corruption.

Cynics may downgrade ethics, dismissing the whole business as a public relations scheme, an alibi, or a handy tool for attacking opponents. At the other extreme are the idealists who want to push too far, too fast. Their impassioned go-ahead usually fails in public service in the United States. But the pragmatists, who back off and go slowly, are aware that ethics proposals in public management can open the door to either misuse and abuse or to best practices.

Public Administration's Track Record

The first step in figuring out how to get there from here is to pinpoint where we are now. A brief review of public service's experience with ethics helps us understand where we stand now, how we arrived, and what that means. (For more on the development of public service ethics as an academic field, see Cooper, 2001.)

There are enough elements in management theory to support pragmatists' caution about administrative ethics. Going back to our theoretical roots, we see that both pre-World War I scientific management and the human relations school of the 1920s and 1930s treated ethical concerns as they did workers: instrumentally, that is, to elicit more productivity. Image, not ethics, was one big difference between the two; the machine vied with the biological organism as the model of a social organization. Chester Barnard's *The Functions of the Executive,* published in 1938 on the eve of World War II, provides a much-cited argument for the instrumental approach to ethics for executives, who should "deal effectively with the moral complexities of organizations without being broken by the imposed problems of choice" (Stillman, 1984, p. 478).

The amoral machine won out in the dogma of public administration that dominates even today. A presidential committee's report issued in 1937 epitomized that view and recommended the establishment of the Executive Office of the President (itself to become a powerful institution and a source of ethical and legal problems). The report announced that "real efficiency . . . must be built into the structure of government just as it is built into a piece of machinery" (Brownlow Committee, [1937] 1987, p. 92). That same year, a core statement of classical public administrative theory enthroned a single overriding value by proclaiming efficiency "axiom number one" in administration (Gulick, 1937).

Having settled on the primary value, public administration could ignore issues of choice, values, and ethics. This was simple to do and comfortably in line with the original posture that neatly removed amoral, technical administration from value-laden politics. The developing social sciences such as sociology, anthropology, psychology, economics, and political science also contributed to the temporary triumph of amoral public management. Social science nurtured a dichotomy between facts and values and rejected the latter as unsuitable for scientific study. As a result, the positivists ignored ethics.

Business Backdrop

When ethics was not banished entirely, the instrumental view held sway. This is hardly surprising, considering the fact that business management was the primary source of theories and empirical research. Much was lifted wholesale; efficiency dominated. With respect to business ethics, "A critical ethical obligation . . . is to fulfill this basic business activity as efficiently as possible" (Rion, 1990, p. 46). The cardinal standard is getting the job done; all else is secondary. Initially, business served as the outright model for public administration, and the mantle of the generic *management expert* was bestowed on business experts. (Max Weber, to whom we owe much of what we know or believe about bureaucracy, judged the distinction between public and private meaningless for understanding bureaucratic authority.)

A letter from Chester Barnard to Senator Paul Douglas hints at the consequences. Barnard declined for reasons of health and schedule to participate in the 1951 Senate hearings on establishing a governmental ethics commission. He wrote, "I have no consistent and worked-out ideas on this subject although it is one to which I have given a good deal of thought from time to time in connection with my experience both in the Federal Government and in that of New Jersey."

Measured by talk (codes, conferences, publications, media coverage), ethics is a hot topic in today's corporate world. The Enron, Worldcom, and Tyco scandals in 2001 pushed it to the fore. Although many corporations already had active ethics programs, government law and regulation are forcing major changes. The Sarbanes-Oxley Act, the Securities and Exchange Commission regulations on ethics, and the Federal Sentencing Commission's Guidelines on Organizational Sentencing have changed the corporate view of ethical responsibilities. Many CEOs now see the purely instrumental view of ethics so dominant throughout the twentieth century as both dangerous and irresponsible.

Business management is not to be faulted for its influence on public management. We—public service professionals and scholars—did it to ourselves. At the inception, Woodrow Wilson (practitioner-scholar *par excellence*, popularly credited with founding the field of public administration in the United States on his way to becoming president) firmly grounded professional public service in making government more "businesslike." Administration, as "government in action" (Wilson, [1887] 1987, p. 11), was formulated largely as a problem of science, technology, or businesslike management. Yet at about the same time, Wilson ([1885] 1956, p. 187) reflected on the value of ethics:

> *Power and strict accountability for its use* are the essential constituents of good government. A sense of highest responsibility, a dignifying and elevating sense of being trusted, together with a consciousness of being in an official station so conspicuous that no faithful discharge of duty can go unacknowledged and unrewarded and no breach of trust undiscovered and unpunished—these are the influences, the only influences, which foster practical, energetic and trustworthy statesmanship.

Rediscovery of the Ethical Enterprise

The private sector has standards, but that they diverge from public sector standards somehow was overlooked. (The difference is not in underlying ethical values and principles but in the number of standards, their emphasis and priority, and the degree of fastidious adherence to them.) Whether standards and aspirations are higher or lower is not the issue here; it's that they are *different*.

Perhaps this was forgotten in the rush to embrace the entrepreneurial spirit so prominent in American myth. Coming from a business background, public service would take decades to reorient and acknowledge that public and private management are alike "in all unimportant respects" (Allison, 1987). As President Jimmy Carter notes in *Why Not the Best?* (1976, p. 132),

> Nowhere in the Constitution of the United States, or the Declaration of Independence, or the Bill of Rights, or the Emancipation Proclamation, or the Old

Testament or the New Testament, do you find the words "economy" or "efficiency." Not that these words are unimportant. But you discover other words like honesty, integrity, fairness, liberty, justice, patriotism, compassion, love—and many others which describe what human beings ought to be. These are the same words which describe what a government of human beings ought to be.

The profession had lost sight of government's fundamental purpose: making and enforcing normatively driven choices and pursuing selected social, political, and economic goals. Still a few practitioners and educators expressed ethical concerns. Years ago, Paul Appleby (1951, p. 171) observed that "the genius of democracy is in politics, not in sterilization of politics."

Yet only now is the profession beginning to air the old philosophical proposition that, ideally, government is ethics institutionalized for pursuing the public good. (A senior federal manager quoted Rousseau's *Social Contract* on this point, and we hereby pass along his recommendation for required reading.)

Public sector ethics began to emerge as a concern in its own right only after catastrophic irrationalities such as two world wars, genocide, and the atom bomb taught us the power of organization; groundbreaking analyses of decision making in organizations by Nobel Prize-winner Herbert Simon (1947) and others taught us its limits. And administrative discretion prospered, thereby relegating the traditional dichotomy between politics and administration to the realm of delusion. At the same time, bureaucratic atrocities, misguided efficiencies, errors, and blind spots begged for explanation (Adams and Balfour, 1998).

The sociological search led to the "organizational man," who is socialized and pressured by and for the organization and thus ethically benumbed. (The Hollywood classic, *The Man in the Grey Flannel Suit,* offers some perspective.) The psychological search associated with names such as Skinner, Piaget, and Kohlberg took behaviorism well beyond the human relations school to learning theory and influential theories of cognitive development.

In public service, the search was not for explanations but for solutions, which led to more red tape instead of an ethical resurgence. Exploding responsibilities, growing staffs, and mounting budgets were transforming public agencies. Responses were keyed to classical public administration, with its emphasis on technical and organizational remedies, plus conventional institutional arrangements in the constitutional tradition. Many jurisdictions responded to new challenges by slapping on ever-more-numerous and sophisticated controls to ease the intensifying risk (and sometimes reality) of fraud, waste, and abuse. The accent on controls and oversight diverted attention from people to dollars and from personnel to more readily controllable financial management.

Some would summarize the result for many agencies as a strangulating, dehumanizing, even less productive work environment. Some would emphasize how we tied ourselves and our employees in knots and forced ourselves to look for ways around the rules. Although some might argue that more controls led to more integrity among public employees, this is a continuing debate in the public administration community.

Professional Legacy

Today's ethics revival in public service grows out of these intellectual roots and practical experiences. It also echoes concerns in the broader society. We acknowledge that legitimate government (meaning public management, too) is in fact an ethical enterprise.

What do managers do with this professional legacy in terms of the ethical side of management? Do we just turn our backs, echoing the sentiment of a character in James Joyce's *Ulysses,* who remarks, "History . . . is a nightmare from which I am trying to awake"? Total rejection sets us up for self-contempt and the urge to throw the baby out with the bathwater. Sanctification is the polar extreme, but here we face the danger of mindlessly repeating old mistakes. That leaves a point in between, calibrated by picking and choosing in a pragmatic, reflective way.

Public service's track record counsels a *go* but *go-slow* attitude toward ethics in the workplace. Wariness, instead of paralyzing us, can short-circuit both excessive regulations and unbridled expectations. A cautious attitude now can prevent the later repudiation that is inevitable if we set ethics up as the single cure for all managerial ills.

Three Roads to the Future

Public management practice and theory offer two often-opposing routes to the goal of encouraging ethical practice and ethical practitioners in public agencies. These routes encourage different behavior, make use of different vehicles, promote different purposes, and lead in different directions. A third path merges the other two and moves public service at slow speed in the direction of moderation and innovation.

The "Low Road" of Compliance

The path of compliance, in the words of the poet, means "dreaming of systems so perfect that no one needs to be good." A largely proscriptive, coercive, punitive, and even threatening route, this approach to ethics is designed to spur obedience to minimum standards and legal prohibitions. It is enforced by controls on the job that ordinarily aim at acceptable levels of risk, not flawless purity. John Rohr (1989, p. 60) calls this the "low road." It features "adherence to formal rules" and a negative outlook. Along this road, Rohr (p. 63) argues, "Ethical behavior is reduced to staying out of trouble" and the result is "meticulous attention to trivial questions." The allure of compliance is both explained and mirrored in the words of a U.S. deputy attorney general in the U.S. Department of Justice: "In the minds of many Americans, public service, government officials, politicians, crooks, and criminal activity are inextricably mixed" (Burns, 1987, p. 46).

A compliance perspective monopolizes thinking about ethical behavior in many quarters, including the federal government and many states and localities. Federal training materials for ethics officials and employees deals with behavior exclusively in terms of legally enforceable standards and as legalistic problems to be solved (by reference, for example, to the U.S. Code and Code of Federal Regulations) rather than ethical dilemmas to be resolved.

In managerial terms, compliance translates into oversight and controls. When it comes to ensuring accountability, these are facts of life in the complex, highly structured, and very powerful organizations we label *bureaucracy.* Nikolai Gogol's play "The Inspector General" is a suggestive description of a response to compliance in the field. This nineteenth-century Russian drama opens with a governor, analogous to a political appointee, announcing the imminent arrival of an inspector! Feeling threatened by impending doom, the governor relates his dream of giant, peculiar rats that sniff and sniff at everything and everyone. Any manager who has undergone an audit probably can relate to his dream.

Realistically, public managers are not about to purge compliance from government operations. Nor should managers want to. Represented by administrative controls and legal sanctions, compliance is fundamental to the way the public's business is conducted. As guardians of political relationships and political goals, *controls are accountability implemented.* For evidence, look on your desk. Controls are ingrained in budgeting and personnel—traditional managerial functions.

The U.S. system has been preoccupied with accountability from its inception. Probably the single most important travel reimbursement in U.S. history shows that colonial controls were enforced even in revolution, when the founders were turning their backs on authority in "the first general crisis of authority in American history" (Lipset and Schneider, 1987, p. 2). Even so, Paul Revere duly submitted his bill for printing and "riding for the Committee of Safety" in 1775. The Massachusetts legislature approved payment "in full discharge of the written account." But reimbursement was for less than the patriot requested. George Washington's detailed account of expenses incurred as commander-in-chief (Jotman, 1988) provides more disillusioning historical evidence of using controls to implement accountability.

The "High Road" of Integrity

The path of integrity is ethics in the raw. Relying on moral character, this route counts on ethical managers individually to reflect, decide, and act. Integrity is a basic ethical value, not limited to public service by any means. Ethical behavior draws on appropriate values and principles, absorbed from upbringing, philosophy, or, in John Rohr's formulation, regime values as constitutionally derived ethical norms. Individual responsibility is both a starting *and* an end point on the integrity route in public service. Along the route lie the normative, voluntary, prescriptive, persuasive, and the positive—but no external inducements or penalties.

Because the integrity route is noninstitutional by definition, public agencies show few signs of it. Examples from the field include the credos (mislabeled as *codes*) adopted by the Government Finance Officers Association, the International Personnel Management Association, and the American Society for Public Administration (GFOA, IPMA, and ASPA, respectively). Relying on persuasion, they cajole members to measure up.

An approach based solely on individual integrity, as upbeat as it sounds, brings its own difficulties. It bypasses unethical behavior entirely and preaches to the believers. When reduced to simplistic do-good exhortation, it overlooks the competing claims that perplex an ethical manager. By neglecting the decision-making environment and focusing exclusively on autonomous moral individuals, the integrity approach sweeps aside organizational and other influences that affect behavior. Given the fact that the organization is an important influence on an individual's behavior, an *exclusive* focus on the individual operates at an inappropriate level of analysis. Perhaps more to the point, the integrity route does not seem to have worked all that well, and abuse and corruption persist.

The "Fusion" Road

The low road of compliance does not care that most people want to make good decisions but only that most people meet minimum standards of conduct. Integrity's high road rejects administrative realities that stem from accountability. Both mistakenly reduce the world to two distinct categories—ethical and unethical—whereas managers actually cope in the gray areas of legitimate-but-competing values, principles, and responsibilities. Neither approach *alone* accomplishes the purpose of spurring ethical practice and practitioners in public service.

This purpose calls for fusing the two standard approaches and moving on both fronts at once—a bipartisan conclusion reached long ago, often repeated but rarely implemented. So we know what we should do. Now all that's left is to follow through. To the extent that public service has moved on both fronts, it results more from default than strategy and is more a hodgepodge than a blending.

Public service and public employees would both be well served by management's merging the best from the compliance and integrity roads. Such a merger fuses forces together to meet energetically the public service purpose stipulated at the start of this introduction. We use a modernistic term on purpose here: *fusion*. But it implies no explosion. Its futuristic orientation has roots deep in Western (and other) culture, reaching back to Aristotle's golden mean, which defines *virtue* as the mean of excess and shortfall. In the familiar context of a balanced budget (less familiar, of course, in the federal context than others), the good outcome falls between surplus and deficit; any other outcome signals trouble.

This is the path of moderation, adaptation, and compromise; it works through phased innovation on both compliance and integrity fronts and at a slow pace. William L. Richter (1989) imparts its tone and direction: "Positive ethics means concentrating a little less on what we must prevent—and a little more on what we want to accomplish." A two-pronged, systematic approach accomplishes that by incorporating both compliance with formal standards and the promotion of individual ethical responsibility.

There is no parade and no intoxicating drumbeat along this road. When public management jumps on the latest management bandwagon, the ancient virtue of temperance is heavily devalued. Ethics demands informed reflection and individual judgment; ethical managers are counted on to make sober decisions. Public service is too important to be swept up in the carnival atmosphere of the hottest fad, where reaching for the golden ring sabotages the golden mean.

PART ONE

ETHICAL RESPONSIBILITIES OF PUBLIC MANAGERS

CHAPTER ONE

WHAT IS IMPORTANT IN PUBLIC SERVICE?

In an examination of ethics and the profession, Part One asserts that ethics and genuine professional success go together in public service. It is the job itself—the ambiguous, complex, pressured world of public service—that presents special problems for people who are committed to doing the public's work and who want to do the right thing. Facing up to the ethical demands on public managers starts with biting the bullet: public service ethics is different from ethics in private life. The reason is that democracy is sustained by public trust—a link forged by stringent ethical standards. This chapter concludes with a diagnostic exercise and a case study; both serve to clarify the contending values and cross-pressures pressing on everyday judgment calls.

Public managers' morale, identity, and capacity for decision making and innovation are entangled in ethics, and rightly so, because public service is our society's instrument for managing complexity and interdependency. The concern with ethics and demands on managerial responsibility extend beyond academic halls to government corridors, public interest groups, and professional associations. Much of the action in the past thirty years—for example, the race to adopt or tighten ethics codes by many jurisdictions and professional associations—translates into new challenges for the public manager. Public expectations and formal standards today demand that managers undertake sophisticated ethical reasoning and apply rigorous ethical standards to decisions and behavior.

Why Me?

Ethical concerns target public managers for two main reasons. One is that having public power, authority, and accountability in a democracy means that the public service's smooth functioning depends on trust. That trust has declined. The second reason is the higher standards earmarked for public service and the public perception of pervasive shortfall.

Need for Public Confidence

"Public service is a public trust. If there is anything unique about public service, it derives from this proposition" (Lewis and Catron, 1996, p. 699). This proposition can be traced back, in the United States at least, to Thomas Jefferson and is the very first provision in the federal Principles of Ethical Conduct for Government Officers and Employees (first issued by executive order in 1989). It can be identified at other times and in other cultures. According to the Organization for Economic Co-operation and Development (OECD, 2000), with its thirty member countries,

> Public service is a public trust. Citizens expect public servants to serve the public interest with fairness and to manage public resources properly on a daily basis. Fair and reliable public services inspire public trust. Public service ethics are a prerequisite to, and underpin, public trust, and are a keystone of good governance.

The relationship between ethics and trust is so widely presumed that it is written directly into professional codes, law, and regulations at all levels of government. (It is also a fruitful area of current policy research.) Our hunch is that public confidence in government is grounded in ethics, carrying with it broad acceptance of public activity. An instrumental approach cultivates ethics as politically useful because it makes collective action possible, desirable, and legitimate. According to the INDEPENDENT SECTOR (2004), for example,

> As a matter of fundamental principle, the nonprofit and philanthropic community should adhere to the highest ethical standards because it is the right thing to do. As a matter of pragmatic self-interest, the community should do so because public trust in our performance is the bedrock of our legitimacy.

Public agencies rely on trust as the foundation for our ability to govern effectively through the voluntary compliance we in democracies prefer to compulsory obedience. All mainstream segments of the political spectrum in the United States share this preference and assume that ethics, trust, and government power are linked. President Ronald Reagan affirmed his faith in this proposition in 1987 by declaring,

> The power of the presidency is often thought to reside within this Oval Office, yet it doesn't rest here. It rests in you, the American people, and in your trust. Your trust is what gives a president his powers of leadership and his personal strength.

Recognized years ago, the "confidence gap" came to symbolize a pervasive erosion of confidence in government and public trust of public institutions, paralleling attitudes toward all institutions (Lipset and Schneider, 1987). The public assessment is that perceived wrongdoing plagues society, from Wall Street to Main Street, from academia to the media, and from evangelical tents and churches to popular charities. No segment is immune.

Public confidence started its downturn in the early 1960s. As shown in Figure 1.1, it continued its plunge through the 1970s and the events of Watergate that climaxed in August 1974, when for the first time an incumbent president resigned. The spirit was dubbed "moral malaise" in the Carter administration. The celebrated turnaround in the early years of the Reagan administration was modest compared with the earlier, precipitous decline, and ultimately many high-level officials left the Reagan and ensuing administrations under an ethics cloud.

This public attitude (coupled with scandal in places high and low) catapulted ethics into a national concern. National Gallup polls have long asked, "What do you think is the most important problem facing this country today?" From April 1990 through April 2004, usually less than 10 percent of respondents have answered with some variant of "ethics/moral/religious/family decline, dishonesty, lack of integrity." Given the circumstances surrounding presidential impeachment, it is not surprising that responses peaked in excess of 15 percent in 1998 and then returned to their usual level. These data suggest that when the noise of scandal subsides, our attention turns to business as usual, meaning concerns such as jobs, prices, and national security.

Attention to ethics, predictably, is scandal-driven and short-lived. In a national poll, 34 percent of respondents replied "restoring moral and family values" when asked, "Which do you think should be a greater priority for the Bush Administration—maintaining economic growth or restoring moral and family values?" (45 percent responded "maintaining economic growth" and 19 percent "both" [NBC News/*Wall Street Journal* Poll, 2001]).

Seasoned political veterans habitually moderate their distress by allowing for the political mileage gained by bemoaning moral deterioration. It is a favorite pastime. (Every administration since Harry Truman has run, at least in part, on cleaning up the ethics mess of its predecessor.) Yet even the most cynical among us must admit that the nationwide, overall decline in trust in government is part and parcel of discussions

FIGURE 1.1. TRUST IN GOVERNMENT INDEX, 1958–2002.

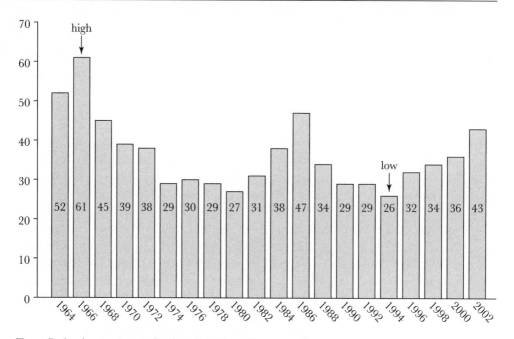

Trust Index is constructed using data from four questions.

Q1: "How much of the time do you think you can trust the government in Washington to do what is right — just about always, most of the time, or only some of the time?"

Q2: "Would you say the government is pretty much run by a few big interests looking out for themselves or that it is run for the benefit of all people?"

Q3: "Do you think that people in the government waste a lot of money we pay in taxes, waste some of it, or don't waste very much of it?"

Q4: "Do you think that quite a few of the people running the government are (1958-1972: a little) crooked, not many are, or do you think hardly any of them are crooked (1958-1972 at all)?"

Source: The National Election Studies, Center for Political Studies, University of Michigan. The NES Guide to Public Opinion and Electoral Behavior, Table 5A.5. Internet [http://www.umich.edu/~nes/nesguide/nesguide.htm] (accessed June 10, 2004).

of contemporary ethics. Low evaluations on ethical dimensions such as honesty and integrity sounded the alarm as the end of the last century neared (Lipset and Schneider, 1987). The alarms continue to ring into the twenty-first century.

There simply are not enough hard data to separate the ratings of those in public service from elected officials and those in state and local service from federal and nonprofit service. (Most available data describe opinions about elected officials but rarely refer specifically to career professionals.) There is evidence that public confidence is associated with the public's overall feeling about the state of the nation (Pew Center for the People and the Press, 1998). In a national survey conducted in 1998, "Three in four said the country's values and morals are in serious decline." Nearly two in three said they were dissatisfied with the "honesty and standards of behavior of the people in this country." The survey also found, "Large majorities of men and women, Democrats and Republicans, liberals and conservatives, blacks and whites, young people and old, the wealthy and the poor sense something has gone terribly wrong with the country's moral compass" (Morin and Broder, 1998, p. A1).

Public confidence in and experience with government's ability to perform and handle problems are different from its confidence in government when ethics is the issue. Performance ratings outstrip ratings on ethics (Goodsell, 2004; Pew Center for the People and the Public, 1998). As a result, the data shown in Figure 1.2 speak to efficiency and competence and are the basis for the following conclusion:

> Today, more people trust their state and local governments than trust the government in Washington. But, it was not always that way. Twenty-five years ago people were more confident in the federal government than in those closer to home. Since then confidence in Washington has eroded, while faith in state and local government has actually grown (Pew Center for the People and the Press, 1998).

Because public confidence is believed to be related to public perceptions of ethical practice, energies shift to improving the ethical posture and reputation of public service in order to increase public trust. Fundamentally, public service is and must be an ethical enterprise. There is and must be an ethical core to public service. Given the resources, power, and uneven sharing of benefit and harm in the governmental enterprise, we cannot afford to lose sight of what is right.

Need for Higher Standards

Despite the ballyhoo, public opinion usually judges public service on the whole as no worse than other segments of society. Of course, there are differences, depending on the field or function (Pew Center for the People and the Press, 1998; Figure 1.3). Sparse data indicate that people in public service are usually seen as about average, meaning no worse but also no better than others. The problem is that average is just not good enough. (See Exhibit 1.1.)

In reality, *average* is not the public's, the profession's, or the public employee's expectation. Falling short of a higher expectation arouses a sense of ineptitude, even betrayal. Whatever the actual or perceived incidence of either corruption or fairness, the

FIGURE 1.2. CONFIDENCE AND TRUST IN GOVERNMENT TO HANDLE PROBLEMS.

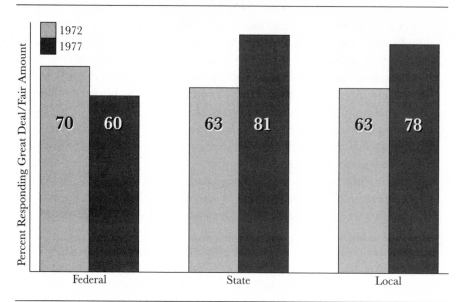

Source: Pew Center for the People and the Press, "How Americans View Government: Deconstructing Distrust." 1998. Internet [http://people-press.org].

simple fact is that public service is expected to operate on a higher ethical plane than other, more garden-variety activities. Decades ago, an eminent practitioner-academic testified at Senate hearings (Appleby, 1951, p. 166):

> It is significant, too, that the American people generally seek and expect from the [g]overnment of the United States higher standards than they expect elsewhere. And on the whole they do receive from elected and appointed officials generally a return of extraordinary devotion, even though the weighing of value questions is so complicated and difficult as to make the judgments reached highly controversial.

Appleby's words ring true for all of public service.

The Latin word *virtu* means *excellence* and summarizes the demands made on those in public service by public opinion, philosophical tradition, historical experience, and professional identity. In actuality, as a special endeavor, public service operates on distinctive standards that reflect particular values.

The proposition is this: public officials and employees truly are expected to conform meticulously to standards higher than those aligned with strictly personal morality or standards associated with the private sector (see Figure 1.3). Both the nobility and the burden of public service are that it strikes a different chord.

The American political tradition resounds with this refrain. It is sounded in the well-known words of Thomas Jefferson: "Where a man assumes a public trust, he should consider himself a public property." Henry Clay echoed it: "Government is a trust, and the officers of the government are trustees; and both the trust and the trustees are created for the benefit of the people."

The interaction of trust, confidence, and governmental integrity is evident in law and regulation. It is conspicuous in governmental codes across the nation. For example, in Austin, Texas, the human resources Web site [http://www.ci.austin.tx.us/hr/policy.htm] announces, *"Citizens must have complete confidence in the integrity of their public servants. The aim . . . is to provide guidance to employees on upholding the public trust through ethical standards and expectations."* The ASPA's code forges the same link: "Demonstrate the highest standards in all activities to inspire public confidence and trust in public service."

FIGURE 1.3. RATING ON HONESTY AND ETHICAL STANDARDS.

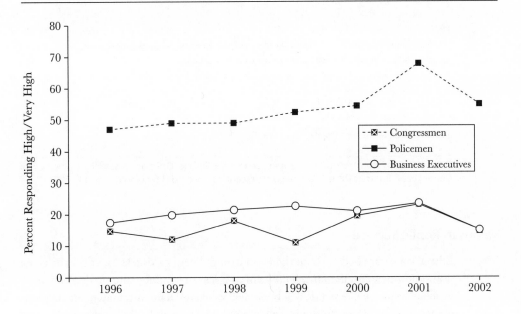

Question: "How would you rate the honesty and ethical standards of people in these different fields?"

Source: Gallup, Nov. 1996, 2002. Data provided courtesy of the Roper Center for Public Opinion Research, University of Connecticut. Internet [http://roperweb.ropercenter.uconn.edu/] (accessed Oct. 17, 2003).

EXHIBIT 1.1. AVERAGE IS NOT GOOD ENOUGH.

2002

"For each of the following, please tell me how you would rate their moral and ethical standards—as excellent, good, fair, or poor . . . members of the Bush Administration."

8%	Excellent
38	Good
34	Fair
17	Poor
3	Not sure

Source: Time/CNN/Harris, 2002

1992

"How would you rate the moral and ethical standards of most . . . members of the Bush administration . . . excellent, good, fair, or poor?"

2%	Excellent
27	Good
48	Fair
22	Poor
1	Not sure

Source: Harris, 1992

1988

"Do you think the moral and ethical standards of the Reagan Administration are higher than those of other recent administrations, lower, or about the same?"

17%	Higher
23	Lower
56	About the same
4	Not sure

Source: NBC News/*Wall Street Journal,* 1988

Data provided courtesy of The Roper Center for Public Opinion Research, University of Connecticut. Internet [http://roperweb.ropercenter.uconn.edu] (accessed June 11, 2004).

Values in Public Service

Ethical values are beliefs about right and wrong. These yardsticks for ethical behavior draw on feeling and thinking. Sentiment and reason combine into predispositions or inclinations to act (Cooper, 1987). But not all values are the same; neither are they necessarily associated with ethical behavior. Some are virtues—the habits of ethical action embedded in moral character that underlie ethical behavior and translate abstract, ethical values into customary, observable behavior. Many ancient traditions stress personal virtue, and Plato wrote of four: courage, wisdom, justice, and moderation.

In Buddhist teachings, "Good men and bad men differ from each other in their natures. . . . Wise men are sensitive to right and wrong" (Bukkyo Dendo, Kyokai, 1987, p. 264). In Exodus 18:21, when Moses sets about forming his administrative hierarchy for the tribes of Israel newly liberated from slavery, his father-in-law, Jethro, advises him to "provide out of all the people able men, such as fear God, men of truth, hating covetousness; and place such over them, to be rulers."

Because not all values are ethical values, contemporary observers of the managerial scene draw up their own lists of requisite values and virtues. Some relate to modern business management, others more directly to democratic ideals. Among those drawn upon in this book, Laura Nash (1981, 1990) and Michael Rion (1990) figure among the former; John Rohr (1989), Michael Josephson (1989), Josephson Institute (1990), and Terry Cooper (1987) are among the latter. Also in the democratic mode, Stephen Bailey—an influential figure in public administration—selected optimism, courage, and "fairness tempered by charity" (1964, p. 236).

The point is that in public service, particular values are of special concern. They are part of the answer to the question, "Why me?" These values support principles of action that distinguish public service from other endeavors.

Why not select a single roster of ethical values? A list—plain-dealing and direct—would be more compelling and maybe even more appealing. The answer lies in what ethics itself is all about:

- Ethical action is reflective; it is based on thought and reason.
- Ethical action is principled; it draws on sound values.
- Ethical action means making normative judgments, and that means choice.

For Adults Only

The hallmark of adulthood is the capacity to tolerate ambiguity, uncertainty, and complexity. Not necessarily liking it, mind you. Just tolerating it. This is the decision-making context of public service, and it demands ethics, maturity, a solid sense of self, and a receptive frame of mind.

Competing Ethical Claims

Rival claims devour a public manager's time, attention, and loyalties. Competing obligations in modern life pull everyone in different directions, while physical mobility disrupts ties that, once upon a time, lasted a lifetime. Ask the city manager or field agent whose career requires periodic relocation. Ask a ranger for the National Park Service who gets transferred from Yellowstone to the Statue of Liberty. The Internet, fax machines, cellular phones, and other technological comforts let competing calls invade every arena, every moment. These demands fragment thinking and can even shatter an undisciplined manager who exercises no selectivity.

Discriminating discipline is imposed by the manager's priorities; they specify what is important to attend to, and when. Choices among priorities and responsibilities are made with an eye to roles—the sources of operative ethical responsibilities—that define one's own behavior and that of others in different circumstances. The demand to play multiple roles causes many of the pressures associated with contemporary public service. By contrast, the acknowledged driver in business is the "bottom line." A business either makes a profit or it doesn't. The public sector's multiple "bottom lines" are far harder to measure than profit. The reality is that "the end of the government-centered public service and the rise of a multisectored service to replace it" has made the public sector's new reality even more complicated (Light, 1999, p. 1).

Different perspectives stress different concepts and responsibilities, but all envelop numerous and varied roles and responsibilities. For example, Dwight Waldo (1981, pp. 104–106) encompasses just about all of them in his unranked catalogue of twelve spheres of ethical claims on the public servant: the constitution; the law; nation; country, or people; democracy; organization-bureaucratic norms; profession and professionalism; family and friends; self; middle-range collectivities such as class, party, race, union, interest group, and church; public interest or general welfare; humanity, world, or future; and religion or God.

This is a lot to absorb all at once, and an analytic handle may be useful. Michael Harmon's "theory of countervailing responsibility" organizes opposing aspects of administrative responsibility into three types: the political, professional, and personal. "Action that is deemed correct from the standpoint of one meaning might very well be incorrect or irresponsible from the standpoint of another" (1990, p. 154); therefore, tension is built into administrative life. Harmon (p. 157) defines each type:

> *Political Responsibility:* "Action that is accountable to or consistent with objectives or standards of conduct mandated by political or hierarchical authority."
>
> *Professional Responsibility:* "Action that is informed by professional expertise, standards of ethical conduct, and by experience rooted in agency history and traditions."
>
> *Personal Responsibility:* "Action that is informed by self-reflexive understanding; and emerges from a context of authentic relationships wherein personal commitments are regarded as valid bases for moral action."

Competing claims and interests are inevitable once the public service role is defined as distinct and different from other roles. The distinction—the separation itself—is what induces conflict. As the National Municipal League points out, "Having a conflict is not, in and of itself, evil, wrong or even unusual. Conflicts may be ethnic, cultural, emotional, nostalgic, regional, financial or philosophical" (Weimer, 1990, p. 16). This realistic perspective suggests that we also take just as realistic a look at multifaceted public managers who inhabit a rich, complex environment and enjoy job, family, friends, community, and other attachments.

The Ethical Claims of Five Different Roles

Figure 1.4 shows the five primary clusters of roles with which managers cope. A role defines the capacity in which the public manager is acting and the behavior suitable to it. Each role signals different bundles of concerns, values, and standards of behavior; each is marked by a mix of ethical claims, or *duties*. Some duties are *responsibilities*, meaning self-imposed, voluntary, and informal; others are *obligations*: formal, externally imposed, and legally or otherwise sanctioned. The fact that both types of claims confront managers invokes the distinction between legality and ethicality, which is explored in the next chapter. (By contrast, Cooper [1990, p. 60] distinguishes obligation as responsibility *for* a task or goal from accountability as responsibility *to* someone.) Responsibilities tend to be broad, even diffuse; obligations, if only for enforcement purposes, tend to be narrow and clearly defined.

The personal role involves self, family, personal beliefs, and community affinity and is the stuff of daily life and emotional bonds. Although its ethical claims are self-imposed, they are still typically compelling. Sometimes this personal role is conceived as an arena protected from intrusion, regulation, or scrutiny and thereby is confused with "the private" and privacy. This confusion breeds misunderstandings about role boundaries (which we examine in Chapter Three). To illustrate, President Chester A. Arthur is quoted as saying, "I may be president, but my private life is nobody's damned business" (Hochschild, 1998, p. 76). Although many Americans value privacy and stress the informal responsibilities associated with the personal role, the equation of personal and private simply does not hold up either historically or contemporarily. Individual, familial, and community obligations have long been written into law and backed by serious sanctions, from the ancient Code of Hammurabi and the Book of Leviticus through today's inheritance, divorce, child abuse, right-to-die, and other laws.

By comparison, the bundle of claims evoked by one's part in humanity is more abstract, by definition more inclusive, usually self-generated, and often less forceful. Figure 1.4 shows the reach or scope of duties as inversely related to their priority and depicts the typical pattern of behavior: the more immediate and personal claims are more compelling (or salient to behavior).

This line of reasoning emphasizes the distinction between the formal obligations imposed by virtue of working in public service and the responsibilities customarily associated with roles outside the profession, agency, or jurisdiction. This emphasis is important because of the cross-pressures induced by the many and often complex roles public managers play in their daily and professional lives. Figure 1.4 depicts public

FIGURE 1.4. ROLE DIAGNOSIS.

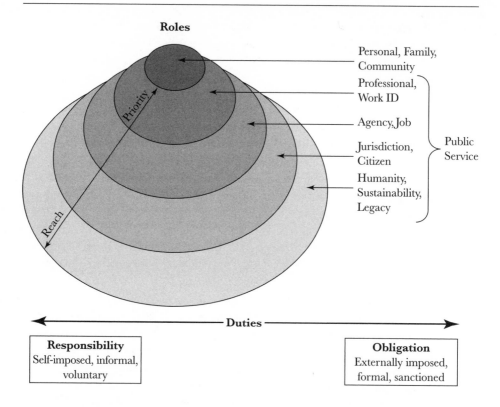

- Begin by assessing the roles you play and the seriousness of competing ethical claims. A role defines the capacity in which one is acting and the behavior befitting it.
- No simplistic trump, please; while there may be strong reasons for opting for one role over another, they need not be ethical reasons.

Graphic courtesy of Brian Baird, doctoral student in engineering at the University of Connecticut and research assistant in the Connecticut Center for Economic Analysis.

service as potentially including all but the personal domain—a core distinction discussed in Chapter Three.

A public service role often invokes legal obligations, in the sense that minimum claims are explicitly specified in written rules and enforced through legal provisions and penalties. Commonly formalized through accountability mechanisms, serving the public interest and legal compliance are central, recurring, but by no means the only ethical claims in public service. Some professional associations, such as the ICMA and American Institute of Certified Public Accountants, self-police members' adherence to formal obligations; other associations, such as ASPA and the GFOA, reject enforcement while articulating relatively broad obligations. The current trend in public service, as discussed in the Introduction, is toward transforming responsibilities into obligations and obligations into legal requirements through the adoption of enforceable standards of conduct.

Given the differences between public service and other roles, as well as among ethical claims, conflicts are bound to provoke pressure at times. Each of the five primary role clusters has numerous facets, and all five are interrelated, sometimes directly; other times they are filtered or mediated through intervening claims. For example, accountability as a formal obligation imposed by the jurisdiction is related to the "appearance" standard of professional public service; asking whether a manager would be comfortable explaining a decision to family members (see the end of Chapter Three) calls on family claims as a support.

Following the trail to its primary source is an instructive exercise for understanding and meeting different claims. For this reason, Figure 1.4 can serve as a tool for role diagnosis. The many different parts we play in our daily lives create many responsibilities and obligations; cases in point include parent, spouse, friend, neighbor, patriot, and professional and public servant. These sometimes conflict. For example, did you ever have to be in two places at the same time?

A public servant is a fiduciary or *temporary* steward of public power, resources, and trust. Although public leaders cannot reasonably be required to abandon other relationships and affiliations, they nonetheless are obliged not to use public positions to serve their personal role. This is what conflict of interest is all about. For example, being a parent does not make nepotism right; owning a business does not wipe out obligations to the town. The separation of public from personal life in modern organizations reinforces a central ethical duty to avoid conflict of interest that injures or appears to undercut independent, impartial, objective judgment. (The positive version of this is *serve the public interest,* which is discussed in Chapter Three.)

Role diagnosis stands guard against conflict of interest. This tool asks, "What hat am I wearing" and "What are my obligations?" It is a good first cut into a dilemma. But beware! Role diagnosis is too crude to be used alone. Ethical problems are *not* solved by a simple-minded winner-takes-all approach. One role may not automatically and thoughtlessly cancel all others without seriously damaging them. (See by way of illustration the case, "The Contract," in Chapter Four.)

Getting It Together

Evidence of the strains caused by vying and often incongruent claims is all around us, especially when it comes to family. Sura IV of the Koran (iv. 1–14) opens with an appeal to the unity of mankind and respect for mutual rights; it goes on to speak of sacred family relationships and their implications for rights, property, and inheritance.

The Universal Declaration of Human Rights, adopted by the General Assembly of the United Nations on December 10, 1948, as "a common standard of achievement for all peoples and all nations" identifies rights and responsibilities on many levels, including the individual, family, community, society, state, and humanity. According to Article 16(3), "The family is the natural and fundamental group unit of society and is entitled to protection by society and the State." Clashes are predictable with Article 29(l), which declares, "Everyone has duties to the community in which alone the free and full development of his personality is possible."

Almost forty years ago, Kenneth Boulding (quoted in Boling and Dempsey, 1981, p. 13) charged that our ethical thinking lags behind social realities. "We are still . . . thinking in terms of a society in which organizations are rather small and weak, and in which the family is the dominant institution." Although the family remains a forceful institution in the United States, extended families, tribes, and even nuclear families are no longer the sole or even dominant relationship in which one lives one's full life. The market economy, physical mobility, geriatric medicine, and many other developments have seen to that. Other institutions, relationships, and roles exert a strong pull on the modern manager, who must either find a way through the maze of competing claims and loyalties or be immobilized.

Override

Fixing exclusively on a single value or role-generated ethical claim is a simple way out but may do serious damage to excluded contenders. "It is unusual that one value or duty obviously 'trumps' another" (Kernaghan and Langford, 1990, p. 30). The tragic tale of Pavlik Morozov, one-time hero of Soviet communism, illustrates the friction between family and public service obligations and between abstract justice and personal compassion. As a youth, Pavlik denounced his father for aiding kulaks when the Stalinist regime of the early 1930s considered it treason to help these rich peasants. They were blamed for Pavlik's murder after he informed on his father and testified against him in court. Pavlik's example became a fable by which to teach children an overriding devotion to law and society.

However, over time the moral changed, and the assault on family allegiance lessened. Although Pavlik's story now is more a cautionary model of ordinary virtues that are unobjectionable even to a Boy Scout, the original version had betrayal distorting relationships and loyalties. Sacrificing individuals to overriding abstract concepts and all values to the public good contributed to developments like the infamous gulags (labor camps) and, according to a Soviet historian, to "deep psychological and moral deformation" (Barringer, 1988, p. Al).

This story warns of the danger of justifying an action *in the name of* a greater good or higher authority rather than taking action *for the sake of* that purpose. The first invokes authority in order to empower the doer and fails to distinguish the deed done from the good being sought. The second pursues the good by exercising its spirit. Doing your duty with public power behind you is heady enough.

Personal Integrity

The tensions aroused by competing ethical claims jeopardize personal integrity, that is, keeping oneself integrated and whole, in balance, and ethically sincere. The cartoon shown in Figure 1.5 makes the point that the core of personal integrity is ethical values, not self-indulgence.

Supporting authentic, unbiased convictions—holding the high ground—is a measure of a manager's administrative skill (Appleby, in Bailey, 1964, p. 237). In President Kennedy's pointed formulation, people of integrity "never ran out on either the principles in which they believed or the people who believed in them . . . whom neither financial gain nor political ambition could ever divert from the fulfillment of our sacred trust" (quoted in Richter, Burke, and Doig, 1990, p. 291). A manual for local administrators-magistrates in seventeenth-century China advises, "An official's first consideration is maintaining his integrity" (Huang Lie-Hung, 1984, p. 141).

J. Patrick Dobel (1990, p. 355) offers an inclusive view of ethical integrity that suits managerial realities in public service. "The ideal of personal integrity describes a condition where individuals can hold multiple realms of judgment in tension while keeping some coherence in their actions and lives." Integrity is more like a web than a hierarchical structure, which is "too static and rigid to account for the way individuals live their lives and keep moral coherence" (Dobel, 1990, p. 355).

FIGURE 1.5. ETHICAL VALUES ARE THE CORE OF PERSONAL INTEGRITY.

BLOOM COUNTY by Berke Breathed

In a national poll, 57 percent of the respondents disagreed strongly or somewhat with the statement, "The world is always changing and we should adjust our morals and values to those changes." Fully 70 percent agreed strongly or somewhat that, "We should be more tolerant of people who choose to live according to their own moral standards even if we think they are wrong" (*Washington Post*/Henry J. Kaiser Family Foundation/Harvard University, 1998). These responses reflect the widespread recognition that integrity requires neither uniform nor static perspectives.

Finally, we are left with ambiguity and choice, which is precisely the point of ethics. Normative rules of ethics help us make choices that demand the exercise of judgment.

Mapping Ethical Obligations

Professional public administration in the United States is more than a century old, and over that time it has adapted to new demands, adjusted to new truths (social, economic, organizational, and technological), and absorbed new values. By way of example, turn to the U.S. Constitution and compare the dissonant definitions of what is *fair* in the Fourteenth Amendment (equal protection clause) and the Sixteenth Amendment (income tax). In the former, *fair* means treating everyone identically, but in the latter, it had come to mean treating people in different circumstances differently.

Today public service is an amalgam of often-discordant values and the action principles they underwrite. All operate at the same time and in tension with one another. Because managers—and services and policies—cannot and should not swing like a pendulum from one to the other, managers daily find themselves reconciling the values and balancing the claims.

Ethics, Democracy, and Professionalism

A public position itself is ethically neutral—used for good or bad, right or wrong—until people use it or, rather, abuse it for something other than solving "people problems" and meeting the mission. To the question, What is important to an *ethical* public manager? we propose three core answers: (1) ethics, (2) democracy, and (3) professionalism. These combine to protect and promote individual and institutional integrity. Exhibit 1.3 lists the many values and virtues associated with each.

Of course, let us not use the formula to misdirect us into rigidity. The point here is to reflect on the many demands made on public managers, not to fix them in place once and for all time for all of public service. In fact, the many alternatives invite you to add your own preferences, delete ours, or shift choices to other categories.

Among the alternatives is the OECD's roster of values. "All OECD countries publish a set of core values for guiding their public servants in daily operations, and they draw these values from the same substantial sources, namely social norms, democratic principles and professional ethos" (Organization for Economic Co-operation and Development, 2000). The eight most frequently cited core values for public service in the OECD countries were, in numbers of countries: impartiality (24), legality (22), integrity (18), transparency (14), efficiency (14), equality (11), responsibility (11), and justice (10). Another option is the list of values approved by the INDEPENDENT SECTOR in January 2004. These include the following:

- Commitment to the public good
- Accountability to the public
- Commitment beyond the law
- Respect for the worth and dignity of individuals
- Inclusiveness and social justice
- Respect for pluralism and diversity
- Transparency, integrity, and honesty
- Responsible stewardship of resources
- Commitment to excellence and to maintaining the public trust

Why do we incorporate democracy in this formulation of public service ethics? Because democracy is the operational framework for public service in the United States. Democracy calls on the values of impartiality, justice, the rule of law, liberty, equality, and human dignity. It also points to the importance of accountability and transparency. ASPA's code urges, "Recognize and support the public's right to know the public's business" and "Promote constitutional principles of equality, fairness, representativeness, responsiveness and due process in protecting citizens' rights."

Professionalism is also part of the answer because credentials and expert knowledge are so important in modern life and to our image of who we are. How many of us think of ourselves as a professional in one walk of life or another? Does anyone we know admit to setting the personal goal of acting *un*professionally? Professionalism calls on the values of excellence, quality, competence, and merit.

What is ethics that it checks self-serving or arbitrary behavior and substitutes instead so many obligations? Ethics is about having an independent place to stand. It is the capacity for making systematic, reasoned judgments about right and wrong and to take responsibility for these judgments. Ethics is about decisive action; it is no armchair activity. But it is a special kind of action, rooted in moral values and principles expressing what is right and important—values and virtues like justice, compassion, honesty, loyalty, and even old-fashioned ones such as humility, temperance, and prudence. Ethics is action that you can defend publicly and comfortably, and the action should be something you and the community can live with.

Because (as the Introduction's cutback exercise illustrates and Chapter Two argues), public service is about power. It is also about survival. The key to the ethical professional's survival is personal integrity, that is, taking a sincere and principled ethical stand. Integrity is important for its own sake, yes! But it is important also because it is necessary as a building block of public confidence and trust in a democracy. And a public servant's own integrity is one of the few things he or she can take away from the halls of public service and into "civilian" life.

So now we have the formula shown in Exhibit 1.2: $D+P+E=I_{ii}$ (institutional and individual).

Here are so *many* values and principles, and they surely lead responsible leaders to different conclusions and contradictory actions. That is what a dilemma is all about. The burden and beauty of ethics is that there is no user-friendly computer program to substitute for personal judgment and responsibility.

So the bottom line is clear. For public managers, the formula means exercising public power as a temporary trust, without privilege, and with an eye on personal and organizational integrity. This power is cut off from personal benefits and perks so that *public* interest dominates. (The next two chapters develop this line of reasoning further.)

A Diagnostic

A roadmap, or diagnostic, is helpful in laying out the numerous, often competing values, standards, and obligations cluttering modern public service and tugging at its members. Exhibit 1.3 and Figure 1.6 impart a sense of what is right and important to us and how that fits into public service generally.

EXHIBIT 1.2. $D+P+E=I_{ii}$

DEMOCRACY
Justice, impartiality, truth (accountability, disclosure), liberty, equity, citizenship (informed participation), responsiveness, transparency, accessibility

+

PROFESSIONALISM
Merit, impartiality, competence, quality, self-awareness, self-understanding, esteem (honor, reputation), responsibility (self-policing)

+

ETHICS
Values and virtues, principles and duties, judgment and responsibility

INTEGRITY *(individual and institutional)*
Authentic, sincere, genuine, sense of being whole and intact

These values and obligations are classified in Exhibit 1.3 into four multidimensional arenas. Each is illustrated by a single dimension depicted as a continuum with the extremes identified. Overlaid on an ambiguous and untidy world, this map is not a universal taxonomy. (We want to be the first to observe that the categories are neither discrete nor comprehensive; classification in particular applications may be problematic.) We oversimplify here for the sake of clarification.

The arenas include (1) types of values and standards, capturing the manager's and government's goals and illustrated by a democracy-productivity continuum; (2) the manager's worldview or units of analysis, with an illustrative continuum running from the general to the individual; (3) a justice-compassion continuum that illustrates the arena focusing on how people are treated and the manager's preferred means, and (4) the manager's own conduct, as shown on a public service–personal continuum that identifies the primary role that generates dominant obligations.

EXHIBIT 1.3. VALUES AND STANDARDS IN PUBLIC SERVICE.

Each of the four arenas listed below is multidimensional and illustrated by a single selected dimension depicted as a continuum with extremes identified.

What counts?	Types of Values and Standards
PRODUCTIVITY . . . . DEMOCRACY	
"Hard," economy,	"Soft," accountability,
efficiency, competence,	representativeness,
expertise, merit,	citizen access, policy advocacy,
Hamiltonian bureaucracy,	Jeffersonian bureaucracy,
technical implementation	volunteerism, public demand

Counting others?	How Individuals Are Treated
JUSTICE . . . . COMPASSION	
Uniformity, standardization, rules,	Responsiveness, equity,
neutrality, stability, precedent,	circumstances, flexibility,
14th Amendment to U.S. Constitution	16th Amendment

Who counts?	Units of Analysis for Identifying and Ranking Interests/Stakes
GENERAL . . . . INDIVIDUAL	
Rights, overarching public good,	Liberty, client claims,
cost-benefit analysis,	majority interest,
allocational issues,	distributional issues,
future generations, global ecology	private property, privacy

Counting source?	Primary Role Generating Obligations
PUBLIC SERVICE . . . . INDIVIDUAL	
Law, public interest,	Self-interest,
regulations, chain of command	career, family

The map points to many different issues and values. That is its purpose. Efficiency is an enduring core value in public administration; social equity was added later. After suffering some depreciation, values associated with compassion were condoned rhetorically by President George H. W. Bush in his inaugural address on January 20, 1989, when he identified the national purpose as "to make kinder the face of the Nation and gentler the face of the world."

Used to organize and make sense of the many different managerial and democratic values mentioned earlier in this chapter, Exhibit 1.3 and Figures 1.4 and 1.6 help us translate abstractions into meaningful, realistic guidelines for public management. (For example, Rion's "avoid harm" principle emerges from humanity as a source of ethical claims in the Role Diagnosis graphic by Brian Baird; Josephson's "excellence" relates to Exhibit 1.3's first category (Productivity). Together, these can be used to probe any proposed litany of public service values and standards.

In this way, we accept public administration's messy inclusiveness and the sundry values that push and pull on public managers. (See the case concluding this chapter for an example of all this in play.) The end-point on each continuum represents legitimate, authoritative positions, but each derives its meaning in actual practice from its position in tension with the other end-point on the continuum. Practical conflicts such as between rights and liberties or freedom and justice are familiar examples built directly into modern democratic political systems.

"The questions that now urgently confront us are as old as the Republic itself. How can we maintain a government structure and administrative system that reconcile liberty with justice and institutional and personal freedom with the general welfare?" (Seidman and Gilmour, 1986, p. 29).

The many values are modified by contending values on the same continuum. "Only from the clash of opposites, contraries, extremes, and poles can come from the accommodations that are themselves American public service ethics" (Chandler, 1989a, p. 613).

The four arenas in Exhibit 1.3 depict not an either-or choice but efforts to moderate the extremes and reconcile different value dimensions. This reconciliation is at the heart of ethical decision making in public service because a complete rejection of other values on the continuum distorts a democratic polity. Pavlik's story warns against a pathological goal displacement that exaggerates solitary values and excludes all other points on the continuum.

Figure 1.6 uses the four continua for a quick diagram of strengths, weaknesses, deficiencies, and excesses. (Dwight Waldo called for mapping public service values in 1981 in *The Enterprise of Public Administration.*) The method here begins with laying out the four continua on a circle. The next step is to identify the approximate location on each continuum that best describes the actual or preferred position, as we see it. The third and last step is to connect the points and show the diamond pattern.

FIGURE 1.6. DIAGNOSTIC: WHAT SHAPE ARE WE IN?

Mapping Public Service Ethics

P — D (Productivity———Democracy)   G — I (General———————Individual)
J — C (Justice————————Compassion)   S — L (Public Service———Personal)

Step 1: Use four continua of values and standards in Figure 1.6.
Step 2: Locate approximate point on each continuum for best fit or description.
Step 3: Use straight lines to connect points and show pattern.

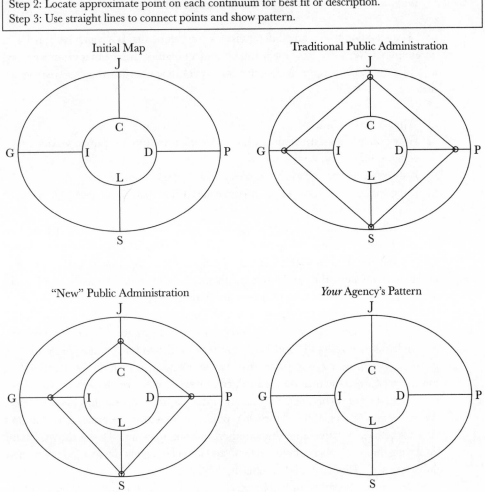

This is an exploratory device, and public service, *not* personal values, is the object of exploration. Figure 1.6 shows four sets of values and standards of behavior:

1. Types: captures the leader's and the government's goals, illustrated by democracy-productivity
2. Public manager's worldview or units of analysis, illustrated by continuum from general to the individual
3. A justice-compassion continuum that puts the focus on how people are treated and the leader's preferred means and style
4. The manager's own conduct, as shown on a public service-personal continuum that identifies the primary role that generates dominant duties

The map points to many different issues and values; that is its purpose. It helps us accept public service's messy inclusiveness and ambiguity and see that we move along a continuum. The mapping is designed for a quick diagnosis of strengths, weaknesses, deficiencies, and excesses.

1. What shape are you in?
2. How does it match up against what you hope is in store for public service's next generation?
3. If there's a mismatch, what should and can you do about it?
4. If there is a match, how can you preserve the current shape as a legacy? Should you?

A radical, ungainly shape is a warning signal that something is wrong, and an exercise in ethical fitness—shaping up—may be in order. That is up to the manager. Despite the kite shape and the fact that managers do not operate at a single discrete point but move along the continuum, the intent of the exercise is to survey the present and anticipate the future with both feet firmly on the ground.

Figure 1.6 prompts managers to describe their agency as it is, but it is also interesting—and challenging—to plot two other maps: (1) the manager's preferred pattern for public service generally and (2) the pattern predicted for the next generation in public service (pushing us to think as stewards, taking care for future generations). A mismatch between the two sounds an alarm. Over the years, public service paradigms have shifted or absorbed new values, and public administration has been *refounded* (Wamsley and others, 1990). Moreover, public outrage over recurring scandals and countless ethics initiatives hint that another shift is in the wind. That is the reason for displaying the "*new* public administration" and for encouraging the mapping of a "new public service" (Denhardt and Denhardt, 2003).

Of course, the shape of public service is molded by the larger society, and career professionals in public service are not a group apart. They inevitably reflect the moral tone of the society in which they live and the institutional contexts in which they work. The problems and challenges are neither light nor likely to disappear. Indeed, public accountability is being reshaped by new technologies, new public disclosure standards, and new demands on ethical professionals in public service. We predict that this development will expand rather than curtail individual responsibility and managerial integrity.

We agree with President John F. Kennedy's message to Congress on April 27, 1961: "The ultimate answer to ethical problems in government is honest people in a good ethical environment." He called on government leaders "to develop in all government employees an increasing sensitivity to the ethical and moral conditions imposed by public service."

Case: Right at Ground Zero

Passed just eleven days after the terrorist attacks on September 11, 2001,[1] the Victim's Compensation Fund (VCF) is the first of its kind.[2] It aimed to protect the airlines (and, by extension, their suppliers and subcontractors) by limiting their liability and providing "a no-fault alternative to tort litigation for individuals who were physically injured or killed as a result of the aircraft hijackings and crashes on September 11, 2001."[3] Victims or their beneficiaries who are willing to waive their right to sue may be compensated for economic and noneconomic loss related directly to physical injury sustained at the World Trade Center, Pentagon, or Shanksville, Pennsylvania (see Exhibit 1.4).

Kenneth R. Feinberg, the unpaid and highly credentialed[4] special master appointed by Attorney General John Ashcroft to oversee the multi-billion-dollar fund, described the VCF as "an unprecedented expression of compassion on the part of the American people to the victims and their families devastated by the horror and tragedy of September 11th." He goes on, "While there is no amount of compensation that can replace a human life, our goal is to aid those who have so greatly suffered as a result of this horrendous act" (U.S. Department of Justice, 2001). The fund surely is a gesture of the American people's compassion and a symbol of the value they place on human life.

A mix of corporate protection and public compassion, the VCF is associated with different and sometimes incongruent goals and values, seemingly inconsistent promises, and, therefore, some misunderstandings and misguided expectations. The contradictions led one legal scholar to plead that we "not continue to confuse the tort system and the inspiriting charitable impulses that infuse both private and public compensation initiatives" (Culhane, 2003, unpaginated). One newspaper headline aptly defines *disaster aid* as "the mix of mercy and politics" and quotes the 1996 congressional testimony of the director of the Federal Emergency Management Agency (FEMA): "Disasters are very political events" (Rosenbaum, 2003).

This is not the first public policy or first governmental process to be grounded in competing values. Contradictions are built right into the federal regulatory process, for example.[5] In fact, a whole literature has developed around the tensions among

EXHIBIT 1.4. WAIVING THE RIGHT TO SUE.

OMB 1105-0078

September 11th Victim Compensation Fund of 2001
Compensation Form for Deceased Victims
Part III - Attestations and Certifications

Victim's SSN or Nat'l ID #

☐☐☐ - ☐☐ - ☐☐☐☐

Personal Representative's SSN or Nat'l ID #

☐☐☐ - ☐☐ - ☐☐☐☐

Part III. b - Privacy Act Notice

The Department of Justice is authorized to collect this information by the September 11th Victim Compensation Fund of 2001, Title IV of Public Law 107-42, 115 Stat.230 ("Air Transportation Safety and System Stabilization Act"). The information you submit in your claim is for official use by the U.S. Department of Justice for the purposes of determining your eligibility for and the amount of compensation you may receive under your claim to the Victim Compensation Fund. Provision of this information is voluntary; however, failure to provide complete information may result in a delay in processing or a denial of your claim. Information you submit regarding your claim may be disclosed by the Government only in accordance with the provisions of the Privacy Act.

Part III. c - Certification of Dismissal of any Legal Action

Have you or any dependent, spouse, or beneficiary of the Victim filed a civil action (or been a party to an action) in any Federal or State court relating to or arising out of damages sustained as a result of the terrorist-related aircraft crashes of September 11, 2001 (other than civil actions to recover collateral source obligations or a civil action against any person who is a knowing participant in any conspiracy to hijack any aircraft or commit any terrorist act)?

Yes ☐   No ☐   If Yes, has such action(s) been dismissed as of March 21, 2002?   Yes ☐   No ☐

                              Initial here _____   *(please attach proof of dismissal if applicable)*

Part III. d - Acknowledgement of Waiver of Rights

I hereby acknowledge that by submitting a substantially complete Compensation Form for Deceased Victims I am **waiving** the right to file a civil action (or be a party to an action) in any Federal or State court for damages sustained as a result of the terrorist-related aircraft crashes of September 11, 2001.

Please note this Waiver of Rights could apply to the rights of individuals other than the Personal Representative. This waiver does not apply to a civil action to recover collateral source obligations or to a civil action against any person who is a knowing participant in any conspiracy to hijack any aircraft or commit any terrorist act.

Signature of Personal Representative   Date (mm/dd/yyyy)

16

caring and compassion (Gilligan, 1982; Noddings, 1984), social equity associated with the *New Public Administration,* and justice (Frederickson, 1974; Frederickson and Hart, 1985; Nozick, 1974; Rawls, 1981; see Resource A). The contradictions also explain why some decision makers, beneficiaries, or even the public may feel swindled or betrayed. Competing values are an inescapable feature of public managers' workaday world, so much so that many seasoned managers think it is prudent to anticipate allegations of hypocrisy or unfairness.

Opposing values mean that different people, with different ideas about what is fair and right, see the VCF in different lights. A leading advocate for victims and their families and self-described as one of Feinberg's "sharpest critics," Charles Wolf, points out that one thing that makes the VCF different is that it is very much in the public eye and the public is not used to seeing such a calculation with disparate valuations (Wolf, personal communication, Sept. 20, 2003; see also http://www.fixthefund.org).

Believing that the principle of compensation means making up for actual loss rather than serving as political symbolism, some claimants advocate steep differences in awards that reflect the wide variations in victims' earnings ("vertical equity," in economic jargon). After all, what's fair is fair, one can almost hear them say, and this is what Congress enacted and the president signed.

Believing that there are some circumstances, such as the events of September 11, when market-based calculations seem inappropriate—even offensive—others argue for equal compensation for all victims suffering similar harm (horizontal equity). A mother who lost her son—a firefighter—says, "It's not about the money. This is not ever about the money" (Belkin, 2002, p. 92). A father protests, "The value of a life is certainly not determined based on earnings. We're talking about my son" (Glaberson, 2001, unpaginated). "Mr. Feinberg, they say, you have undervalued our loss, your cold calculations have come up short" (Chen, 2003, unpaginated). "I don't care how much money it is. I just want fairness" (Chen, 2003, unpaginated).

An argument grounded in the inherent value of all human life would have everyone treated about the same, or at least awards would have been kept within a narrow range. (Others argue on behalf of the value inherent in all life, human or otherwise.[6])

Still others object to valuing life in dollars. "But the very idea of giving human life a monetary value has struck many as not merely difficult but repugnant" (Kleinig, 1991, p. 147). Rejection of any monetary valuation at all on human life would have shifted the public purpose from compensation to providing a measure of financial security.

Assigning a monetary value to life is part and parcel of standard evaluation techniques such as cost-benefit analysis and environmental assessments in the United States and elsewhere (Gillette and Hopkins, 1988; Linnerooth, 1975). For example, in considering road construction,

> [T]he monetary value of fatalities . . . is what the economist means by "the value of life." The term is almost a joke, a bit of gallows humor to exorcise the ghoulishness that inevitably clings to analysis of life and death in monetary terms.

The problem is unavoidable. The road will be built or it will not be built, and a decision either way is a statement about the value of life. . . .

Governments cannot avoid the trading of lives for money, but they may establish the terms under which that trade takes place. The trade is unavoidable because governments take responsibility for activities—health, transport, environmental protection, civil order, and especially national defense—where lives can be saved at a price (Usher, 1985, pp. 168, 185).

In an interview with Feinberg, it was noted that the Federal Aviation Administration's cost-benefit analyses (for deciding on safety procedures) uses a value of a life saved at $2.7 million (Public Broadcasting Service, 2002). This is also the approach taken in tort claims.

For centuries, civil lawsuits have tried to answer such questions in dispassionate economic terms. . . . In measuring the value of a lost life, lawyers often say that dollars are inadequate, but that they are all there is. In addition to damages for economic losses, intangible things, like the suffering before an inescapable death, are given a price tag (Glaberson, 2001, unpaginated).

Objecting to computational methods derived from tort law and thereby undervaluing nonmonetary aspects of a human life, some might argue that "someone's own worthwhile life is a good thing in itself, not merely an instrument for creating benefits for others" (Rhoads, 1980, p. 242).

Despite the different views, it is the statute that defines the fund. The statute directs the special master to devise all the rules and procedures governing the fund's administration, to determine awards, and oversee appeals. Wolf (undated) notes,

With a sparsely written law, Feinberg was forced to write most of the details himself in the form of regulations. Then, he has to implement what he just wrote, pointing back to those same regulations as unbendable rules. Finally, he is the final adjudicator as the law prohibits judicial review by the courts. Feinberg has the power of King George III; he is lawmaker, administrator, judge and jury.

Asked how he calculated the value of life for purposes of compensation, Feinberg replied, "We went to the Bureau of Labor Statistics and the Bureau of the Census, and we developed a methodology . . . based on salary, age and number of dependents, came up with presumptive awards. . . ." (Public Broadcasting Service, 2002).

Although the awards themselves are not subject to judicial review, the rules for making them can be contested in court. With the power to make irreversible multimillion-dollar decisions, Feinberg exercises extraordinary discretion: "The buck stops with me, and me alone" (Chen, 2002a).

Yet the statute constrains Feinberg in at least three fundamental ways. First, the fund's method of valuation is specified by statute and mimics the assessment of economic and noneconomic loss associated with tort awards. The special master is directed to consider economic loss, defined by statute as "any pecuniary loss resulting from harm (including the loss of earnings or other benefits related to employment, medical expense loss, replacement services loss, loss due to death, burial costs, and loss of business or employment opportunities) to the extent recovery for such loss is allowed under applicable [s]tate law." When making awards, he is obligated to consider noneconomic loss, statutorily defined as "losses for physical and emotional pain, suffering, inconvenience, physical impairment, mental anguish, disfigurement, loss of enjoyment of life" and all other "nonpecuniary losses of any kind or nature."

Second, the statute stipulates that the award shall be reduced by collateral compensation, defined as "including life insurance, pension funds, death benefit programs" and governmental payments associated with the terrorist-related airplane crashes. Third, the deadline for filing a claim was set at two years from the promulgation of regulations, which occurred on December 21, 2001.

Most simply, awards are based on actuarial estimates of lost income over one's lifetime, minus likely living expenses and collateral compensation. "Over the years, Feinberg has worked out a method for dealing with sprawling, complex cases, the key element of which he describes as stripping away the complexities. Under this method, individual circumstances are reduced to numbers, so that the whole settlement can be expressed in a set of tables" (Kolbert, 2002, unpaginated). According to Feinberg, "The way you divvy up the money is to come up, to the extent you can, with an objective allocation formula" (Kolbert, 2002, unpaginated). (See Exhibit 1.5.) Because the fund has no statutory cap, the special master in effect "has been granted what amounts to a blank check on the federal Treasury" (Kolbert, 2002, unpaginated).

Numerous complaints and objections have arisen over Feinberg's methodology and other aspects of the fund. Compensation for economic loss means that low-income earners are eligible for lower awards. "At first glance, the tables defy most notions of equity; the more needs a family is likely to have, the less well it fares" (Kolbert, 2002, unpaginated). A minimum award adopted by the special master addresses this concern to some small degree. At the same time, the special master has so far refused to compensate the beneficiaries of the highest-income earners with full economic compensation that would amount to tens of millions of dollars each. "Feinberg counters that Congress vested him with enormous discretion in making payment decisions, and that he is striving for a more democratic apportionment of the taxpayer money that funds this compensation initiative" (Culhane, 2003, unpaginated).[7]

A strict application of the rules that contain neither minimum nor cap (and therefore do not set limits on outcome) would lead to a large disparity among awards. The special master appears to have opted for compressing the range of awards.

Some beneficiaries decry the collateral offsets, which strike them as unfairly penalizing the family of a victim who conscientiously and responsibly paid life insurance premiums or pension contributions. Appealing an offset, one attorney protested, "This

EXHIBIT 1.5. EARNINGS FIGURE INTO CALCULATION.

September 11th Victim Compensation Fund of 2001
Compensation Form for Deceased Victims
Part II - Compensation

OMB 1105-0078

Victim's SSN or Nat'l ID #

☐☐☐ - ☐☐ - ☐☐☐☐

Personal Representative's SSN or Nat'l ID #

☐☐☐ - ☐☐ - ☐☐☐☐

Part II. f - Compensation Information

Compensation typically includes base salary and wages as well as other sources of earned income such as commissions, bonuses, incentive pay, etc. Please provide the Victim's complete compensation history below. Please note that passive sources of income, such as income from rental properties or investments, are not considered in the calculation. For salaried victims please provide their base salary at the end of each listed year. If the victim was both employed and self-employed complete both lines. For 2001, indicate salary for period up to September 2001. If additional amounts were due please describe at part II.k.

Compensation Amount
(Please provide currency if other than US Dollars _____)

	2001 (to 9/2001)	**2000**	**1999**	**1998**
Was the Victim self-employed? If yes, enter total yearly compensation amount here.				
If not self-employed, enter **Base Salary/Wage** information here. Indicate whether figure provided is a yearly, monthly, bi-weekly, weekly, or hourly figure.				

Additional Compensation - Please provide information for all other compensation including, but not limited to, incentive pay, bonuses, overtime, commissions, tips, shift differentials, longevity, and honoraria. For 2001, indicate salary for perod up to September 2001. If additional amounts were due please describe at part II.k.

For Victims who were in the armed forces - Please include housing, subsistence, TAD, re-enlistment, and other compensation by each category. However, if you want the Special Master to rely on published compensation and benefit scales please check the box at the end of this statement. If you do so, there is no need to complete this section, but please attach a copy of the Victim's Military Leave and Earnings Statement indicating the pay level and benefit information. ☐ I wish to rely on published data regarding U.S. military compensation.

	2001 (to 9/2001)	**2000**	**1999**	**1998**
Other Compensation (Please describe)				
Other Compensation (Please describe)				
Other Compensation (Please describe)				
Other Compensation (Please describe)				
Other Compensation (Please describe)				

is about the principle of fundamental fairness" (Chen, 2003, unpaginated). Some refuse to file because they thereby lose their right to sue the airlines or governmental entities involved. These issues are dictated by the statute, not the award regulations or methodology, and are not subject to the special master's discretion.

Perhaps the most fundamental questions are built right into the fund by the statute and center on the very spirit of the fund. They have to do with fairness and how justice and compassion push in different directions. In Feinberg's words, "What you're really asking is: All lives are equal, why isn't everybody getting the same amount of money? . . . . A very fair question, ladies and gentlemen. The answer is: Congress told me that is not the way to compute these awards. Congress said you must take into account the economic loss suffered by the victim's death" (Kolbert, 2002, unpaginated). When asked in the spring of 2003 how he would change the fund, Feinberg responded, "Give everyone the same" (Culhane, 2003, unpaginated). This solution certainly would have made his job easier (and suggests that public managers may pay a price for broad administrative discretion).

All told, almost 3,000 people died at the three sites; there is no official tally for the number of injured. More than 2,830 applications for deaths and more than 3,600 injury applications met the midnight deadline on December 22, 2003. A last-minute surge pushed the application rate up more than 30 percentage points, to a 95 percent rate (and rising) and well above the 90 percent mark Feinberg set as the program's goal. The jump in applications in part is attributable to "a massive turnaround in the popularity of the fund, which had drawn applications from fewer than half of the eligible families as recently as the second anniversary of the terrorist attacks" (Hirschkorn, 2003, unpaginated).[8] About seventy-three families have opted to file lawsuits against the airlines (Barrett, 2003, unpaginated). The average lump-sum, tax-free[9] award for a death claim stands at $1.8 million, with "the highest award, about $7.9 million, going to one of the badly injured victims who survived" (Barrett, 2003, unpaginated).

The public certainly has a stake in the fund and in other governmental and nongovernmental responses to the events of September 11. (See the case featuring the Red Cross in Chapter Three.) After all, the public is who public managers are supposed to serve, and the public is at the heart of the definition of democratic accountability. But the public's responses to the VCF reveal the fundamental problem: contending values confound simple solutions and offer little or no clear-cut direction. When asked in January 2002 whether the offsets for insurance and pensions should reduce awards, 35 percent of the respondents said yes (thereby agreeing with the statutory requirement), but 59 percent said no, and 6 percent were not sure (*Time*/CNN/Harris, 2002). When a national sample of registered voters was asked in February 2002 how awards should be structured, 15 percent opted for potential earnings (the statutory criterion), 32 percent chose families' needs, 50 percent responded that all "should get about the same, and 4 percent gave no answer or did not know (Quinnipiac, 2002). Neglected is the question of whether government should compensate victims in these sorts of circumstances.

The tensions among values emerge in nonmonetary ways as well. A poll released in September 2003 shows that 54 percent of registered voters in New York City believe that the names of all victims of the attack should be displayed together on the memorial at Ground Zero in New York City. However, 38 percent responded that there should be a separate listing differentiating uniformed emergency workers. Their losses were so great: 343 firefighters, 23 city police officers, and 37 Port Authority police. Although taking no position on the matter, New York Governor George Pataki observes, "It's one thing to deal with the tragedy as America had to after September 11. It's another to run into the buildings while they're still burning" (Hirschkorn, 2003, unpaginated). It also is true that fewer than 300 bodies were recovered from Ground Zero, and the remains of 1,521 victims have been identified by the city medical examiner's office (Hirschkorn, 2003).

◆ ◆ ◆

Discussion Questions

1. In your opinion, is it possible to avoid a clash of values in public service? Is it desirable?
2. If you were the special master, would you compress the range of awards? How would you justify your answer *in ethical terms*? (See Chapter Five.)
3. Sometimes a professional in public service has to implement an imperfect law. Is this ethical? Does compliance with statute trump every other consideration? (See Chapters Four and Six.)
4. The case suggests that public managers may have to pay a price for broad administrative discretion. What price? Does the exercise of public authority carry with it any ethical obligations? What objections to administrative discretion should a prudent public manager anticipate?
5. Should public opinion influence ethical professionals in public service? Why? (See Chapter Three.) Explain your answer *in ethical terms*.
6. Take the NYC poll. How would you have responded, and why? What should you think about as a citizen? As a professional in public service?

Note: Exhibit 5.3 examines alternative ethical perspectives that help sort out the different objections to the VCF as a public policy and to decisions made by the special master.

◆ ◆ ◆

Notes

1. The fund was signed into law by President George W. Bush on September 24, 2001, as a subsection of the Air Transportation Safety and System Stabilization Act (P.L. 107-42).

2. A 1986 federal statute provided compensation in the amount of $50 per day plus interest to military and civil service members held hostage in Iran from November 4, 1979, to January 21, 1981. See National Victim Assistance Academy by Internet at http://www.ojp.gov/ovc/assist/nvaa2002/chapter22_9.html (accessed Nov. 13, 2003).

   Although numerous support, insurance, and disaster mitigation programs exist, governments in the United States ordinarily do not compensate for natural disasters, contagious illness, or other socially shared risk.

3. For a synopsis of the VCF, see http://www.usdoj.gov/victimcompensation/faq1.pdf (accessed Sept. 12, 2003). For the law, final rule, and other documents, see http://www.usdoj.gov/victimcompensation/civil_01.html (accessed Sept. 13, 2003).

4. Among Feinberg's credentials are his settling the Agent Orange case for Vietnam veterans and the suits against the Dalkon Shield IUD and Dow Corning over breast implants.

5. Executive Order no. 12866, issued on September 30, 1993, by President William Jefferson Clinton directs, "When an agency determines that a regulation is the best available method of achieving the regulatory objective, it shall design its regulations in the most cost-effective manner to achieve the regulatory objective. In doing so, each agency shall consider incentives for innovation, consistency, predictability, the costs of enforcement and compliance (to the government, regulated entities, and the public), flexibility, distributive impacts, and equity." Seehttp://reginfo.gov/eo12866.htm (accessed Sept. 10, 2003). On an overview of the federal regulatory process, see http://www.archives.gov/federal_register/tutorial/tutorial_000.pdf (accessed Sept. 15, 2003). On the value of statistical life, evaluation of life-saving benefits, and federal environmental, health, and safety rules, see, for example, Shogren and Stamland, 2002, and Viscusi, 1993. For the most comprehensive federal study yet of the cost and benefits of regulatory decision making, see OMB's 2003 report to Congress (Office of Information and Regulatory Affairs, 2003).

6. This perspective is associated with, for example, Deep Ecology, commonly dated to 1976. See http://www.cyberus.ca/~sustain1/deepE.html (accessed Aug. 3, 2003). See also Resource A.

7. This hits hardest the beneficiaries of deceased employees of Cantor Fitzgerald, the brokerage firm whose casualties represent nearly a quarter of all those killed in the attack on the World Trade Center (Chen, 2002b and Cantor Fitzgerald, 2002).

8. Attributing his change of heart to Feinberg's own changes in the program and attitude, Charles Wolf submitted his application to the VCF in November 2003 (Wolf, 2003b). Over 97 percent of the World Trade Center families applied, compared to 70 percent of Pentagon families and 30 percent of Shanksville families (Hirschkorn, 2003). "Plaintiffs' attorneys have said the Pentagon and Shanksville families would have stronger wrongful death claims against the airlines and would be impacted less by the legislative cap on damages per airplane" (Hirschkorn, 2003, unpaginated).

9. See Victims of Terrorism Tax Relief Act (P.L. 107-134, 115 Stat. 2427), at http://www.usdoj.gov/victimcompensation/civil_01.html (accessed Sept. 12, 2003).

CHAPTER TWO

OBEYING AND IMPLEMENTING THE LAW

L et us start out by admitting that being a public manager brings with it real power. Wielding power and public authority entails special ethical obligations. This asymmetrical power relationship—the power of people in public service relative to the power of those they serve—is behind the idea that, as Thomas Jefferson wrote, "public service is a public trust."

In this chapter, the obligation of legal compliance derives from the mix of power, public trust, and promise keeping. Its knotty spin-offs include differentiating among legal obligations, disobeying illegal orders, and engaging in personal dissent. A fundamental decision model that concludes the chapter centers on legal obligations without devaluing other core managerial concerns.

Public managers work with public power at their backs. They actually implement decisions through the compulsory powers of legitimate government authority. The public relies on law to tame arbitrary power. The rule of law effects justice and produces predictability and reliability in public programs and in society more generally. Otherwise unfettered discretion is tied by law to authorized, permissible public purpose and procedure.

> Administrative discretion refers to the degree of latitude or flexibility exercised by public administrators when making decisions or conducting any agency business. The chief source of administrative discretion comes from legislative bodies that have drafted vague laws. These skeletal statutes essentially allow public administrators

the discretionary power to interpret laws as they see fit, as long as their discretionary interpretations do not contradict specific statutory provisions (Warren, 2003, unpaginated).

Government authority gives public servants power over ordinary citizens. Dependent on government services, including the administration of justice, citizens are vulnerable to public servants' decisions, from program eligibility to arrest, taxation, and more. According to many governmental and professional codes, special obligations are the result of unequal power and of public managers' exercising public authority. Along these lines, ASPA's code commits members to "Exercise discretionary authority to promote the public interest."

This power imbalance between the public manager and the citizen is the reason ethical duties are so often framed in terms of (1) not doing harm, (2) taking care of those depending on us, and (3) taking into account ethical claims such as promises made. The link between power and ethics goes back to ancient times. In *The Peloponnesian War,* Thucydides wrote, "You know as well as we do that right, as the world goes, is only in question between equals in power, while the strong do what they can and the weak suffer what they must." Democracy depends upon law to equalize power so that *right* dominates decisions and interactions.

The whole political system turns on trust, public confidence, and faith in the fairness of public servants and institutions. Democracy relies on public trust to accomplish civic purposes through voluntary compliance. The reciprocal is that public *managers are obligated to implement and comply with the law.* Failure to do so is a legal and ethical violation. The law draws boundaries around public power; it curbs commitments to mission, client, or personal claims. Two broad boundaries compel public servants to take action *(mandamus)* and forbid action beyond legal authority *(ultra vires).*

Taking the Job and the Pledge

The ethical values of truth telling and promise keeping underlie citizens' faith. They place their trust in public servants who have sworn to uphold the law. Like so many ideas in public service, the idea of taking an oath can be traced to the roots of Western civilization; the Pledge of the Athenian City-State (see Exhibit 2.1) reveals the idea's durability.

By taking the job, you have given your word. The promise to obey and implement the law is part of taking a public position. The promise may be unspoken, but it is still understood. Many public service employees, such as those in nongovernmental agencies, do not actually take an oath. Yet the implicit promise underlies the public's grant of trust. Reinforcing the commitment to special ethical principles, the promise functions

EXHIBIT 2.1. PLEDGE OF THE ATHENIAN CITY-STATE.

We will never bring disgrace to this our city
by any act of dishonesty or cowardice,
nor ever desert our suffering comrades in the ranks;

We will ever strive for the ideals and sacred things
of the city, both alone and with many;

We will revere and obey the city's laws
and do our best to incite to a like respect and reverence
those who are prone to annul or set them at naught;

We will unceasingly seek to quicken the sense
of public duty;

That thus, in all these ways, we will transmit this city
not only not less, but greater, better and more beautiful
than it was transmitted to us.

as a symbol of conferring public power on the one hand and, on the other, agreeing to exercise it within permissible boundaries. This function is obvious in ceremonial oaths, of which the presidential oath of office, set forth in the Constitution, is an outstanding example: "I do solemnly swear (or affirm) that I will faithfully execute the Office of President of the United States, and will, to the best of my ability, preserve, protect, and defend the Constitution of the United States."

Many government employees do take a formal oath. Newly appointed federal executive, legislative, and judicial appointees swear "true faith and allegiance" to the Constitution by taking the oath of office. The oath is required by Title 5, Section 3331 of the United States Code (hereafter, U.S.C.) for all individuals (except the president) "elected or appointed to an office of honor or profit in the civil service or uniformed services." Federal civilian employees complete the appointment affidavits (Exhibit 2.2) when appointed and take an oath to uphold the Constitution.

By taking the military oath of office, military personnel swear (or affirm) to defend the Constitution and "bear true faith and allegiance to the same." Donning the uniform means accepting its terms. This promise induces the ethical obligation for military personnel to abide by civilian authority and the rule of law.

Those in public service in all branches of state (and, by extension, local) government also give the promise by assuming the office or taking the job. Article VI, Clause 3 of the Constitution states:

EXHIBIT 2.2. FEDERAL APPOINTMENT AFFIDAVITS.

APPOINTMENT AFFIDAVITS

_____   _____
(Position to which Appointed)   (Date Appointed)

_____   _____   _____
(Department or Agency)   (Bureau or Division)   (Place of Employment)

I, _____ , do solemnly swear (or affirm) that--

A. OATH OF OFFICE
I will support and defend the Constitution of the United States against all enemies, foreign and domestic;
that I will bear true faith and allegiance to the same; that I take this obligation freely, without any mental
reservation or purpose of evasion; and that I will well and faithfully discharge the duties of the office on which
I am about to enter. So help me God.

B. AFFIDAVIT AS TO STRIKING AGAINST THE FEDERAL GOVERNMENT
I am not participating in any strike against the Government of the United States or any agency thereof,
and I will not so participate while an employee of the Government of the United States or any agency
thereof.

C. AFFIDAVIT AS TO THE PURCHASE AND SALE OF OFFICE
I have not, nor has anyone acting in my behalf, given, transferred, promised or paid any consideration
for or in expectation or hope of receiving assistance in securing this appointment.

_____
(Signature of Appointee)

Subscribed and sworn (or affirmed) before me this____ day of _____ , 2_____

at _____   _____
       (City)   (State)

_____
(Signature of Officer)

(SEAL)

Commission expires_____   _____
(If by a Notary Public, the date of his/her Commission should be shown)   (Title)

Note - If the appointee objects to the form of the oath on religious grounds, certain modifications may be permitted pursuant to the
Religious Freedom Restoration Act. Please contact your agency's legal counsel for advice.

The Senators and Representatives before mentioned, and the Members of the several State Legislatures, and all executive and judicial Officers, both of the United States and of the several States, shall be bound by Oath or Affirmation, to support this Constitution.

These oaths spell out the foundation of duty in public service. By taking the job, office, or position, the public servant promises legal compliance. The federal ethics code (P.A. 96–303, unanimously passed by Congress and signed into law by the president on July 3, 1980) spells out a simple standard: "Uphold the Constitution, laws, and regulations of the United States and of all governments therein and never be a party to their evasion."

This grounding in law applies to all in public service, including nonprofits. The model value statement and ethics code approved by the INDEPENDENT SECTOR in January 2004 states, "Adherence to the law is the minimum standard of expected behavior. Nonprofit and philanthropic organizations must do more, however, than simply obey the law. We must embrace the spirit of the law" (INDEPENDENT SECTOR, 2004).

The principle sounds simple, but it raises practical (and philosophical) questions that managers are bound to face. Laws and regulations with the force of law may push managers to behave in a personally objectionable way. And sometimes laws or regulations conflict. At other times, the spirit and purpose of public service is undercut by to-the-letter or by-the-book legal obedience.

The difference between ethics and legality is an inescapable challenge in public service, as Figure 2.1 points out. Sophocles' *Antigone* is a classic statement of this difference, but let us not forget that not so long ago our predecessors enforced Jim Crow laws.

Two questions in particular have hounded public service for centuries: (1) What are a manager's obligations in the face of an illegal directive? and (2) What if the manager dissents and sincerely believes a law is unjust, wrong, or immoral?

The Force of Law

Not all legal formulations are of equal weight. The oaths noted earlier reflect the primary position of the Constitution. Public service is both rooted in and bound by the Constitution's provisions (Rohr, 1989, 2003; Rosenbloom, 1992). They are the ethical manager's framework for action and the citizen's basis for trust.

The responsibility for seeing that lesser laws conform to the Constitution lies with the Supreme Court. A public servant who renders a legal opinion on unconstitutionality to justify his or her own noncompliance goes far beyond official competence and legal boundaries. When the elected chief justice of the Alabama Supreme Court in 2003 defied a federal district court order to remove a monument depicting the Ten Commandments from public display in the courthouse rotunda, the issue was *not*

FIGURE 2.1. SPIRIT AND CHALLENGE OF PUBLIC SERVICE.

whether the monument was in violation of the First Amendment's establishment clause. Courts recently have issued conflicting rulings over such displays, and the debate continues over whether they violate separation of church and state (Associated Press, 2002; Roig-Franzia, 2003). The issue simply was whether the display was lawful. The state court's associate justices ordered compliance, cited Article VI of the Constitution, and wrote that they were "bound by solemn oath to follow the law, whether they agree or disagree with it" (Alabama Supreme Court, 2003). A special nine-member judicial court removed the chief justice from the bench (Gettleman, 2003).

In a real sense, usurping the Supreme Court's role is abuse of office. When, who, and how the law is tested against the Constitution is a matter for negotiation in the agency and litigation in the courts. Yet in the face of a conflict between the Constitution and a statute, a regulation, or a supervisor's command, the ethical public manager is committed to the Constitution. This double-bind is part of public service reality.

Reading the Rules

An agency's *rule* has the force of law, but it should not be confused with the law itself. Further, there are rules, and there are *rules*. According to the federal Administrative Procedure Act, Section 551(4), *rule* "means the whole or part of any agency statement of general or particular applicability and future effect designed to implement, interpret, or prescribe law or policy or describing the organization, procedure, or practice requirements of any agency." (For details on U.S. federal rules and regulations, see http://www.archives.gov/federal_register/tutorial/tutorial_000.pdf, http://www.regulations.gov, and http://www.archives.gov/federal_register/index.html.)

A document submitted to a congressional hearing (U.S. House of Representatives, 1990) describes the Supreme Court's formulation governing review of an agency's deviation from its own regulations. A reviewer should

> determine whether the regulation was intended (1) to require the agency to exercise its independent discretion, or (2) to confer a procedural benefit to a class to which complainant belongs, or (3) to be a "mere aid" to guide the exercise of agency discretion. If the first or second, invalidate the action; if the third, a further determination must be made whether the complainant has been substantially prejudiced. If he has, invalidate the action; if not, affirm.

Thus justice for a potential casualty of government discretion leads to the differential weighing of rules.

How does one read the rules? It depends. Existing agency rules entail legal liability, but the ethical obligation based on the oath to uphold the Constitution is of a different order altogether. With that obligation in mind, rules are narrowly or broadly interpreted, loosely followed, or scrupulously obeyed. With effort, rules can be waived or changed.

A discriminating manager distinguishes the standard way of doing business in an agency from formal procedure, regulations, and law. The obligation is legal compliance, not the manager's or client's slavery to routine. The distinction between organizational habits and substantive regulation is important if managers are to retain their capacity for adaptability, innovation, and leadership (see Chapter Six).

Disobedience Before Illegality

Legal compliance imposes on managers the heavy burden of refusing to obey a superior's illegal order or directive. For each manager empowered to guard the legal basis of citizen trust, disobedience is preferred over illegality. Admittedly, the disobedient manager "practices civil *obedience* under particularly stressful conditions because he upholds the rule of law against his lawless superior" (Rohr, 1989, p. 12).

The principle extends to military service. During the nationally televised Iran-Contra hearings in the mid-1980s, Senator Daniel K. Inouye (D-Hawaii), himself a wounded veteran, asserted for the nation to hear that even military orders do not take priority over law.

> An order which is unlawful not only does not need to be obeyed, but obeying such an order can result in criminal prosecution of the one who obeys it. Military courts have long held that military members are accountable for their actions even while following orders—if the order was illegal (Powers, 2004, unpaginated).

Nonetheless, military law "now generally excuses soldiers who obey a superior's criminal order unless its illegality would be immediately obvious to anyone on its face. Such illegality is 'manifest,' on account of its procedural irregularity, its moral gravity, and the clarity of the legal prohibition it violates" (Osiel, 1998, unpaginated). Moreover, and according to the manual for courts-martial (pt. IV, ¶ 14c(2)(a)(i) (1998), "When an accused is charged with willful disobedience of a lawful order under Article 90, UCMJ, the order is presumed to be lawful, unless it is patently illegal" (quoted in Osiel, 1998, note 74). A courtroom defense based solely on the "following orders" defense dates back to 1799 in U.S. military history and was rejected by the Supreme Court; it was similarly rejected at the Nuremberg tribunals in the wake of World War II (Powers, 2004; see also Chapter Four).

What about disobeying lawful orders? One view on this is expressed in the military context. The official reprimand when a U.S. Air Force major refused an order to submit to an anthrax vaccine in 2000 reads, "Your disobedience of the lawful order of a direct superior commander undermines the very essence of military good order and discipline. Your failure to live up to these standards cannot be condoned" (Vela, 2000; see also Katz, 2001; Powers, 2004; Wenker, 1981).

Exhibit 2.3 shows a civilian version, where an unqualified *no* is overly formalistic and uselessly simplistic, given what public managers know. Managers cannot afford the self-indulgence of sentimentality or sanctimoniousness. Realistically, in the field and in the central office, we know managers bend, twist, curve, and break laws and regulations. This is what selective enforcement is all about: facing an ethical dilemma and blinking. The blink may be for pragmatic reasons—to accomplish the mission and get the larger job done. Or there may be an imperfect fit between by-the-book and public purpose. Sometimes judgment rests on rival values or contradictory laws or regulations. At other times, faulty judgment or even downright ignorance is at work. Managers understand this, but they should not celebrate it.

Judgment, it often is argued, rests on fulfilling a superior's underlying intention and purpose, that is, the spirit rather than the letter of the order. This leeway enables flexible, instant response to changing circumstances. The same reasoning (spirit

EXHIBIT 2.3. TO OBEY OR NOT TO OBEY!

Imagine you are an inspector in the engineering department and have the responsibility to inspect the sidewalks of residents whose streets are being resurfaced. The policy is clear—residents who live on streets that are partially resurfaced must pay up to $1,000 per home for their sidewalks to be replaced. But residents on streets that are fully resurfaced are not required to pay. Your job is to determine how much a resident who lives on a partially resurfaced street must pay to replace the sidewalk. Sounds straightforward enough. Not so. Why? Because the technical criteria for determining the difference between a full resurface and a partial resurface are murky. Moreover, as the inspector, you have suffered for many years trying to explain the system to residents who are impacted. And it is your strong belief that the required fee is too great of a burden, particularly as it is not applied in all cases and a large percentage of the residents are retired. After years of expressing your concerns to the director of the engineering department and having them ignored, you decide to take the matter directly to the mayor.

The engineering director does not find your conversation with the mayor amusing. Indeed, he becomes quite angry with you for going to the mayor and having his policy decision questioned. He instructs you to proceed with collecting money from residents and lobbies the mayor to support the current policy. You continue collecting checks and contracts from residents but decide not to cash them or process the contracts because you feel the mayor will rule in your favor. And you are right. The mayor concludes the system is unfair, and resident contributions are eliminated for all sidewalk replacement projects.

Upon hearing the mayor's decision, you return the unprocessed checks and destroy the contracts. The director, not having budgeted for the change, instructs you to continue with the old policy for the upcoming construction season and to initiate the new policy the following year. Concerned about losing your job, you lie and say that you had not collected any money. You feel it would be impossible to collect the money for the upcoming project year, as the change in policy had already been announced in the local press.

In the meantime, the director investigates and finds that the money has indeed been collected and subsequently returned. In his opinion, this was contrary to a direct order. You admit lying but claim that you had merely followed the wishes of the elected officials. The director gives you a pink slip, thus terminating your employment. You decide to appeal the decision to the assistant administrator.

1. Now imagine you are the assistant administrator. What should you do?
2. Was the director right to fire the employee for her behavior?
3. Was the director acting out of his anger at having his decision overturned?
4. Was the employee acting in the best interest of the community?
5. Is it sometimes ethical to disobey an order when you feel it is the "right" decision? Should the employee have been disciplined?

Reprinted with revision by permission of the American Society for Public Administration. Anonymous author. Originally published in *PA Times,* "Ethics Moment" column, edited by Don Menzel, Sept. 2002. Internet [http://www3.niu.edu/~tp0dcm/aspa/ethicsec/moments/moments.htm].

and purpose over knee-jerk obedience) lies behind determining legislative intent. Different from discretion, intent really narrows wiggle room because it calls on managers to abide more fully by the law.

Disobeying for Good Reason

We are not about to tell public managers that it is ethically defensible to break a law. Given their promise to comply with the law, it is not. Moreover, those who do break the law may be personally liable. This is not to say that managers do not and will not do it; they do and will. Their reason is usually a *good* one, but it cannot serve as an excuse whereby the offenders seek to be held blameless.

When other ethical claims push in the direction of illegality, the manager confronts a true ethical dilemma. Any decision in this situation stirs controversy; people of good character and strong principles will disagree. The argument here is that the law is the center of gravity in public service, and the Constitution is the touchstone.

Abusing Public Office for Personal Dissent

If a public manager believes a law is unjust or immoral, is he or she ethically obligated to comply? Or does another, higher law prevail? Managers today know there exists the possibility of an unconstitutional political order as, for example, symbolized historically by Nazi Germany. This argument is a red herring. It changes the subject from legitimate government to illegitimate regime. It changes the question from *What now?* to *What if?* It is irrelevant to the contemporary constitutional system of American public service.

Then there is the likelihood of unjust human law to consider. When ethical judgment conflicts with legal compliance in major matters, conscientious dissent or civil disobedience substitutes a standard from outside the administrative system. Religion (as in the case concluding this chapter) or philosophy may provide standards for judging whether a human law is just or not. "Civil disobedience rests its case on a higher moral or natural law not on positive law" (Rohr, 1989, p. 12).

Civil disobedience is defined as follows:

> [Civil disobedience is] a violation of law with the intent of effecting a change in current policy, regarded as unjust by the citizens taking action. Important issues involved in civil disobedience include fidelity to the state, publicity of the disobedient act, the permissibility of violence in civil disobedience, and the acceptance of punishment on the part of the protesters (Tedesco and Harris, 2002, unpaginated).

These factors distinguish civil disobedience from acts of terrorism.

Plato's *Crito* and *Apology* present Socrates' take on the issue. As chronicled in Resource A, current politics is well versed in peaceful and not-so-peaceful civil disobedience, thanks to Gandhi's struggle against colonialism, the sit-ins and freedom rides of the civil rights movement, and the antiapartheid and antinuclear campaigns. In a famous act of civil disobedience in December 1955, Rosa Parks disobeyed segregation laws in Montgomery, Alabama, by refusing to give her seat to white passengers.

In his renowned "Letter from Birmingham City Jail" (1963, p. 6), the Reverend Dr. Martin Luther King Jr. explained:

> Since we so diligently urge people to obey the Supreme Court's decision of 1954 outlawing segregation in the public schools, it is rather strange and paradoxical to find us consciously breaking laws. One may well ask, "How can you advocate breaking some laws and obeying others?" The answer is found in the fact that there are two types of laws: There are just laws and there are unjust laws. [O]ne has a moral responsibility to disobey unjust laws. . . . A just law is a man-made code that squares with the moral law of the law of God.

King (p. 7) goes on to state a central tenet of ethical civil disobedience, which is taking responsibility for one's actions. "One who breaks an unjust law must do it openly, lovingly . . . and with a willingness to accept the penalty." Similarly, John Rawls sees civil disobedience as an open political act—"an appeal to the majority and its sense of justice, and by engaging in civil disobedience, one hopes to show the majority that the policy or law in dispute is inconsistent with the society's shared political values" (Tedesco and Harris, 2002, unpaginated).

Contrast this with *conscientious refusal*, which "is not necessarily a political act and thus may be grounded in one's personal moral, religious, or philosophical convictions" (Tedesco and Harris, 2002, unpaginated), which is illustrated by the case at the end of the chapter. In *A Matter of Principle,* Ronald Dworkin examines "integrity-based civil disobedience" and justifies refusal to obey the law "because when people violate their morals, conscience, or integrity in order to obey a law, they suffer immediate, irreparable harm by doing so" (Tedesco and Harris, 2002, unpaginated).

Dissenting as a Citizen

May a public servant ethically engage in conscientious dissent *outside* his or her office? This question accents professional and organizational roles, but these are not the only roles, which is the point of Figure 2.1. How should a city manager respond to an urban planner who takes part in a peaceful demonstration opposing abortion? How should a state finance analyst decide to participate in an antiwar protest? There are two issues when the action is not related to official duties: (1) responsible citizenship and the

(2) legality of the mode of dissent. (See Chapter Eight, where Exhibit 8.4 portrays these issues in action.)

When the actions are legal, a *yes* underwrites important citizenship obligations and reserves rights already limited by ethical standards, laws, and regulations discussed throughout this book. In practice, the answer is often modified by the appearance standard discussed in the next chapter. Unwelcome professional consequences will likely vary according to the visibility of the administrator and the action. Part of ethical action is a willingness to take responsibility for it.

Not all modes of dissent are legal. Respect for democratic processes, public trust, and the promise of legal compliance ethically constrain the public servant. As a result, the ethicality of dissent outside of office turns on the action's legality. A county hospital administrator who challenges nuclear weapons by refusing to pay personal income taxes is breaking the law and shrugging off the ethical value of promise keeping. Bear in mind that a sincere ethical argument can be made (as did Henry David Thoreau in his 1849 essay that came to be called "Civil Disobedience"); the dissenter may believe that public interest is paramount in this instance.

Dissenting in Office

It may be ethically permissible or even imperative for a citizen to break a law. Yet that does *not* extend to public servants the privilege of using government authority and public position to do so. *The ethical manager may not use public office to dissent as a citizen.*

By definition, civil dissent or disobedience is not possible through a public position that draws on government authority. Nor is it an option for an ethical public manager, who would thereby violate an important value and break the prior promise of legal compliance. Pursuing conscientious dissent through public office, for whatever reason, makes a liar of the public servant and a lie of public service. Were managers to use public office to break the law at will, public trust would be broken as well. (Again, we are speaking of routine circumstances, not an "evil empire" but a constitutional system with implemented safeguards and exercised rights.)

What does an ethical public manager do when faced with a choice between legal compliance and violation of a central, personal, ethical belief? (Granted, a choice this clear-cut is rare.) The answer lies *outside* public position. Because no organization or law should dictate central ethical choices, if the choice is truly that momentous and stark, then the preferred option may be to resign. In this case, walking away from the job exercises and tones personal integrity.

If some misguided public servants try to have it both ways—to justify illegality and to use public authority—then they are operating under the delusion of moral superiority and disguising it as legal authority. Having it both ways is inherently antidemocratic and unethical, and such individuals will find themselves caught in a vise of unethical behavior and public censure as a result. Grabbing for power under cover of public position undercuts the very foundations of constitutional democracy. (A pragmatic note: managers also open themselves to legal action.)

Dissent through public position such as described in the case at the end of this chapter reveals public servants disobeying the law on grounds of religion, conscience, or superior knowledge.

Instances of this kind of personal dissent have been sobering experiences for the public and for the players.

Go/No-Go Decision Model

In public service, the law prevails. From the Athenian pledge, "we will revere and obey the city's laws" (Exhibit 2.1), to contemporary standards and professional codes, additional ethical questions arise only after the legality of the action is settled. For example, the code of the Government Finance Officers Association of the United States and Canada (GFOA) identifies legal compliance as an ethical responsibility; its members shall "uphold both the letter and the spirit of the constitution, legislation and regulations governing their actions and report violations of the law to the appropriate authorities." (Consider also the price tag of personal and organizational liability.) Accepting the law's priority is the first step in making routine decisions in public service. The obligation to make a legal decision is hardly enough justification; the scope is still too broad. A narrowly legalistic perspective may pervert rather than implement the law's purpose. This is what is offensive about legal manipulations to circumvent the appropriations process. The case, mentioned in the Introduction, of running up the postage meter to expend funds at the end of the fiscal year illustrates that maneuver. Ethical decision makers, sensitive to ethical concerns, aim at *good* decision making. Action should be both legal and ethical.

There is also a third consideration: the job to be done. Effectiveness matters *because* there's a job to be done; there's a service component to public service. Decisions must be realistic and useful. Public managers are not in this business to spin wheels but to solve the problem, meet the mission, deliver the service. Rational and busy managers take action not for its own sake but for the purposes they are trying to accomplish. There should be a logical link between the objective and the decision. Although management without ethics is purposeless or worse, impractical public management is doomed to failure. *Useful* action adds the element of pragmatism to decision making: action should be legal, ethical, and effective.

Simply giving up on an ethical, legal, but ineffective course of action can stifle creativity or justify immobility. Therefore, not all matters should stop here. The next step is to innovatively redesign the proposed action so that it meets all three criteria. Likewise, if action is ethical and effective but illegal, it may warrant a place in the agency's legislative package.

The three questions asked in sequence in Figure 2.2 function as a first cut for decision making. The go/no-go decision-making model aims at immediate action and puts ethical concerns on the table as legitimate in decision making. This model is elementary but hardly simplistic; it helps decision makers act on legal obligations without devaluing other core concerns. Is the decision legal? Ethical? Effective? A *no* to any

FIGURE 2.2. GO/NO-GO DECISION MODEL.

Three judgment calls on immediate action:
1. Is it legal?
2. Is it ethical?
3. Is it effective?

	Ethical	Unethical
Illegal	*no action**	*no action*
Legal and Ineffective	*no action†*	*no action*
Legal and Effective	*action*	*no action*

* Pursue change in law? † Innovative redesign?

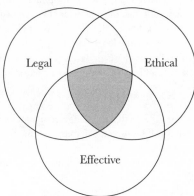

*Take immediate action
only at the intersection.*
(Proportions do not depict number
or scope of activities or decisions
each arena represents.)

one question flashes a red light. Because only a *yes* response leads to the next question and a *no* ends the matter (pending alterations), this approach is efficient and managerial. Immediate action is taken only if the answer is yes to all three questions in turn. The model is given a workout in Exhibit 2.4.

This model is useful in thinking through the falsification of public documents. Undeniably, this is illegal. Although there may be situations in which a *small deception* seems an acceptable price for a greater good (as the third scenario in Exhibit I.2 illustrates), the point of this venture is to undercut accountability, avoid taking responsibility, and evade the test of publicity (described in Chapter Four). The cumulative impact of each instance is unknowable because the record is, in fact, bogus.

Leaving a false trail via protective communication may become habitual or be abused for personal purposes. A classic example is the defensive report—an informal mechanism for reconstructing reality for purposes of self-protection. Perhaps a police officer files charges of resisting arrest because the suspect sustained injury during a botched arrest. Or perhaps a performance appraisal reflects spurned sexual overtures. Although fiction may be effective, it is neither legal nor ethical.

A related twist is passing bad news up the hierarchy, an unenviable task. It tests courage by pitting self-protection against misrepresentation and points to the difference between truth and candor. (By contrast, the issue is competence, not courage, when an analyst or subordinate fails to scrutinize and evaluate data carefully, systematically, and in accord with rigorous standards.) A former assistant to President Carter describes "the government's version of the law of gravity that bad news never flows up. The only

EXHIBIT 2.4. USING THE GO/NO-GO DECISION MODEL.

The cab of a chemical truck overturned on a back-country road, trapping the driver in explosive fumes and precipitating an immediate threat. Although untrained and ill-equipped for the specific hazard, the local volunteer emergency service was first on the scene and went in for an immediate rescue. At the inquiry conducted by the state board, the local chief insisted that the successful rescue was anything but reckless or irresponsible. "I sort of weigh the risks. I wouldn't do anything that could hurt my people more than the good we might do. But we know that our job is to help people, so what else could we have done?"

1. Should the chief have attempted the rescue? Use the go/no-go decision model.
2. Suppose you know that the jurisdiction will be sued for damages by the trucking company and driver. Would that alter your assessment? Why?
3. Suppose you know that a volunteer emergency responder will be injured during the rescue. Would that alter your assessment? Why?
4. Wear the chief's hat. What else should you think about before acting?

times I saw anyone struggle to warn his superior of impending trouble . . . were on those occasions when the superior was sure to find out anyway" (quoted in Patterson, 1988, p. 47). Of course, the silent subordinate is not performing the job, despite the promise implicit in taking it. Therefore, although the behavior may be legal and personally expedient (although risky, if discovered), it is not ethical. Presuming discovery, how would you handle a silent subordinate? What is it about the behavior that offends you? Is it that the behavior is unethical or organizationally ineffective, or that it shows a lack of trust in you?

The case that ends this chapter illustrates duty-based reasoning in which opposing duties face off. (See Chapter Five.) These duties stem from religion, professional medical tradition and practice, and the basic ethical injunction against doing harm. Also, in biomedical ethics the duty to do no harm often is balanced with the duty to do good (beneficence). Utilitarian reasoning is also evident in the effort to balance the needs of both patient and provider through accommodation, referral, and grievance or complaint procedures. Matters such as legal and organizational compliance in public service also rear their heads. The topic is birth control, over which there is national consensus, with 94 percent of respondents in a national poll conducted in October 2003 responding that they "personally" find using birth control [the pill or condoms] "morally acceptable" (ABC News/*Washington Post* Poll, 2003).

As you read the case, if you find yourself immediately and without reflection coming down on one side or the other, try substituting another issue. How would you respond to the case and the questions if religion mandated a practice that is commonly accepted, such as dietary practices. What about abortion—an issue so divisive that it typifies a *cleavage issue*: public opinion is about evenly divided and feelings run strong (Gallup, 2004; Gallup/CNN/*USA Today*, 2004)?

The case also raises the question, What role should individual conscience play in public service? Should appeal to religion or individual conscience trump other concerns? A birth control advocate argues, "The way we look at it is this: whose conscience takes precedence? . . . The interest of the patient is at least equivalent, if not superior, to the person providing service. . . . The conscience to be considered is the person receiving care, not the person providing it" (Hamilton, 2004, unpaginated).

Is this viewpoint right, wrong, or neither? Why? (See the stakeholder analysis in Chapter Seven). In his column, a retired senior navy medical officer asserts that the case is unique in his experience and quotes the Hippocratic oath's injunction to do no harm (Johnson, 2004). (He does not quote the oath's next sentence, which prohibits giving abortions or even counsel about deadly medicine.) He also turns to the American Board of Internal Medicine: "Professionalism . . . comprises those attributes and behaviors that serve to maintain the interest of the patient above one's own self-interest." Is this formulation in the public interest? (See Chapter Three.)

Case: A Matter of One Man's Faith

As a primary care doctor at the U.S. Naval Submarine Base in Groton, Dr. Thomas V. Messe sees patients who include women seeking birth control. But Messe is a devout Catholic who believes that contraceptives are wrong and that to help patients get them violates his religious beliefs.

Rather than participate in what he calls "a sinful act," Messe arranged with the Navy to be allowed to refer patients seeking birth control to other physicians. "I would simply say to the patient, 'Because of my religious beliefs, I don't prescribe contraceptives. I will send you down the hall to my nurse's office, and she will find a doctor who can write a prescription for you,'" said Messe, 35.

The informal arrangement worked—for a while. But when the Navy questioned it, then stipulated that Messe would have to make direct referrals to other doctors rather than go through a nurse, he balked. Navy officials accused him of "patient abandonment"—deliberately leaving a patient in harm's way.

Now Messe has filed a complaint insisting on his right to have the Navy accommodate his religious beliefs and alleging harassment and discrimination.

Navy officials declined to comment on the specific complaint, but said the service balances the needs of its patients and its health care providers.

"Medical personnel who object to participating in specific procedures of family planning would not be required to do so," said Lt. Cmdr. Joe Carpenter, a Navy spokesman in Groton, "unless their refusal poses an immediate threat." Carpenter said others involved in the matter would not be allowed to comment on Messe's complaint because of the ongoing investigation.

A Thorny Issue

The Naval Ambulatory Care Center in Groton, where Messe has worked for four years, is an outpatient facility serving more than 12,000 active duty members and their families, as well as reservists and military retirees.

Messe said that for about three years, the clinic would give a printed handout to female patients before their exam, which read:

"Dr. Messe does not prescribe artificial contraception for personal reasons, but after your visit you can meet with the nurse to arrange for contraception."

Messe said most patients who wanted a birth control prescription could get it that same day; occasionally a patient had to return if the nurse couldn't find a doctor. And, he said, most—though not all—patients accepted the situation.

The text of this case is reprinted by permission from TMS Reprints for the ***Hartford Courant.*** The text is from F. G. Taylor, "A Matter of One Man's Faith, Sub Base Physician Files Complaint against Navy after Clash over His Birth Control Views," ***Hartford Courant,*** Jan. 25, 2004. Internet [http://www.ctnow.com] Jan. 25, 2004.

"It's a thorny issue, and you try to be as tactful as you can," he said.

Messe also said the doctors and nurses in the clinic supported him and did not feel overburdened by the arrangement, although he knows one nurse strongly disagreed with his views.

The arrangement worked for about three years, Messe said, until a new director of clinical services, Capt. H. A. Taylor, was assigned to the health care facility last year. About the same time, a male patient filed a complaint when Messe declined to discuss the man's request for information on a vasectomy and sent him to a nurse for a referral. A few months later, Messe told a female patient who was taking a medication that could cause birth defects if she became pregnant she should abstain from sex. He did not give her any information about birth control.

Messe said Taylor told him that his arrangement was a burden to patients and to other physicians.

"He said, 'If you were the only doctor on a ship, you would have to prescribe contraception,'" Messe recalled. "And I said, 'No sir, I don't have to, and I wouldn't.'"

Things went downhill from there. Messe said Taylor also suggested that perhaps his practice should be limited to men and to women over 40.

In September, Messe said, he was called to the regional headquarters in Newport, R.I., to meet with Taylor and with Capt. F. R. MacMahon. They offered repeatedly to limit his practice, Messe said, and also discussed a possible transfer to the all-male Marines, which would have separated him from his wife, Charnette, who was fighting breast cancer, and their two children.

Messe said he felt both his career and his wife's health were in jeopardy. Fearing he could be kicked out of the Navy and lose the family's health insurance, he said, he felt coerced to accept a new arrangement they ordered: He would have to make "physician to physician" referrals, rather than send patients who wanted contraceptives to a nurse.

Those referrals involved more than just writing a prescription: Before sending a patient to another doctor, Messe had to determine whether she had a condition such as liver disease or hypertension that could affect the type of birth control she could use.

Each day he came home more guilt-ridden and depressed, he said, because he believed his direct involvement contradicted his faith.

"I could stop seeing women under 40 or continue to sin against my God," Messe said. "That's when everything blew up."

On Jan. 2, Messe said, Taylor told him, "You are a wheel on the train that doesn't spin, so now the whole train won't move."

The next day, Messe filed charges against the two superior officers. Under Article 138 of the Uniform Code of Military Justice, charges can be filed if a soldier or sailor believes he or she is being harassed or abused by a commanding officer.

A mediator was called in, beginning a process that could take several months. In the meanwhile, Messe is again sending patients who want birth control to a nurse for referral to a physician.

Fast-Growing Cancer

For Messe, his passionate stand is not solely about religion. It's also personal.

A day after his wife, Charnette, then 31, discovered she was pregnant with their second child, she was diagnosed with a fast-moving form of breast cancer.

The couple blame her cancer at such an early age on the fact that she used contraceptives, including birth control pills and Depo-Provera, in her teens and 20s.

A mammogram revealed that the cancer had spread to her lymph nodes. Their son, Christian, was born prematurely in 2002. Charnette Messe had chemotherapy and a modified radical mastectomy last May.

Her cancer is now in remission, but she is tearful at the memory. "It was all so unbelievable," she said. "I told the doctor I had a 3-year-old daughter at home, and I asked him if I was going to get to see her grow up. He said possibly not."

The story of Charnette Messe's battle to survive breast cancer and deliver her baby led to an appearance on "The Oprah Winfrey Show" and was chronicled in a number of publications.

"Women want their contraception because they don't know the risks," she said. "People like my husband are refusing to prescribe birth control because they know what it can do."

"There is a link between contraception and breast cancer," Thomas Messe said. "My wife is a classic example."

The Word *'Referring'*

Under the guidelines of the Navy Bureau of Medicine and Surgery, contraception will be provided to patients upon request, but the rules also give physicians with moral or religious concerns the option not to participate:

> Medical personnel who object to participating in specific procedures related to family planning services on moral, ethical, or religious grounds shall not be required to perform or assist in such procedures unless their refusal poses an immediate threat to the health of a patient. However, [as] a practitioner they are responsible for referring the patient for services required.

The stumbling block, Messe said, "is that word 'referring.'"

Capt. Jane F. Vieira, regional chaplain for Commander Navy Region Northeast, would not comment directly on the case, but spoke about the right of religious accommodation.

"The most common religious accommodation requests revolve around issues of worship, religious dietary requirements, the wearing of religious apparel," Vieira said. "Every effort is made to accommodate requests of religious practice when the accommodation will not have an adverse impact on military readiness, unit cohesion, discipline, standards or discipline, or otherwise interfere with a member's military duties."

Vieira would not speculate on how frequently religion and contraceptive issues collide. She suggested that Navy chaplains would view a case such as this one according to their specific religious beliefs. But, she added, "As far as Navy medical professionals, they are instructed through Navy Bureau of Medicine instruction."

Pat Gillen, an attorney for the Thomas More Center, a public interest law firm in Ann Arbor, Mich., specializing in religious liberty issues, said he is monitoring the case. Messe contacted the center for advice before filing charges.

Though disputes concerning religious accommodation may occur with some regularity, Gillen said, this case is the first of its kind that he knows of. "The issue probably comes up a lot, but commanders might handle it in a more respectful way," Gillen said. "You can also see that the matter is systemic because of the way the regulation is written. It acknowledges that he should not be compelled, yet it does require him to cooperate in a referral."

As for the possible burden that accommodating Messe's beliefs might impose on his colleagues, Gillen said, "Administrative inconvenience is not a justification to strip someone of their constitutional rights."

Messe puts it more simply: "I just need some justice and for people to wake up."

◆ ◆ ◆

Discussion Questions

1. Although the U.S. Constitution guarantees the separation of church and state, this case seems to have far more to do with ethical issues than legal ones. What is the difference, and where do they overlap in this case?
2. How far should the navy (or any public organization) go in making religious accommodations? Are the accommodations that were offered to the doctor reasonable?
3. Would the issues be different if the case occurred in the civilian public sector?
4. A local newspaper reports, "He said people who criticize him for using his faith as a reason not to prescribe birth control contend he should not use his position to stake out a political stand. . . . His commanding officer, he said, 'is using this as a platform for his bias on contraception'" (Hamilton, 2004). Does his view of his superior's alleged bias justify Dr. Messe's taking a counter position? Why? (See Chapter Nine.)
5. Regulations and standard operating procedures are not neutral but implicitly bear ethical values and call on selected duties and principles. (See Chapter Ten.) One of the central issues in this case is *referral*, obligatory under navy guidelines. Is there a difference in terms of values, duties, or principles between prescribing contraceptives and referring patients to other staff? Is complicity an issue, given that the patient requests the service?

6. Should personal religious beliefs play a role in a public manager's decision making and service delivery? Why? Is the doctor's behavior here any different, from an ethical perspective, from the chief justice's defiance of a court order, as related in Chapter Three?

7. You are the new director of clinical services and Dr. Messe's superior. How would you handle this, and why?

CHAPTER THREE

SERVING THE PUBLIC INTEREST

Another public service obligation is to champion the public interest. Invoked by democratic imperatives, interdependency, and shared concerns, as well as empathy and respect for future generations, this obligation generates three standards: (1) avoiding conflict of interest, (2) maintaining impartiality, and (3) avoiding the appearance of impropriety. This chapter proposes a model for exploring what *public interest* means and confronts the realities of public scrutiny by offering practical guidelines for working with the media.

The use of a public position to pursue *any* personal agenda is unacceptable ethically (and politically) in public service. Public managers wield other people's power and authority. That these are on temporary loan is simply a fact of life in public service. Managers do much of the choosing in the *authoritative allocation of values* that is the standard definition of what government is all about (as the case concluding Chapter One and Exhibit 10.3 illustrate). A mission related to the public good is part of the definition of a nonprofit agency. To keep the citizens' trust, public managers are charged with pursuing the public interest.

Trade-offs and paradoxes top today's political agenda: the environment competes with economic interests; public health programs and insurance proposals face off against medical technology and an aging population; donors' preferences clash with recipients' needs; deficits challenge tax preferences; and so on. Resolution carries with it considerable ethical content and fallout.

The paradox is that private self-interest—selfish, greedy, and unrestrained or, more technically, maximizing short-term, individual utility—plunders the common pot. Unbridled self-interest threatens shared resources, often the very source of the prize. Bounty becomes booty, and the whole community is at risk (see Exhibit 3.2 later in the chapter).

Protecting common assets is a governmental purpose. In the conventional contractual view, we voluntarily submit to coercion and establish government to restrain liberty from destroying us all. Public service obligations derive from this creation myth. Public servants ideally mold and sustain the links to our future and to the whole, without unduly curbing liberty.

In Hot Pursuit

The problems on the public service agenda call for "a fundamental extension in morality" (Hardin, 1972, p. 250). These problems have no technical solution. Public interest cannot be laid out on a spreadsheet or figured on a calculator. Public interest mandates the forging of a link between the short term and the long term and between individually rational self-interest and the aggregate, common good. (See Chapter Five on rationality in decision making.) The agency's mission statement is a sensible place to start in understanding what public interest entails.

What does the injunction, "serve the public interest," really mean for public managers, and why is it important? Often an answer draws on the definition by the U.S. journalist, essayist, and social critic, Walter Lippmann (1889–1974): "The public interest may be presumed to be what . . . [people] would choose if they saw clearly, thought rationally, acted disinterestedly and benevolently. . . ." (Bell and Kristol, 1965, p. 5). Yet we need to ask, "How do we know the public interest when we see it?" (Morgan, 2001, p. 153).

As a public service duty, pursuing the public interest is conceptualized more fruitfully as a process, not as an objectively identifiable endpoint. An elusive and sweeping obligation, its pursuit is a never-ending process made meaningful more by practice than by a product. "It can be simultaneously seen as both a state of being and an ongoing process. Its quality and significance are bound up in both the process of seeking it and in the realization that it must always be pursued" (Denhardt and Denhardt, 2003, p. 67). Terry L. Cooper (1998, p. 77) asserts, "The function served by the concept of public interest is not so much one of defining specifically what we ought to do or even providing operational criteria for particular decision-making problems. Rather it stands as a kind of question mark before all official decisions and conduct." It is a moving target in the sense that its content changes along with timeframe and condition.

For purposes of practicality and reasonableness, the duty to pursue the public interest is defined here by two demands it makes on professionals in public service. One demand is to reflect on its many facets, as disclosed through broad representation and dialogue. The second demand is to engage genuinely the duties and values associated with four aspects of public interest: democracy, mutuality, sustainability, and legacy. Selected as the common core in many formulations, these four aspects of public interest are arrayed in Exhibit 3.1, which packages public-interest issues the way they often come to managers concerned with who, when, democracy, and ethics; the *what*, of course, is the public interest. It asks us to address sincerely each aspect in sequence and to dismiss none.

EXHIBIT 3.1. PURSUE THE PUBLIC INTEREST.

Step 1. Touch Four Bases in Sequence . . . Dismiss None

1. *Democracy:* delegate, agent
   How? Listen and respond, balance competing popular preferences
   Values: responsiveness, receptiveness
   Tools: cost/benefit analysis, public opinion polls
2. *Mutuality:* statesman, trustee/steward
   How? Create and define community, use moral imagination and dialogue
   Values: inclusion, ethics, impartiality, civic virtue
   Tools: analysis of constitution, mission statement, regime and professional values
3. *Sustainability:* steward, sustainer
   How? Preserve, protect, anticipate
   Values: empathy, benevolence
4. *Legacy:* steward, custodian, legator
   How? Preserve, transmit, educate, cherish
   Values: empathy, benevolence

Step 2. Reflect on Four Principles

- **Trustee Principle**—Protect future generations' interests.
- **Sustainability Principle**—Secure future generations' opportunity for comparable quality of life.
- **Chain of Obligation Principle**—Provide for the needs of current and coming generations and give near-term concrete risks priority over long-term hypothetical risks.
- **Precautionary Principle**—Absent compelling need, avoid imposing risk of irreversible harm or catastrophe.

Step 1 is adapted from C. W. Lewis, "In Pursuit of the Public Interest," delivered at the 2004 Ethics Forum, national conference of the Ethics Section of the American Society for Public Administration, Portland, Oregon, March 27, 2004; the four principles in Step 2 are from the National Academy of Public Administration, 1997, p. 7.

Across Time

Two of the four umbrella categories in Exhibit 3.1 relate to public managers' responsibilities to the present: democratic concerns and individual or private interests on the one hand and, on the other, mutual interests and ethics. The other two speak to public managers' responsibility to future generations: ensuring a viable future and preserving and transmitting civilization's legacy. These four categories obviously cross-walk to the many roles, values, and duties associated with public service (discussed in Chapter One).

The centrality of democratic values, especially as a constraint on administrative arrogance, excess, or incompetence (Morgan, 2001), drives the sequence in Step 1 in Exhibit 3.1. Starting from a democratic base, the public manager as agent or delegate aggregates into public action the individual, private interests articulated as political demands. In a democracy, managers *must* remain responsive to citizens, or the public interest idea degenerates into irresponsible justification of antidemocratic action. Beware of those who wrap themselves in the common good or confidently assert future interests; demagogues or scoundrels may try to use these to justify current oppression and repression. The key is the context and accommodating rather than spurning the important values, principles, or interests at stake.

By itself, this first take on the public interest is inadequate to the manager's task as trustee or steward. (The distinction sometimes made in the literature between *trustee* and *steward* is not useful here, so we use the terms interchangeably.) Henry Kass (1990, pp. 113, 129) defines *stewardship* as the "administrator's willingness and ability to earn the public trust by being an effective and ethical agent in carrying out the republic's business" and "signifies the achievement of both effectiveness and ethicality." (This is the theoretical underpinning of the go/no-go model shown in Figure 2.2.)

So now the manager shifts to mutual or community concerns. The buzzwords "the public interest" encode the obligation to search for the common ground, to find the common threads that bind us together. We read in the Federalist Papers no. 57: "The aim of every political constitution is, or ought to be, first to obtain for rulers men who possess most wisdom to discern, and most virtue to pursue, the common good of the society. . . ." Louis Gawthrop (1998, p. xiii) asserts that "the ethos of public service, so essential for the spirit of democracy to flourish, can be realized only if directed by a moral imperative bound to the common good." Here, then, is added an explicit and focused moral aspect, along with a more inclusive approach to public service (but we argue that there are moral aspects to all four categories).

The method we recommend has two components. One is community dialogue, in part to safeguard democratic values and in part to stimulate creative resolutions. From the postmodern or discourse perspective, "the public interest has to be socially constructed through a dialogical process that is open and free from all forms of oppressive constraints" (Morgan, 2001, p. 172; on dialogue and accountability, see Harmon, 1995, and Roberts, 2002). The public interest is well served when the manager adds a dose of creativity to the dialogue. Public managers are expected to "search imaginatively for a public-will-to-be. In this search, the public servant is often a leader in the creation of a new public will" (Bailey, 1964, p. 235; see also Chapter Six on moral imagination). The second component is to draw on constitutional, regime, and professional values. Of course, expert knowledge also is called into play.

The "public interest" idea urges public managers to live in a dynamic time warp, with a foot in the future. Therefore, one simple test of public interest is respect for future generations, which is simple to understand but not necessarily simple to do. For this reason, the third aspect of public interest in Exhibit 3.1, sustainability, spotlights biological and ecological viability. The moral responsibility here rests on future generations' vulnerability to current decisions with irreversible repercussions. Public service in its finest sense demands looking at the long-term implications of today's decision. This obligation is expressed with elegant simplicity in ancient Athens' pledge (Exhibit 2.1): "We will transmit this city not only not less, but greater, better and more beautiful than it was transmitted to us."

Legacy, the fourth obligation, speaks to matters of culture, civilization, and history. It is fourth because it is logically dependent on viability. The legacy aspect of public interest is illustrated in Exhibit 3.2.

George H. Fredrickson (1994) asks, "Can public officials correctly be said to have obligations to future generations?" In answering, he cites the future orientation in the pledge of ancient Athens. Let us now fast-forward to a more recent example: the founding of the United Nations Educational, Scientific and Cultural Organization (UNESCO, http://portal.unesco.org) in 1945 and the adoption in 1972 of its World Heritage Convention that seeks to protect cultural treasures and natural habitats (and boasted 754 properties on the World Heritage List as of 2003). In his speech, "Conservation as a National Duty" to the First Conservation Conference in 1908 President Theodore Roosevelt spoke as follows:

> [He remarked] on the anomaly whereby man, as he progressed from savagery to civilization, used up more and more of the world's resources yet in doing so tended to move to the city, and lost his sense of dependence on nature. Lacking that, he also lost his foresight, and unwittingly depleted the inheritances of his children. "We cannot, when the nation becomes fully civilized and very rich, continue to be civilized and rich unless the nation shows more foresight than we are showing at the moment" (Morris, 2001, pp. 516–517).

EXHIBIT 3.2. FROM BOUNTY TO BOOTY.

Perhaps no recent event better illustrates the worldwide recognition of the legacy obligation to future generations than the reaction to the looting of Iraq's National Museum of Antiquities in Spring 2003. When the news broke, the media, international and professional associations, and museum and archeology sites on the Internet blazed with concern and condemnation of the U.S.'s failure to safeguard the museum. Originally, 170,000 artifacts and art treasures were reported lost, and an archaeologist described it as "a rape of civilization" (Booth and Gugliotta, 2003). In May, the UN Security Council's Resolution 1483 imposed a world-wide ban on illicit trade in Iraqi cultural property [http://www.un.org/Pubs/chronicle/section/080103_unesco.as]. By June it was known that "only" 33 important pieces from the main collection were missing. A senior official at the Baghdad Museum and respected archeologist, Donny George, noted, "But look, these things can never be replaced. That is why they call them priceless" (Booth and Gugliotta, 2003, p. A12). By September, the total count of missing pieces was reduced to about 10,000 (Bogdanos, 2003).

UNESCO, international experts, Iraqi cultural experts, INTERPOL, and others have been active in efforts to restore and preserve the artifacts. According to Col. Matthew Bogdanos, head of the U.S. investigation into the looting (as a marine reservist called from his work as a public prosecutor in New York City and armed with degrees in law and classical studies), of the more than 3,400 items recovered as of September 2003, more than 1,700 were returned by Iraqis under an amnesty program, and other items have been seized in Baghdad, at checkpoints and borders, and in Jordan, Italy, Britain, and the United States. His analysis of the evidence "suggests three dynamics at work," including professionals targeting more valuable items, indiscriminate looters, and insiders with access and keys. He observes, "It must be stressed that the loss of a single piece of mankind's shared history is a tragedy. It is equally clear that numbers cannot possibly tell the whole story. Nor should they be the sole determinant used to assess the extent of either the damage done or the recovery achieved" (p. D6). Bogdanos articulates the legacy obligation when he states that the pieces "are indeed the property of the Iraqi people, but, in a very real sense, they are the shared property of mankind. I speak for all when I say we are honored to have served" (Bogdanos, 2003, p. D6).

Exhibit is adapted from C. W. Lewis, "In Pursuit of the Public Interest," delivered at the 2004 Ethics Forum, national conference of the Ethics Section of the American Society for Public Administration, Portland, Oregon, March 27, 2004.

We conclude that it is widely accepted practice to extend the *public* for whom public interest is being explored to encompass future generations (for this reason, future generations are included in Figure 1.1).

Across Condition

Public interest mandates that the public manager take an empathic leap across time, yes, but across condition as well. Empathy is another test of public interest and decrees open-mindedness and participation. (The latter is an important part of ethical public service and is built directly into the agency ethics process presented in Chapter Ten.) Even Attila the Hun, "a dubious character upon whom to base a metaphor on leadership," is credited with this: "Chieftains must develop empathy—an appreciation for and an understanding of the values of others, a sensitivity for other cultures, beliefs and traditions" (Roberts, 1987, pp. xiii, 19).

The empathy component means that public managers are stewards for all the public, including (and, some might argue, especially) the vulnerable, dependent, and politically inarticulate—those most likely to be overlooked in formulations of the public interest. The result is that public managers are responsible for hearing otherwise silent voices in the process through which the public interest is defined. Now *us* is broadly defined to include future generations for whom current public service is a steward.

Empathy may demand an inventive resolution needed to overcome an "ethical impasse" (Hart, 1974) that can otherwise paralyze decision makers. Here again we call on the moral imagination. The downside is that *new* means untested, and this implies risk. Step 2 in Exhibit 3.1 discriminates between the near-term and long-term future and between concrete and speculative risks. Very much to the point, it has been argued, "Most risk problems can be solved only by ethical analysis and democratic process: the most important aspect of risk is not scientific but ethical" (Shrader-Frechette, unpaginated, 1998).

The "new public administration" of the 1970s (Frederickson, 1987; Hart, 1974; Marini, 1971) reactivated the value of benevolence (Frederickson and Hart, 1985). The ancient obligation to do good is found in the ethical complexion of most of the world's religions and so is not as radical as was thought at the time. It established social equity as a "third pillar" in public administration (Frederickson, 1990), right alongside efficiency and economy, and was elevated to another "basic operational guideline" (Hart, 1974, p. 3).

This move was heavily influenced by John Rawls's *A Theory of Justice* (1971), in which the philosopher provides an idealized method for arriving at the public interest or general welfare. By abstracting oneself from one's own class, status, and social circumstances, one discusses and reflects behind a "veil of ignorance"; because decision makers do not know how they would be affected by decisions, they are persuaded to minimize their own (and descendants') risk by choosing truly just arrangements and institutions (Heichelbech, 2004).

The voluntary assumption of social conscience by professional public managers was also heavily influenced by the racial, economic, and intergenerational turmoil of the 1960s. President Lyndon B. Johnson captured the ethical content in his "War on Poverty" and "Great Society" speeches. In calling for economic and racial justice—a new social order—he declared a war on poverty on March 16, 1964: "Because it is right, because it is wise, and because, for the first time in our history, it is possible to conquer poverty."

An unrealistic timetable and other factors (such as the escalation of the war in Vietnam and racial protest) bred disillusionment and a turnabout in public—especially government—programs and duties. The rapid reversal saw the realists (cynics, some would say) among us reject public service's competence and therefore its legitimate intervention in the pursuit of social justice. Inescapably, however, present-day interactions and modern interdependencies speak for coexistence. They beg for an inclusive, empathic stance.

Is the notion of empathy idealistic? Yes, intentionally so. Idealism, too, is a public service trait mirrored in the Athenian pledge. It has been said that the notion of ethics itself "derives from man's imaginative power, from his tendency to idealize, to envision perfection, to extend his selfhood in identification with humanity as a whole" (Bergson, quoted in Boling and Dempsey, 1981, p. 14).

Is the principle of public interest antipragmatic? No, because ethical public service rejects both naïveté and cynicism. The essential moral qualities of the ethical public servant include optimism, the faith that things can be improved, and the courage to act on that faith (Bailey, 1964, p. 236). Optimism—pragmatic, realistic, confident—combines *can do* with *should do*. Public service is privileged to retain an old-fashioned and hard-headed belief in the possibility and desirability of progress.

Avoiding Conflict of Interest

Public interest, like law, draws a boundary between public and personal life. As a result, conflicts among competing roles and claims are predictable in public service. The very separation of public from personal roles induces the potential for conflicts of interest. (Remember that secondary relationships are among the traits of Max Weber's ideal-type bureaucracy.) It is the logical and practical by-product of the multiple roles shown in Figure 1.1.

Managers are ethically obligated to act through their public position on behalf of the public interest. This standard is a public service rudder by which public managers are expected to steer. They are expected to have personal interests but are ethically constrained from using public office to pursue them. Public managers should anticipate conflicts and temptations but not indulge them at public expense.

The separation of public from personal often translates in practice into an ethical (and legal) prohibition against the sale of office, as Exhibit 2.2 illustrates. The fact is that "no public official or administrator, high or low, owns the government, his organization, or his office. The government belongs to the public, and the administrator's role is that of a trustee, not a proprietor, in the use of his authority" (Graham, 1974, p. 92). This formulation depends on the legitimacy of property and ownership (which opens it up to distributional questions beyond the scope of our discussion). Article 17 of the Universal Declaration of Human Rights formalizes a universal right to own property privately and collectively. This right has meaning only if theft is prohibited. The United Nation's Anticorruption Convention, adopted in October 2003, refers to "the principles of proper management of public affairs and *public* property" (italics added). Because, whether by bribery, extortion, or otherwise, use of office for personal gain is theft, this posture effectively enthrones a prohibition against the sale of office to a global standard. It is outright abuse of office.

The principles behind prohibiting conflict of interest include the following: maintaining impartial and independent judgment, being responsive to public interest, rejecting private gain from office or duties, and upholding public confidence in the integrity of public service and public servants. Russell L. Williams (2002, unpaginated) writes,

> Some consider conflicts of interest to occur only when specific conflict of interest rules or laws are broken. Many of those laws are aimed at specific issues, such as financial disclosure, nepotism, improper use of public resources, or influence peddling. However, in the larger sense, if an individual (or group) functioning under governmental auspices, responsible for making decisions or taking actions affecting the public, places self-interest ahead of public interest in exercising authority, then a conflict of interest exists.

(On how this concept has shifted toward impaired judgment or a subjective definition of interest, see Stark, 2000.)

The avoidance of conflict of interest by public servants is so widely accepted in different societies that it ranks as orthodoxy. It persists as a standard precisely because violations continue and typify conflicts between public and personal claims. At its most minimal, the standard is this: use of office for personal gain for oneself or others is unethical (see Exhibit 9.4). Usually, it is also illegal.

Outright bribery—a form of sale of office—usually is prohibited outright. Exhibit 3.3 points to its historical role and political implications. According to one government definition, "A bribe is an offer to employees of something of value to (a) do something they should not do or (b) fail to do something they should do, in their official duties. The something of value need not be money; it can be anything of value" (U.S. Department of Defense, 1984, p. 40). Bribery competes for the title of most unambiguous ethical offense. There is evidence of a worldwide rejection of official bribery (Gilman and Lewis, 1996).

Some temptations do not and will not ever disappear; individuals succumb, no matter how widely accepted the ethical standard. One example is *nepotism*, meaning favoritism shown to relatives. The word's derivation reflects its longevity and persistence. It comes from the old Italian word for *nephew* and refers to special favors in job placement shown church dignitaries' relatives in Europe centuries ago. A more recent is from Mayor Richard J. Daley of Chicago. Asked about awarding a contract to his son, Daley reputedly said, "If you can't help your family, who can you help?" (Chicago Metro Ethics Coalition, 1989, p. 4). Today, nepotism is prohibited widely and outright. In public service, preferential treatment for personal gain, even if not one's own immediate gain, is unacceptable.

EXHIBIT 3.3. READ ALL ABOUT IT.

Why does corruption capture the headlines today, when it is such an old story?

If it were a new story, we would not read this in Deuteronomy 16:18–20: "You shall appoint magistrates and officials for your tribes . . . and they shall govern the people with due justice. You shall not judge unfairly; you shall show no partiality; you shall not take bribes. . . . Justice, justice shall you pursue."

More evidence of corruption's durability comes from ancient Athens, whose citizens pledged, "We will never bring disgrace to this, our city, by any act of dishonesty or cowardice." And one keystone of the British and U.S. legal systems, the Magna Carta, stipulates, "To no one will we sell, to no one will we refuse or delay right or justice."[1]

A late-seventeenth-century manual on local administration in China advises: "The magistrate is obliged to remain impartial and render judgments strictly in accordance with the law. If, unfortunately, the magistrate is fatuous enough to accept a bribe, his impartiality will be compromised" (Huang, 1984, p. 114).

And this is the point precisely: corruption undermines justice in principle, in fact, and in the public's perception of its government.

Again: If it is not new, why is corruption newsworthy? One answer is this: corruption is newsworthy when it appears systemic, endemic, and at high levels. On the scandal sheet over the past decade, we find elected officials, appointed officials, senior staff, civil servants, nonprofit managers and board members, educators, scientific researchers, contractors, and others. For government, corporations, foundations and charities, academia, and the media, an abbreviated list of offenses includes bribery, influence peddling, plagiarism and research falsification, and violations of contract procedures and gift bans.

We discover a culture of corruption in our leading institutions, and this discovery is greeted with outrage. This outrage surely is another part of the answer as to why corruption rates headlines. Now we are betrayed. We are victims of corruption, and the cost is more than dollars—it is our confidence and trust (see Figures 1.1 and 1.2).

Politicians and pundits across the country deplore the damage done by ethical lapses to the trust deemed fundamental to a democratic political system. The data presented in Chapter One on the "most important problem" from Gallup polls suggest that attention to corruption is scandal-driven and short-lived. Public corruption is newsworthy and attention short-lived in the United States because corruption is, in fact, uncommon in the more than 87,000 state and local governments. From 1980 to 2001, the number of state officials indicted for corruption in public office (a federal crime) increased from 72 to 95 individuals; indictments of local officials declined by about 9 percent to 224 (calculated from U.S. Census, 2003, Table 340).

When our attention is once again diverted, what can we do to prevent systemic, high-level corruption? The answer relies in great measure on constitutional checks and balances among the branches of government. Arguing in support of the U.S. Constitution, James Madison cautioned in Federalist no. 51, "If angels were to govern men, neither external nor internal controls on government would be necessary. . . . A dependence on the people is, no doubt, the primary control on the government; but experience has taught mankind the necessity of auxiliary precautions." So we also rely on robust, independent watchdog institutions such as ethics commissions and campaign finance commissions. The latter need strengthening and deserve our support. We depend on their independence, strength, and expert staffs to combat corruption so ancient and durable that its reappearance is a sure thing.

If we so depend on institutions, then, in the words of another ancient, Juvenal, "Who guards the guardians?" This is the citizen's responsibility in a democracy: to demand accountability, hold leaders' feet to the electoral fire, clamor that the link between government and justice remain uncorrupted, and refuse to tolerate the sacrifice of public interest to personal or political gain.

The headlines inevitably remind us that this responsibility cannot be transferred, delegated, or forgotten.

---

[1] *Note:* The Great Charter of English liberty was granted (exacted by the barons, given the threat of civil war) by King John in 1215 at Runnymede. U.S. law derives from English experience, so it is hardly surprising that Article 2, Sec. 4 of the U.S. Constitution stipulates bribery among the grounds for impeachment.

Standard of Impartiality

The impartiality standard, which is closely tied to avoiding conflict of interest, speaks to the possibility, even the likelihood, of bias. Public managers are ethically obligated to promote the public interest, which demands impartiality. Because competing claims make impartiality problematic, ethical public managers bend over backward to retain objectivity and reduce bias in action and decision making. This can be done by steering away from any avoidable influence that may cloud vision, bias decision, or appear as if it may.

Exhibit 3.4 illustrates this routinely frustrating, yet invariably tough, standard. West Virginia's Governmental Ethics Act of 1989 (Chapter 6B, Section B1.2) speaks directly to this matter, as shown in Exhibit 3.5.

Bias stemming from political party affiliation has had a long and altogether infamous career in American public service. President Grant's administration even today epitomizes the problems: ineptitude, preferential treatment, and public contempt. Terms such as *party boss* and *machine politics* conjure up the old images of public employees being required to toe the party line and donate time, money, and even votes to partisan campaigns. Spearheading the professionalization of public service over a century ago, the move to civil service began the divorce of public administration from partisanship by interposing the concept and practice of "merit" (Williams, 2002).

The federal Hatch acts, enacted on the eve of World War II, sought to protect further the public interest by forbidding partisan political activities by federal employees and, by extension, all government employees whose jobs touch federal programs or money. Many state and local jurisdictions followed suit. The generally recognized public service standard of impartiality rejects bias in action or decision making for reasons of political party affiliation or preference.

That the impartiality standard, like so many other things, is easier said than done does not diminish the obligation. This is widely recognized among senior managers.

EXHIBIT 3.4. NYC CONFLICT-OF-INTEREST BOARD'S ETHICS GUIDE FOR PUBLIC SERVANTS.

The City's Conflicts of Interest Law prohibits public servants from using or appearing to use their City positions for their own personal benefit. To comply with the law, you cannot:

- Use your City position to gain any private advantage for yourself, a close family member, or anyone with whom you have a financial relationship.
- Use City resources for any non-City purpose, or disclose confidential City information to any private person or firm.
- Accept any valuable gift from someone doing business with any City agency, or from anyone for performing your City job.
- Take a second job with a firm, or own all or part of a firm, that has business with any City agency, unless you receive approval from the Board and your agency.
- Enter into any kind of private financial relationship with a superior or subordinate.
- Ask a subordinate to work on a political campaign or make a political contribution.
- Take part in a not-for-profit organization's business dealings with any City agency.
- Discuss possible future employment with a firm you are currently dealing with in your City job.
- Communicate with your former agency on behalf of a private firm for one year after you leave City service, or ever work on a matter you personally and substantially worked on while with the City.

Source: City of New York, undated. Internet [http://www.nyc.gov/html/conflicts/downloads/pdf/ethicsguide.pdf] (accessed Feb. 15, 2004). Used with permission of the NYC Conflicts of Interest Board. ©1999, 2004. All rights reserved.

> While some acts are clearly wrong (where the individual uses his or her office for private gain, or for the benefit of someone with whom he or she has a private relationship), others are not so easy to characterize, such as those occasions when the official believes he is acting in the public interest *despite* a private relationship (Cowan Commission, 1989, p. 145).

The argument holds for personal policy preferences as well.

Appearance of Impropriety

Publicity is an evaluative test regularly applied to ethical choices in all spheres of life (Rawls, 1971, p. 133). It is particularly meaningful in public service, where obligations are linked to public confidence and trust. Public servants are expected to attend to the public's perception of the way their activities and decisions look and the public's response. It is not enough for managers *just* to uphold the law and be ethical. Public service must look right, smell right, feel right; in short, it must avoid the appearance of impropriety.

On the one hand, the appearance standard is rarely, if ever, defined. On the other, it operationalizes public confidence and public scrutiny at the level of community

EXHIBIT 3.5. FROM MONTGOMERY COUNTY'S ETHICS CODE.

Sec. 19A-2. Legislative findings and statement of policy.

(a) Our system of representative government depends in part on the people maintaining the highest trust in their officials and employees. The people have a right to public officials and employees who are impartial and use independent judgment.

(b) The confidence and trust of the people erodes when the conduct of County business is subject to improper influence or even the appearance of improper influence.

Sec. 19A-14. Misuse of prestige of office; harassment; improper influence.

(a) A public employee must not intentionally use the prestige of office for private gain or the gain of another. Performing usual and customary constituent services, without additional compensation, is not prohibited by this subsection.

(b) Unless expressly authorized by the Chief Administrative Officer, a person must not use an official County or agency title or insignia in connection with any private enterprise.

(c) A public employee must not use any County agency facility, property, or work time for personal use or for the use of another person, unless the use is:

    (1) generally available to the public; or

    (2) authorized by a County law, regulation, or administrative procedure.

(d) (1) A public employee must not appoint, hire, or advocate the advancement of a relative to a position that is under the jurisdiction or control of the public employee.

    (2) A relative of a public employee must not be employed in a position if the public employee:

        (A) would exercise jurisdiction or control over the position; and

        (B) advocates the relative's employment.

Source: Ethics Code of Montgomery County, Maryland. Internet [http://www.amlegal.com/nxt/gateway.dll?f=templates&fn=default.htm&vid=alp:montgomerycounty_md] (accessed Apr. 19, 2004). Used with permission.

standards. Although *appearance* is often defined as "what a reasonable person could reasonably believe," this definition leaves a good deal to the imagination (see Exhibit 3.6). What is an impropriety? As it appears to whom? Do facts count? In its best form, this standard reciprocally obligates the public to be informed, which is not always the case.

    Some managers interpret this appearance standard to imply that looking good is as important as doing good. They see it as offensive, intellectually barren, or practically bankrupt. For some, it recalls the old quip about obscenity—"I can't define it but I know it when I see it"—and represents an unjust basis for civil or even administrative sanctions. A book on the subject is subtitled *How the Ethics Wars Have Undermined American Government, Business, and Society* (Morgan and Reynolds, 1997). Because others, such as management guru Peter Drucker (1981, p. 28), question whether the standard involves leadership or hypocrisy, it is important to note that the American Bar Association (1980, p. 47) cautions against subordinating duty to potential misunderstanding or criticism. It also is important that the standard in Common Law for appearance demands that the observer making judgments be both *reasonable and informed*.

EXHIBIT 3.6. APPEARANCE OF IMPROPRIETY.

One of the most controversial concepts in public service ethics is the notion of the appearance of impropriety. Whereas few would question the evil of impropriety in carrying out one's public duties, many have great difficulty with the modifier "appearance." After all, some might argue, cannot any action be falsely perceived? Does not the appearance standard leave anyone open to attacks by the most excessive elements of the community? Is not appearance an excuse for subjective extremism? Even if all these questions are answered affirmatively, reality for those who serve the public is that the appearance of impropriety is a critical standard by which to evaluate public officials. . . . [A]t the end of the day, it might be the most important standard by which to judge the actions of public officials.

Appearance standards are not limited to public administrators, but also extend to legislators and judges. In fact, many professional associations [including ASPA, ICMA, and the Association of Government Accountants] . . . have codes that have appearance as one element. Recently, the appearance of impropriety has even been raised for private-sector companies whose multiple business lines seem to conflict with each other (e.g., public auditing companies and their consulting firms).

Appearance standards are all derived from the English Common Law Standard of the Common Man Rule, or in its modern incarnation the Prudent Person Rule: Historically known as the prudent or reasonable man rule, this standard does not mandate an individual to possess exceptional or uncanny investment skill. It requires only that a fiduciary exercise discretion and average intelligence in making investments that would be generally acceptable as sound. The Prudent Person Rule provides a model test: Would a reasonable person armed with all the facts conclude that an action or inaction was inappropriate?

TOWARD A DEFINITION

Appearance of a conflict of interest, appearance of the loss of impartiality, and appearance of impropriety often are used interchangeably. Although some might claim that it is valuable to refine the differences among them, for our purposes these concepts are synonymous. A claim can be made that conflicts of interest are a subset of impropriety; however, in applied, practical cases it is almost impossible to support the distinction. Andrew Stark has argued that appearance of impropriety can either take "a factual or a normative caste (or sometimes both). Either (a) it looks like the official did something wrong or (b) the official did something that looks wrong" [Stark, 1995, p. 328]. In other words, an official's action is questioned; however, no law was broken and no broadly agreed-on mores were violated. Instead, people feel there should have been a law against the action (or result), or it should be defined as an actually improper action (or result).

On a number of levels such judgments seem unfair. They are prejudiced (decided before the facts are actually known) and also seem to smack of ex post facto laws (laws made after the action). Following Stark's argument, in civil matters such standards of legal fairness are excessive because they assume protections inherent in criminal prosecutions (e.g., innocence until proven guilty).

. . . . In the vast majority of cases, appearance issues do not rise to criminal standards. Most often, they are punished either politically or administratively, with the most extreme penalty being removal from office. In addition, we assume that public officials will be held to supererogatory standards, thereby justifying the public's trust.

Another argument against an appearance standard is that it rests on knowing one's intention. . . . [But] . . . as Dennis Thompson pointed out, "because appearances are often the only window that citizens have on official conduct, rejecting the appearance standard is tantamount to denying democratic accountability" (Thompson, 1993, p. 376).

. . . . [I]f we understand appearance not in its juridical form, but as a way of clarifying values, it seems to take on a wholly different character. Where a law, regulation, or rule would emphasize a "bright-line" test of whether you violated the precept, a values approach requires balancing various principles and interests.

An additional dimension of appearance is that it is dynamic, often varying with historical tides, scandals, and changing societal mores. For example, the press and public often ignored sexual peccadilloes in the nineteenth century when "affairs of the heart" seemed to be part of the privilege of the ruling class. Well into the twentieth century, both Franklin Roosevelt and Dwight Eisenhower were purported to have long-term relationships with mistresses. Today, the slightest hint of such a relationship would be front-page news. . . .

SPECIFIC RULES

Attempting to clarify the concept of appearance of impropriety, numerous governments codified the concept in the 1990s. Although this is true for a number of federal, state, and local governments, as well as Canada and Australia, the paradigm case is the executive branch of the U.S. federal government. In 1989, . . . President George H. W. Bush issued Executive Order 12674, which articulated 14 general principles of government conduct, including "employees shall endeavor to avoid any actions creating the appearance that they are violating the law or the ethical standards promulgated pursuant to this order." In the executive order, President Bush further ordered the U.S. Office of Government Ethics (OGE) to promulgate regulations to clarify and allow for enforcement of these standards, including appearance. . . .

[OGE's] . . . regulation . . . provides several vignettes to illustrate how to apply the regulation, for example: An employee of the Internal Revenue Service is a member of a private organization whose purpose is to restore a Victorian-era railroad station and she chairs its annual fund raising drive. Under the circumstance, the employee would be correct in concluding that her active membership in the organization would be likely to cause a reasonable person to question her impartiality if she were to participate in an IRS determination regarding the tax-exempt status of the organization. . . .

CONCLUSION

The appearance of impropriety is both a vexing and illuminating concept. It is vexing because, although it appeals to fundamental values, it also undermines fairness. It is illuminating because it points to the extraordinary set of responsibilities of public servants, and the growing expectations around those responsibilities held by the public. In a sense, the appearance of impropriety is the leading edge of the organic expansion of public service ethics. Impropriety acts as a sort of tidewater mark, to which laws and regulations ultimately rise. Dennis Thompson (1993, p. 376) calls this phenomena mediated political corruption. . . .

Reprinted courtesy of Marcel Dekker from S. Gilman, "Appearance of Impropriety," *Encyclopedia of Public Administration and Public Policy,* edited by Jack Rabin. New York: Marcel Dekker, 2004a. Internet [http://marceldekker.com] (accessed Apr. 26, 2004). Notes omitted.

Despite criticisms and cautions, the standard that calls for avoiding the appearance of impropriety drives public service. In no small measure, it even defines it. But the obligation to avoid the appearance of impropriety is not intended to substitute for ethical action. Instead and ideally, it points to the public manager's obligation to reinforce public perception of legitimate authority exercised on behalf of the public interest.

How are we doing in this realm? The data in Chapter One suggest the answer: not nearly *good* enough. It is not just that more needs to be done in this area but that avoiding the appearance of impropriety is an ongoing and never-ending challenge. Three decades ago, in his 1961 message to Congress on codifying standards in federal service, President Kennedy noted,

> There can be no dissent from the principle that all officials must act with unwavering integrity, absolute impartiality, and complete devotion to the public interest. This principle must be followed not only in reality but in appearance.

Public Duties, Private Lives

Media revelations about U.S. Supreme Court nominees, members of Congress, presidential candidates, religious leaders, and others have embarrassed and even brought low many in high places in recent years. Entire books have been written about the role of scandal in U.S. politics (Garment, 1992).[1] Offenses include smoking marijuana, hiring illegal aliens, plagiarizing, sexually harassing others, engaging in pedophilia, having government workers *volunteer* to do work in a private home, and attempting to hide unsavory personal histories; other violations are petty and repeated theft, campaign finance violations, adultery, and perjury. . . . And the list goes on. These incidents are newsworthy because they raise issues of judgment and character (as well as illegal behavior in some instances), and sometimes eclipse questions of policy and beliefs.

Many city managers, police chiefs, state commissioners, and others can testify that the spotlight shines on appointed officials and career professionals as well. The impact of public scrutiny was aptly summarized almost a half-century ago: "[E]very governmental executive lives and moves and has his being in the presence of public dynamite" (Appleby, [1945] 1987, p. 162).

Recent events trigger thoughtful but still inconclusive probing into the distinction between public roles and private lives, a subject that has sparked debate for millennia. Does the public's right to know mean there is *no* realm of wholly private behavior unrelated to job performance and, more broadly, public trust? (See the scenario in Exhibit 1.2.) In this light, consider the case of a second-shift maintenance worker with several years of service with the county; the employee is convicted on a minor gambling charge. Are you *ethically* justified in dismissing the worker?

Disclosure Standards

There really is no consensus here. Frequently, standards are limited to *official* action or public activities. Federal administrative standards fall in this category. Alternatively, standards may extend to personal realms as well. This is an ancient idea. The Oath of

Hippocrates, the fifth-century B.C. Greek physician, stipulates, "With purity and with holiness I will pass my life and practice my art." The International Association of Chiefs of Police's Oath of Honor states, "On my honor, I will never betray my badge, my integrity, my character, or the public trust. Its Law Enforcement Code of Ethics says, "I will keep my private life unsullied as an example to all and will behave in a manner that does not bring discredit to me or to my agency." The ICMA's ethics code (2002) obligates members to "Be dedicated to the highest ideals of honor and integrity in all public and personal relationships in order that the member may merit the respect and confidence of the elected officials, of other officials and employees, and of the public."

In 1974, Washington State's Supreme Court articulated a standard that is readily extended beyond elected officials to appointees and employees. In some respects, it amounts to the *compelling interest* justification:

> The right of the electorate to know most certainly is no less fundamental than the right of privacy. When the right of the people to be informed does not intrude upon intimate personal matters which are unrelated to fitness for public office, the candidate or officeholder may not complain that his own privacy is paramount to the interests of the people (quoted in Weimer, 1990, p. 15).

When the Connecticut Supreme Court upheld the disclosure of a teacher's sick-leave records, Chief Justice Ellen A. Peters declared, "We note that when a person accepts public employment, he or she becomes a servant of, and accountable to, the public. . . . As a result, that person's reasonable expectation of privacy is diminished, especially in regard to the dates and times required to perform public duties." And the Freedom of Information Commission's executive director opined, "While some say it's a privacy issue, I see it as a public accountability issue" (Tuohy, 1993, pp. C1, 13).

Dennis Thompson (1981) suggests that high office and high visibility march in step with the public's right to know. Recent experience suggests these same factors affect the likelihood of public disclosure. Some of these issues are illustrated in an administrative setting described in Exhibit 3.7.

The Press Pass

What makes a person fit or unfit for public service is a consideration for the media no less than for the public person who works under the glare of the spotlight or the threat of disclosure. Visibility cues vulnerability; exposure increases the higher one climbs in public life. Other determining factors may include public and private, youth and adult, community standards, public record, and character indicators. Although the media exercise selectivity, nothing is inherently excluded. According to the Society of Professional Journalists' code of ethics (1996), "Ethical journalists treat sources, subjects and colleagues as human beings deserving of respect." Members should "[r]ecognize that private people have a greater right to control information about themselves than do public officials and others who seek power, influence or attention. Only an overriding public need can justify intrusion into anyone's privacy." The preamble states, "Members of the Society of Professional Journalists believe that public enlightenment is the forerunner of justice and the foundation of democracy."

For the media, self-censorship means filtering the public's right to know. The competition over news—to break a story or at least not be caught napping—is also compelling. People make a better "story angle" for television viewing than abstract ethical or technical issues. Hypocrisy, greed, sexual exploits, and the like give events a "personal touch." They help an exposé "reach a critical mass," allowing that the "ability to reduce complicated events to colorful drama is the key to a scandal's market value" (Kurtz, 1989, p. D5). As a result, the civics conversation tends to be "conceptually narrow and impoverished" (Jennings, 1989b, p. 23). "The quality of deliberation in a democracy is debased when sensationalist exposés of private activities displace discussions of questions of public policy" (Thompson, 1981, p. 225).

EXHIBIT 3.7. PUBLIC WORKS.

Joe has lived in this city of 25,000 residents most of his life, and now he is a civil engineer and the public works director. He's invited several neighbors and friends, some of whom work with him at City Hall, to his home for cocktails to mark the holiday season. He agrees cordially when a neighbor asks whether she may bring along her dinner guest—a reporter for the local newspaper. Unfortunately, Joe succumbs to too much holiday spirit and drunkenly collapses in the kitchen before the guests depart.

- Has Joe done anything unethical, or has he just been stupid?
- Should the reporter print the story?
- Is Joe's home a protected reserve?

Changing the circumstances clarifies the mode of reasoning and pinpoints critical factors in making judgments. Closed questions force decision making; open-ended questions encourage analysis.
   Would your answers to the three preceding questions change if

- Joe's drinking were habitual, perhaps affecting his performance on the job?
- Joe had made several racist remarks during the party?
- Joe were chief administrative officer in a city of 300,000?

Would your answers to the first two questions change if it had been an office party in a local restaurant?
   Do the public opinion polls affect your answers? Should public opinion affect a manager's ethical choices?

Do people in public life have a right to any privacy? Balancing privacy with the public's right to know becomes more troublesome as the speed, capacity, and standards of disclosure change. Today so much *is* public record that it is hard to distinguish privacy from anonymity. The functional equivalent of puritan New England's public pillory is the nightly news, but with at least one big difference. Not too long ago, private peccadilloes were isolated from public responsibilities. Public scrutiny (and public voyeurism) was limited by technology and convention. At one time, living a lifetime in a small town meant that friends and neighbors knew everybody's secrets, but anonymity was within a few day's ride on horseback. Today our neighbors may not know our names, but personal matters are headlines for the entire world to see. In some respects, modern life has turned the public and private domains inside out.

Public-Private Boundary

Although it is squarely in the American political tradition to apply one set of standards of behavior to the private citizen and another to a public figure, we have not yet developed selective material criteria. Beginning with George Washington, presidents have made great public contributions more significant historically than their private mischief, including their love lives. Ralph Chandler (1989b, p. 1) calls for "moral grandeur" in making judgments rather than in making grand demands on someone else's behavior. On the other hand, historically the criticisms of the president (even George Washington) have been harsh. The accusations made by the Federalist press during the Jefferson administration would make even today's caustic commentators pale.

Is "appearance of impropriety" a code term (pun intended) for higher standards or double standards? Is it an excuse for titillation at the expense of public officials and employees? Can we separate what is trivial or irrelevant from what is meaningful? Should we distinguish a youngster's misstep from a character defect in the mature manager? Some have suggested that we apply to those in public life a statute of limitations or proclaim an amnesty (Raspberry, 1987, p. A27). The courts use a "least restrictive means" test for curbs on individual liberties. Cannot a comparable standard be developed for public appointees and employees? Should a line be drawn between pertinent public and private behavior? If so, where? And by whom?

When ethics is politically—and cynically—abused for partisan purposes, public managers and employees, their morale, and the image of government all get hit in the crossfire. Who gets blamed and takes the heat? Which agency, which manager, which political party? The current stew is heavily spiced with partisan ingredients. Given ethical charges and accusations, "the very language of political judgment has become suspect and subsequently debunked" (Jennings, 1989a).

If the test of competence includes perfection, then we are doomed to disillusionment and to the loss of public confidence. Therefore, the obligation to maintain the public trust must not degenerate into spouting sanctimonious platitudes or feeding vulgar curiosity. The genuine obligation depends on meeting meaningful standards and intelligible guidelines.

Pressing Business

There are at least five lessons for the public manager in all this: (1) use common sense, (2) go on record, (3) establish ethical credibility, (4) tell it as it is, and (5) tell it as it should be. Let us take them one at a time.

1. *Use common sense.* Be realistic. Learn what to expect from the media—nothing; that is its calling and professional duty. Be prepared for special scrutiny, not special treatment.

2. *Go on record.* Professional survival skills include making it difficult to be misinterpreted, misunderstood, or misquoted. Giving good interviews and writing good press releases are useful professional skills. Although professional standards may urge anonymity, a public manager may not always have a choice in the matter.

3. *Establish ethical credibility.* Take a hand in training; help break in media novices to establish a good working relationship and personal rapport and to expose them to the legal and professional standards operating in the jurisdiction. This exposure can include workaday ethical choices and even a crisis or two. (See Chapter Ten, concluding this book.)

4. *Tell it as it is.* Tell the truth. Let the media know they are dealing with a person they can trust. Lying is both unethical and impractical. Surely, we all make mistakes; the key is to admit them and not repeat them. Ethics restrains deception but does not prevent error.

5. *Tell it as it should be.* The fifth and final proposal shifts from self-protection to plea bargaining. It invokes a senior manager's responsibility to protect a blameless subordinate who is unjustly accused. It also invokes the value of compassion, which is more compelling when not self-serving. If an otherwise promising subordinate with a valid excuse (meaning a reason to be treated as if innocent) is threatened, a manager can call out the artillery: reason. One forceful argument is that only hypocrites will respond to a call for perfection. Another is the need to allow for human error and personal growth. The public manager can also urge caution along with compassion by suggesting that even when moral judgments are wrong, the personal damage persists. Also the senior manager is responsible for who does what on his watch. The senior manager's purpose here is to speak up, not cover up, and keeping subordinates' trust demands both charity and courage.

When operating under public scrutiny, the manager's acid test is whether he or she would like to read all about it on the front page of the local newspaper. Imagine, too, explaining that behavior or decision to family and friends. To safeguard personal integrity in the face of public disclosure, another important test consists of asking and answering some hard questions. What kind of person would do this? Do I want to be and be known as this kind of person? This approach is shown in Exhibit 3.8.

Nonprofit organizations and charitable organizations in particular have been in the spotlight in recent years. Among them is the American Red Cross (the subject of the case concluding this chapter) and the U.S. Olympic Committee, which concludes Chapter Ten. The INDEPENDENT SECTOR, Better Business Bureau, Urban Institute's Center on Nonprofits and Philanthropy, and scholars (for example, Light, 2002) have scrutinized fundraising, finances, and more. (See Resource B for nonprofit Internet sites.) In response, national umbrella organizations developed model codes and accountability standards that recognize that these organizations' lifeblood is donors' confidence and trust.

EXHIBIT 3.8. AUDIT DECISIONS AGAINST FOUR STANDARDS.

☑ The mirror test for integrity asks,
  "What kind of person do I admire and want to be?"

☑ The publicity test for accountability asks,
  "Am I willing to read about this in the newspaper? Tell my family?"

☑ The visceral test for implementation and authenticity asks,
  "Am I willing and likely to follow through? Can I live with this?"

☑ The signature test symbolizes personal responsibility and asks,
  "Do I take public responsibility for this recommendation, analysis, or decision?"

Signed _____

Date _____

Case: In the Black with the Red Cross

September 11, 2001, is scarred into the contemporary consciousness. The horrific images simply are unforgettable; symbols of U.S. economic and military power were attacked, and thousands of innocent victims fell to terrorism.

The American Red Cross (ARC) was there, helping tens of thousands of people made homeless and families in despair because of the loss of loved ones, and providing support to an untold number coping with this national tragedy (see Exhibit 3.9).

EXHIBIT 3.9. SNAPSHOT OF THE RED CROSS.

In 1863, Henri Dunant and other Swiss nationals established the International Committee for Relief to the Wounded and initiated the humanitarian movement now known as the Red Cross. The International Federation of Red Cross and Red Crescent Societies was founded in Paris by five national societies (Britain, France, Italy, Japan, and the United States) in 1919 and has 178 recognized societies today.

Founded in 1881, the American Red Cross has been operating under congressional charter for more than a century. The avowed mission of the American Red Cross is to "prevent and alleviate human suffering wherever it may be found" and its "purpose is to protect life and health and to ensure respect for the human being" (American Red Cross, 2002a).

Propelled by a desire to help somehow, Americans and people from all over the globe responded by sending money to the Red Cross. In the first six months, over $850 million had been donated to the Red Cross's 9/11 relief fund, the Liberty Fund.

In the past, Red Cross executives have steadfastly said the organization's policy was to state in its appeals for funds that money collected in the wake of an event would be used for "this disaster or similar disasters." Some community groups countered that the statement often was overwhelmed by gripping images of local victims and the use of local addresses as mail-in sites. The implication in the Red Cross advertising was that the money was to be used to address the tragedy of 9/11 in some way. Some cosponsors also emphasized this theme, for example, by saying "A portion of the profits from X will go to Red Cross' Liberty Fund to help survivors of 9/11."

Local Red Cross leaders in at least a half-dozen areas of the country hit by large disasters in the past decade have said they have had to pressure the Red Cross to release millions of dollars in donations that the public intended for their communities. Criticism dates to at least 1989, after the San Francisco Loma Prieta earthquake, and continued through the 1995 Oklahoma City bombing and the 1997 Red River flood in parts of Minnesota and North Dakota. In these cases, local officials said the Red Cross launched emotional appeals after each disaster that tapped into a charitable outpouring, and then delayed spending portions of the money locally until community leaders protested. In early 2001, victims of San Diego wildfires waited for money earmarked for them while funds were spent on vehicles and a telephone system upgrade for the local Red Cross chapter, an audit found.

The Donor Expectations Survey—a national survey sponsored by the Better Business Bureau's (BBB) Wise Giving Alliance and conducted by Princeton Survey Research Associates in Spring 2001—finds,

When people are asked to weigh the importance of many different kinds of information, they rate two other areas almost as important to their giving decisions as charity finances—the accuracy of a charity's advertising and promotion

(73% very important) and the effectiveness of a charity's programs (70% very important). The public's broader informational agenda is underscored by the finding that two-thirds (67%) of adults would not want an independent watchdog organization that monitors charities to focus exclusively on charity finances, but instead report on many different aspects of charity operations. The public's other priorities include information about the truthfulness and accuracy of fund-raising appeals (rated "very important" by 81%), willingness to disclose information about operations (80% "very important"), and the effectiveness of a charity's programs in achieving their purpose or mission (70% "very important")" (Better Business Bureau, 2001, p. 2).

The report concludes, "Public trust in charities today is stable, an improvement from the declining confidence that characterized the public mood in the early 1990s" (p. 5).

The Red Cross reversed course in November, 2001, in its handling of a fund drive for victims of the 9/11 terrorist attacks (American Red Cross, 2001). Responding to public criticism, the Red Cross backed off plans to reserve some of its so-called Liberty Fund for long-term projects, promising that all donations would be used for the victims of terrorism. Its board of governors adopted the changes on the recommendation of the organization's new chief executive officer in charge of a $3 billion operation. Active fundraising ceased for the Liberty Fund, now pledged to remain a separate, segregated fund. By this time, $137 million of the $543 million raised had been spent from the Liberty Fund.

Acting on complaints from donors to the Red Cross and critical reports about its post-September 11 fundraising (*Washington Post,* 2002a), the BBB asked the Red Cross in February 2002 for information to help determine whether it still meets bureau standards for charities. The Red Cross was criticized for initially saying it would use some money for projects unrelated to the attacks.

By June 2002, the fund had raised almost a $1 billion. That same month, in response to criticism from the BBB and other charitable watchdog groups, the Red Cross issued a press release that tried to put these concerns to rest (American Red Cross, 2002b). The organization's external auditor, KPMG, issued an unusual audit statement that covered the disbursements from the 9/11 fund through October 31, 2001, and another audit of fund activities for the period September 11, 2001, through June 30, 2002. The unqualified audit statements ("no material weaknesses in internal controls") were used to buttress the Red Cross's argument that it was discharging its fiduciary responsibility (or proper stewardship) of the funds. It was certainly the case that professional accounting rules were followed.

This did not satisfy external watchdogs. In August 2002, the BBB's Council released its evaluation of the Red Cross (Better Business Bureau, 2002). Using its twenty-three criteria for charitable solicitations, the BBB determined that the Red Cross failed to meet two of these criteria, thereby losing its status as an approved charity of the BBB.

Criterion 1:

1. 9/11 donations were being used for broader purposes than solicitations indicated.
2. Appeals that did disclose the Red Cross's intention to spend funds on broader purposes did not do so in a clear and conspicuous manner that would be reasonably understood by potential donors given the circumstances of 9/11.

Criterion 5:

Some corporate sponsors that the Red Cross made agreements with did not disclose what portion of the profits would benefit 9/11 victims and their families but nonetheless used the fund as a marketing tool.

Hard on the heels of criticism that it should be clearer about how it uses disaster donations, the Red Cross announced significant changes in its advertising and public solicitations. A major policy shift saw the Red Cross acknowledge that it had not clearly explained to donors that funds contributed to a local disaster could wind up being used anywhere in the country for other relief efforts. Now the charity will notify the public when the costs of a disaster have been met, and it will stop using prominent references to local disasters in fundraising for its national Disaster Relief Fund.

"One lesson from that controversy," Red Cross Chairman David McLaughlin said, "is that the public expects greater accountability from the Red Cross and other large charities. We need to be more transparent. We need to be totally clear in our message. We need to clarify donor intent, document that donor intent and affirm that donor intent so there is no misunderstanding" (*Washington Post,* 2002b).

As part of the group's new program, donors who make undesignated contributions to the Disaster Relief Fund will be asked to confirm that they understand how their donations will be used before the money is accepted. They also will receive a written acknowledgment to reconfirm their intent.

Charity watchdogs and members of Congress generally applauded the changes. Senator Charles E. Grassley (R-Iowa) said, "People think hard about how much they can afford and where their money will do the most good. Charities should treat them accordingly" (*Washington Post,* 2002b, A9).

The BBB's Standards for Charity Accountability went into effect in March 2003 and "recommend ethical practices beyond the act of disclosure in order to ensure public confidence and encourage giving. As voluntary standards, they also go beyond the requirements of local, state and federal laws and regulations" (Better Business Bureau, 2003b). In May 2003, the BBB's reevaluation found that the Red Cross meets its solicitation standards. "After a review of copies of recent Red Cross appeals, the Alliance concluded that the Red Cross has demonstrated it has implemented its previously announced plans to change its disaster appeal language to help donors understand how their gift will be used" (Better Business Bureau, 2003a, unpaginated).

As of March 2003, the Liberty Disaster Relief Fund had received more than $1 billion in donations and had disbursed about 77 percent (Better Business Bureau, 2003a).

◆ ◆ ◆

Discussion Questions

1. Should nonprofit and charitable organizations be held to a high fiduciary standard? Why? Is the Red Cross being held to an unreasonable standard in this case? What should one consider in answering these questions?
2. Should charities, if they are given more money than they need for one project, shift the funds to other worthy projects that are underfunded? Otherwise, what should they do? Return it or spend it needlessly? What principles and ethical perspectives apply here?
3. What ethical obligations do nonprofit organizations and charitable organizations in particular owe to donors?
4. Often working closely with government agencies when responding to emergencies and a *federal instrumentality* by virtue of its congressional charter (1905), the American Red Cross is required to fulfill responsibilities delegated by the federal government (including providing family communications for U.S. military personnel). The IRS gives charities nonprofit status (501c3), which means they are exempt from taxes and some other forms of government regulation. (See Figure I.1.) Given this special relationship and the need for public confidence and trust, does government have an obligation to ensure proper stewardship, or should this issue be worked out without government intervention, perhaps in the marketplace?
5. In this case, did the Red Cross operate in the public interest? Why should or should not this be among its concerns? Some might argue that, for nonprofits, "The challenge . . . is for the board of directors to provide direction and leadership while meeting the competing needs of multiple stakeholders, as well as reconciling the rival demands of both the fiduciary principle and the common good principle" (Groudine and Miller, 2002, p. 124). Do you agree or disagree, and why?

◆ ◆ ◆

Note

1. If the truth be known, the only dirty book in our offices is Kenneth W. Starr's report on alleged financial improprieties (Whitewater) and perjury and obstruction and obstruction of justice (Lewinsky scandal) delivered by the Office of the Independent Counsel to the U.S. House of Representatives. The *New York Times* Web site devoted to the Starr Report (http://www.time.com/time/daily/scandal/ starr_report/files) shows the following warning: "The following report contains sexually explicit language."

CHAPTER FOUR

TAKING INDIVIDUAL RESPONSIBILITY

This chapter converts public service obligations into general guides to ethical action in public agencies by drawing on the idea of individual responsibility in both everyday and extreme bureaucratic experiences. The chapter confronts central facts of managerial life: individuals work in organizational settings, exercise discretion, and ply their expertise. We start by warning against substituting scapegoating for problem solving. Then we move from individual responsibility to responsibility for means and ends and, finally, to professional competence. A concluding case puts the action guides to work.

Ethical principles are guides to action; they operationalize values and cue behavior that is befitting public service. Three clusters of action-driving principles stem directly from legal compliance and public interest, core ethical obligations in public service, and the definition of *ethics*. These action guides point to individual responsibility, substantive responsibility, and competence. The level of generality thwarts a formula-like application, which is all to the good. Ethical decision making demands individual judgment, and workaday problems are so diverse and so complex that even an encyclopedic compilation would not cover all possibilities. The goal is to guide action, not stymie or dictate it.

Searching for Demons

Most principles, in their exaggerated or absolutist versions, are shaky, even suspect. Thus demanding individual responsibility can decline into preoccupation with allocating blame, ferreting out the guilty, and finding the one at fault. This outcome is encouraged by the fact that individual wrongdoing is easy to understand, or at least easier than legalistic abstractions or systemwide flaws. As a result, we occasionally try to dodge difficult issues by finger-pointing. Sometimes we *use* a person as an example or escape hatch: victor, villain, or victim. Diversionary tactics and scapegoating are ethically unsound. Often they are not even very useful in the long run and are trivial subplots in passionate dramas over profound ethical issues.

Three incidents corroborate the generic quality of the diversion-scapegoat proposition. In 1968, almost six hundred largely unarmed and unresisting civilians were massacred at My Lai in Vietnam. U.S. soldiers in Charlie Company under platoon leader Lieutenant William L. Calley were directly responsible. The ex-serviceman whose letter originally provoked the investigation, Ron Ridenhour, said in an interview two decades later (Cockburn, 1988, p. 403), "The important thing is, this was an act of policy, not an individual aberration. My Lai didn't happen because Lieutenant Calley went berserk. There were similar acts of policy all over the country. I mean, every once in a while they decided they would make an example." (Note that Ridenhour's letter begins the ethics chapter in West Point's 1985 textbook on leadership [U.S. Military Academy, 1985, pp. 21–1]).

In time, the army charged about two dozen officers and enlisted men with direct involvement in the massacre but convicted only Calley, who wound up serving three years under house arrest. William Wilson, the army colonel in the inspector general's office who handled and later wrote about the investigation, quoted General Peers: "The failure to bring justice to those who inflicted the atrocity casts grave doubts upon the efficacy of our justice system." Wilson concludes, "I do remember being startled when the public seemed to make a hero out of Rusty Calley, or at the least a victim. It sure didn't look that way from up close" (Wilson, 1990, p. 53).

The American response to the massacre at My Lai is worth comparing to the then-Soviet Union's response to the disaster at Chernobyl. *Pravda*, the Soviet Communist Party's newspaper, blamed plant managers for ignoring safety measures in "cleaning up" after the nuclear accident at Chernobyl in April 1986. Although charges ran the gamut from nepotism and drunkenness to management abuses, the main point is that blaming plant managers for stressing power production at any cost," including repair and maintenance, obscures the realities of pressure from *Moscow* to increase energy output (Keller, 1988). Undoubtedly, that pressure was linked to the accident in the first place. Although many acts of personal courage marked the events, the irresponsibility and ineptitude of scientists, senior officials, and government workers in the planning, construction, and operational phases contributed to the tragedy to which Soviet physicist and then-dissident Andrei Sakharov attributed universal significance (Sakharov, 1991, p. viii).

In May 2004, the U.S. Senate unanimously passed a resolution condemning the abuses of Iraqi detainees at Abu Ghraib prison and calling for a full investigation.

The U.S. Army general, whose March 2004 report described abuses by American soldiers and interrogators, "was shaped by that strong moral compass and by his vision of the Army as a noble calling" (Jehl, 2004, unpaginated). In his May 2004 testimony before the Senate Armed Services Committee, he identified the cause: "Failure in leadership from the brigade commander on down, lack of discipline, no training whatsoever, and no supervision" (quoted in Jehl, 2004, unpaginated). "At the end of the day, a few soldiers and civilians conspired to abuse and conduct egregious acts of violence against detainees and other civilians outside the bounds of international laws and the Geneva Convention" (quoted in Branigin, 2004, p. A04). Secretary of Defense Donald Rumsfeld said, "It is a body blow when we find that we have . . . a few who have betrayed our values by their conduct" (quoted in Semple, 2004, unpaginated). The individuals charged with misconduct are on trial. It is too soon to tell whether organizational responses will be taken. The fact that, as one journalist points out in the headline, "Only a Few Spoke Up on Abuse as Many Soldiers Stayed Silent," suggests that an organizational response is needed (Zernike, 2004).

The purpose behind the storytelling is not to defend the indefensible; in fact, some individual public servants have committed reprehensible deeds. The infamous Ramparts scandal in the Los Angeles Police Department in the 1990s started with the arrest of "one bad cop" but spread so far and swept up so many that the department came under federal supervision (Cannon, 2000). The central allegations revolve around revelations provided by former LAPD officer Rafael A. Perez, who stole eight pounds of seized cocaine from a department locker and received a lighter sentence in exchange for information about police corruption.

Most of the charges involve the anti-gang CRASH (Community Resources Against Street Hoodlums) unit operating in a neighborhood just west of downtown, known as the Rampart Division (Booth and Sanchez, 1999). Our purpose here is to emphasize that *individual responsibility is by no means identical to sole responsibility.*

These stories have a perverse ending: a search for demons functions as a sorry substitute for solving systemic shortcomings or organizational flaws. (By way of contrast, see Exhibit 4.1.) According to the U.S. Military Academy text (1985, pp. 21–23),

> Whether the My Lai incident . . . is interpreted as simply the fault of a few weak or flawed characters who happened to hold key leadership roles or is seen instead as symptomatic of a complex organizational phenomenon, moral failure on such a scale . . . illustrates the awesome importance of the ethical dimensions of organizational leadership.

Accountability is not just a military or government problem but a bureaucratic one. The Columbia tragedy in 2003, like the Challenger disaster in January 1986 in which corporate executives and engineers played a crucial role, testifies to its immediacy and magnitude. Melvin J. Dubnick (personal communication, June 15, 2004) argues:

Accountability matters, but not in the way most people think. Those who believe that greater accountability is the key to justice, democracy, ethical behavior or better administrative performance have yet to prove their case. They have little to offer except rhetoric and unsubstantiated assumptions to support their calls for reform. What we do know is that accountability in its many and varied forms can provide effective protection against the thoughtlessness that Hannah Arendt warned against in her elaboration of the "banality of evil." On those grounds alone we should make every effort to enhance accountable governance.

(On public service accountability, see Behn, 2001; Bovens, 1998; Gormley and Balla, 2004; Romzek and Dubnick, 1987.)

EXHIBIT 4.1. THE TRAGEDY OF MISSION STS-107.

The Columbia Space Shuttle Mission STS-107 was lost on February 3, 2003, sixteen minutes before scheduled touchdown. In one journalist's eyes, "In so many ways, the shuttle was a machine made from the raw material of the American character. Columbia embodied calculated risk" (Hotz, 2003, unpaginated). Sean O'Keefe, the relatively new head of NASA, within hours appointed an independent investigatory panel—the Columbia Accident Investigation Board (CAIB [http://www.nasa.gov/columbia/home/index.html]). Its head, Admiral Harold Gehman (who had led the panel investigating the bombing of the U.S.S. Cole) testified before the Senate Commerce Committee on May 14, 2003: "If we find that something could have been done, then the benign bureaucratic decisions made earlier take on a whole new significance."

Some questions asked during the Senate Commerce Committee's hearing centered on just who in NASA was responsible for rejecting the offered satellite images of possible damage to the shuttle. Gehman spoke of "missed signals going up and going down" NASA's hierarchy. He "blamed NASA's system, not any individuals, and said there was 'not one person responsible'" (Recer, 2003, unpaginated).

The CAIB report concludes that NASA's "failings include an institutional culture that plays down problems, as well as constraints from Washington that may have reduced the ability to reach space safely" (Schwartz, 2003, unpaginated; currently unavailable).

On what it terms NASA's *organizational culture,* CAIB (2003, notes omitted) reports,

> The CAIB also investigated communications procedures between NASA engineers and managers. The nature of [the] Shuttle program is complex, given the high level of technology used and the multiple civilians, contractors, and Centers involved, each integral to the success of the program. CAIB found the need to communicate effectively between the individuals and organizations involved in the Shuttle program to be paramount, given the technology, and risk involved.

Pressure to stay on an existing launch schedule and inadequate resources also are considered to be contributing factors of the STS-107 accident. CAIB also found that NASA's safety program falls short of achieving the level of safety necessary for the shuttle program. As a result, CAIB recommended that the safety system at NASA be restructured.

A public manager's first task is to fix the problem and only secondarily to fix the blame. These incidents demonstrate the need for both ethically supportive organizations and ethically responsible individuals.

We Are Individually Responsible for Our Decisions and Behavior

Ethics rests on voluntary moral judgment, with the individual as ethical player. Rephrased, this idea means individual responsibility for making judgments and choices. Logically, decision making turns on selecting and accepting responsibility. The problem of individual responsibility within an organizational framework is often referred to as the problem of "many hands" (Thompson, 1980). However, individual responsibility is *not* obliterated by collective decision making in organizations and agencies. Because most of us work in organizations most of the time, arguing otherwise would put ethics (along with contemporary civilization) on the endangered species list.

The organizational habitat of public managers affects decision making, action, *and* ethical analysis. The ecology features implicit norms, predominant values, established routines, underlying decision premises, and pressures for obedience and loyalty (for example, rewarding the team player). To these are added explicit policies, procedures, and routines. Public administrators need to be and usually are attuned to the organizational context of decision making.

Through selective recruitment and the imbibing of organizational habits and group norms (socialization processes), many—but not all—organizational members come to identify strongly with the organization and absorb its standards as their own. Hierarchical, peer, and career pressure is not just a classroom theory, as the case concluding this chapter illustrates. Many public managers have recounted to us the pressures they feel to compromise their personal values and standards of behavior. And they are not alone.

Harvard researchers found in their study of one hundred young professionals that the subjects professed themselves willing to compromise their integrity to advance their careers (Rimer, 2003). In its 2003 National Business Ethics Survey of 1,500 U.S. private sector workers, the Ethics Resource Center (Ethics Resource Center, 2003) found, "Nearly a third of respondents say their coworkers condone questionable ethics practices by showing respect for those who achieve success using them." ERC describes "observed misconduct" and "pressures to compromise ethics standards" as "key indicators of ethics-related problems in the workplace." It reports that both have declined since the 2000 survey: observed misconduct from 31 percent to 22 percent and pressure from 13 percent to 10 percent.

In some cases, the identification becomes extreme. "Their job contract with bureaucracy soon becomes a psychological contract" (Hummel, 1987, p. 7). As a result, "what is likely to be *substituted* for ethical deliberation is an application of the individual's understanding of the norms and values of the organization" (Denhardt, 1988, p. 91).

The bureaucratic mentality (or, more accurately, *bureaucratic dispositions*; Heclo, 1987) applies to large-scale corporate cultures and nonprofit organizations, along with governmental ones. Bureaucracy is not solely a governmental trait; it is the way contemporary society organizes joint action to perform complex tasks. Some experts view bureaucracy as inherently constricting, pathological, amoral, or even immoral. Others, such as Charles Goodsell in *The Case for Bureaucracy* (2004) and James Q. Wilson in *Bureaucracy* (1990), counter with contrary evidence and arguments. Beneath these broad generalizations lies a mix of cultures, missions, procedures, and other characteristics. Bureaucracy is neither uniform nor monolithic, and bureaucrats are not of one face or one mind.

Although stereotyping does injustice to all employees, organizations do exert pressures on members to conform. *The pressures can be for better or for worse.* A public position itself is ethically neutral—used for good or bad, right or wrong—until people use it or, rather, abuse it for something other than solving people problems and meeting the mission. Peter Drucker (1989, p. 229) explains: "Management is about human beings. Its task is to make people capable of joint performance, to make their strengths effective and their weaknesses irrelevant."

Mutually restraining interaction between the individual and organization is an institution's danger and its promise, and it is precisely the point of building ethically supportive agencies. At any rate, while organizational demands may challenge individual responsibility, they do not erase it.

The ethical benchmarks of the twentieth century (itemized in Resource A) teach us that bureaucracy is powerful, but power is neutral, that is, it can be used for great good as well as great evil. The very fact that these benchmarks are extreme cases helps crystallize issues and clarify thinking. By definition, they do *not* reflect daily routine in public service. The distance and magnitude of awesome events sometimes make them useful learning devices. Both heroic behavior and heinous behavior direct our attention to the interplay between individuals and organizations and their capacity for good and evil.

In this light, consider the Nuremberg Charter of 1947. It specified the procedures and principles underlying the trial of the major Nazi war criminals by the victorious allies (the United States, France, Great Britain, and the former Soviet Union) after World War II. On making decisions and giving orders, Part II, Article 7 of the charter states, "The official position of defendants, whether as Heads of State or responsible officials in Government departments, shall not be considered as freeing them from responsibility or mitigating punishment."

SO IT FOLLOWS THAT WE CANNOT HIDE BEHIND OUR BOSS
OR OUR DESK TO ESCAPE RESPONSIBILITY.

In the organizational habitat, the manager's niche is defined as a particular spot in the chain of command, the hierarchy of legitimate authority. Here deference to superior-subordinate relations generally and routinely prevails. It is supposed to do so. But neither discipline nor obedience defines the boundaries of subordinates' ethical responsibility. (See the section "Disobedience Before Illegality" in Chapter Two.)

Moral outrage, incomprehension, or both are usual responses to the notorious words of Adolf Eichmann, the Nazi official kidnapped to Israel, tried by an Israeli court, then hanged in 1962. Denying legal culpability and ignoring ethical responsibility, his defense is popularly rendered as "I was only following orders." On taking orders, Part II, Article 8 of the Nuremberg Charter states, "The fact that the defendant acted pursuant to order of his Government or of a superior shall not free him from responsibility, but may be considered in mitigation of punishment."

The former prison psychologist at Nuremberg notes the *"psychologically* aberrant nature of an adult person who defines good and evil merely as synonyms for obedience and disobedience to one's superiors" (Miale and Selzer, 1975, p. 6). Hannah Arendt's thesis in *Eichmann in Jerusalem: A Report on the Banality of Evil* (1964) is that ordinary people are capable of doing evil. Stanley Milgram's well-known psychological experiments on obedience in the early 1960s required subjects at Yale University to inflict painful electric shocks that were, unknown to them, counterfeit (Milgram, 1983, and Ochs and Whitford, 2004). Arendt's and Milgram's works are often marshaled as evidence of how easy it is to unthinkingly obey authority and ignore questions of right and wrong, good and evil.

Maybe so on both counts, but that does not justify the behaviors or make them ethical. Guy B. Adams (personal communication, June 16, 2004) notes,

> When the damaged or dead human beings are visible in the managerial rear-view mirror and colleagues reassure you that it was the *right* thing to do or that you were "just following orders," it is too late for you to reflect on whether "marking" a group of people as "superfluous" (less than human, a "disease," or "insects," or "vermin") might lead to administrative evil.

(On administrative evil, see Adams and Balfour, 1998).

Although few indulge themselves in outright evil and fewer still in righteousness, people are evidently influenced by authority, by apathy, by thoughtlessness, and by their environment. Take a moment to think about the results of ceding responsibility for moral reasoning. Renowned Italian author and Holocaust survivor, Primo Levy, draws on his experience as an inmate at Auschwitz: "Monsters exist. . . . But they are too few in number to be truly dangerous. More dangerous are . . . the functionaries ready to believe and to act without asking questions" (quoted in Hochschild, 1998, p. 121).

Think about the willingness of many, though not all, of Milgram's subjects to inflict shocks on human subjects who were already in pain. (The shocks were sham, as was the participants' pain, but the subjects didn't know that.) As a counterbalance, keep in mind that a member of Calley's platoon refused to shoot; Sherron Watkins blew the whistle on Enron (Solomon, 2004); some speak up (Zernike, 2004), and some step up. The individual and the setting interact. But whether that setting is a help or a hurdle, the individual is still the responsible agent.

Blaming one's own unscrupulous behavior on circumstance or other people is a well-worn excuse, summarized by Machiavelli in *The Prince:*

> A man who wishes to make a profession of goodness in everything must necessarily come to grief among so many who are not good. Therefore it is necessary for a prince, who wishes to maintain himself, to learn how not to be good, and to use this knowledge and not use it, according to the necessity of the case.

Even if one accepts the personal utility argument, being coerced into it by rogues, villains, or one's boss does not make the behavior any more ethical.

To act as ethical agents and retain personal integrity, public managers must avoid the trap of what Dennis Thompson (1985) calls the *ethic of structure.* Here responsibility is defined by the job description, and to say "it's not my job" lamely justifies irresponsibility. ("The Contract"—the case concluding this chapter—illustrates this, as does Maria's problem in the Introduction's first bullet.) Inaction or looking the other way is a choice but not necessarily an ethically neutral one. Invalidating moral reasoning and responsibility altogether, the claims are (1) "not administrators but the organization (and its formal officers) should be held responsible for its decisions and policies" and (2) "personal moral responsibility extends only to the specific duties of their own office for which they are legally liable" (Thompson, 1985, pp. 555, 559). By shedding the burden and possibly the onus of organizational outcomes, this argument denies individual responsibility, efficacy, and ethics. Even were these claims valid, the manager could not duck responsibility: What is one doing working in that agency?

Responsibilities and loyalties to the boss complicate the cross-currents of obligations. One pitfall is exaggerated personal allegiance. Aaron Wildavsky (1989, p. 779) puts it this way: "What is the temptation of administrators? By confusing their patron with their God, they mistake serving their superior with helping their people."

Despite the boss's relative power, successful managers are fully aware that the boss does in fact depend on them. Management pundit Peter Drucker (1986, p. 16) defines a manager as "someone who is responsible for the performance of all the people on whom his own performance depends. The first person on whom a manager's performance depends is the boss, and the boss is thus the first person for whose performance a manager has to take responsibility. Managing the boss means, above all, creating a relationship of trust." Although Drucker is speaking of business managers and has rejected the notion of distinctive business ethics (1981), the implication for public managers is that mindlessly following orders serves neither ethical nor managerial purposes.

SO IT FOLLOWS THAT WE CANNOT HIDE BEHIND OUR SUBORDINATES.

President Ronald Reagan dramatized the principle that we cannot hide behind our subordinates in his response to the critical report issued by the Tower Commission he appointed to investigate the Iran-Contra affair in the mid-1980s. In a nationally televised address on March 4, 1987, Reagan said, "First, let me say I take full responsibility for my own actions and for those of my administration. As angry as I may be about activities undertaken without my knowledge, I am still accountable for those activities. . . . [T]his happened on my watch." By publicly and personally taking responsibility and despite his disengaged management style that abetted the activities, the president went a long way in the minds of many toward separating this affair from Watergate. The principle guiding action is echoed in Senator Howard Baker's famous question, asked during the Watergate hearings: "What did the president know and when did he know it?"

The idea is far older and broader than American public administration, however. The advice given Moses in Exodus 18 about designing an administrative structure emphasizes Moses' responsibility for recruiting subordinates of good character and for retaining the hard cases for himself. In a change of venue, consider that *negative responsibility* in the Tokyo war trials (after World War II, in 1946–1948) held that a superior can be guilty for failing to prevent subordinates' actions that were preventable. The results of two national surveys, shown in Exhibit 4.2, provide a more workaday example of managerial responsibility.

Reasonably, a city manager is not directly answerable for a road crew's unauthorized coffee break any more than the president is answerable for what goes on deep in the innards of a cabinet-level department. Commonsense yardsticks such as proximity, saliency, and gravity rightly affect our assessment of managerial responsibilities. Reasonable people would take a hard look at chain of command and span of control. A key in the question posed by the *New York Times* surveys shown in Exhibit 4.2 is the word *widespread*. Although managers may not know what is going on, shouldn't they? What about managerial responsibility for supervision?

The principle of responsibility for subordinates' actions is tied to the principles introduced next, which involve knowledge and competence. For example, in the July

EXHIBIT 4.2. SHOULD THE AGENCY HEAD RESIGN?

Question: If an investigation reveals widespread corruption at low and middle levels of a government agency, but it is clear that the head of the agency was not corrupt and did not know about it, should the head of the agency resign, or not?

Responses	December 1985	April 1986
Should resign	16%	19%
Should not	75	75
Depends	4	2
Don't know/No answer	5	4

- Do you agree with the majority response?
- Managers may not know what is going on, but shouldn't they?
- Although the agency head may not be corrupt, is that person acting responsibly and doing the job?

The question and responses came from *New York Times* surveys conducted in 1985 and 1986.

1987 congressional hearings on the Iran-Contra affair, John M. Poindexter, former national security adviser to President Reagan, testified that the president was misled or lied to by omission to protect him: "I made a very deliberate decision not to ask the president so that I could insulate him from the decision and provide some future deniability." The end result is that *plausible deniability is* usually implausible, and its costs are figured in terms of credibility.

SO IT FOLLOWS THAT WE CANNOT HIDE BEHIND OUR IGNORANCE.

Because serving the public interest means, in part, identifying the public interest, getting the facts is an important and often first step in thinking through ethical problems. Usually, there is not enough information or time to guarantee being absolutely certain of all spin-offs and side effects, as Exhibit 4.3 suggests. Yet public managers cannot be paralyzed. They must make decisions as best as they can. Unanticipated or unintended results, if by-products of indifference, thoughtlessness, or carelessness, point to *inexcusable* ignorance. Here the rule of reason applies, and ethical people *can* make mistakes. There is an obvious kinship between this principle and competence. "Where the welfare of so many is at stake, officials must make exceptional efforts to anticipate consequences of their actions" (Thompson, 1985, p. 560).

A profession is defined largely by its specialized knowledge, on which its privileges rest. Ignorance undercuts all members. Many professional codes incorporate standards that require the continuing professional training and tutoring of junior colleagues. The

EXHIBIT 4.3. IMPROVISING A HOMELAND DEFENSE.

The National Commission on Terrorist Attacks on the United States (9–11 Commission [http://www.9–11commission.gov]) was established by law in 2002 as an independent, bipartisan commission.

> Neads [Northeast Air Defense Sector] did not know where United 93 was when it first heard about the hijacking from F.A.A. at 10:07. Presumably, F.A.A. would have provided the information, but we do not know how long it would have taken, nor how long it would have taken Neads to find and track the target on its own equipment.
>
> Once the target was known and identified, Neads needed orders to pass to the pilots. Shoot-down authority was first communicated to Neads at 10:31. Given the clear attack on the United States, it is also possible—though unlikely—that Norad's [North American Aerospace Defense Command] commanders could have ordered the shoot-down without the authorization communicated by the vice president.
>
> Norad officials have maintained that they would have intercepted and shot down United 93. We are not so sure. We are sure that the nation owes a debt to the passengers of United 93. Their actions saved the lives of countless others, and may have saved either the U.S. Capitol or the White House from destruction.
>
> The details of what happened on the morning of September 11 are complex. But the details play out a simple theme. Norad and the FAA [Federal Aviation Administration] were unprepared for the type of attacks launched against the United States on September 11, 2001. They struggled, under difficult circumstances, to improvise a homeland defense against an unprecedented challenge they had never encountered and had never trained to meet.

Excerpt is from National Commission on Terrorist Attacks on the United States: Staff Statement No. 17, "Improvising a Homeland Defense." June 2004. Internet [http://www.9–11commission.gov/hearings/hearing12/staff_statement_17.pdf] (accessed June 18, 2004).

most elementary standard of required knowledge springs from the obligation of legal compliance: know the law. (Chapter Two lays this out.)

Even more to the point is the fact that specialized knowledge is a source of substantial power in today's information society, and its manipulation increases the handler's exploitative potential. Many professional codes stress confidentiality and the public's right to privacy. North Dakota's 1999 Code of Professional Conduct for Educators declares that educators "shall disclose confidential information about individuals, in accordance with state and federal laws, only when a compelling professional purpose is served or when required by law" (Section 67.1–03–01–01, http://www.state.nd.us/espb/practices/ethics.htm).

The *danger zones* in information handling are outright deception; prejudicial distortion; inaccuracy; spurious accuracy and false certainty; proprietary, privileged, and confidential information; disclosure, public access, freedom of information, and privacy; and data integrity and computer security. There are so many first-rate negative examples of how defective disclosure degenerates into abuse of information and deception that it would be superfluous to provide one here.

Public managers are responsible for actions undertaken under the umbrella of their authority or in their name. Expert advice, professional judgments, and policy recommendations—all part of the daily routine—ideally rest on up-to-date information and assessment techniques. Getting the facts is logically part of many ethical decision-making models. In direct contrast to the nonchalance exhibited in Figure 4.3, responsible information management demands honoring basic standards. Checking against the seven questions in Exhibit 4.4 should help minimize bias and error.

We Are Responsible for What Is Done Along with How It Is Done

With the traditional boundary between politics and administration routinely breached by discretion (decisions made) and expertise (decisive influence), responsibility extends to both meaning and method, to substance as well as technique. Most managers perceive some scope and clout (Warren, 2003). More than a half century ago, at hearings on establishing a commission on ethics in government before a Senate subcommittee on June 27, 1951, Paul H. Appleby related the cross-pressures to hide behind impotence and to duck managerial responsibility for building an ethical work environment.

> Public officials dealing with public programs struggle with problems . . . constantly in the business of drawing the line between desirable considerations of citizen concerns in a somewhat flexible and sympathetic way and carrying on systematically in pursuit of the general public interest without discrimination and without favoritism.

EXHIBIT 4.4. GETTING THE FACTS.

Yes	
☑	1. Are underlying analytic assumptions known and open?
☑	2. Are significant omissions disclosed?
☑	3. Are reliability or error estimates provided?
☑	4. Are factual disagreements declared?
☑	5. Is information appropriate for the intended use and user?
☑	6. Are available consequential data or views included?
☑	7. Are data sources credible? Independently corroborated?

Checking *yes* to all seven questions conforms to basic standards.

In one sense these problems are most acute for low ranking officials engaged in operational dealing with the citizens and groups most directly concerned. They often feel weak and insecure as minor cogs in a great machine, and may on that account bend too easily to importunities from groups which seem to them powerful; they may feel unable to guess what backing they will get at higher levels if they hold firmly what would appear to them to be the general public-interest line. They may also be so closely associated functionally with such groups as to mistake them for the public. These subordinates can act reasonably well only with institutional patterns of responsibility laid down, and constantly supported and developed by officials at higher levels.

Discretion and expertise obviously operate in policy analysis and at the higher administrative ranks, where broad policy decisions are made. Legal, budget, and personnel decisions affect everything that goes out the door. But think of the many daily decisions made at the operational level, especially by those line employees who are direct service providers, or "street-level bureaucrats"—a term Michael Lipsky (1980) contributed. Here are the building and health inspectors, zoning enforcement officers, lifeguards at county parks, police officers, emergency dispatchers, air traffic controllers, park rangers, and even teachers. Away from the central office and often unsupervised, they meet the citizen, treat the citizen, and teach the citizen about government on the justice-compassion continuum shown in Exhibit 1.3. Each transaction shows the human face of government through *individual but not arbitrary treatment.*

Discretion

Line employees dispense services by making choices every day. These choices are constrained to a limited range of responses by standard operating procedures (SOPs; see Exhibit 10.3, "Hardly Neutral") dictated by the agency or supervisor, intergovernmental mandate, judicial directive, legislative oversight, professional association, and other sources, including the organization's informal culture. As a result, operational employees interact with people by *case management,* according to categories assigned by that public employee but defined by procedure. That the categories themselves, the assignment of them, and interactions based on them have profound ethical content is often dramatized by triage in medical services. Discretion is all about rationing resources, time, and attention, with serious ethical content and grave practical outcomes. Many professional codes of conduct recognize the power inherent in administrative discretion and the responsibility that power entails. Rules and resources must be selectively, sensibly, and sensitively applied in day-to-day operations. (Note that *discretion* has been called "a structural invitation to corruption" [Chambliss, 1988, p. 96]).

Means and Ends

Martin Luther King Jr. (1963, p. 13) argued that "it is wrong to use immoral means to attain moral ends [and] it is just as wrong, or even more so, to use moral means to preserve immoral ends." In its ethics code, ASPA bids members, "Exercise discretionary authority to promote the public interest." This requires Aristotle's *practical wisdom*, meaning "the ability not only to know the means to certain desired ends, but also to know what ends are desirable (worthy of desire)" (Tong, 1986, p. 88). As Aaron Wildavsky (1989, p. 787) sees it, "For public administrators, the second question is how well you accomplish objectives; the first is which objectives it is right to try to accomplish. Answers to the second question matter, but only after the first is settled."

Both public purposes and managerial practices have ethical dimensions. Often managers do what they can rather than what is best according to some objective standard. Contemporary thinking about decision making views the connection between ends and means as part of the routine decision-making process. According to Charles Lindblom (1959), goals and methods are intertwined, not distinct.

A 1988 administrative decision illustrates how ethical considerations about method can temper an otherwise single-minded commitment to meeting goals and getting the job done. A protest letter from scientists at the Environmental Protection Agency (EPA) prompted the agency's chief to ban data from Nazi experiments on humans from an EPA report. The use of data on phosgene (a toxic gas) provoked a debate about benefiting from unethically obtained information, along with questions about its reliability. One toxicologist argued that use of the data threatened to "condone taking some lives in order to save others," while an opposing opinion argued that "when data is [sic] collected in an unethical fashion, if it is important in protecting public health and is not available in any other way, I would use it" (Shabecoff, 1988, p. A17). Is the use of tainted data ethical, if it promises benefit to society (Alt and Weinstein, 2003)? Is the use or the disregard of such data tantamount to confounding means and ends?

Ethical neutrality is different from policy impartiality, unbiased treatment, and nonpartisanship. The "ethic of neutrality" denies that morality is possible in public bureaucracies by asserting that public managers "should follow not their own moral principles but the decisions and policies of the organization" (Thompson, 1985, p. 555). Ethical neutrality takes bureaucracy and transforms it into an assembly line. It means working in one's own little cubicle or with blinders on. It fosters refusing to admit or act on the implications of one's decision. Such a posture attempts to transform human beings into technical problems of transport, timetables, case quotas, check processing, and so on. Ethical neutrality strips the humanity from both the manager and service recipients. Dehumanizing the players serves to deny the ethical element. Blaming the victim generally accomplishes the same thing.

By ousting the individual ethical agent who thinks through ethical problems and makes judgments, this reasoning also jettisons ethics. A famous quotation from the great American nineteenth-century essayist Ralph Waldo Emerson sums it up perfectly: "We must hold a man amenable to reason for the choice of his daily craft or profession. It is not an excuse any longer for his deeds that they are the custom of his trade. What business has he with an evil trade?"

Incompetence Is Abuse of Office

Today's professional public service is based on competence, in contrast to the old patronage and citizen-volunteer methods of staffing. (Although there is no test of competence for political appointees in the executive branch, the United States survives a large number of political appointees without massive corruption.) According to President George H. W. Bush (Volcker Commission, 1989, p. 2), "How well the tasks of government are done affects the quality of the lives of all our people. Moreover, the success of any political leadership in implementing its policies and objectives depends heavily upon the expertise, quality, and commitment of the professional career employees, of government." Mary Ellen Guy (1990, p. 15) asserts, "The pursuit of excellence means striving to be as good as one can be. . . . It is not enough to be content with mediocrity," and puts that pursuit on her list of essential ethical values. A posture of competence ("we can do it") implies a commitment to needed change and demands a good-faith effort.

Competence is an ongoing aspiration, a moving and therefore always unmet goal, and a professionally decreed ethical obligation. Applying to public service generally, this standard is a heavy payload because it means, by definition, that managers permanently fall short.

Professional public service is rooted in making government more *businesslike* (as discussed in the introduction), and productivity and efficiency remain pivotal (see Chapter One). The general standard in federal service from 1965 to 1989 specified that employees avoid any action or appearance of "impeding government efficiency or economy." Its successors, signed by President Bush in 1989 and 1990, stipulate: "Employees shall put forth honest effort in the performance of duties." Quality and continuous improvement figure among the contributions of Total Quality Management and its derivative management reforms (Deming, 1986; Osborne and Gaebler, 1992).

Competence in public service turns on more than just these values, however. APSA's code commits members to "Strive for Professional Excellence" as well as to "[t]ake responsibility for their own errors." The competence standard is related logically to responsibility for the specialized knowledge associated with a profession. Professional competence is obligatory in many professional codes.

Perfecting, Not Perfection

Incompetence is an intolerable condition, a breakpoint or floor below which an action is unacceptable. For professionals pledged to strive for competence, operating below the floor delineates unethical action (or inaction). "Incompetence can lead to such catastrophes as the failure of a bridge, the spreading of epidemic or endemic disease, the growth of narcotics addiction, playground accidents and fatalities, and the 'blighting' of urban areas" (Graham, 1952, p. 262). Incompetence traced to pressures to contract out can result in disaster (Cohen and Eimicke, 1996). The problem is that outcome, over which managers may have little control, is part of the public's competence test. (See Exhibit 4.1.)

Within the agency, fairness demands that due consideration be given employee performance. Expectations of infallibility serve no good purpose and do no one any good. Being wrong for the right reasons is quite different from behaving unethically; allowance for error is imperative. Here it is fitting to cite Murphy's Law: "If anything can go wrong, it will." Fortune may play a role in outcomes, but in public service, competence plays the lead.

The competence standard demands from public managers not perfection but perfecting, that is, an effort to do the best that can be done, given the state of the art and within reasonable limits. Expert judgment is, after all, still judgment. In a world of scarce resources, uncertainties, and unknowns, performance as well as product and effort as well as outcome define competence. The competence standard is bounded by realistic limits and driven by high expectations, as a comparison of Exhibits 4.1 and 4.3 suggests.

A fair standard of performance distinguishes incompetence from a professional, good-faith effort that proves to be erroneous by subsequent events. The standard allows that being wrong or falling short does not necessarily translate into being unethical. There are four parts, then, to a fair competence standard: (1) perfecting, not perfection; (2) performance and product; (3) effort and outcome; and (4) doing the best that can be done, given the state of the art and reasonable limits.

Self-Victimization

Bureaucrat bashing is an all-American spectator sport. Yet it is unjust and demoralizing for public managers and employees to accept bureaucracy's *inaccurate* street image. Three well-known maxims about bureaucrats' alleged incompetence communicate the image: slouch, bumbler, bungler. The Peter Principle (Peter and Hull, 1969) couples eventual inadequacy with promotions until a bureaucratic organization is inherently inept. Parkinson's Law sights inefficiency: "Work expands so as to fill the time available for its completion" (Parkinson, 1957). Boren's testimony (1971), a parody presented as irreverent testimony to a House subcommittee, counsels, "When in charge, ponder; when in trouble, delegate; when in doubt, mumble." A can-do attitude of competence rejects that image; there is no reason for managers to disparage public employees by accepting satire as gospel.

There also is no excuse for managers' tolerating incompetence as business as usual. Perhaps a good start is owning up to the pressures pushing against it: a manager who allows employee incompetence to protect the agency in the short run ends up embroiled in cover-up and deception; a supervisor's easygoing leniency is misread as a go-ahead. Here the manager is letting compassion or caring subvert other values.

Forbearance and leeway make daily routines flexible, bearable, and humanistic, but the point is to enable public employees to do their job, not dodge it. Providing some maneuvering room should coincide with communicating the message that competence is the standard of performance. Organizational competence and individual competence are supported directly by "responsible communication habits" (Brown, 1990, p. 168).

Impossible Promises

Incompetence may be organizationally induced by managers' own exaggerated promises and underestimated costs—manipulative deceits designed to bypass full disclosure. (Padding budget requests may be a commonplace practice, but it is deception nonetheless.) Substituting strategy for neutrality and accuracy, managers are then forced to follow through on the proverbial shoestring. Cutting corners is an illusory response to cutting budgets when making do slides into gross negligence, as well as when planning is shortchanged, corrective steps are not taken, or testing goes undone.

Nothing symbolizes public service's competence more than the phrase "the eagle has landed," radioed back from the first manned lunar landing. It took less than two decades to descend from this to the Challenger disaster and then later, the Columbia, as described in Exhibit 4.1. An agency commitment to competence as an ethical standard is needed as much as the routine remedies of staff and budget increases.

In actual practice and public perception, public management operates—or should operate—in a "culture of performance" (Volcker Commission, 1989, pp. 13, 47). An all-too-frequent scramble to *prove* competence rather than *improve* it, individually or organizationally, revives the issue of blame raised at the beginning of this chapter.

Leave Responsibility Where It Belongs

Responsibility for ethical decision making belongs in the hands of individual managers. Detailed, hard-and-fast rules preempt individual responsibility and may chain, rather than empower, public service. Ralph Chandler (1989a, p. 605) notes that "certain ethical precepts have guided American public administrators from the earliest days of the republic. Some are implicit, some are explicit, and several are contradictory to each other, and all are subject to differing interpretations." It is hardly surprising, then, that many alternative game plans for ethical behavior have been spelled out over the years. Knowing this, some managers ask for more direction, for definite rules based on duty or law.

George Graham's "rules of the game" for professional administrators strikes a middle ground. Relatively clear-cut and concrete, this formulation demands impartial open-mindedness. Graham divides "the hard questions" into three categories: participation, compromise, and implementation. Each is related to "accepting the melding process as a necessity in organized representative government in a democratic society, and guided by the principles of due process which are embedded in the public law of the land" (Graham, 1974, p. 91). Accordingly, the administrator's role summons three sets of standards and obligations: participation, compromise, and implementation.

1. *Participation.* Inform participants of significant information relevant to their role. Interpret and explain data and policy impact, while ensuring no personal conflict of interest and revealing personal values. Advocacy is guided by the issue's importance and the administrator's cognizance and competence. "Accept decisions made within the 'rules of the game' . . . made rationally by informed persons, acting within their authority, and attempting to be fair and reasonable" (p. 91). Defend such a decision, but remember that one is "not required under any circumstances to testify falsely" on facts or personal judgment.
2. *Compromise.* Contest provisional decisions outside routine channels only when assured the mistake is significant, judgment is unbiased, and the issue's gravity justifies personal risk and potential contributions. Sign only documents one approves. Obey and enforce the law. Resign if controlling orders cannot be accepted.
   A correlate of this is that administrators are forbidden to order a subordinate to take illegal action; suppress significant information, distort facts, or deceive; take responsibility for an opposed decision for which the superior can take responsibility; or sign unapproved documents.
3. *Implementation.* Implement a legal, final decision whether agreed with or not. If legality is in doubt, "'go slow' until legality is determined" (p. 92). Alternatives are to request a transfer or to resign.

Like our approach in this book, Graham's formulation calls for legal compliance and action in the public interest.

Many managers prefer guidelines over rules because they equip managers to make decisions in varied, everyday situations and keep responsibility in the managers' hands. Many may agree with one manager's appeal: "I want guidelines—not rules—and I want them to say, 'Here's how we do business around here'" (Rice and Dreilinger, 1990, p. 103). We prefer guidance as key to the fusion route because it bridges compliance and integrity and keeps responsibility with the individual decision maker.

The action guides in this chapter are geared to summarizing and sorting public service obligations and responsibilities so that they are linked logically and practically, retain their intellectual content while broadly guiding behavior, and can be mustered from memory. We believe they represent consensual ethical guidelines developed over more than a century of professional public administration in the American democratic context. Their practical ramifications are explored and refined time and again in the cases and discussions in this book. The case that immediately follows (and Exhibit 2.3) depicts this chapter's principles at work.

Case: The Contract

An influential community leader lets you know that you are expected to sign off on a shoddy job by an independent contractor with political connections in towns across the state. You suppose that this leader sincerely wants to avoid a public ruckus that could embarrass your municipality and believes that a possible malfunction wouldn't really *hurt* anyone. Although you genuinely disapprove, as a sole-supporting, single parent you can ill-afford the luxury of intemperate indignation or sentimentality. *How should you handle this?*

1. Working in an organization (and for other people) takes compromise, so why not just sign off?

   This irresponsibly hands ethical judgment over to others.

2. What about signing and covertly filing a dissenting memorandum to protect yourself?

   Irresponsible, ineffective, cowardly, and fails tests for making ethical decisions.

3. Why not cooperate because you must support your child?

   A shrug and easy calculation that one must cooperate in order to support one's child express the market price, not the ethical position. Of course the parental obligation is serious, but it does not automatically cancel all others.

   Reject the following excuses:

- Everybody is doing it.

   People sometimes blame others to get off the hook by pointing to common practice as an excuse. Because responsibility is fundamental to ethical reasoning, this is an ethically bankrupt argument.

Thomas Paine: "A long habit of not thinking a thing wrong gives it the superficial appearance of being right."

- I did it in self-defense.

A related excuse forecasts others' wrongdoing, which in turn prompts anticipatory action. This argument often justly triggers charges of hypocrisy. Try using a classical yardstick from Duc de La Rochefoucauld (1678): "Hypocrisy is the tribute which vice pays to virtue."

Points to Ponder

Purchasing Department Head in Meriden, Connecticut, Wilma Petro (personal communication, May 2004), advises that reasoning and response may depend on how high in and how new to the organization the public servant is. Higher management may try to blame those below for their approvals, while subordinates may, rightly or wrongly, perceive pressure to please the "powers that be." On this very point, see Paul H. Appleby's testimony earlier in this chapter.

The Ethics Resource Center's 2003 National Business Ethics Survey of American workers finds that younger, newer managers were less likely to report workplace misconduct than older employees and more likely to feel pressure to compromise company ethics standards (Ethics Resource Center, 2003).

"Compared with other employees, younger managers (under age 30) with low tenure in their organizations (less than 3 years) are twice as likely to feel pressure to compromise ethics standards (21% versus 10%)."

"Younger employees with low tenure are among the least likely to report misconduct (43% as compared with 69% for all other employees). They are also among the most likely to feel that management and coworkers will view them negatively if they report."

◆ ◆ ◆

Discussion Questions

1. What guidance does your official code offer?
2. What does your professional code offer?
3. What do you recommend? _____
   _____
   _____

PART TWO

TOOLS FOR PERSONAL
DECISION MAKING

CHAPTER FIVE

FINDING SOLID GROUND

Ethical Standards and Reasoning

Earlier chapters expose the problems, conflicts, and claims shouldered by public managers. Here we work to reconcile and sort them ethically. Part Two provides the techniques and tools to use in doing that by turning to how individual managers make ethical decisions.

This chapter looks at how ethical reasoning is grounded in common sense and two broad philosophical perspectives: (1) duty, or principle underlying an action and (2) the consequences of action, or results. Overlaid with the clash between the *delegate* versus the *trustee* roles for public servants, these perspectives lead to very different outlooks on what is ethically important in a given decision. The ethical public manager draws on impartial open-mindedness to overcome an ethical impasse or resolve an ethical dilemma. Political traditions and practical experience counsel moderation and reconciliation in preference to ethical extremism. In the case at the chapter's end, different ethical postures lead to different stands on an everyday problem.

The public manager must act quickly in a gray, marginal area where laws are silent or confusing, circumstances are ambiguous and complex, and the manager is responsible, well-meaning, and perplexed. Consider the first four cases in the Introduction. These examples summon honesty, justice, impartiality, loyalty, fairness, confidentiality, public interest, and prudence, which pull the manager in different directions.

Where does the manager turn? Ethics commissions or designated agency ethics officers (see Chapter Eight) are not available in all jurisdictions; where they do exist, their emphasis on compliance means that the legal staff may not be able to help; they also take time to respond. What other resources are there? A friend? The boss? Religion? Philosophy?

A survey conducted by the *Wall Street Journal* (1988) asked one thousand corporate executives to name their most trusted confidant when faced with an ethical situation. The single largest category (44 percent of all responses) was "myself." In 1993, a national adult survey posed the question, "Do you agree or disagree that when it comes to morals and ethics [that], people must decide for themselves what is right and wrong, there are no absolute standards that apply to everybody in all situations?" More than seven out of ten agreed "strongly" or "somewhat" (Barna Research Group, 1993).

Although this kind of self-sufficiency may be popularly admired, ultimately—what ethical integrity boils down to—it is inadequate in a head-on collision over contending ethical values and principles. Accountability precludes public managers from playing cowboy, shooting from the hip, and roaming where they please. Ethical benchmarks and philosophical sounding boards keep managers in tune with public service.

Common Sense and Character in Decision Making as Guides to Action

The manager may prefer to rely on character and upbringing for a commonsense, visceral choice between right and wrong. (This is, after all, the point of Figure 1.2.) In fact, we make most of our ethical choices this way: in the pit of the stomach, automatically, reflexively, intuitively in the popular sense, by common sense, and in tune with the first category in Exhibit 5.1. We must do this, or contemplative demands would bring the office to a standstill and suspend our daily lives.

Going with how the situation *feels* is a suitable and efficient method for making relatively straightforward, routine choices between right and wrong. Having faced these predicaments before, we use our experience again. Of course, this problem-solving approach can only be as good as the character and common sense of the decision maker.

Dating back to Aristotle, "virtue ethics" stresses character and values. James Bowman (2003) explains:

> Goodness is the result of internal imperatives to do right, not sanctions from moral rules or rewards from expected consequences. Formulation of a problem can never be a purely technical procedure. People do good not because of reasoning about moral dilemmas . . . as a result of personal conviction, incremental development, behavior patterns, and the everyday choices stemming from them. Sound judgment is based on good character; beliefs, sensitivity, and experience are key in ethical life and should not to be taken for granted.

EXHIBIT 5.1. HOW DO I MAKE ETHICAL CHOICES?

If I believe
>   I learned to tell right from wrong as a child and that does not change
>   an itch, warning bell, or uncomfortable feeling tells me it is wrong
>   What is there to think about? I have to live with myself and my conscience
>   sophisticated arguments are used to justify unethical behavior

then I may be using a commonsense approach.

If I believe
>   some principles like the sanctity of human life must not be compromised
>   fundamental right and wrong never change, only excuses change
>   the way we do something is more important than what we do
>   there are certain things I would never do or condone, for any reason
>   it is my responsibility and no other reason is needed; it is that simple

then I may be using a principle-based approach.

If I believe
>   it is not fair to treat people in different circumstances the same; rules are rigid;
>   we need flexibility to respond to changing situations
>   what matters is people; we do not agree on principles anyway
>   government should be efficient and effective; it is results that count
>   noble principles are fine, but I have to be practical when I spend taxpayers' money

then I may be using a results-oriented approach.

The role of character in leadership and management is widely recognized as important, but its practical bearing remains unsettled. A 1998 survey "showed Americans sharply divided on what to expect from a political leader. Half of those interviewed—49 percent—say it is performance alone that counts in a president, agreeing that 'as long as he does a good job running the country, whatever he does in his personal life is not important.' But just as many disagree: They say the president has a 'greater responsibility' to set 'an example with his personal life'" (Morin and Broder, 1998).

A commonsense or character-based approach works well on routine problems and moral choices. These are the ones amenable to President George H. W. Bush's advice, "It's not really very complicated. It's a question of knowing right from wrong, avoiding conflicts of interest, bending over backwards to see that there's not even a perception of conflict of interest" (Volcker Commission, 1989, p. 14). This is the approach presumed in the argument, "Ethical government means much more than laws. It is a spirit, an imbued code of conduct. It is a climate in which, from the highest to the lowest ranks of policy and decision-making officials, some conduct is *instinctively sensed* as correct and other conduct as being beyond acceptance" (Volcker Commission, 1989, p. 1; emphasis added).

But what about other problems less readily susceptible to commonsense solutions? How best to grapple with dramatic, compelling matters that defy commonsense and demand moral reasoning? Exhibit 5.2 presents such a problem. With blurred boundaries and mixed messages, some issues are messy, perhaps when they invoke self-interest or seem to have nominal impact. Other issues might focus on *right-versus-right* decisions as when, for example, a health-care provider has a limited number of vaccines and faces the choice of inoculating the elderly (who are most vulnerable) or first responders (who are needed to help the elderly and others who get ill or hurt). In these kinds of cases, it is imperative to have managerial tools that allow effective moral reasoning (see Resource C).

Philosophical Perspectives at Work

Well-meaning managers sometimes find themselves sincerely baffled and needing to bounce decisions off someone or something else. The philosophical concepts that have penetrated our society and culture over thousands of years are rich resources. But is this an unfashionable topic? Apparently it is. An annual survey shows a decline in the proportion of college freshmen for whom developing "a meaningful philosophy of life" is essential or very important. With the proportion falling from three-fifths in 1976 to two-fifths in 1989 ("Fact File," 1990, pp. A33–A34) and to less than two-fifths in 2003 (Young, 2004), new recruits into public service are unlikely to bring philosophical proficiency with them. Granted, a busy manager may dismiss philosophy as artificial and impractical—an abuser's guide to reality. And agency problems do not always fit neatly into standard ethical categories.

EXHIBIT 5.2. TOUGH CALL.

In 1996, the Unabomber suspect was arrested as a result of information given to the FBI by members of his family. The next week, a national adult survey (Gallup/CNN/*USA Today*, 1996) asked, "If you were faced with the same decision, would you have provided the F.B.I. with information about a member of your own family, or not?"

How do you respond as a private person? What should you think about?

- Those who said they would have provided the FBI with information were asked, "Would that have been an easy decision for you to make or a hard decision?"

As a private person, what do you say and why?

Fully 88 percent of respondents answered *yes,* while *no* (at 6 percent) tied with *don't know* and refusals. The majority (71 percent) described their decision as *hard,* compared to 28 percent who responded *easy.*

- Now revisit the questions, first wearing the hat of a state manager and then a local police officer. Do your answers change? Should they? Why?

Sometimes the administrative world is complex, circumstances ambiguous, and the situation new; thoughtful reflection is needed for ethically sound decision making. In that case, when bumping against a true dilemma we need expert advice. Philosophy is the expert in ethics: a "systematic attempt to understand, establish, or defend basic moral principles or rules of conduct, judgments about what is right and wrong" (American Society for Public Administration, 1989, p. 101). Our thinking about ethics rests on two broad philosophical traditions, one based on the duty or principle underlying action (deontological) and the other on the consequences of action (teleological). The case at the end of this chapter brings both into high relief in an administrative setting; Exhibit 5.3 shows the perspectives at work in our daily decisions. A brief review serves as a reminder of their main features. There is no need to repeat at length what is readily available in many philosophy and ethics texts.

Duty or Principle as Guide to Action

According to deontological frameworks based on duty or principle, some types of behavior or acts are either good or bad in themselves, and the outcome is irrelevant to moral judgment. As its name implies, this approach uses duties or moral rules or principles as guides to action. The Golden Rule is a familiar example. Another comes from Le Chambon, France, whose residents, community leaders, and public officials defied Nazi orders and saved thousands of people. According to the pastor's wife (recorded in Johnson, 1989-1990, p. 19), "Sometimes people ask me, 'How did you make a decision?' There was no decision to make. The issue was: 'Do you think we are all brothers or not?'"

Immanuel Kant (1724–1804) provides the categorical imperative, a rational rather than a religious formulation whereby one should only act as if one were legislating a universal law for everyone to follow in a preferred world; people are never treated instrumentally, as a means, but only as ends in themselves (Heichelbech, 2003a). The categorical imperative is a simple thought experiment: if you generalize any action to everyone in society, what would be the impact? An insistence on human beings' dignity and worth is central to Kant's ethical perspective.

EXHIBIT 5.3. EVERYDAY USE OF PHILOSOPHICAL PERSPECTIVES.

Put yourself in the driver's seat of the only car pulling into the parking lot. The night is dark, and rain is pounding on your windshield; little wonder that no one else seems to be around. You must run into the convenience store for just a minute to pick up a carton of milk. The vacant parking space right in front of the store entrance is reserved for handicapped parking and you do not qualify. What should you do? What should you think about?

Deontological reasoning comes in many shades, depending on whether the rules of behavior are seen as permanent and universal, knowable or unknowable, derived from revelation, human law, or community norms, and so on. All permutations dictate that there are certain underlying principles by which behavior is judged, and no matter how desirable the consequences, there are certain things the manager (and government) may not do.

Results as Guide to Action

The results-based or teleological approach judges ethical worth by an action's consequences (Heichelbech, 2003b). Because this standard is frequently applied to international affairs, U.S. power on a global scale makes it especially important to understand.

In results-based reasoning's most familiar form—utilitarianism—ethical action means utility maximization, defined as society's net benefit over harm. An excessively simplistic formulation would have it that the ends justify the means, but Figure 5.1 sounds the imperative warning against this caricature. More sophisticated formulations speak on behalf of impartiality and benefiting all concerned. John Stuart Mill argued, "As between his own happiness and that of others, utilitarianism requires him to be strictly impartial as a disinterested and benevolent spectator."

Variations within the results-based approach stem from the good to maximize happiness or pleasure and whether the rule or the act drives the utility calculation. According to *rule utilitarianism*, "Each act, in the moral life, falls under a rule, and we are to judge the rightness or wrongness of the act, not by its consequences, but by the consequences of its universalization—that is, by the consequences of the adoption of the rule under which this act falls" (Hospers, 1986, p. 108). *Rule utilitarianism* begins with the greatest good but generalizes it as a rule across society and time by developing a rule to balance immediate needs with future needs. However, *act utilitarianism* looks at an act in terms of its immediate consequences for the greatest good. "An act utilitarian judges the rightness or wrongness of actions by the goodness and badness of their consequences" (Smart, 1986, p. 80). Exhibit 5.4 looks at these alternative ethical traditions in the context of the case that concludes Chapter One.

Accommodating the Two Traditions

Contemporary democratic society has been unable or unwilling to reconcile the deontological and teleological traditions or to choose between them. So our ideology accommodates both. The American political system operates according to two different ethical standards within constitutional and legal limits. Teleology's utilitarian principle is deeply embedded in American culture and politics, as illustrated by the widespread use of formal and informal cost-benefit analysis. The Bill of Rights

FIGURE 5.1. SELF-CENTERED RATIONALIZATION IS A SORRY SUBSTITUTE FOR ETHICAL REASONING.

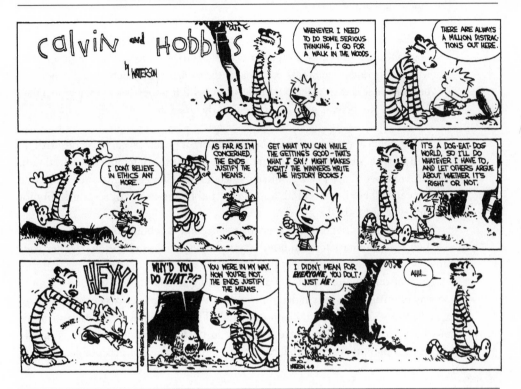

EXHIBIT 5.4. ETHICAL PERSPECTIVES IN ACTION.

Let us revisit the case concluding Chapter One to examine alternative ethical perspectives that help sort out the different objections to the Victims Compensation Fund as a public policy and to decisions made by the special master. *Act utilitarianism* triggers concerns of fairness, equity, and responsibility. *Rule utilitarianism* eliminates certain objections (such as the insurance offset) but, as important as it may be to a public servant, it hardly satisfies grieving stakeholders unimpressed by seemingly formalistic statute and regulation and personally searching for something emotionally more satisfying. And last, from a duty-based or deontological approach, it appears that the fund is compassionate but misguided; its very structure violates the notion of respect for people *simply as people* by discriminating among them through a differential valuation of loss. (See Kleinig, 1991, and Rhoads, 1980, as illustrations.) Because this case presents real ethical dilemmas, no formulation may satisfy all ethical objectives and objections. This defines the reality of the job for many professionals in public service.

represents deontology's alternative of underlying principles. Their joint role in political discourse is invoked by President Kennedy's appeal to both duty and results in his 1961 inaugural address:

> To those peoples in the huts and villages of half the globe struggling to break the bonds of mass misery, we pledge our best efforts to help them help themselves, for whatever period is required—not because the communists may be doing it, not because we seek their votes, but because it is right. If a free society cannot help the many who are poor, it cannot save the few who are rich.

Other political systems also call on these different philosophical traditions. Exhibit 5.5 from Canada's Institute on Governance shows how the different ethical traditions influence managers' perspectives and ethics codes (see Chapter Eight). The result is to burden each elected, appointed, and career public servant with responsibility for deciding which standard applies and when.

The scope for disagreement is evident in arguments about, for example, acceptable police and military force and interrogation tactics (as examples in Chapter Four show). Concern with the ethical principle to sustain human dignity vies with the "urgency of obtaining information about potential attacks and the opaque nature of the way interrogations are carried out can blur the line between accepted and unaccepted actions" (van Natta, 2003, unpaginated). That thoughtful people may not agree on what constitutes appropriate behavior in particular circumstances is hardly surprising; different ethical standards lead to different views of acceptable behavior.

EXHIBIT 5.5. ETHICAL TRADITIONS.

Responses to the Task: "Describe the Good World" and Implied Focus

The good world is . . .	Focus
. . . a world populated by virtuous people	(1) Attitude or character
. . . a world in which the use of, e.g., the Golden Rule is pervasive	(2) Rules to guide actions
. . . a world in which, e.g., overall happiness is maximized	(3) Goals to guide actions

Ethical Traditions in Relation to Language Used in Ethics Codes and in Management

Tradition	Focus
Virtue Ethics	(1) Values (character, intentions, motives, attitudes)
Deontology	(2) Standards (compliance), duty, rules, means (emphasize consistency)
Utilitarianism	(3) Outcomes, consequences, goals, ends (emphasize context and flexibility)

Source: Saner, 2004, Tables 1–2, pp. 3–4. Reprinted by permission.

Some argue on principle and underlying duties, and dismiss the results. Others appeal to opposing, results-based standards, sometimes irrespective of underlying ethical boundaries or law, and argue for doing whatever it takes to accomplish policy goals. The two ways of thinking induce different responses to problems and offer competing premises on which to make decisions.

These lopsided arguments blindside the public manager and damage public service. *Ethical public service demands that public servants touch base with all ethical perspectives.* This is why changing decision-making premises, meaning the philosophical framework, is so useful in thinking through ethical dilemmas (and underlies the go/no-go model in Figure 2.2.) The questions that follow are designed to trigger the open-mindedness that incorporates both impartiality and responsibility:

1. What philosophical tradition underlies your proposal or posture?
2. What other moral principles could guide action and alter the proposal or decision?
3. What considerations emerge from alternative philosophical positions?
4. Why would a public manager try to design a proposal that reconciles different philosophical perspectives?
5. Should anything else be considered?
6. In your view, is the proposal personally acceptable and ethically persuasive?

Try applying these questions to the cases that conclude subsequent chapters in this book.

In the end, the individual decision maker is left with the judgment and the responsibility for exercising it.

Different Views of Public Service

Examining different ideas enriches our thinking by providing nuance and depth. At the same time, these ideas complicate matters by offering different views of public service and behavior befitting different roles. Ideologically, contemporary public service follows the Platonic tradition that stresses public interest as distinguishable from self-interest. According to Bruce Jennings (1989a, p. 175), this is precisely what judgment entails in the political arena within which public service operates. "Political judgment, in the classical sense of the term, is the capacity to tell the difference between public and private ends. It is also the ability to spot a private interest masquerading as a public good." Machiavelli's very name has come to signify the opposite: rational, self-interested decision making conducted in the long and short term. (In contrast to the classical Platonic tradition of abandoning personal interests, the rational self-interest theory underlies arguments for pay parity with private sector counterparts.)

Contrasting notions of organizational and professional roles complicate matters further. Chapter Four treats this issue in some detail. Again, American democratic and bureaucratic practice combines main ideas—the trustee and the delegate—associated with philosophers such as Locke, Bentham, and Mill. As interpreter, the steward or trustee acts statesmanlike in the community's best interest, as the decision maker sees it. The U.S. Supreme Court, the U.S. Senate, political executives, and senior administrative generalists fit this category, as do claims of electoral mandate. A famous speech by English philosopher Edmund Burke coincided with the American Revolution: "Your representative owes you, not his industry only, but his judgment." The delegate, on the other hand, is more like a conduit who purposefully brings the constituency's views to bear and faithfully reflects them. This stance is typified by public opinion polls and some elements of populist and representative bureaucracy.

In sum, we have an ethics stew simmering on the back burner for every public manager. Ethical choices bubble up from ideas about morality, about public service, and about organizational and professional roles derived from classical philosophy and political thought. The sheer number of options drawn from philosophical traditions indicates that philosophy will not make our choices for us. Instead, it clarifies the reasoning behind our choices. The burden of multiple sets of ethical standards is all the heavier because the public manager uses public authority and enormous government power to back up decisions. As a result, the obligation for *informed* ethical reasoning—thinking through a dilemma and making a morally reasonable decision—falls on the shoulders of the individual public manager.

Purity Versus Receptivity

The purpose behind mastering the conceptual tools of ethical analysis here is to make moral judgments about one's own actions and decisions, not to evolve into a judgmental, self-righteous arbiter of other people's behavior. (See the section on vigilante ethics later in the chapter.) Imputing intent and motivation is dangerous business. Although this is a traditional element in judging legal culpability in the courtroom, a jury is used, along with confronting accusers, advocacy representation, and other safeguards. Because true motives may be camouflaged from the decision maker—never mind an observer—accurately tracing back from action to intent is tricky at best. We therefore conclude that *ethical judgment is best when it is self-applied.*

If we allow for human error, faulty reasoning, or incorrect facts, then what we observe may not be what is intended. There are observational snags, too. What we witness as an isolated action in fact may be part of a series and therefore we misinterpret the single data point. Also we sometimes may confuse an excuse with an explanation. An excuse states why one should be considered innocent or blameless *despite* an action; an explanation cites the reason for *choosing* that action.

Because it is so difficult to confidently distinguish surface from substance at a distance, judging others' behavior easily degenerates into charges of selective enforcement or casual labeling: Unethical! Hypocrite! There are many reasons for apparent inconsistencies and contradictions in ethical reasoning and behavior, including the following:

1. *Courage.* The problem may be more a matter of following through on what one knows to be right when it is unpleasant or costly or demands sacrifice.
2. *Multiple roles.* We may adjust our behavior and reasoning to conform to different roles with different but associated standards, and when incompatible claims (such as public interest and family loyalty) clash, the choice of an appropriate primary role may lead to behavior that would otherwise be unacceptable.
3. *Camouflage.* Motivation is a tough call, and the underlying reason may not be clear, even to the decision maker.
4. *Rhetoric.* An appeal to noncontroversial, vague values (such as justice or honesty) is quite different from an explanation of ethical reasoning. For example, what values are tapped by arguing that "the most important thing about government is democratic process"? Moreover, this statement obscures the mode of reasoning.
5. *Confusion.* Public interest has been defined as the majority (sum of individual interests) and the shared (overarching interest). Representation can mean being a delegate or a trustee. Conceptual ambiguity may lead to misunderstanding and mixed signals.
6. *Excuse, not explanation.* Offering an excuse (reason one should be held blameless) instead of an explanation (reason for a choice) is a common source of confusion.
7. *Consensus.* Agreement is intuitively satisfying, and there is a temptation to claim all ethical ground in order to satisfy everyone. This may communicate unsound reasoning or political expediency.
8. *Hard but different choices.* Not all ethical problems are the same. If the dilemma is real and values or standards do conflict, then choices may reflect different assessments of, for example, the stakes or values involved. Immediate life-and-death issues are often treated differently, or at least more carefully, than others.
9. *Error.* Reasoning may be faulty or partial. Intention may be undermined by factual error or omission.
10. *Selectivity.* If every decision warranted and received thorough analysis, we would be immobilized. Pressures on time and attention mean that many decisions and actions are prompted by common sense or conscience rather than reflection or deliberation; sometimes we choose to downplay the wrong issue and fail to see a choice's serious ethical implications.

These ten reasons for seeming inconsistencies and contradictions induce a wise manager to *reserve most moral judgments for self-application* and to leave some matters to psychologists or clergy. Emphasizing a strong moral commitment, President George H. W. Bush took a forbearing stand in his 1989 inaugural address when he said, "A president is neither prince nor pope, and I don't seek a window on men's souls. In fact, I yearn for a greater tolerance, an easygoingness about each other's attitudes and way of life." A 1998 national survey shows that the American public reflects this forbearance. Fully 70 percent of respondents agree with the statement, "We should be more tolerant of people who choose to live according to their own moral standards even if we think they are wrong" (Morin and Broder, 1998, p. A01).

Appeal to Consensus

When it comes to giving explanations, consensus is intuitively satisfying, perhaps because public service is concerned with appearance and widespread public support. There is a temptation to claim all ethical ground in order to satisfy everyone, including oneself. "Most people . . . will move across ethical systems and use more than one approach to grapple with an ethical dilemma. We feel more ethically certain when we derive a common answer using two or more different ways of moral reasoning," according to Stuart Gilman (1989, p. 21). Also, as problems vary from the trivial to the significant, we may shift from one ethical basis to another. Table 5.1 shows the six main bases public managers may wish to touch. (Touching different bases is different practically and analytically from moral relativism.)

In a historic specimen of ethical explanation (excerpted in Exhibit 5.6), President Gerald R. Ford explained his decision to pardon President Richard M. Nixon in 1974 on grounds of secular duties and religious rules, pragmatic effects and political results, and an intuitive appeal to conscience. He asserted a commitment to ethical integrity by seeking "to be true to my own convictions and my own conscience." Conforming to the ethical reasoning model laid out in the next chapter, he explicitly accepted responsibility on the basis of his public role as president rather than on friendship. He noted his fact-finding efforts, referred to advice, and cited preeminent values of substantive justice (which President Ford defined as equal treatment) and procedural justice (due process). He spoke of moderating justice with compassion and exhibited empathy for the affected party.

TABLE 5.1.   TOUCHING SIX BASES.

	Trivial Concern	Significant Problem
Common sense or character		
Duty		
Results		

EXHIBIT 5.6. PRESIDENTIAL EXPLANATION.

It is interesting to compare the explanation offered here with President Abraham Lincoln's Second Inaugural Address of March 4, 1865; with President Clinton's statement of apology on December 11, 1998 (http://www.npr.org/news/national/981211.apology.html); and with Clinton's letter of December 3, 1969, to Col. Eugene Holmes, director of the ROTC program at the University of Arkansas (http://www.pbs.org/wgbh/pages/frontline/shows/clinton/etc/draftletter.html). Try comparing them in terms of role diagnosis (Chapter One), ethical perspective, stage of moral development, use of explanation versus excuse, and stakeholder analysis (Chapter Seven).

Following are excerpts from President Gerald R. Ford's Explanation to the Public of his Pardon of Richard M. Nixon, September 8, 1974:

> I have come to a decision which I felt I should tell you and all of my fellow American citizens, as soon as I was certain in my own mind and in my own conscience that it is the right thing to do. . . .

> My customary policy is to try and get all the facts and to consider the opinions of my countrymen and to take counsel with my most valued friends. But these seldom agree, and in the end, the decision is mine. . . .

> I have promised to uphold the Constitution, to do what is right as God gives me to see the right, and to do the very best that I can for America. . . .

> The Constitution is the supreme law of our land and it governs our actions as citizens. Only the laws of God, which govern our consciences, are superior to it. . . .

> Theirs [Nixon and his family] is an American tragedy in which we all have played a part. It could go on and on and on, or someone must write the end to it. I have concluded that only I can do that, and if I can, I must. . . .

> I deeply believe in equal justice for all Americans . . . The facts, as I see them, are that a former President of the United States, instead of enjoying equal treatment with any other citizen accused of violating the law, would be cruelly and excessively penalized. . . .

> During this long period of delay and potential litigation, ugly passions would again be aroused. And our people would again be polarized in their opinions. And the credibility of our free institutions of government would again be challenged at home and abroad. . . .

> As President, my primary concern must always be the greatest good of all the people of the United States whose servant I am. As a man, my first consideration is to be true to my own convictions and my own conscience. . . .

> My conscience tells me it is my duty, not merely to proclaim domestic tranquility but to use every means that I have to insure it. I do believe that the buck stops here, that I cannot rely upon public opinion polls to tell me what is right. I do believe that right makes might and that if I am wrong, 10 angels swearing I was right would make no difference. . . .

> Now, therefore, I, Gerald R. Ford, President of the United States, pursuant to the pardon power conferred upon me by Article II, Section 2, of the Constitution, have granted and by these presents do grant a full, free, and absolute pardon unto Richard Nixon for all offenses against the United States which he, Richard Nixon, has committed or may have committed or taken part in during the period from July (January) 20, 1969, through August 9, 1974. . . .

The subsequent drop in the president's standing in opinion polls suggests that even a beautifully crafted ethical explanation may not work. People may still think you are wrong, or worse. A universal claim to being right may backfire by undermining credibility and conveying unsound reasoning, self-interest, or expediency. Ethical explanation may smack of a public relations campaign. Justifying decisions on ethical grounds is no guarantee of professional or political success or approval. But that is not the point; if success governs ethical choices, then standards and principles (and codes of conduct) apply only if they produce tactical advantages. This Machiavellian argument would have public managers strong like a lion, wily like a fox, and devoted exclusively to results.

Over the Long Haul

Long-term purity—indelible, unmixed, and unchanging adherence to a single way of thinking—is unlikely if public managers are like other people, whose capacity for thinking abstractly and applying general principles varies over time. Despite methodological and epistemological criticisms (Gilligan, 1982; Hirschmann, 1989), research by psychologist Lawrence Kohlberg and his colleagues has deeply influenced contemporary thinking about cognitive development (White, 1999).

Kohlberg identifies six general, universal patterns that are sequenced in invariable stages of cognitive development, based on the individual's use of generalizable abstractions (1981). These six orientations or "total ways of thinking" he terms "stages of moral development" (1980, p. 31). The stages progress from the pre-conventional level (stages 1 and 2), which is concerned with physical and hedonistic consequences, to the conventional level of conformity and loyalty (stages 3 and 4), and finally to the post-conventional level of autonomous, principled reasoning (stages 5 and 6). According to Kohlberg (1980, pp. 91–93 and 1981), the stages are these:

Stage 1. Punishment and obedience orientation

Stage 2. Instrumental relativist orientation (market relations)

Stage 3. Interpersonal orientation (intention, pleasing others)

Stage 4. Law-and-order orientation (authority, duty, order)

Stage 5. Social contract legalistic orientation (utilitarian overtones, procedural rules)

Stage 6. Universal ethical principle orientation (logical comprehensiveness, universality, consistency of abstract ethical principles)

Grouping the stages in levels of moral development, Table 5.2 relates the levels to self-perception and the value accorded to human life.

TABLE 5.2. KOHLBERG'S STAGES OF MORAL DEVELOPMENT.

Level	Self-Perception	Stage	Value of Life
Preconventional	Outside group	1. Obey or pay, punishment orientation. 2. Self (and sometimes others') satisfaction.	1. Confused with physical objects. 2. Instrumental to needs of possessor.
Conventional	Inside group	3. Win others' approval by helping them. 4. Law-and-order mentality. Doing one's duty.	3. Based on empathy of family. 4. Based on legal rights and duties.
Postconventional	Above group	5. Respect individual rights. Accept critically examined values. 6. Act with logically developed and universally accepted principles.	5. Life is universal human right. 6. Life is sacred.

Source: White, 2003. Reprinted by permission of Marcel Dekker.

In looking over this list, it is useful to bear in mind the following: "It is not the invoking of 'high principles' that credits a subject with high-stage thinking, but rather the way that a subject sets up the problem and deals with the claims of all participants in a dilemma" (Rest, 1980, p. 121). "Kohlberg insists on a close relationship between the level of moral development and procedural justice to insure a moral baseline for his body of theory. To him, moral development theory is grounded upon a Rawlsian concept of morality about how humans cooperate, how they manage conflicts, and what concepts of fairness they adopt" (White, 2003, unpaginated). This formulation stimulates objections and disagreements over moral content (Wilson, 1980), over invariable evolution, over the relative weight assigned to the use of abstract principles in lieu of humanistic concerns, and over the theory's usefulness for predicting or understanding behavior. Each stage is identified via expressed reasoning rather than actual behavior. "The first, and in some sense the most basic, continuing issue in assessing the moral stage theory approach in public administration relates to whether the underlying assumption of 'principled reasoning' as the normative ideal is the right assumption for public administration" (Stewart, Sprinthall, and Shafer, 2001, p. 473).

Kohlberg (1980, p. 92) identifies the fifth stage as the "official morality" of the U.S. government and Constitution. Recent research has sought to establish a "baseline measurement of moral reasoning" (Swisher, Rizzo, and Marley, 2001) among public managers.

This research draws on the Defining Issues Test (Rest, 1986), as tailored specifically to public management by Debra Stewart and Norman Sprinthall. Although their findings show a tendency among U.S. public managers toward conventional reasoning's Stage 4—the law-and-duty orientation (Stewart, Sprinthall, and Shafer, 2001)—other research shows a tendency toward post-conventional moral reasoning (Swisher, Rizzo, and Marley, 2001).

Also important to understanding ethical reasoning is the fact that "people at different developmental stages perceive moral dilemmas differently," and empirical tests confirm that a person's orientation is not permanent (Rest, 1980, pp. 109, 113). "Instead of existing as fixed traits, moral character occurs in a series of developmental stages" (Sprinthall and Sprinthall, 1988, p. 17). Furthermore, stages are *orientations*, meaning that, at any one time, an individual mixes the current, preceding, and next stages. Whether one agrees with Kohlberg or not, it is useful for understanding ourselves and working with others to allow that we are all engaged in an ongoing process of moral development. (This is the reasoning behind the memorandum exercise concluding this book.)

Impartial and Open-Minded

Purity in ethical judgment is hard to come by. Motives and reasoning usually are mixed and are bound to change over circumstance or time. *In public service, the search is for compatibility and balance, reconciliation and accommodation.*

Moral absolutism rejects alternatives; moral relativism fails to distinguish among them. Public service rejects both by combining empathy, responsibility, and receptivity. The moorings for action are secured in moral character, and thinking is anchored in moral principles, including obligations to implement and comply with the law and to promote the public interest.

Our passionate, messy world of public service violates purity and precision at every turn. The way Debra Stewart (1984, p. 20) sees it, "Most managers are neither pure deontologists, nor pure utilitarians, but rather operate according to a kind of ethical pluralism . . . [a] synthesis of moral systems." The recommendation is not for fickle or expedient reasoning but rather that alternative perspectives be used so managers can see their behavior as others do. This "double focus" would have each of us "strain to experience one's act, not only as subject and agent, but as recipient, sometimes victim" (Bok, 1978, p. 30). (See Chapter Seven on stakeholder analysis.)

Many managers' judgments change with circumstances. A flexible manager, responsive to human distress, may not see all ethical problems as identical and amenable to a single, invariable verdict. He or she may prefer to blend consistency and flexibility, along the lines of mitigating factors in courtroom sentencing. Different values and stakes may alter the calculus as when, for example, an immediate threat to life out-weighs the otherwise cherished value of telling the truth.

An unyielding, adamant position represents moral absolutism, which always applies timeless principles to every situation. Seductively simple, this view by and large negates individual judgment (not to mention compassion, mercy, and other unexceptional values).

By contrast, many managers pursue accommodation or reconciliation. They distinguish between "the principle of compromise and the compromise of principle," and understand that "willingness to compromise in order to reach an agreeable, ethical solution is very different from a willingness to jettison ethics altogether in a compromise of principle" (Guy, 1990, p. 19). According to Tom Peters (1987, p. 241), author of management books that have topped the bestseller lists,

> The reality—whether you are in the executive branch of government or the legislative branch or the private sector—is that there has never been an effective leader yet who has not devoted 90 percent of his time to consensus building. All effective managers spend most of their life building consensus around the key issues where they want to make a difference.

Managers put it all together by selecting pragmatically from a number of right choices as they shift from abstraction to practical problem solving. What is needed to overcome an ethical impasse or resolve an ethical dilemma is *impartial open-mindedness*. This is individual ethical pluralism that tolerates moral ambiguity (Denhardt, 1989). It recognizes the acceptability as well as the probability of varying standards, principles, and rankings of what is right and important in different ethical choices. (See Chapter Six's decision-making model and Chapter Ten's agency process.)

Receptivity is distinct from promiscuity—the ethical relativism that rejects the validity of ethical judgment in the belief that right and wrong are only culturally defined or simply idiosyncratic personal opinions. Relativism leads to indiscriminate decision making. In its highly reduced version, relativism tumbles into the wanton, amoral "do your own thing."

Nor does sincere open-mindedness mean plugging in theories until one finds the perfect rationalization. This is the charade of sifting through ethical arguments until an appropriate justification is found for a decision already made (the "linear reasoning" described in French, 1983). Ethical locus remains an unsettled issue in American society. In an opinion poll conducted by Kane, Parsons, and Associates (1989), 48 percent of the respondents said that there are absolute standards of right and wrong, whereas 44 percent said that right and wrong are related to the specific society a person lives in. In 1998, when a national survey asked whether respondents agreed or disagreed with the statement, "The world is always changing and we should adjust our morals and values to those changes," 42 percent agreed strongly or somewhat, while 57 percent disagreed strongly or somewhat (*Washington Post*/Henry J. Kaiser Family Foundation/Harvard University, 1998).

Open-mindedness allows "that there might be diverse traditions, beliefs and opinions about morality within a society but that this does not preclude widely shared agreement on the morality of certain basic practices" (American Society for Public Administration, 1989, p. 102). In that spirit, these authors suggest altering decision premises and circumstances to double-check ethical judgments or reconcile different philosophical perspectives to imaginatively resolve a thorny problem. (See "moral imagination," discussed in Chapter Seven.)

What does this open-mindedness do to personal integrity? Being true to oneself does not mean shutting others out in order to sleep at night; it means managers seeing themselves the way managers actually live, that is, related to other people and ideas. *Impartial open-mindedness is the first-order test of genuine empathy in public service.* The decision calculus calls for bending over backward to compensate for bias. Astute managers take care not to see *only* what they are told; empathy is balanced with analysis. Public service mandates thinking inclusively, listening closely (which begins with fact-finding), and striking a balance among competing ethical perspectives (and values).

The impartial public manager is ethically driven, not ethically empty. Unfortunately, a habit of empathy and concern for facts and legal obligations may be condemned as alleged *bureaucratic caution.* The manager in public service is often on the receiving end of ethical judgments. A decision maker bent on moderation, inclusiveness, and reasonableness may appear hypocritical, indecisive, or self-serving for those very reasons. Tolerance, breadth, and delay—byproducts of the search for balance—may be interpreted as lack of conviction, as well as lack of resolve. It may be small consolation to remember that a temperate inclination is not temporizing, that looking around is not at all the same as looking over one's shoulder.

An inclusive perspective aims not at stopping action but at making action *and* integrity possible. It is part of the definition of integrity, of being whole, of what it means "to serve with honor" (the title of the 1989 report of the President's Commission on Federal Ethics Law Reform).

Vigilante Ethics

A danger here is that we will abuse ethical judgment by being too hard on ourselves or on others, by using ethics to intimidate instead of inspire. Using ethics like a vigilante's rope in an old film version of the American West, we can wield ethical judgment to bludgeon public service into submission by demanding perfection or lifelong uniformity. Lord Acton's observation in the nineteenth century that "power tends to corrupt and absolute power corrupts absolutely" emphasizes the danger of militant claims to moral superiority. Excess is a real threat in relations with employees, with dependent service recipients, and even with the boss.

The American tradition of public service sees both "rule" and "result" postures as dangerous when they are exaggerated and alienated from each other. From a stand usually rejected in American administration, ideologues justify wiping away all concern for the opposing ethical standard. This runs contrary to consensual accommodation—the customary composite of American politics. The dogmatist is a true believer for whom ethical rules are untempered by pragmatism and who sacrifices policy objectives to first principles and rules of conduct at whatever cost. Zealots, by contrast, sacrifice principles to policy, and their appetite for results cancels out all rules of acceptable behavior. (The key, of course, is having the power to choose the particular purposes that justify neglecting all principles.) Reduced to simple extremes, both lead to fanaticism.

In American public service, uncompromising visionaries, whatever their vision, are restrained by law, limited and shared power, and *moderating virtues*. Humility and charity are unfashionable but not outdated virtues for public managers plying public power for public purpose. Years ago, Stephen K. Bailey (1964, p. 235) specified three "essential mental attitudes" in public service, including recognition of "the moral ambiguity of all men and of all public policies," "the contextual forces which condition moral priorities in the public service," and "the paradoxes of procedure." By adopting (or resigning ourselves to) impartiality and open-mindedness, we can draw on the philosophical traditions to inform ethical judgment but not replace it. Ambiguity is the price of flexibility, and responsibility is the price of reason.

Case: A Matter of Convenience

Here is the problem. Both you, a senior manager, and your newly hired assistant, a newcomer to the county, commute separately every day from a suburb not too far from the airport; the major highway runs past it. This evening you will be detained unexpectedly at an important meeting called by your boss, the commissioner. As luck would have it, you have promised to pick up your spouse at the airport tonight. The arrival was scheduled deliberately to coincide with the office's regular closing time. Do you ask your assistant to pick up your spouse?

This case highlights incongruent obligations, conflicting loyalties, clashing values—the stuff of ethical dilemmas. But it is purposefully small stuff, with personal convenience an underlying issue. Practicing on low stakes, the decision maker echoes the daily choices that sum to a habit of ethical behavior. Many ethical dilemmas are part of daily routine.

Do you ask your assistant to pick up your spouse?
Check the responses you agree with:

No, because

1. It is coercive to request personal favors from subordinates.
2. The employee may expect a job-related favor in return.
3. The assistant is not a friend, so a personal favor is out of order.
4. Your prior promise to your spouse means you cannot attend the meeting.

Yes, because

1. The assistant is passing right by the airport, it is no big deal, and you would do it for someone else.
2. You made clear that it is voluntary and purely personal.
3. The problem is job-related.
4. You are in a jam, and it is not your fault.

The familiar context in this case shows how different modes of ethical reasoning lead to different resolutions.

Examine the *no* responses.
1 = apply rule derived from role
2 = result is critical factor
3 = apply rule derived from role
4 = rule applies (prior promise), not role

Examine the *yes* responses.
1 = nonreflective, commonsense response
2 = mix rule and result
3 = irresponsible—abdicates to organization
4 = irresponsible—substitutes excuse for explanation

◆ ◆ ◆

Discussion Questions

Would your obligations or preferred responses change if

1. The assistant volunteers to help?
2. A routine obligation such as day care is substituted?
3. A houseguest is substituted for your spouse?
4. The assistant is a friend?

Why? What is the reasoning that guides your response?

CHAPTER SIX

RESOLVING ETHICAL DILEMMAS

Strategies and Tactics for Managers

Using a decision-making model that is open to contending viewpoints and values, we show in this chapter how managers can tool up for fact finding, accommodating, and using selective trade-offs that lead to informed, principled choices. With thinking anchored in moral principles and values, the manager now is asked to do three things: (1) take a harm-averse stand, (2) admit that collective action is bound to hurt someone in some way, and (3) reconcile steps 1 and 2. Using tools for deciding *what* counts, the manager reconciles the responsibility to avoid doing harm with collective action and selective action. Central guidelines developed throughout the book are synthesized in this chapter for ready reference. Using a checklist, an application melds models and tools together to resolve a case on friendship and impartiality. The chapter concludes with a device for taking personal soundings on ethical responsibility and a case for exercising ethical reasoning.

Ethics must not be reserved for experts or philosophers. If practitioners do not practice it and if decision makers ignore it, then public service and the public are in real trouble. For managers, ethics is only ethics when they are doing it. Public managers must be equipped to do what they cannot afford to eliminate and cannot legitimately delegate.

Question: What does a public manager do when a weighty problem refuses to disappear and routine solutions do not work satisfactorily? Answer: Mull it over, seek advice and information, apply specialized knowledge and analytic techniques, and reason it out. The same is true for ethical problems. Ethical reasoning is a form of specialized problem solving. Its methods provide tools for making choices, and equipment is standard on all models. The package includes public service values, a systematic perspective, fact-finding and screening tools, and feedback devices and assessment tools. Of course, like all crafts, public service depends on the qualities of the craftsperson wielding the tools; fine equipment works best in the hands of someone with personal virtue, professional courage, and a decisive turn of mind.

Decision-Making Models

The three models discussed in this chapter expose managers to different ways of thinking through ethical problems. Because they help clarify a manager's cognitive reasoning process, they are useful for reconstructing and then polishing one's own rational model. They also offer the manager some elbowroom to make an individual choice.

We now know that linear models of rational decision making based on a calculus of costs, benefits, probabilities, and risks do not describe the way human beings make decisions. Research in cognitive psychology such as Daniel Kahneman and Amos Tversky's *Prospect Theory* (1979) undermines the applicability of the rational-actor model of decision making under conditions of uncertainty (Kahneman, Slovic, and Tversky, 1982). The research suggests that, instead of analytic processing and cognitive operations, decision making is a matter of determining categories and matching patterns, which helps explain the "powerful impact of contextual factors on decision making." "Risk taking, time discounting, and interpersonal decision making . . . are much more a function of how people construe situations than of how they evaluate and weigh attributes" (Lowenstein, 2001, pp. 500–501, notes omitted). It seems that a choice heuristic that favors improvement over decline kicks in, along with decision biases toward seeking or avoiding risk that very much depend on decision makers' understanding of the situation. All this suggests that decision makers draw on their experience and expertise first "to figure out what kind of situation they are in and then adopt choice rules that seem appropriate for that situation" (Lowenstein, 2001, p. 503).

Further research needs to be done that applies relatively new developments in cognitive psychology to the context of public service and that relates risk of gain or loss to the likelihood and size of benefit (Douglas and Wildavsky, 1982; Fischhoff, Lichtenstein, Slovic, Derby, and Keeney, 1981; Green, Kahneman, and Kunreuther, 1994; Green, Jacowitz, Kahneman, and McFadden, 1998; Kahneman and Lovallo, 1993; and Kahneman, Slovic, and Tversky, 1982). Our understanding of ethical reasoning and anticorruption systems may be well served by incorporating, for example, the idea of "anchoring," that is, using a reference point.

[T]he concept of a reference point, an innovation central to recent models of decision making under uncertainty, can also be applied to intertemporal choice. . . .
[T]he reference point reflects a simple insight: people evaluate the outcomes of gambles as gains or losses, or departures from some psychologically relevant point of reference, rather than as final levels of wealth (Loewenstein, 1988, p. 200).

The best problem-solving method is the one the decision maker uses. Ethical analysis is not menu-driven, like computer software: if this, then that—then hit the key. There is no mechanical procedure, no automatic scheme, no standardized bubble sheet of correct responses to ethical dilemmas.

Instead, choices, nuances, and fine-tuning favor individual tailoring. A manager might initially select among the analytic frameworks discussed here on grounds of practicality, theoretical appeal, or situational fit. Some managers may wish to try several models if the problem is truly momentous. The choice among models turns on the manager's assessment of suitability and affinity. Is it appropriate? Satisfying? Does it square with time, resources, inclination, and circumstance?

Our preference for merging the three models is shown in the application that follows. A compound method has it all; that is its strength and weakness. On the one hand, some managers reject testing decisions against several standards because, having selected a preferred ethical stance, they object to a combination (recall the discussion in Chapter Five about appealing to consensus). On the other hand, the genuine flexibility and built-in expansiveness may attract other decision makers who are not put off by complexity, factual and intellectual demands, or the time required. A composite may be best reserved for the truly exceptional dilemma.

An analytic framework lets the decision maker break down a problem into manageable parts in order to examine them, then re-synthesize them and make better decisions. Sorting out and selecting among ethical claims—for what, to whom, and why—are central tasks in ethical analysis. The ethical values and principles at risk and the decision's consequences are figured in. Some decision-making models (including Nash's, which we discuss later) explicitly wed duties and outcomes; some models diverge over an accent on results for affected parties. Still others, not shown here, emphasize personal morality (Denhardt, 1988, for example).

Calling on Integrity and Imagination

Terry Cooper (1990) tells us that the ethical process means examining and ranking what is important (values) and general rules for guiding action (principles) in a given decision. Accepting the emotional component of people's decision making, Cooper sets two goals for the ethical manager. The first is to maintain a sense of integrity and avoid an "ethical hangover" when a decision incongruent with our self-image begets anguish (p. 24). The implication is that most of us would like to look in the mirror and see someone we can respect. (Oscar Wilde's *The Picture of Dorian Gray* depicts progression in the opposite direction.)

Cooper's second goal is stretching "the moral imagination" (p. 22; see also Chapter Seven). A series of steps generates alternative solutions through serial reasoning from a results-based perspective.

1. Specify all conceivable alternatives.
2. Match probable positive and negative consequences with each alternative.
3. Identify principles related to each alternative.
4. Rank principles or values at stake and justify priorities as if to someone else or publicly.

With choices generated, the task now is to select among them. Working on the assumption that public service role obligations are accepted, the decision-making method can be summarized in four steps (Cooper, 1990):

1. Review the facts and get what you need to know.
2. Understand roles and values, both your own inclinations and imposed obligations.
3. Consider all possible options and possible results.
4. Anticipate how you would feel about it and explain your decision.

The fourth step, in part, parallels the publicity tests suggested at the conclusion of Chapter Three. According to Cooper (p. 24), "Resolution is reached when we discover an alternative that satisfies our need to have sound reasons for our conduct and our need to feel satisfied with the decision."

Accommodating Duties and Results

Laura Nash proposes twelve questions that are grounded in the two broad philosophical traditions discussed in Chapter Five but that are expressed concretely and designed for practical business decisions. Substitute *agency* for *corporation* in the fourth question and add *legislative body* to the tenth, and public sector applications become apparent.

1. Have you defined the problem accurately?
2. How would you define the problem if you stood on the other side of the fence?
3. How did this situation occur in the first place?
4. To whom and to what do you give your loyalty as a person and as a member of the corporation?
5. What is your intention in making this decision?
6. How does this intention compare with the probable results?
7. Whom could your decision or action injure?
8. Can you discuss the problem with the affected parties before you make your decision?
9. Are you confident that your position will be as valid over a long period of time as it seems now?
10. Could you disclose without qualm your decision or action to your boss, your CEO, the board of directors, your family, society as a whole?
11. What is the symbolic potential of your action if understood? If misunderstood?
12. Under what conditions would you allow exceptions to your stand?

Nash's method combines major (simplified) traditions in formal moral reasoning to explore the ethical content of workaday decisions in organizational settings and in language meaningful to a manager. Loyalty conflict (question 4) "is a workable way of smoking out the ethics of a situation and of discovering the absolute values inherent in it" (1981, p. 84), and disclosure or scrutiny (question 10) "is a way of sounding those submarine depths of conscience and of searching out loyalties" (p. 86). Nash sees the symbolic message as being aimed at domestic consumption within the organization and for external communication with the public. Questions 9, 10, and 12 test decisions against change. As in several cases in this book, changing selected circumstances clarifies reasoning, may alter the decision maker's anchor or reference point, and reveals critical factors in making moral judgments. These three questions are especially suggestive from the standpoint of the public interest and public service.

On the job, when demands prohibit delay, a mental checklist is a useful device for filtering and organizing information quickly. A checklist modeled on Nash's framework is given in Exhibit 6.1, with an abbreviated version, designed for easy recall, shown in Figure 6.1. Together they represent a useful and inclusive method for making ethical decisions. The elementary standard—know the law—from Chapter Four is the starting point.

Decisions are made with the heart and the mind but sometimes rejected in the pit of the stomach. The visceral test—Can I live with this?—serves as a final check, a precaution with the force of feelings behind it. The question taps into anticipated consequences and the likelihood of follow-through. Then it remains to monitor and evaluate the decision as it is implemented.

EXHIBIT 6.1. DECISION-MAKING CHECKLIST.

☑ 1. Facts (including law)
☑ 2. Empathy and inclusion
☑ 3. Underlying causes and precedents
☑ 4. Stakeholders and responsibilities
☑ 5. Motives and objectives
☑ 6. Possible results and rationality
☑ 7. Potential harm (stakeholders)
☑ 8. Participation
☑ 9. Long-term timeframe and anticipated change
☑ 10. Disclosure and publicity
☑ 11. Appearance and communication
☑ 12. Universality and consistency

FIGURE 6.1. ABBREVIATED DECISION-MAKING MODEL.

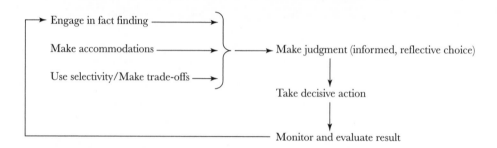

Questions for the Manager

The abbreviated version of the decision-making model shown in Figure 6.1 combines the inclusiveness of Nash's model with pointed questions from Michael Rion's *The Responsible Manager* (1996). Rion builds a framework for practical decisions by business managers under severe time pressures. His construct poses six questions.

1. Why is this bothering me? Is it really an issue? Am I genuinely perplexed, or am I afraid to do what I know is right?
2. Who else matters? Who are the stakeholders [affected interests, individuals, or groups] who may be affected by my decisions?

Reprinted by permission of Michael Rion. *The Responsible Manager. Practical Strategies for Ethical Decision Making.* West Hartford, Conn.: Resources for Ethics and Management, 1996, pp. 13–14; original emphasis deleted.

3. Is it my problem? Have I caused the problem or has someone else? How far should I go in resolving the issue?
4. What is the ethical concern—legal obligation, fairness, promise keeping, honesty, doing good, avoiding harm?
5. What do others think? Can I learn from those who disagree with my judgment?
6. Am I being true to myself? What kind of person or company [or agency] would do what I am contemplating? Could I share my decision "in good conscience" with my family? With colleagues? With public officials?

The first question highlights the difference between a real ethical dilemma and the courage to follow through on ethical obligations. It is especially handy for short-circuiting evasive waffling used to postpone unpleasant or costly action. In Rion's approach, ethics is not just a rational process, although it is a deliberative one. Because they have to live with the outcomes, managers should be comfortable with them.

The third question needs to be distinguished from the excuse that "it's not my job" or from the argument that no one is responsible for collective decisions in a public agency. This question adds an element of reasonable selectivity to the proposition in Chapter Four: "We cannot hide behind our supervisor or our desk to escape responsibility." A public manager wantonly doing *good works* would soon burn out or exceed both legal authority and the budget. The question now is how to opt reasonably and selectively for responsibility.

Opting for Responsibility

Recall the old story about a government employee who complains to the teacher that someone at school is stealing his child's pencils. The father explains that it is the *principle* that bothers him, not the pencils—he gets all the pencils he needs at the office! Of course, behavior is not always this transparent, but it does seem easier to pin down, without qualification or queasiness, someone else's responsibility than one's own. When it comes to tough calls, it may also be easier to get bogged down in nuances and definitions as a way of bypassing decision making. At any rate, responsibility is not as difficult to define as to exercise.

An earlier discussion organized ethical claims according to roles from which they stem and depicted them, for simplicity's sake, as five separate clusters (see Figure 1.1). By extending that image, responsibilities can be visualized along a vector that runs from the informal, personal, and self-imposed responsibility to the formal, public, and externally imposed obligation. In actuality, roles are interrelated; they interact, overlap, and sometimes conflict, blotting out or magnifying segments of other multifaceted clusters. The result is a profusion of dos and don'ts, not all of which can be acted on simultaneously.

Daily events activate multiple responsibilities; they create dilemmas and spark the need for selectivity when a manager cannot meet all responsibilities at the same time. From harassment, racial bias, or preferential treatment to "managing romance at the office" (Exhibit 6.2), the public manager is embroiled in human drama, the law, agency pressures, and core values such as fairness and trust. The many responses from readers to the case concluding this chapter reflect the reality and controversy sparked by these multiple responsibilities.

The decision-making model we adopt affects the responsibilities we accept and the way we choose among them when choice is necessary. Decision makers must use some sort of framework to sort and accept ethical claims, with the framework acting as a decision-making model. Our adopted model cues and sorts claims (Are they legitimate? Are they compelling?) and keys our choices among them. Figure 6.2 illustrates this idea in one clean thrust.

Avoid Doing Harm

In many models, the number one concern is how people are affected (leading to stakeholder analysis, discussed in Chapter Seven). A typical starting point is accepting the minimum prescription to avoid harming others. "Customarily, ethics in public administration means the obligation to avoid injury" (Stewart, 1984, p. 19). To avoid doing harm or inflicting injury is crucial for Rion, Nash, and others. It tops unobjectionable lists of commonsense moral values and rules (Goodpaster, 1984, p. 4) and, rendered as caring, is among the values around which there is general consensus (Guy, 1990, p. 14). It is a stringent standard under ordinary circumstances and even more so when regulatory and redistributive effects guarantee that people are helped and hurt differentially.

The harm-averse stand is so important in public service that we add it to the ranks of basic guides to action. Exhibit 6.2 shows these essentials of ethical performance in public service. They serve as general guides by which to order competing ethical claims.

EXHIBIT 6.2. DOING PUBLIC SERVICE.

Principles
1. Obey and implement the law (Chapter Two).
2. Serve the public interest (Chapter Three).
3. Avoid doing harm (Chapter Six).

Action Guides
1. Take individual responsibility for decisions and behavior (Chapter Four).
   No escaping responsibility by
   hiding behind the boss or the desk,
   hiding behind subordinates,
   hiding behind ignorance.
2. Take responsibility for what is done and how it is done (Chapter Four).
3. Treat incompetence as abuse of office (Chapter Four).

FIGURE 6.2. DECISION MAKERS USE A FRAMEWORK TO SORT AND ACCEPT ETHICAL CLAIMS.

Doonesbury   **By Garry Trudeau**

Although the dictum of doing no harm deeply influences ethical reasoning and action, an ethical and pragmatic regard for competing claims forces us to moderate it through selectivity and trade-offs, as discussed in the next chapter. Selectivity calls for ranking the ethical claims on the manager as a way of establishing priorities.

Rank Roles

In some instances, a manager may prefer to set priorities according to the source of the claim and the operative roles (see Exhibit 1.2). To do this, the decision maker selects one ruling cluster and sidesteps or downplays others. (This is behind the argument about citizen versus official dissent in Chapter Two.) Although this works well for fundamental obligations in public service, other applications may produce crude oversimplifications that lead to the Morozov-like deformations described in Chapter One.

The potential damage to important values and ethical claims can be minimized by making several checks. Anticipate followthrough by inquiring, "Can I live with this?" Apply the acid test of prospective publicity and ask what kind of person would do this and whether you want to be and be known as that kind of person. (See Chapter Three and the memorandum exercise in the Afterword.)

Rank Responsibilities

Given the actual prospect of exceeding legal authority, budget, energy, credibility, and more, what do you do when you can't do it all? When avoiding harm is at issue, a useful approach to setting priorities and making trade-offs draws on (1) the type of ethical claim and (2) taking responsibility for one's actions. The lower the claim on the list, the more appropriate is a *principled no*. Ranked in order of diminishing strictness, ethical claims are shown in Exhibit 6.3.

EXHIBIT 6.3. RANK RESPONSIBILITIES.

When you must make a trade-off, think about this:

   Given the very real prospect of having to exceed legal authority, budget, energy, credibility, and more, what do you do when you can't do it all?

The lower the claim on the list that follows, the more appropriate is a *principled no:*

   Avoid harm, the most stringent and the negative obligation
   Remedy or relief for problems we provoke
   Affirmative help for problems others cause
   Voluntary charity, the least stringent, doing good works

Public service's posture of avoiding harm begets an obligation to correct direct or indirect problems we create. In thinking about the effects of actions or decisions, the ethical manager applies the rule of reason rather than conjecture but is obligated to examine reasonably foreseeable consequences and disclose analytic and informational limitations undermining certainty.

A third and less rigorous claim moves the decision maker from the realm of obligation to responsibility and states it positively: to help. This line of reasoning is by no means unique to public service; many religions teach, first, not to do evil and, second, to cultivate good.

Charity, the fourth ethical claim, is the least stringent. It is voluntary, self-generated, and dictated by time, energy, and personal inclination. Although doing charitable deeds is commendable, it is not necessarily ethical to do them at public expense or through public office.

Thoughtfulness propels managers to distinguish charity from the obligation to do good (or *beneficence*, mentioned in Chapter Five). Doing good is defined by statutory mission for government and public purpose for nonprofits. It is especially important in public management to recognize the dual principles: "do no harm" and "beneficence." Sometimes they must be balanced against each other. (Note that beneficence is not on the list in Exhibit 6.3 but figures strongly in Exhibit 2.4 as effectiveness.)

Use the Threshold Test

What about a problem a manager did not cause? Usually, this is the most challenging dilemma a manager faces. Apply a threshold test: the more that each of the following four factors applies, the more punch behind the obligation (Rion, 1996, pp. 64–65; Stewart, 1984, p. 21). As shown in Exhibit 6.4, a *principled yes* emerges from considering as many factors as possible.

EXHIBIT 6.4. USE THRESHOLD TEST.

If you're dealing with problems others cause, consider this:

A *principled yes* emerges from considering as many factors as possible. The four listed are the most pertinent.

1. Vulnerability: potential injury, risk to affected party
2. Proximity: know or should know, access, authority, competence, span of control
3. Capability: can help without excessive risk, danger, liability
4. Dependency: no place else to turn, weak or needy with few options or advocates, and low probability of alternative remedies or services

These factors elaborate on the commonsense yardsticks of proximity, saliency, and gravity that are used in Chapter Four to discriminate among top management's responsibilities. The multifaceted notion of proximity can be broken down further by distinguishing among physical access, reporting lines, structure of authority, and cognizance.

Although the threshold test is most commonly applied when immediate physical danger is threatened, it easily extends to injury of any sort, from material loss to severe violation of basic ethical values or principles. It is especially relevant to sorting out self-generated ethical claims. Although not everyone would agree that "[t]hese conditions provide a warrant to inject personal judgments" (Dobel, 1990, p. 360), they do promote vulnerability and dependency as critical factors in assessing ethical responsibility. At minimum, they should trigger earnest reflection.

Ranking responsibilities and applying the threshold test reveal the dilemmas in the case at the end of this chapter. They also explain our emphasis on a *future generations* test. With neither voice nor vote to participate or to protest irreparable harm, future generations are the most dependent stakeholders of all, and public officials are their only institutional trustees.

Realistically, because the point of all this is ethical action, time constraints and urgency are part of a manager's calculation of priorities, even—or especially—ethical ones.

Of course, managers can fine-tune any assessment technique by refining or adding criteria by which responsibilities are selected and ranked. Some possibilities are mandated mission and legislative intent, cost, reversibility, and future effects and beneficiaries.

Application

With the help of the foregoing tools, we can use an amalgam of the three approaches (from Cooper, Nash, and Rion) to resolve a perplexing case. Picture the scene: as personnel director, you learn at a top-level staff meeting that the municipality's retrenchment plan calls for reorganization and cuts in managerial staff. The tentative blueprint has the city's Department of Community Services absorbing the small elderly services unit, whose program director, a close friend of your family, is slated for termination. The city manager, whose judgment you respect, mentions the program director's poor performance and, as the meeting adjourns, reminds everyone that the discussion is confidential as usual. As you leave, you remember that your friend is about to make a substantial down payment on a new home. *How would you handle this?*

Reviewing the decision-making checklist shown in Exhibit 6.1 is a good beginning. By putting ourselves in the personnel director's role, we can use the checklist to elicit acute considerations.

1. *Facts.* Does the city manager know about the imminent down payment? (No) Is the city manager aware of the friendship? (Yes) Is your friend aware of prospective termination? (No) Are you sure your friend depends on her municipal salary to finance housing? (Yes)

Is information confidential just because the city manager says so? Is a strictly legalistic view right or an excuse? You strike a middle ground by asking yourself, "Is this privileged information, known to me through my job but not known generally?" (Yes) Confidential information, oral or written, generally is that which is not currently a matter of public record or public knowledge.

Does your jurisdiction prohibit using public office for *anyone's* personal gain and divulging confidential information? (Perhaps) But either way, you know confidentiality is a widely accepted administrative value because federal and many states' laws and many nonprofits' standards forbid the use of confidential information.

2. *Empathy.* How would you feel if financial ruin threatened you? Can you put yourself in the city manager's shoes? How important is confidentiality in *your* job? How are other people in the community affected by your helping or not helping your friend?

3. *Causes.* Thinking about causes helps you define the problem and solutions. Your friend brought her termination on herself through poor performance but not the retrenchment's coinciding with the new house. Therefore, the problem is not keeping the job but avoiding financial disaster.

4. *Stakeholders.* Friendship does make ethical claims on you, but the difficult part of public service is that personal friendship is rejected as a legitimate basis of action. It is nontransferable from the personal to the public realm. (See Dobel, 2001, on friendship and public leaders.) You must weigh responsibilities and obligations to *all* affected parties, including these: the city manager, who unknowingly put you in a difficult position; your family friend; yourself, spouse, and family; the municipal organization, and residents and taxpayers.

5. *Objectives.* The city manager's motives are not clear, but because he did not know about the down payment, because confidentiality is standard procedure at these staff

meetings, and because you trust his judgment, you assume he intends to act for the best. You even may feel that he knowingly put you on the spot and ought to do something about it. The obligation to prevent injury emerges from checklist items 2 and 3, but what about *your* objective? Are you acting to protect a friend through special treatment?

6. *Possible results.* What happens if your friend loses her job and cannot make the mortgage payments? How can you face her accusation of betrayal? What happens if she learns about the retrenchment plan from you, does not buy the house, but then does not lose her job? If you were to betray a trust for friendship's sake and your friend knows you have other friends, too, can she ever trust you again? Can you be effective in your job without the city manager's trust? What if everyone disclosed confidential information on whim? Can government function if public trust takes second place to employee needs? To personal friendship?

7. *Potential harm.* Your friend faces financial harm. The city manager's trust is at issue. You also realize that the organization is at risk. Do you want to work in an organization that would allow something like this to happen to an employee, even one being fired? Does the city deserve an administration like this? You decide something should be done to prevent injury.

8. *Participation;* 11. *Appearance.* Because of the friendship, you conclude it would be best for communication to come from someone else. Given the fact-finding in Exhibit 6.1, you begin to think about bringing the city manager into the picture.

9. *Change;* 10. *Disclosure.* You do not see these items as directly applicable to the problem you face.

12. *Universality and consistency.* At this point you skip to checklist item 12 in Exhibit 6.1 because you realize that you happen to have specific information that warrants consideration on behalf of *anyone* in a precarious situation, not just your friend. Your intention *is not* to use privileged information from public office solely to protect a friend.

Next, you turn to assess the options stimulated by your thinking:

1. Do nothing, say nothing.
2. Tell your spouse, who is not bound by confidentiality.
3. Tell your friend immediately and directly.
4. Inform the city manager of your friend's impending down payment.
5. Say nothing, but be prepared to help your friend financially.
6. Casually hint to your friend about impending shake-ups.
7. Leak the retrenchment plan to the media.
8. Tell your friend and other municipal employees that budget cuts mean that a shake-up is imminent and suggest that they avoid new commitments at this time.
9. Say nothing, and help your friend get another job when the time comes.

Can you stand by and do nothing? Is this your problem? The obligation to keep confidentiality (involving legal compliance, loyalty, and trust) clashes with another top-ranking obligation: to refrain from doing harm. Although you are not directly causing the problem, inaction or silence could result in serious injury. Therefore, your obligation is reduced but still compelling. You may remember the story about George Washington refusing to help a job-seeking friend: "As George Washington, I would do anything in my power for you. As President, I can do nothing" (Bailey, 1964, p. 241). You feel that *his* obligation of affirmative help was lighter than the one you face, which is the obligation to avoid doing harm.

Pragmatism affects your choice among alternatives. Given your municipal salary, the remedy or relief of supporting your friend's new home is not realistic; financing your own mortgage is hard enough each month, and soon both families would be insolvent. Helping in the job hunt does not mean omitting the friendship or poor performance appraisal from a reference, but you know of many publicly advertised openings, and your expertise can really help a friend here.

You can think of no way to sidestep the conflict. Embroiling your spouse unties no ethical knots and is itself unethical. Even a hint or two to your friend ("cutbacks in towns across the region counsel postponing life choices") abides by the letter more than the spirit of the obligation. Even worse, ignoring other employees possibly in comparable positions results in favored treatment for a friend. Leaking the story as an unidentified source means breaking confidence on a grand scale, plus trying to escape personal responsibility. A general tip-off to employees personally or through the media still breaks confidence, stimulates gossip, and would cause anxiety and distress. Inflicting minor injury on many, including the innocent (those with good job performances), to protect a friend from more serious harm makes you uncomfortable. (See the fourth scenario in Exhibit I.2.)

Using the threshold test, you determine that there is a need or problem, you do know something, and you are capable of helping but at either some professional or some personal cost. However, you are not the last resort, and this realization, along with considerations of participation and appearance, lead you to speak with the city manager. You request that he inform your friend and the others targeted in the retrenchment plan.

Now comes the hard part. Assume that the city manager, whose judgment you respect, declines to make the retrenchment plan public, citing potential employee demoralization, as well as the need to avoid giving advance notice; affected agencies could then undercut the plan by soliciting citizen opposition. He explains that the decision is still tentative, and he does not feel that widespread employee stress is a reasonable price for your friend's financial security. He also refuses to give your friend special treatment. Empathically, you reconsider obligations and options from the city manager's perspective.

If you still believe that his response fails to meet the ethical claims that are emerging from your analysis, and you genuinely believe that anyone should be told, not just your friend, then you decide to go farther. You try to persuade the city manager and explain your ethical posture. Your task is to convince him that the information should be disclosed to those at severe risk; the city has a responsibility to employees, too. You point to the prescriptions of your professional code and argue that information deeply affecting people ought to be made public or at least available to directly affected parties, especially when withholding it causes serious harm.

If that fails, you acknowledge that the city manager's ethical preference or lapse does not absolve you of the responsibility that you have already determined is yours. You then reassess capability in terms of *excessive* risk to yourself (job, integrity, family, friendship, professional identity) and the values and principles associated with all participants, including your good friend, the municipal organization, city residents, the profession, and others.

Presuming an authentic assumption of ethical responsibility in this case, you decide that legal compliance and avoidance of a conflict of interest represented by respecting privileged information are preeminent obligations in public service. Your professional code reinforces your commitment to treat confidential information as privileged and given in trust. You decide to say nothing, to help your friend in her job search, and to initiate an outplacement program for all municipal employees. (This last idea illustrates inventive resolution—the *moral imagination* at work—as discussed in Chapter Seven.)

You conclude by asking, "Can I live with this?" You test the emotional components of your decision and assess the likelihood that you will follow through. To find out, you decide to let the decision sit for a time, but you feel pushed by the pace of events. You audit your decision by testing it against the *mirror test for integrity,* the *publicity test for accountability and appearance,* and the *visceral test for implementation and authenticity,* as shown in Exhibit 3.8.

Your personal anguish is sincere, and you ask yourself, "Am I right?" Insofar as you attempted to use reasoned, unbiased judgment in an informed, systematic way, yes. Does everyone agree with your resolution? No. That is why this dilemma recurs with different faces and different choices at all levels of public service.

Accepting Responsibility (Self-Testing)

Given the principle of individual ethical claims, accepting and selecting responsibilities are critical to a public service built on accountability. Moving from the abstract idea to the concrete heightens the noncognitive aspects of decision making. Can you live with this? Take responsibility for it? And the consequences? This applies the visceral test and makes tangible an abstract or general decision.

The symbolic template shown in Exhibit 3.8 can be laid over decisions as a self-testing device. A streamlined version is shown in Exhibit 6.5. We are not recommending that it be adopted as a public communication or official routine by an agency or office. Rather, public managers can scan the ethical soundness of their decisions against their willingness to sign—as if for the public record—the ethics responsibility statement.

No Closure

The exercise in Exhibit 6.6 asks you to put it all together. Is this all there is? Of course not. But this book is for public managers, who are not and do not want to be philosophers or theologians. Managers prefer other pursuits, which is easy to understand and respect. Just turn on a faucet, cross a bridge, or buy a home.

EXHIBIT 6.5. ETHICS RESPONSIBILITY STATEMENT.

(Not intended for agency adoption)

I take personal responsibility for making this recommendation or decision in the public interest, with consideration given to future generations.

_____   _____
(signed)   (date)

I am prepared to explain this recommendation or decision publicly, to the press, and to my agency, service recipients, and collaborators (if a public-private partnership, inter-jurisdictional project, or government-nonprofit project).

_____   _____
(signed)   (date)

I take personal responsibility for making this recommendation or decision in an ethical manner.

_____   _____
(signed)   (date)

EXHIBIT 6.6. TEST ETHICAL DECISIONS.

Impelled by severe financial straits, the municipal council agonizes and by majority vote stops funding the community alliance that runs the homeless shelter. You are sincerely distressed on three counts: (1) the homeless have nowhere else to turn; (2) you believe you are in public service to help people, not hurt them, and (3) the administration publicly is committed to being responsive to community projects like the shelter. As a public leader, it is your job to see that council decisions are implemented, but you think this one is a disgrace.

How should you handle this?

Mirror Test for Integrity	Publicity/*Mama* Test for Accountability, Appearance	Visceral Test for Implementation, Authenticity
What kind of person do I admire? Want to be?	Do I want to read about this in the newspaper? Tell my family?	Am I willing and likely to follow through? Can I live with this?

WHY? Ethical reasoning. What values or principles are at stake? What claims? (Claims include roles, values and virtues, principles and duties, and affected parties and interests.)

Try accommodating all concerns in a creative proposal. What resolution produces the best mix? If you can't do it all, aim at minimizing damage to competing claims and responsibilities.

_____

_____

_____

Do you take public responsibility for this decision?

Signed _____

Date _____

Why not adopt a few authoritative rules and settle the problems once and for all? Because simplistic rules are no solution in our complicated world and are not the point anyway. Judgment and action are. Not everything can or should be reduced to a snappy slogan on a bumper sticker or a twenty-second sound bite. The polar extreme of hairsplitting and quibbling over exquisite niceties does not help managers either. Remember Lewis Carroll's *Through the Looking Glass?* Tweedledee says, "Contrariwise . . . if it was, it might be; and if it were so, it would be: but as it isn't, it ain't. That's logic."

After thousands of years of discussion and tons of paper, closure is improbable—and impossibly arrogant. Then, too, anyone promising the *last* word on the subject rejects the challenging future anticipated for public service.

Case: A Late Night Surprise

Dennis, the city manager of a financially strapped municipality, is working uncharacteristically late at night. The offices are empty and quiet as he is leaving. He notices a sliver of light coming from the door of the new budget director, Susan. He decides to stop in and praise her for her excellent report in which she discovered errors that will save the city millions of dollars, projecting for the first time in many years a budget surplus. As he approaches her office, he can see through the few inches the door is open that she is in a passionate embrace with Gary, the assistant city manager. Employment policy strictly forbids dating between employees, threatening dismissal to those who do.

Dennis's code of ethics requires him to enforce this policy, yet at the same time he does not want to lose either or both of his valuable employees. It would be difficult, if not impossible, to bring in someone else with their experience and credentials for the amount of money the city is able to pay. What should Dennis do? Should he report Susan and Gary, in accordance with policy? Should he overlook the situation, believing the city will be best served in the long run? Should he speak to each of them and threaten to tell if they don't end the relationship?

Readers' Responses

The city manager, Dennis, "should look outside of the current policy box and analyze all of his alternatives. If legislating morality worked there would be no need for vice squads. In my opinion, you should not come between two people who are in love or are falling in love even if they happen to be public officials. Instead, if he feels he needs

Reprinted with revision by permission of the American Society for Public Administration. Case by Carole L. Jurkiewiez. *PA Times,* "Ethics Moment" column, edited by Don Menzel, Mar. 1998. Follow-up material, Apr. and Aug. 1998. Internet [http://www3.niu.edu/~tp0dcm/aspa/ethicsec/moments/moments.htm]. Based on an actual case.

to do something about Susan and Gary, he should work to change the policy prohibiting dating between employees. Is an embrace in a public office after hours in the bowels of a government building considered dating or is dating seen as an open affair in public? Either way, who cares? The ethical thing to do is to have the guts to eliminate a staid and outdated policy. Ethics is a matter of judgment about doing the right thing and then having the guts to take responsibility for your actions and standing behind your decisions."

"The assistant city manager and finance director are key members of the city's executive management team. They and the city council set the tone for city employees and the public's perception of what behavior standards are acceptable for the organization."

"The city manager must, at a minimum, notify the assistant and the finance director in writing that the behavior will cease immediately and result in termination if it occurs again. The notice and counseling should focus on the employees' excellent work records and [their] value to the city. But their responsibility for setting behavior standards takes priority over their administrative competencies."

"It is too easy for the city manager to overlook behavior by the executive team that is not tolerated for line employees. Being 'valuable' to the organization should not be a license to deviate from behavior standards. If anything, they should be held to a higher level since they set the standard for other employees and send a message to the employees about what is acceptable. The manager needs to think about what type of message he wants to send down the line!"

"The manager's alternative in this case is to officially authorize everyone to play 'Bob and Carol, Ted and Alice'."

Managing Romance in the Office

Dennis did not speak to them directly. He used the next staff meeting (with Susan and Gary in attendance) as an opportunity to discuss the policy and introduced a hypothetical situation for discussion that closely mirrored the one he was in. After discussion about alternative approaches to handling the situation, the staff agreed that they would tell if in the same position. Business went on as usual, and he never encountered Susan and Gary in a romantic embrace again. He doesn't know if they understood the veiled warning he was trying to give them or they simply ended the relationship. He's generally happy about the outcome.

Reader's Response

"This solution . . . has several problems. First, the leveling of discipline (warnings) upon the whole to reach the few may be a diplomatic and perhaps innovative solution, but it may open up the manager to unexpected consequences and organizational resentment, thereby impacting the agency's morale. 'It occurs to me that the age-old management tool of bringing the offenders to task, given the existence of the rule forbidding dating, would be to present his hypothetical case in private to the offenders.'

"Second, honesty or the fear of confronting issues head on may be problematic in this case. Using my approach leaves no doubt in anyone's mind about appropriate behaviors and would have involved as few people as possible in resolving a disciplinary issue.

"Regardless of which approach might be taken, consider what might happen to employee morale should the following also have occurred: the city manager was not the only late-night worker to observe the passionate embrace, and the word gets around about the romance [and] neither of the top managers are fired."

◆ ◆ ◆

Discussion Questions

1. What should Dennis do? What should Dennis think about?
2. Try using the checklist in Exhibit 6.1 and decision-making model in Figure 6.1 to work through this case and evaluate the proposed alternatives.

CHAPTER SEVEN

UNDERSTANDING WHO AND WHAT MATTERS

Stakeholder Analysis

In this chapter, stakeholder analysis operationalizes open-minded reasoning. A diagnostic tool helps answer the question of who counts and what counts. Because they are significant players in ethical dilemmas, ethical managers count as well. Principled discrimination in responding to ethical offenses equips managers to discount trivialities and survive professionally with their integrity intact. A case calling for stakeholder analysis concludes the chapter.

Ethical analysis is all about ambiguity and confusion; that is what the word *dilemma* implies. Stakeholder analysis is a method of viewing a scenario from the potential victims' perspectives, for taking the empathic leap to public interest without sacrificing too much or too many.

Stakeholder analysis has a duty-based core, although at first glance it may appear wholly and solely focused on results. The underlying reasoning draws on both of the philosophical perspectives discussed in Chapter Five, but results do play a leading role in the analysis. A manager, acting on the principles of reciprocity in human relations and respect for the other person, searches for some way to bring practice in line with principle. This often demands creative leadership and moral imagination. The task, then, is to specify who and what is threatened by adverse repercussions in order to lighten or relieve them. (Admittedly, it may be used self-servingly to predict likely response or possible opposition; this conjures up suspicion about mixing pragmatic and ethical rationales.)

Deciding Who Matters

Many factors, many actors, and many effects thicken the plot. Stakeholder analysis is a tool for identifying and sorting them out. Likely as not, the stakes are numerous, complicated, and important.

Ethical managers exercise reasonable selectivity among responsibilities and choose their battles in a principled way. The principle proposed in Chapter Six of abstaining from doing harm is moderated by the need for collective action that actually may inflict some injury. The task of ethical analysis now shifts to pinning down the potential injury and victim. Although more is involved than a simple calculation of net good over harm, public service requires one to act in the public interest, and general harm bars action. However, decisions rarely reduce neatly into no-harm/go choices. Instead, particular groups, regions, sectors, individuals, interests, or values are vulnerable to someone's good idea or good intentions, as the case at the end of this chapter dramatically illustrates.

Self-interested resistance is the crux of the not-in-my-back-yard (NIMBY) attitude, which can be summarized this way: "Yes, we need a new recycling facility, but don't put it near my property." NIMBY rejects solutions that sacrifice one locale or group to a common good more broadly enjoyed. NIMBY and similar attitudes are compelling reasons for examining basic assumptions (What would happen were there no backyard?) and innovatively redesigning alternatives.

Because collective action in an interdependent world is bound to hurt someone's pocketbook, sensitivities, surroundings, values, or principles, collective problem solving is possible only if we allow for the possibility of someone getting hurt in some fashion and to some degree. Collective or government action is possible only through a combination of sacrifice (often involuntary), relief or compensation, and trade-off. This very trade-off allows for acting in the public interest and distributing costs and benefits differently to different segments of the public.

Need for an Expansive Reach

To serve the public interest, public managers extend their analytic reach to encompass as many and as much as needed to dismantle bogus barriers imposed on public problem solving by limited viewpoints and biased perceptions. How? Often through expertise, experience, and reflection, as well as very important dialogue with the public, officials, and peers. Logically, then, there may be no *a priori* exclusion of a class of *others*. Only broad inclusion can begin to satisfy the injunction, pursue the public interest.

Figure 7.1 transforms Figure 1.4 to highlight the expansive reach demanded of public managers. Notice how Figure 7.1 scrupulously preserves the impermeable boundary between personal roles and public roles. The point of the boundary is

FIGURE 7.1. EXPANSIVE REACH OF PUBLIC SERVICE.

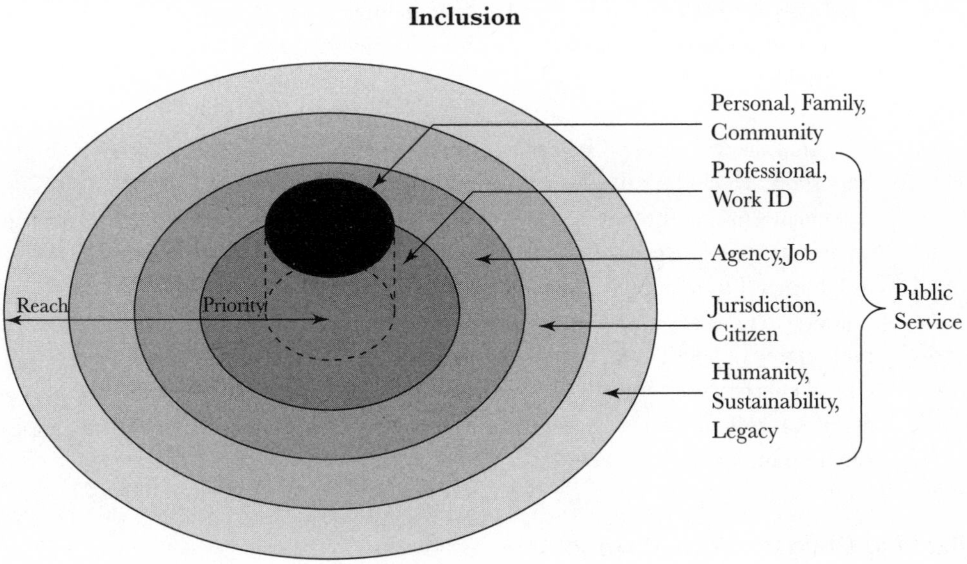

Inclusion

Graphic courtesy of Brian Baird, doctoral student in engineering at the University of Connecticut and research assistant in the Connecticut Center for Economic Analysis.

twofold: (1) to stress the imperative of using public office for the public interest and (2) to remind us how we are so strongly attached and give such high priority to our personal perspectives and attachments. Pursuing a public rather than a personal agenda, ethical managers expansively reach out in order not to allow bias in reasoning to blur their view or partiality in treatment sneak into their behavior.

The Need to Define "We"

Stakeholder analysis helps decision makers define the *we* in "We, the people" (from the preamble to the U.S. Constitution) as broadly as possible. Stakeholder analysis is a method of specifying who and what is affected, *not* a search for interest groups couched in the rhetoric of ethics. It asks, "Who else matters?" (Rion, 1990, p. 46). Three categories provide an answer (Rion, 1990, pp. 43–55). The point is to be as inclusive as possible and consider the long and short terms. Affected stakeholders include the following:

1. *Internal:* The organization or agency, including mission, superiors, employees, and the decision maker

2. *External and direct:* Clients and suppliers, lawmakers, taxpayers, and community residents and businesses

3. *External and indirect:* Those keyed to general interests, spillovers, and the long term, including citizens and society, other jurisdictions, the private sector, and future generations

Analysts will surely disagree about particular classifications, but that is not as important as including all affected parties. Stakeholder analysis can also assist decision makers in working through controversial environmental problems. The link between environmental concerns and ethics is in extending our reach to future generations, as Chapter Three argues. Here they enter the calculus as external, indirect stakeholders. Where environmental degradation is concerned, future generations are both highly dependent and highly vulnerable. Also bear in mind the three levels of ethical effects: the decision maker or individuals affected, the organization or policy, and the system or society. By changing the level of abstraction, stakeholder categories can account for all three levels.

Ranking Obligations to Stakeholders

Once affected parties and potential adverse effects (who is being hurt and how much) are identified, the next step is to rank the weight of obligation to each. A simple but unworkable method is to choose one of the three categories and base priorities on it. That makes a sham out of the exercise, leaves out too many stakeholders, and treats all stakes the same.

A more useful alternative is to rank the stakes—the values associated with interests—and to come up with a composite gauge of adverse impact. This is the first step in Exhibit 7.1. Using a stakeholder diagnostic along the lines of the one presented in Exhibit 7.1, the decision maker can assign scores to selected factors. The stakeholder diagnostic is a practical tool for aiding deliberation, not a quick fix for ending it.

Although the stakeholder diagnostic shown in Exhibit 7.1 uses six *equally weighted* factors in the index, the decision maker can adapt it to different ethical concerns by varying the weight of different factors or adding new ones. For example, if the weight assigned to the sixth factor strikes you as double-counting (tipping the scales, as it were), then delete it and substitute another factor chosen *on ethical grounds.* The decision maker or manager selects the factors and assigns the values. For example, a high score on policy impact (the fifth factor in the sample diagnostic) suggests injury for trivial results and explicitly factors in utility gauged by aggregated effects. Although duty-oriented purists may drop it from the calculation, some analysts would consider tolerating any harm at all for only material, nontrivial reasons.

EXHIBIT 7.1. STAKEHOLDER DIAGNOSTIC.

Category (check one)   *Description of Stake*
☐ Internal   _____
☐ External and direct   _____
☐ External and indirect   _____

Step 1. Score each factor.
      High = 3
      Medium = 2
      Low = 1
      None = 0
    The higher the score, the less acceptable the decision for that stakeholder.

Factors	*Score*
Dependency on agency—inaccessible alternative services	_____
Dependency—improbable relief or remedy from harm/injury	_____
Vulnerability to decision—likelihood or risk of potential harm/injury	_____
Vulnerability—gravity (*versus* triviality) of effect	_____
Scope—broad policy impact (*versus* negligible)	_____
Risk to fundamental ethical value, duty, or principle	_____

                           Add column for total score:

Step 2.
Repeat the scoring for each of the stakeholders to allow comparisons among them.
Next, add all stakeholders' scores together for a measure of the overall potential.
    A decision that causes severe permanent harm or injury receives a high score.

Step 3. *Action*
A high score across the board should prompt managers to reject the proposal outright
    (#1, below).
A high score for some stakeholders coupled with a low score for others may prompt managers to
    recommend alternatives or targeted relief (#2, below).

1. Manager recommends obligatory action or relief?   ☐ Yes ☐ No
2. Score triggers manager's considering alternative action or relief? ☐ Yes ☐ No

The second step is to repeat the scoring for each of the stakeholders, in order to allow comparisons among them. The higher the score—at or approaching 18—the less acceptable the decision for that stakeholder. Adding all the scores together furnishes an aggregate gauge of the overall potential harm. A decision that causes severe, permanent harm to the dependent (service recipients) or vulnerable (ill, poor) and damage to crucial values receives a high score. A high score across-the-board should prompt managers to reject the proposal outright. The intention here is to provoke rethinking, as well as some reflecting on the meaning of public interest.

A score of 18 for individual stakeholders in the sample diagnostic could trigger thinking about modification, mitigation, remedy, or relief. A high score for some stakeholders, coupled with a low score for others, may prompt managers to recommend alternatives or targeted relief. Although this is surely a burden, the effort could restrain action at deviant points on the continuum shown in Chapter One. By way of precedent, there are monetary compensation, job retraining, outplacement programs, affirmative action, and programs for reducing health and safety risks to employees.

Individual responsibility, truth telling, and publicity combine into an obligation to accept willingly the responsibility for one's actions. Add to this the obligation to modify behavior if the results are harmful. Consequently, feedback is important to building in the capacity to monitor and modify. The willingness to listen is a component of ethical decision making.

Appetite Curbs

Two problems cause indigestion if stakeholder analysis is swallowed whole in a single gulp. One is a matter of concepts and principles of justice, such as distribution, re-distribution, compensation, and others the case concluding Chapter One touches on. The notion of compensation is too often reduced to financial payoffs. We should know better; even the ancient idea of *lex salica* (a sixth-century penal code also including some civil law acts) allows for payment or atonement (Pollock-Byrne, 1989, p. 47). The ethical (and political) ramifications of buying off the injured party or buying citizen cooperation are all too obvious. Is it too harsh to wonder whether what is being bought off sometimes is the decision maker's guilty conscience? Duty-based reasoning argues that some things or people should not be bought; the price is never *right*.

For those with an eye on results, reducing harm via compensation raises the specter of discriminatory, class-based problem solving disingenuously rationalized on ethical grounds. Because the price of a rich injured party is higher than a poor one's, economical implementation of ethically justified solutions targets the poor. If public service sincerely values social equity, why should poor neighborhoods, or poor countries for that matter, get the solutions to society's problems (prisons, nuclear waste dumps, and so on)? Because they are poor? Weak? What level of economic distress transforms compensation into coercion? An opposing sentiment clarifies this line of argument. If the value of efficiency prevails in tax policy, assuming the diminishing marginal utility of money, do we really have an *ethical* rationale for taxing the rich?

The second problem is a problem only if one objects to a results-based, somewhat utilitarian view that condones, although under constrained circumstances, the involuntary sacrifice of individuals, their interests, or values to some *greater* good. This is, of course, a problem with all collective action that parcels out costs and benefits to different members and in different degree. A primitive duty-based critique may protest that the trade-off means *using* another person, and any price for human dignity is ethically intolerable. This kind of moral absolutism freezes government and other public organizations into immobility.

Amplifying Standard Analysis

Stakeholder analysis is a powerful analytic tool. With appropriate research and inclusive participation, authentic empathy replaces patronizing paternalism or self-interested projection. It can be an effective counterbalance to elitist planning and arrogant policymaking that imperiously assign pros and cons and define the public interest expertly but autonomously. Duty-based reasoning can use stakeholder analysis as a net to capture the affected principles and values. Results-based thinking can use it to tally and trade off the effects of a decision (or of indecision).

Stakeholder analysis is also a powerful decision-making tool. Although not speaking of stakeholder analysis itself, Thomas C. Schelling (1981, p. 37) explains how hard decision making is:

> I have often been glad that I wasn't in charge. It is easy enough to see plainly that there is too much inequality (or illiteracy, or ill health, or injustice) and to help to reduce it, knowing that despite all efforts too much will remain. But if it were up to me to decide *how much* inequality is not much, or how much injustice, or how much disregard for the elderly or for future generations, I'd need more than a sense of direction.

Cost-Benefit Analysis

Probing devices such as stakeholder analysis correct for some analytic distortions and omissions in cost-benefit analysis and other analytic techniques by adding ethical dimensions of action, inaction, and delay. (The case at the end of this chapter demonstrates the potential for doing so.) Originally applied to public works by the U.S. Army

Corps of Engineers in the pioneering days of American public administration, cost-benefit analysis now is relatively refined but still ethically lopsided. The technique garnered new clout in the privatization initiatives and deregulatory push of the 1980s. (In 1981, President Reagan issued Executive Order 12291 [46 CFR 13,193], according to which major rules proposed by executive agencies are required to undergo cost-benefit scrutiny.)

Public policy analysis and regulatory review routinely use cost-benefit analysis to examine decisions in which lives, health, safety, and quality of life are expressed in dollars. One issue is the *elastic nature* of the value put on human life; broadly disparate dollar values are assigned by different federal agencies. Analytic limitations are exposed in regulations governing environmental impact statements, as well as the arguments and counterarguments that surface in "Right at Ground Zero"—the case in Chapter One. As a reminder: "The translation of all good things into dollars and the devaluation of the future are inconsistent with the way many people view the world" (Ackerman and Heinzerling, 2002, p. 1562). Stakeholder analysis encourages decision makers to broaden their worldview.

Moral Imagination

Another way of expanding reach that works well in conjunction with stakeholder analysis is exercising the moral imagination to break out of a mind-set, strip off the blinders, weigh the anchor. In the discussion of decision-making models in Chapter Six, we note that decision makers first categorize a situation and then adopt rules for making choices that fit the selected category. To use your moral imagination means to change the "mental model" context and devise another perspective to creatively resolve a dilemma or break an impasse.

Consider the training exercise shown in Figure 7.2. Finding a solution depends on going outside the unreal boundaries we ourselves superimpose on the problem. In fact, there is no square, and we can solve the problem only by breaking out of the self-imposed analytic limits. Similarly, it has been argued in a business context that most managers are moral and public-spirited, but missing the developed moral imagination needed to change their mind-set (Werhane, 1999).

Exhibit 7.2 suggests a way to break out of the box with an eye on the ethical aspects of the problem *and* the ethical dimensions of the solution. This checklist merges four core ethical principles and directs attention to those with a stake in the decision or outcome, such as the town, taxpayers, voters, residents, elected officials, colleagues in the office, and professional associates. Using the list stimulates creative leadership by calling up the moral imagination in order to redefine the problem, as ethical leaders try to satisfy, or at least touch base with, as many ethical principles and values as possible.

FIGURE 7.2. CONNECT THE DOTS.

Connect the dots using four straight lines,
without lifting your pencil from the paper.

According to Exhibit 7.2, moral, democratic, public leadership offers ethical compromise and values principled judgment. This kind of leadership is responsive, open, and accountable. It mixes and harmonizes different, rightful claims, instead of shutting out people and their concerns. The option of fixing single-mindedly on one's personal preferences often means great cost or harm to others.

> The notion of living according to ethical standards is tied up with the notion of defending the way one is living, of giving a reason for it, or justifying it . . . the justification must be of a certain kind. . . . Self-interested acts must be shown to be compatible with more broadly based ethical principles if they are to be ethically defensible, for the notion of ethics carries with it something bigger than the individual. If I am to defend my conduct on ethical grounds, I cannot point only to the benefits it brings me. I must address myself to a larger audience.
>
> From ancient times, philosophers and moralists have expressed the idea that ethical conduct is acceptable from a point of view that is somehow *universal* (Singer, 1979, p. 10).

Is it sermonizing to suggest that self-righteousness is a public service vice (Lewis and Catron, 1996)? Because public officials and employees are *temporary* stewards of public authority, arrogance is out of order. Some degree of humility encourages self-restraint, especially when we admit the possibility of human error. Yet the leader's ethical concerns also count, or personal integrity no longer does. The result: ethical leadership proposes principled, creative solutions when rival claims threaten ethical gridlock.

EXHIBIT 7.2. CREATIVELY LEAD.

Redefine the problem to satisfy as many ethical values and principles as possible. Instead of stopping at doing as little harm as possible (the usual minimum duty), a public manager with moral imagination seeks to reconcile and execute four time-honored ethical principles and harmonize duties and values:

1. *Reciprocity* signals respect for human dignity and rights and to avoid doing harm; the Golden Rule is a familiar example.
2. *Reversibility* (or empathy) calls for seeing oneself as subject or victim, trading places, or walking in someone else's shoes.
3. *Utility* (or net good results, however defined) urges concern for the number of people affected and how deeply, in both the long and short term.
4. *Universality and consistency* block arbitrary, haphazard, or unscrupulous behavior in favor of impartiality, fairness, and predictability.

The Personal Stake

Public managers do not need stakeholder analysis to tell them that *they* are affected parties, too. Integrity, reputation, financial security, and career prospects dictate a genuine and legitimate concern for oneself. In his influential *Inside Bureaucracy*, Anthony Downs (1967, p. 53) argues that "every official acts at least partly in his own self-interest, and some officials are motivated solely by their own self-interest." Although personal cares are not permitted to usurp public interest or disable impartiality, ignoring them altogether may undermine analytic integrity and ultimately impede followthrough (as the "price tags" in Exhibit I.2 suggest). Unless altruism is the standard in all things and all cases, a manager can better identify and separate out personal stakes by considering them than by ignoring them. Stakeholder analysis permits a manager to own up to self-interest and personal costs. It clarifies general issues, undercuts hypocrisy and self-deceit, and avoids later paralysis or regrets.

Personal Qualms

Sometimes an ethical manager is the object of unethical behavior, sometimes a witness to it, or occasionally even an active party (however unwilling or accidental) in it. The manager then is in the uncomfortable position of either tolerating his or her own unethical conduct or that of others, or doing something about it. Here we revisit the themes raised at the beginning of this book: What counts? What is at stake? How can managers ensure both professional success and ethical survival?

Here again, the individual and the setting interact. The innumerable examples of heroism and steadfast resistance to injustice in Resource A remind us that even passive acceptance or inaction is a choice, although not necessarily an ethically neutral one. Of course, they remind us as well of the personal risk and potential cost. Assuming that we work without blinders on, the choice is among eight general options:

1. Denying the problem
2. Being hypocritical
3. Conducting sabotage
4. Electing disqualification (recusal)

5. Notifying a supervisor
6. Working for change
7. Blowing the whistle
8. Resigning

The fact is, none of the options is fully satisfactory for figuring out which way to turn.

Filtering Offenses

Denying the problem is probably used as often as any other single option, but denial is self-deceit. It works nicely for petty conveniences and immaterial human error (we forget that he put that pen in his pocket). The idea that ethical offense is a matter of degree, of gradations, is the point of the exercise given in Exhibit 7.3. Managers routinely sort misdeeds by discounting for imputed motive, intent, impact, and widespread agreement (in the agency or community) about wrongdoing and other factors. *Selectivity*—choosing your battles in a principled way—*does not change the ethics of the violation but does affect the response* (reaction, remedy, penalty).

Where do you draw the line? Judith N. Shklar (1984, p. 8) observes, "Most of us may intuitively agree about right and wrong, but we also, and far more significantly, differ enormously in the ways in which we rank the virtues and the vices." What is the difference between pocketing a pen and taking home a PC? The dollar value? Only in part; the smaller infractions have a huge aggregate impact. Similarly, is the *number* of pages duplicated on the office machine the issue, or is it the principle of personal use of public property? Are effects measured as one-shot, cumulative, or aggregate, and does the result affect a manager's response?

Reasonable selectivity runs the risk of appearing to be arbitrary enforcement of standards or preferential treatment of individuals. Problems arise precisely because it is so hard to specify decision-making criteria in advance. Yet these criteria are important precisely when the manager is picking and choosing.

To think that everyone makes mistakes or has a price does not entail equating all offenses. A working proposition is that *the more unethical we judge a behavior to be, the less likely we are to practice it or tolerate others doing it.* For example, many people would agree that endangering a child's life is far more offensive than lining one's pocket. The problem is that seeing ethical offense as a matter of degree may carry a high emotional price tag when trivialities descend into transgressions.

EXHIBIT 7.3. DRAWING THE LINE.

Given the actual prospect of exceeding legal authority, budget, energy, credibility, and more, what do you do when you can't do it all? The objective here is to polish principled thinking about the ethical dimensions of public leadership and to take personal responsibility for everyday practices.

> Even when upstanding people agree on right *versus* wrong, they may weigh ethical claims differently and sort offenses by discounting for: the hat one wears and place in the organization; imputed motive, intent, and likely impact, and norms, habits, and customs in the community. When response, remedy, or penalty turns on your assessment of degree or gradations of ethical offense, a key to keeping personal integrity intact is to draw the line *in a principled way.*

Working proposition: the more unethical we judge a behavior to be, the less willing we are to practice it or to tolerate it when others do it.

Please do each step quickly, spontaneously, using common sense and gut feel.

Step #1. Call it as you see it. Tease out ethical facets of behavior by classifying practices.

A = highly unethical	C = not especially wrong
B = moderately unethical	D = not at all wrong

Public Scrutiny

__ 1. To counteract an untrue charge, accuse the media of cynically distorting reality for political purposes.

__ 2. In response to a scandal, prove that blame actually lies with your predecessor's lax management and inattentive leadership.

__ 3. In a serious policy dispute, threaten to disclose an opponent's real personal indiscretions.

__ 4. At a meeting with a supportive reporter, put an unreleased document on your desk and leave the office momentarily.

__ 5. Claim public support without any factual basis.

__ 6. Prepare a news release supporting the mayor's claims with inventive statistics.

__ 7. Although you have some unannounced information, tell an unsympathetic reporter that you don't know when asked about some shenanigans in City Hall.

__ 8. On a council member's suggestion, *build a case* for dismissing a capable employee whose media disclosures embarrassed the jurisdiction.

__ 9. Take public credit for someone else's idea.

__10. Create an air of acute crisis to dramatize your own policy position.

__11. Cover for a well-meaning colleague's mistake.

__12. Propose canceling a popular program if a low-income program is targeted for cuts.

__13. Delay announcing the bad news to avoid distorting the election.

__14. _____

(a practice you identify)

Some people see ethics as a toggle switch—on or off, right or wrong—and refuse to consider any mediating factors or pragmatic issues in an assessment or reaction.

Do you agree? Did you select only A and D categories?　☐ Yes　　☐ No

Step #2. Look only at your A choices.

Star the three you consider the most serious wrongs.

Then double-star the single most serious offense.

Why are your starred items so offensive? A line may be drawn at a grave offense that

☑ purposefully causes harm to innocent parties　　☑ indulges conflict of interest
☑ fails to remedy a problem one directly caused　　☑ fails to help weak or needy
☑ nullifies accountability　　☑ injures or neglects the public interest
　　　　　　　　　　　　　　　　　　　　　　　(through deception or irresponsibility)

☑ your view:　　☑ your view:

Step #3. In your experience, are any of your A and B choices common practice? Circle these.

> *As a public manager committed to the highest ethical standards and integrity,*
> *What is your responsibility*
> *for starred practices?*
> *For circled practices?*

Discussion

The first step in "Drawing the Line" asks you to go down the list of actions and write the letter that you think best describes each action. The choices run from A (highly unethical) to D (not at all wrong); B and C provide some wiggle room. For example, the fifth entry reads: "Claim public support without any factual basis." Because, in fact, this is lying, many people would assign it an A as highly unethical or B as moderately unethical. Step 1 is to write your choice in the space next to the fifth action.

In numerous professional training and classroom settings, relatively few people assign one letter to all the behaviors. Rather, we see an inclination to make distinctions. Now the question is, How?

This takes you to the second step, where we revisit the list of actions to look only at the A choices. Star the three that you consider the most serious wrongs. Then select from among these three the single most serious offense and give it two stars.

Now examine the starred items to see what makes certain actions so offensive. Often a line is drawn when behavior has serious results or ignores important duties. Also a person's motivation comes into play. (See Exhibit I.2.) Here are the six boundaries that we have found to be the most often-cited reasons for giving an action two stars. Representing the common ethical standards used to filter action and modulate response, these six are critical boundaries for ethical public leaders.

Let us take a closer look at some of the choices. The eighth entry frequently rates a star or two because it (1) seems to purposefully cause harm to innocent parties, (2) fails all the audit tools for testing ethical decisions in Exhibits 3.8 and 6.7, (3) neglects correcting the problem, and (4) raises questions about an organization in which loyalty to the organization outguns loyalty to the public and is rewarded over competence. What kind of an organization is being built here?

It is reassuring to note that many (many!) elected officials in numerous forums have awarded the thirteenth entry two stars as the most offensive behavior. This action not only hurts the innocent opposition candidate and fails to help the voters, it also prevents accountability and informed citizen participation. The third entry is seen as complicated, neither an easy A nor an easy D. It highlights the difference between truth and candor.

Some of us may hesitate because a personal indiscretion may not be related to the official position or public policy. (See the third scenario in Exhibit I.2.)

Other issues: number 4 is a breach of the confidentiality the public leader promises to keep; number 9 is theft, of intellectual property but theft nonetheless; numbers 5 and 6 are lying, and numbers 10 and 12 imply some intimidation or threat, which is hardly an ethical use of one's power. What is at stake in number 11? Does the practice you wrote in for the fourteenth entry breach one of the six boundaries?

As for the third and last step, when a practice is common, the question becomes, What is my responsibility? This question is central to ethics, professionalism, and citizenship in a democracy.

Exhibit is heavily adapted by permission of American Management Association. Derived from W. A. Ruch and J. W. Newstrom, "How Unethical Are We?" *Supervisory Management,* 1975, *20,* 16–21.

One risk is that by looking the other way too much and too long, we end up teetering precariously on that infamous slippery slope—the gradual numbing of ethical discrimination. Watergate figure Jeb Stuart Magruder described his slide down that slope, along which ethical judgment about right and wrong is lost. In his words, "It's a question of slippage. I sort of slipped right into it. Each act you take leads you to the next act, and eventually you end up with a Watergate" (quoted in Terkel, 1973, p. 15).

Magruder was not the only one to have lost a sense of right and wrong. At Watergate hearings in 1973, Senator Herman Talmadge asked John Ehrlichman, a senior White House aide, "If the president could authorize a covert break-in, you don't know exactly where that power would be limited. You don't think it could include murder or other crimes beyond covert break-ins, do you?" Ehrlichman replied, "I don't know where the line is, Senator" (quoted in Moyers, 1988, p. 94). "No man ever became extremely wicked all at once," wrote Juvenal in the second century. Thomas Paine, the U.S. Revolutionary War pamphleteer, observed, "A long habit of not thinking a thing wrong gives it the superficial appearance of being right." At some indeterminate point unknowable in advance, we can lose altogether the capacity to make moral judgments. Or act upon them.

Deception

Michael Walzer argues on behalf of accepting necessary lapses for public purposes as part of the job. "Here is the moral politician: it is by his dirty hands that we know him. If he were a moral man and nothing else, his hands would not be dirty; if he were a politician and nothing else, he would pretend they were clean" (1973, p. 168). Walzer's words apply to politicians, but his reasoning extends to public managers. (For counterviews on deception, see Sissela Bok's *Lying*, 1978.) This kind of reasoning is used to justify sting and covert operations as authorized forms of lying and deception.

A second option—being hypocritical—is denial on a public level. It is designed to deceive. It sometimes degrades into slurs against opponents. Pretense, often justified by loyalty to clients or colleagues, induces cover-ups as, for example, in Watergate or the "blue code of silence" in some police departments. By definition, hypocrisy is terminal for ethical integrity. In the seventeenth century, La Rochefoucauld said, "Hypocrisy is the tribute which vice pays to virtue."

Sabotage is also a public lie but one often undertaken in the name of ethical principle. It is contrary, however, to ethical values such as truth telling and loyalty and to administrative principles such as legal compliance and accountability. The contradictions are so intense that behind sabotage there may be a disgruntled employee indulging in personal retaliation.

Going Through Channels

Disqualification (or recusal, in formal terminology) lets a biased decision maker off the hook by keeping the job *and* the interest that presents a conflict. Blind trusts and negotiated agreements are other forms of excusing oneself, but from the other end of the conflict. Requiring procedures for recognition, disclosure, and substitution, disqualification is essential, unless public service recruits automatons unconnected to family or community.

From experience as an elected official in a small town, one of us (Lewis) knows that in small, stable communities or company towns, where everyone is acquainted with each other or connected to an interest, sidestepping conflict through strict disqualification criteria means that nothing ever gets done and government decision making is crippled. Of course, interwoven relationships may also arise in large jurisdictions.

From the outside, it is hard to differentiate the option of working for change within the organization from self-serving compromise. It may also be hard from the inside. Magruder pointed out that the hired hand or aide tends to go along. "It's very difficult to set your own standard and continue in the power structure. I always felt I could do more by staying in the system. Maybe that's just the way of satisfying my conscience" (quoted in Terkel, 1973, p. 15). This may be just the time to hold up a mirror and review Chapter Five's ten reasons why ethical arguments are so difficult to assess accurately.

It may also be the time to think of the story of General Harold K. Johnson, the Vietnam-era army chief of staff. As a prisoner of the Japanese, a survivor of the Bataan Death March in World War II, and a commander during the Korean War,

General Johnson's physical courage cannot be disputed. Colonel Harry G. Summers Jr. (1989, p. xviii) tells how, during the Vietnam War, Johnson went to tell the president

> [that] the United States had no strategy worth the name in Vietnam, that all the principles of war were being violated, and that American soldiers were being killed needlessly. On the way there, however, he thought better of it and convinced himself that he could do more by staying on than he could by resigning. "And now," he said, "I will go to my death with that lapse in moral courage."

Formerly holding a chair in military research at the Army War College, retired colonel and journalist Summers (p. xvii) concludes, "Everyone knows that taking a moral and ethical stand may have disastrous consequences for one's career ambitions. But General Johnson's comments are testimony that the consequences of not taking such a stand may be far worse."

Going to one's supervisor, another option, also presents problems. Although it is true that federal and many state and local standards obligate disclosure of fraud, waste, or abuse, it is also true that these rules run counter to our indoctrination as team players, starting with Little League, 4-H, and scouting. Sometimes disclosure is even called *ratting*—a term no more complimentary than *snitch*. A humane and human manager, making allowances for trifles and petty errors, lapses into denial on occasion (see entry 11 in Exhibit 7.4). Nonetheless and despite personal discomfort, a public manager has a responsibility to the agency and the public that preempts individual loyalty.

Blowing the Whistle

"Blowing the whistle" means going outside routine channels. It means making an end-run play by using special reporting channels (for example, ombudsman, hotline, inspector general) or even going to the media. We prefer Alan Campbell's definition: "a popular shorthand label for any disclosure of legal violations, mismanagement, a gross waste of funds, an abuse of authority, or a danger to public health and safety, whether the disclosure is made within or without the chain of command" (quoted in Bowman, 1980, p. 13).

Whistle-blowing is *not* a casual choice. It is imperative that everyone—the organization and the individual—see whistle-blowing as a last resort. There is simply too much evidence of personal pain and retribution by peers or superiors in public agencies and corporate life for any other view of whistle-blowing. It continues to rank as "one of the most threatening forms of organizational dissent" (Jos, Tompkins, and Hays, 1989, p. 552), and managers who elect this option are advised to prepare for criticism, ridicule, and ostracism. A good illustration is what Sherron Watkins, the whistle-blower at Enron, says of getting another corporate position: "In terms of the bigger corporations, I have had people talk to me about various things, and then the door gets

slammed. When it comes down to the final decision, there's probably one or two peo-
ple who say: 'Are y'all crazy? She's a whistle-blower'" (Solomon, 2004, unpaginated).
The firing of Jennifer Long, who testified at hearings before the Finance Committee in
September 1997 that focused on accusations that taxpayers were abused by the Inter-
nal Revenue Service, was only halted by congressional intervention (Johnston, 1999).
Nevertheless, whistle-blowing is done (Johnson, 2003).

Of course, there are formal protections in many jurisdictions; federal employees
theoretically are protected against reprisals for making complaint; many state and local
employees are similarly protected. The other side of the coin is protecting the alleged wrongdoer against the unscrupulous or mistaken who would damage a reputation and career anonymously and at low cost (and in contrast to civil disobedience).
Sometimes the protections work. Yet personal costs, factual disputes, impugned
motives, and ruined careers are permanent fixtures. They are evident in a whistle-
blowing case over Alaskan land claims from the Taft administration, as recounted in
an early casebook in public administration (Stein, 1952). Despite today's formal protections, recounted repercussions belie an automatic victory for truth and justice. To
this add the anguish over self-image and identity when a loyal team player with strong
institutional ties breaks ranks—with no guarantee of effectiveness.

Because of the risk potential for the organization and individual on many levels,
the whistle-blowing option demands rigorous procedural protections for both the complainant *and* the accused. Otherwise, whistle-blowing is subject to abuse in personal
vendetta, partisan conflict, or policy dispute and looms as an administrative scourge.
All in all, whistle-blowing is suitable only after the facts are verified, the soul is searched,
and administrative channels are exhausted. Before reaching for the whistle, managers
are advised to answer the six questions posed in Exhibit 7.4.

Are you ready to accept the consequences if you are right but fail to act? The
adage, "The only thing necessary for the triumph of evil is for good men [and women]
to do nothing," synopsizes the results of everyone's silence. Taking action means taking responsibility and showing courage.

Resignation

When personal integrity is, in fact, compromised (and each manager must make this
decision personally), the resignation option separates public service from forced servi-
tude. But before making a rash decision, later regretted, a manager can secure time
for deliberation by submitting privately to a self-audit. Redraw the maps in Figure 1.6,
and verify the mismatch between "acceptable" and "actual" diamond shapes. If the
distortion is either intolerable or unalterable from your office, or both, do what you
have to do. An *ethical career professional* puts the emphasis on the first and third words.
There is a quiet heroism in that.

EXHIBIT 7.4. BEFORE YOU BLOW.

Given the high risk and no guarantee of effectiveness, when should a loyal team player, with strong organization ties, break ranks? Whistle-blowing is suitable only after

> Facts are verified.
> The soul is searched.
> Organizational channels are exhausted.

Before reaching for the whistle, ask

1. Is the violation serious enough to warrant the risk to self and to the organization?
2. Are you prepared for this action to become known and for heroism to mutate into betrayal?
3. Are you sure of your facts? Are you sure you are right?
4. Are you sure that superiors or colleagues are not trying to correct the situation?
5. Is your motive purely in the public interest?
6. Are you ready to accept the consequences if you are wrong?

Six *yes* answers signal ethical leaders to do the right thing.

Case: Valor, Compliance, and Compassion

The deadliest incident of *domestic* terrorism in the United States, which occurred on the morning of April 19, 1995, has special significance for public administrators because the target was government employees, working in the Alfred P. Murrah Federal Building. Fully 60 percent of the 168 fatalities and 40 percent of the 647 injured were federal and state government employees in Oklahoma City, the state capital and twenty-ninth most populous U.S. city. Words and numbers inadequately depict the tragic human toll of this unnatural disaster and its intense effect on many lives.

The long, dangerous, and frustrating rescue operation generated significant and complex ethical issues, such as an emphasis on body count as a proxy measure of an incident's significance and the preeminence of the privacy of survivors and victims' families over other values. When it comes to emergency management, Waugh and Hy (1990, p. 1) point out,

> One of the more telling applications of the fundamental values of a society can be found in how that society responds to risk, particularly risk that may result in major losses of human life and/or property. How society prepares for and invests

Case is excerpted and revised by permission of *Public Personnel Management*. C. W. Lewis, M. J. Tenzer, and T. Harrison. "The Heroic Response to Terror: The Case of Oklahoma City." *Public Personnel Management*, 1999, *28*(4), 617–635.

in programs to prevent or lessen the effects of such disasters demonstrates the values placed on safety and security, the capacity of its political and administrative structures, the dominant political and economic interests in the decision making process, and the technical expertise that can be brought to bear.

As Peter May (1985, p. 46) notes, emergency management is "a function of values (what ought to be done) and of capability (what can be done)."

Early in the rescue, emergency responders confronted a profound ethical dilemma that pitted valor against obedience and personal compassion against professional duty; disinterested expertise serving the public interest vied with the urgency of immediate, individual need. Eighty-six minutes after the blast, all personnel were ordered directly and repeatedly to evacuate the Murrah Building and immediate area because a possible secondary explosive device was spotted; rescue operations resumed after 54 minutes.

◆ ◆ ◆

Discussion Questions

1. *Who are the stakeholders in this case?* The answer to this helps answer another question: Should firefighters and police officers follow orders, evacuate, and thereby safeguard the operation, or remain with and try to rescue victims?

There is no easy answer to be found in manuals or codes of professional conduct. Standard emergency response procedures emphasize the safety of responders as the first concern, in order to protect the organizational capacity to pursue the rescue (Clark, 1998). The assistant fire chief articulated the managerial perspective: "The decision to pull our people was made quickly. In truth, there was no choice to make. The first rule for those responding to an emergency is not to become victims themselves" (Hansen, 1995, p. 18).

2. *Is this rule sound on ethical grounds?* Note that orders and standard procedures notwithstanding, emergency personnel in the field are expected to exercise discretion within the bounds of law, professional norms, and reason. The police department's emergency planning coordinator notes, "The guidance is general in nature, not all encompassing, and its applicability should be evaluated on a case-by-case basis by the first responders" (Clark, 1998).

Fire chief Gary Marrs applied a decision rule of timeliness during the evacuation: where rescuers were close to removing the victim, he urged speed; where the rescue appeared likely to take some time, he ordered the rescuers to evacuate, even against their wishes. "Although moved by their professionalism and willingness to stay, we were not going to take such a risk" (Oklahoma City, 1996, p. 131). Of his own response, Marrs says, "I wanted to stay, but I also knew my duty." He asks, "What was a supervisor to do? Can you allow your people to stay and be subjected to the risk. . . ? Or, do you make them leave?"

3. *Can answers be formulated that meet ethical and practical concerns?* Marrs notes, "You really tried not to hear the cries for help, begging us not to leave, coming from behind us" and concludes, "Some of the things I witnessed during the first hours of the incident were predicated on the duty we felt toward the people we serve—not on what we were being prompted to do in our hearts. Duty had to override emotion in an operation such as this" (Oklahoma City, 1996, p. 131).

4. *Do you agree? Why?* A clash of core values created a profound ethical dilemma. An officer who left a victim explains, "I have been a police officer for twelve years, and I always follow orders, but leaving that young woman under those conditions is the biggest regret I've had. Given another opportunity, that is one order I would disobey" (Ross and Myers, 1996, p. 75).

Three other officers made a different decision; they remained with victims despite the personal risk and successfully brought them to safety. (Others also remained in the area or at nearby sites, despite the evacuation order [Knight, 1998, p. 59].) The question arises whether the officers who remained and rescued two women actually disobeyed orders. The evacuation order was broadcast on radios and public address systems, passed by messengers and word-of-mouth, but no one in the chain of command directly ordered them to desist and evacuate. The issue, then, is less one of disobeying a direct order than failing to comply with standard emergency rescue procedure.

Hansen (1995, p. 19) writes, "We later learned that some of those rescuers opted to stay with the injured and ride out the threat. We didn't reprimand any of them for their decision. We felt it was one of those few times in life where there wasn't a right or wrong choice. Whatever each rescuer personally chose to do given each specific situation was the right thing to do."

5. *Do you agree with Hansen? Why?* He adds, "The rescuers who saw . . . [the victims'] faces caught glimpses of pure terror, and those expressions are something they will carry with them for the rest of their lives" (Hansen, 1995, pp. 19–20).

In May 1996, the Oklahoma City Police Department (OCPD) for the first time in its history awarded its highest service award, the Police Medal of Honor, to the three who remained with victims for their courage and voluntary assumption of personal risk. According to the OCPD procedures manual (procedure 164.50), "this medal is awarded to an OCPD officer who voluntarily distinguishes himself-herself conspicuously by gallantry and extraordinary heroism. The act must be in excess of normal demands and of such a nature that the officer was fully aware of the imminent threat to their [sic] personal safety and *acted above and beyond the call of duty* at the risk of their life."

6. *Would you have awarded these medals? Why?* Did success play a role here? What would be a reasonable organizational response, had their rescue efforts failed or a secondary device put them among the casualties?

The organization's awarding medals to rescue workers whose valorous deeds, in effect, meant deviating from basic emergency rescue procedure exemplifies the value conflict. The OCPD chose to acclaim heroism on an individual level that is deemed unsuitable on an organizational or policy level. The awards indicate that the professional standards expected of emergency workers can—and should—conflict with the emotions aroused in the immediate context of rescue operations. Because courageous action—beyond the call of duty and at grave personal risk—meant disregarding standard emergency rescue procedure but was rewarded with the highest organizational honor, emergency personnel are left with no clear operational and ethical guidelines for the future. Although ethics is not simply about rules, ethical management should provide some direction.

PART THREE

ETHICS AND THE ORGANIZATION

CHAPTER EIGHT

DESIGNING AND IMPLEMENTING CODES

Part Three moves from the individual to the workaday organizational level and examines ethics in the agency. This chapter compares governmental standards of conduct (often referred to as ethics codes) and model statutes by type, function, and provisions. The chapter also offers a benchmark for current practices, a forecast of likely developments, and adaptable innovations. Highlighted provisions run from the typical to the exceptional and include conflict of interest, financial disclosure, the appearance of impropriety, post—employment curbs, and blanket coverage. After recommending guidelines for developing a viable code and managing it effectively, the chapter ends with a case study on the guidance offered by standards of conduct.

Since Hammurabi, Moses, and Hippocrates, we have operated on the theory that it is easier to do the right thing when we know what the right thing is. As a result, codifying standards of conduct has become a popular way to clarify at least minimum expectations about acceptable behavior. In the United States, Postmaster General Amos Kendall developed the earliest code for government in the nineteenth century (see Exhibit 8.1.). Codes are now being adopted, refined, or strengthened in jurisdictions all over the country and in many parts of the world.

Dialogue over the years has produced prototypical arguments for and against codes. Rigorously implemented codes are coercive and spawn more red tape; they reduce managers' maneuverability and restrict practical options. An unenforced code symbolizes a weak message—just a piece of paper scribbled over with platitudes. In fact, the disturbing picture painted by Donald Menzel (1997) shows ethics commissions possibly

EXHIBIT 8.1. CODE FOR U.S. POSTAL WORKERS, 1829.

Issued by Postmaster General Amos Kendall

  I. Every clerk will be in his room, ready to commence business, at nine o'clock A.M., and will apply himself with diligence to the public service until three o'clock P.M.

 II. Every clerk will hold himself in readiness to discharge any duty which may be required of him in office hours or out, in no case where by laboring a short time after office hours an account can be closed or a citizen released from attendance at this city, must he refrain from continuing his labors after three o'clock.

III. Newspapers or books must not be read in the office unless connected directly with the business in hand, nor must conversation be held with visitors or loungers except upon business which they may have with the office.

 IV. Gambling, drunkenness, and irregular and immoral habits will subject any clerk to instant removal.

  V. The acceptance of any present or gratuity by any clerk from any person who has business with the office, or suffering such acceptance by any member of his family, will subject any clerk to instant removal.

 VI. The disclosure to any person out of the office of any investigation going on, or any facts ascertained in the office, affecting the reputation of any citizen, is strictly prohibited without leave of the Auditor.

VII. No person will be employed as a clerk in this office who is engaged in other business. Except the attention which the families of clerks require, it is expected that all their time, thoughts, and energies will be devoted to the public service.

VIII. Strict economy will be required in the use of the public stationery or other property. No clerk will take paper, quills, or anything else belonging to the government from the office for use of himself, family, or friends.

Source: White, 1954, pp. 434–435.

contributing to public cynicism. Codes alter the course from aspiration to asphyxiation, from ethics to obedience; they substitute rules for reasoning. But must we rely on mysteries, guiding behavior by unspoken, axiomatic norms?

The controversy spawns four general choices. First, we can adopt intricate rules with interpretations, advisory opinions, and complex enforcement mechanisms and protections. Alternatively, we can elect blanket prohibitions that are simple to understand and apply but inflexible and difficult to live with. Third, we can adopt fundamental principles as a way of allowing public employees to aspire to higher standards and base enforcement on these broad expectations. Or, finally, we can select no explicit rules, no categorical prohibitions; we can choose to articulate no standards. Figure 8.1 mirrors these choices.

FIGURE 8.1. DIFFERENT APPROACHES TO STANDARDS OF CONDUCT.

As they more and more often choose the first option, many governments today seem to respond to the questions, If not cure-alls, then what good are codes? What can they do? with a simple answer. Ethics codes do *less* than everything and *more* than nothing. Proposing the first codification of federal conflict-of-interest statutes, President Kennedy outlined the pros and cons of ethics codes in his message to Congress on April 27, 1961.

> The ultimate answer to ethical problems in government is honest people in a good ethical environment. No web of statute or regulation, however intricately conceived, can hope to deal with the myriad possible challenges to a man's integrity or his devotion to the public interest.
>
> Nevertheless formal regulation is required—regulation which can lay down clear guidelines of policy, punish venality and double-dealing, and set a general ethical tone for the conduct of public business. . . .
>
> Criminal statutes and presidential orders, no matter how carefully conceived or meticulously drafted, cannot hope to deal effectively with every problem of ethical behavior or conflict of interest. Problems arise in infinite variation. They often involve subtle and difficult judgments. . . . And even the best of statutes or regulations will fail of their purpose if they are not vigorously and wisely administered.

Experience in federal, state, and local governments has proven him correct on every count. Some current samples (see www.stateandfed.com/weekly_updates/email_4_42.htm) illustrate the potential, complexity, loopholes, and even perverse outcomes of writing and implementing standards of conduct. They also illustrate the variability in standards among the more than 86,000 government units in the United States. Formal standards, legal sanctions, public expectations, and acceptable administrative behavior vary significantly across the country.

1. A top San Francisco public works official, under an ethics investigation by the city attorney, is receiving some highly unusual help—a fundraiser organized by members of the Board of Supervisors to pay his legal bills. He came under scrutiny after nine street sweepers for a city-funded nonprofit organization said he had pressured them to vote and distribute campaign literature in the mayoral election campaign. Investigators also are reviewing complaints that he misappropriated city funds to benefit the nonprofit, where he was executive director for six years before being appointed to the public works department ("Supervisors Plan to Aid S.F. Official," 2004).

2. In November 2003, the Illinois legislature revised the state's ethics laws to require that all units of local government, including cities, counties, and school districts, adopt regulations to conform to the new rules. The law spells out clear restrictions on political activities of public employees and also regulates the receiving of gifts by

public officials and employees. The chairperson of Quincy's ethics commission said the commission would do whatever is necessary to make sure the city's ethics ordinance, adopted in 1999, complies with the new state law ("City Must Comply with New Ethics Law," 2004).

3. A New Britain, Connecticut, alderman wants to toughen local ethics rules to bar former city officials and employees from immediately working for city vendors once they leave their municipal posts. Under the proposal, former city officials or employees who had a hand in city contracts cannot immediately go to work for the contracted companies once they leave public service but would have to wait at least one year to begin work with such companies if their departure comes less than a year after the signing of the city contract ("New Ethics Rule Sought," 2004).

4. In Wilmington, North Carolina, a member of the city council proposed an ethics policy to address inappropriate behavior by council members who berate city officials or police officers. Although a code of ethics exists, the council has no way of enforcing it. This would put "teeth" into the code ("Council Ethics Policy Proposed," 2003, p. B1).

5. The New York State Ethics Commission has moved to electronic filing of financial disclosure forms. "Last year, almost 9,500 individuals filed. . . . When academic filers at the State University of New York filed . . . 73% chose to e-file. . . . Whether one files electronically or uses the paper form, the statements are due May 15" ("Popularity of Electronic Filing Saves State Resources," 2004, p. 1).

6. A 2002 *Informal Advisory Opinion* from the OGE responded to an ethics official's request for guidance as to whether an administrative law judge (ALJ) is permitted to use the title of Judge or ALJ on personal stationery or in personal activity. "Two sections of the Standards of Ethical Conduct for Employees of the Executive Branch (Standards of Conduct) are applicable to your question. . . . If an employee used his official title in a personal letter to his sister, it would not violate these provisions. However, if an employee were to use his title in a letter to a local police department challenging a traffic ticket, it might well appear that the employee was using his public office for private gain. . . . Because of this inability to predict all possible circumstances, we advised in a 1994 letter to an ALJ at your agency that he should not use the title U.S. Administrative Law Judge on his personal stationery" (U.S. Office of Government Ethics, 2002, unpaginated).

Given the variability, why bother with what is going on in other jurisdictions and professions, when keeping up-to-date locally is hard enough? One reason is that practices elsewhere provide benchmarks against which to compare current local practices—a way to take a sounding and to gauge future direction. Learning from others' mistakes is more efficient than repeating them. Permutations among states, localities, and nonprofit agencies represent adaptable innovations in a domestic version of technology transfer.

By the beginning of the twenty-first century, the vast majority of states, large U.S. cities, and all Canadian provinces had adopted codes of conduct, and there are hundreds of ethics programs in countries throughout the world. One of the first steps in writing codes is scanning other jurisdictions for ideas about standards and procedures. In 1990, Alaska did it, and the year before, Los Angeles did it. The Council on Governmental Ethics Laws (COGEL) compiles a state-by-state catalogue annually— *The Ethics Update* (Freel, 2003). National public interest organizations are proposing model statutes, while professional associations, research institutes, and national consulting groups contribute to the inter-jurisdictional give-and-take.

In a recent survey, 90 percent of government employees reported operating under written ethics codes (Ethics Resource Center, 2003a). Although codes can also be found at every government level throughout the United States—federal, state, municipal, and county—their applicability varies widely. Some codes cover all three branches of government; some apply only to the executive branch. Some codes apply only to civil servants (executive, legislative, and judicial), but others extend to anyone working for the government, including part-time employees.

Before moving inside government codes and processes, public managers may wish to glimpse them from *the other side*. What is serving on a commission like? Professor Sarah P. Morehouse recounts her experiences as chairperson of an ethics commission in a New England town (Lewis, 1986, p. 45):

> Being on the commission means having to rack your brain for solutions to problems very, very real to the participants and the answers aren't easy . . . and both sides think they are so right. Here we are, sitting in judgment and the answers are painful to come by. This is an area of conflict and questions where everybody wins because of the nature of the questions raised and publicity surrounding them. Also, I think this is some the gutsiest stuff you can do.

J. Patrick Dobel, who chaired the ethics board in King County, Washington, reflected on the importance of such institutions when he wrote, "Public integrity also needs strong institutional support. . . . Those of us who have human scale integrity need the sustained support of people and institutions in order for it to flourish" (Dobel, 1999, p. 220).

There also is a broad difference between commissions (usually individuals on commissions are appointed through a political process) and an agency responsible for ethics code interpretation and enforcement. For example, the states of Wisconsin and New Jersey have ethics agencies with a single appointed head and a professional staff. At the federal level, the executive branch's agency, the U.S. Office of Government Ethics (OGE) has only one political appointee, but Congress has two different committees made up of a partisan balance of members and a small professional staff. Individual states and local jurisdictions in the United States display a rich variety of standards of conduct and ethics institutions (as shown in Exhibit 8.3, later in the chapter). So do standards and systems in other countries.

Code Objectives and Types

Codes have a variety of objectives. Some are designed to clarify the minimal standards expected of public servants within a government. Often these minimal standards are formalized in law or regulation. Violation of these codes can be criminally, civilly, or administratively punishable, depending on the scope of the offense. A violation of criminal ethics codes can result in significant time in jail (for example, a violation of the federal conflict of interest statute can result in up to five years in prison); administrative violations might be punishable by forcing an employee to take time off without pay. For many critics of these kinds of codes, they are at best deterrents of the most terrible forms of behavior, and at worst they encourage bad behavior that is not clearly "outlawed" in the code. For these critics, the purpose of a code should not be describing the minimal but rather should focus public employees on the highest forms of public service. These two different objectives result in very different types of codes: ideas about training and notions of enforcement.

Implementation of Codes

Codes have long been associated with three general but realistic objectives: (1) to encourage high standards of behavior, (2) to increase public confidence, and (3) to assist in decision making (Zimmerman, 1976). Different objectives lead to different models. Legislated codes provide legal penalties and protections as necessary and effective constraints on official power, public authority, and the potential for abuse of administrative discretion. Administrative standards and procedures assist decision making and managers by providing an operational framework tied to workaday realities. "Managers need to know what is regarded as acceptable and what is not. Can an organization afford to have its members trying to guess what its standards are?" (Bowman, 1981, p. 61).

In a nationwide survey, ASPA members asserted that "properly designed codes of ethics have a crucial role in fostering integrity in agencies" (Bowman and Williams, 1997, p. 522). Clear ethical standards actually give public employees more workplace self-rule by ensuring that they know the standards to which they will be held accountable. This limits the pressures supervisors and political leaders can put on public employees to act in ways contrary to the code and limits an agency or department's vulnerability to charges of corruption. (By way of illustration, see "The Contract" in Chapter Four.)

A credo (for example, the Athenian pledge, the federal Code of Ethics for Government Service, or the ASPA code) is both aspirational and inspirational—more a positive statement and pledge of commitment than a list of dos and don'ts. A combined approach encompasses sanctioned aspirations (shoulds), minimum standards (shalls), and prohibitions (shall nots). The American Bar Association's Model Rules of Professional Conduct (which replaced its Code of Professional Responsibility in 2003) is a composite, with three parts: (1) canons, stating the norms or general standards, (2) ethical considerations, stating aspirational principles, and (3) disciplinary rules, which are mandatory minimum rules of conduct. The International City Manager's Association goes beyond these elements with a strict investigative and enforcement mechanism for both its members and the cities that would hire them.

A productive starting point is realistic managerial objectives: the internal, direct clients are the ethical managers and employees; the purpose is to assist them in ethical behavior and decision making. Judith Lichtenberg (1996, pp. 13–27) persuasively argues that codified standards can have an impact both on behavior and decision making:

- Codes of ethics can increase the likelihood that people will behave in certain ways, partly by bringing to consciousness the character of their actions, partly by attaching sanctions to noncompliance.
- Furthermore, the existence or validity of a code of ethics never constitutes a decisive, nonrebuttable reason to act. As in the case of law, it provides at most a strong prima facie reason to act, rebuttable by conscientious objection.
- Codes of ethics, like laws, can also fulfill the function of publicly expressing a group's commitment to some moral standard.

Codes have been used to identify a range of unacceptable behaviors in an agency, but often this is not enough. The best public codes focus on prohibited conduct and a clear set of values to guide public servants to principled behavior.

In the 1980s, with the advent of state codes in the United States, one state-local report predicted that code, disclosure, commission, and penalties "will improve the moral climate and contribute to the prevention of corruption in government in the future" (quoted in Common Cause, 1989b, p. 6). However, it is naïve to assume that the best ethics code can influence all behavior and eliminate corruption. Ethics codes do *not* prevent conflicts of interest. These are inherent in public service (see Chapter One). If duly enforced, codes give guidance on avoiding some transgressions, working out some problems, and detecting violations. Codes also contribute to professional identity, which in turn encourages individuals to ascribe to higher standards. Jeremy Plant (2003, unpaginated) writes,

Professionalism affects standards of conduct in many ways. Professionals share a common identity, which is based not just on shared knowledge but also shared norms and values. They interact on a regular and lasting basis, often through associations that represent their interests and serve as a forum to share knowledge, insights, and experience. Professionals often are guided and governed by codes of ethics that apply general norms of right and wrong behavior to the work context.

Some professional managers in public service may not think of their role in public administration as their profession but rather see themselves as, for example, lawyers, engineers, or planners. Codes are often an excellent vehicle to get professional buy-in by people who come to public management as their second profession.

No code will turn willful crooks into law-abiding public servants. Consider the words of T. S. Eliot, in Choruses from *The Rock* (VI, lines 021–023):

> They constantly try to escape
>
> From the darkness outside and within
>
> By dreaming of systems so perfect that no one will need to be good.

Although the limited research suggests that code enforcement affects the amount of misconduct an employee observes (Ethics Resource Center, 2003a), it is foolish if not downright dangerous to even think that a code will deter all corruption. In regard to overhauling the Senate's code, Senator Adlai Stevenson of Illinois once remarked, "If there are culprits in our midst, they are unlikely to be deterred by ethics codes" (U.S. Senate, 1980, p. 137). In its report, *To Serve with Honor*, a presidential commission studying ethics law reform in 1989 observed:

> Laws and rules can never be fully descriptive of what an ethical person should do. They can simply establish minimal standards of conduct. Possible variations in conduct are infinite, virtually impossible to describe and proscribe by statute. Compulsion by law is the most expensive way to make people behave (President's Commission on Federal Ethics Law Reform, 1989, p. 1).

Exhibit 8.2 shows what it takes for a code to be manageable, realistic, and useful. Workable codes speak directly to public managers and employees and draw on their active involvement in development and enforcement. Too often, codes are written exclusively by attorneys who may write in technical legal language, try to account for the majority of contingencies, and are tied exclusively to a legal context. Effective codes usually are written in partnership with legal expertise but recognize that a purely legalistic code will at best be confusing and at worst ignored. The best codes actively involve employees in their development and implementation (Ethics Resource Center, 2003a).

EXHIBIT 8.2. WORKABLE AND EFFECTIVE STANDARDS OF CONDUCT.

Build on five critical elements:
1. Reasonable, comprehensible objectives
2. Affirmative values to guide action
3. Coherent set of understandable standards, including dos and don'ts
4. Set of enforceable, meaningful sanctions
5. Procedural safeguards

Depend on general processes and effective mechanisms:
1. Enforcement procedures: disclosure, impartial commission; investigation, audit
2. Protections for all concerned: grievance and appeal procedures, help-lines, hotlines, whistle-blowers' protections
3. Meaningful sanctions and penalties: recusal, administrative intervention, noncriminal civil or administrative penalties
4. Agency implementation: orientation, training, evaluation and outside dissemination, self-governance

Commonly cover some or all major categories:
1. Fundamental, understandable prohibitions (conflict of interest, abuse of office)
2. Financial disclosure
3. Appearance-of-impropriety standards
4. Impartial commission or agency (with investigatory or advisory authority)
5. Supplementary restrictions (outside income, postemployment)
6. Criminal sanctions and administrative penalties
7. Procedural protections for complainant and employee

Speak to the public manager:
1. Clarity
   • Do I understand the standards?
2. Simplicity
   • Do I remember the standards?
3. Ties to administrative realities in the organization
   • Are the standards meaningful to my work?
4. Active employee involvement in development and implementation
   • Are the standards meaningful to me?

Demand sound management:
1. Show hard evidence—top management's ongoing, serious commitment to standards and to implementation.
2. Show the flag—immediate superiors' and line managers' integration of ethical concerns into the routine work environment.
3. Link ethical concerns and behavior with career path and with the agency's reward structure.
4. Safeguard against arbitrary or selective enforcement, favoritism, or abuse.
5. Communicate standards and expectations publicly and repeatedly to employees, vendors, clients, the media, and others.

Codes are best written in the spirit of Alexander Hamilton's comment about the newly proposed Constitution: "I never expected a perfect document from imperfect men." At best, a code is a mechanism for communicating and enforcing minimal standards (at least conflict of interest) and highlighting commitment to them. It has long been recognized that, to convey standards, codes should be "simple and straightforward, and should focus on the affirmative values that must guide public servants in the exercise of their responsibilities" (Volcker Commission, 1989, p. 14).

Overzealous codes, or situations in which agencies try to "out ethics each other" can create administrative gridlock and ultimately make the code ineffective (Gilman and Denhardt, 2002).

Creative administrators, confronted with a code of conduct with pages (and more pages!) of rules, may develop a code or value statement that complements (rather than complicates) the legal structure. It can be tailored to the particular organizational challenges confronting the agency and elicit support by involving agency staff in its development.

On the other side of the argument (Mackenzie, 2002), there are three negatives to consider when implementing standards of conduct. First, in a study of the New York City Police Department, Anecharico and Jacobs (1996) argue that ethics rules spawned by an aggressive interpretation of a code resulted in managerial stagnation. The rules had become so limiting that senior police officials found it easier to do nothing than to try and figure out what they could do. Second, the code may be implemented by an office subject to less-than-effective oversight and unfettered authority exercised when interpreting and implementing codes of conduct can lead to grotesque abuses of the administrative process and political power.

Third, commissions can become hostage to partisan disputes. The classic case is the Committee on Standards of Official Conduct in the U.S. House of Representatives. In 1997, the committee fined former Speaker Newt Gingrich $300,000 for using charitable funds for political purposes. Since that date, the committee has taken only five actions through early 2004 ("Groups Seek 2 Probes by House Ethics Panel," 2004, p. A11.) Typically, if a Democratic member suggested that someone (usually of the other party) be investigated, the general response was for a Republican representative to say if you are going to investigate Member X then we will insist on investigating Democratic Member Y. And if a Republican suggested it, the Democrats would respond in kind. Under this kind of perverse blackmail, it is almost impossible for an ethics commission to be effective.

Even the best code will not substitute for good government or good people. Sissela Bok (1978, p. 250) cautions that "codes must be but the starting point for a broad inquiry into the ethical quandaries at work." Unfortunately, most public agencies do not expend the effort to use codes as the beginning of an ongoing ethical dialogue that makes raising ethical questions in the normal course of business an everyday occurrence.

Current Practices in the States

When the first edition of this book was written, only about one dozen states had "something comprehensive enough to be called a state code of ethics" (Weimer, 1990, p. 2). Today a comprehensive code of ethics is almost a given, with forty-six states having ethics commissions (see Exhibit 8.3) and over fifty individual governmental authorities (counties and cities) having independent codes of ethics. In addition, there are often separate codes and systems of implementation for the executive, legislative, and judicial branches (Freel, 2003).

Thirty-two states require some form of financial disclosure (Freel, 2003). Ideally, a financial disclosure system should reveal potential conflicts or other ethics issues, be reviewed in a timely manner, and prevent the public servant from accidentally violating an ethics law or regulation. By preventing infractions, these systems serve to reinforce the confidence of citizens in their governmental institutions. In practice, the ideal is seldom met. Many disclosures go unexamined because of limited staff in the ethics office or are not looked at until the employee is suspected of misconduct. Disclosure varies widely, as do the details required, who must file, availability to the public, and use.

In addition, over fifty cities and counties require some type of financial disclosure from their public employees (Freel, 2003). States are far more likely to ask for financial disclosure reports from their executive branch employees, both elected and civil service, than from their legislators. The number formally required to file varies from 150,000 in Pennsylvania to 30,000 in Alabama and Florida and 6 in Arizona; some states focus in on senior-level officials, but others include a broad array of filers (Freel, 2003). The COGEL, the National Municipal League, and Common Cause have long called for a commission's jurisdiction to extend to elected or appointed officials *and* employees in *all* government branches; actual practices vary among the states.

Diversity best describes the overall pattern of state ethics laws and practices. (Variability and experimentation in public service ethics are good examples of federalism as a "laboratory of innovation.") Coverage, jurisdiction, organization, and specific prohibitions vary from state to state. COGEL data for the past decade and more reveal only a few standard practices. For example, twenty-six states have jurisdiction over appointed officials *and* state employees.

States differ markedly in enforcement mechanisms and procedural protections as well. Except for Idaho, Mississippi, and Virginia, state ethics offices are authorized to issue advisory opinions, declaratory rulings, or interpretive statements. This function allows for variability and adaptability and is vital if either the code or administrative structure is complicated. As proactive protection for the ethical manager, before-the-fact advice helps the individual find a path through what can be a confusing labyrinth. In practice, advice directly supports the code's core: the conflict-of-interest rules.

The "scandal trigger" is apparent from initiation dates. Only four state codes predate 1973; nineteen states adopted codes in response to Watergate between 1973 and 1979; and the rest adopted codes during the following twenty-five years. Most federal ethics legislation—the creation of the Office of Government Ethics, Inspectors General, Independent Counsels, and the Office of Special Counsel (for whistle-blowers)—were all passed in 1978 as a direct response to Watergate. As a matter of fact, scandal still prompts efforts to tighten standards of conduct; this response often leads to a haphazard array of prohibitions dictated by history rather than by principle. Often, too, the goal is to let the public know that ethics is on the front burner. Scandal and political pressure may also trigger efforts to change the administrative framework (Fillo, 2003).

Conflict of Interest

To ensure that the public interest is pursued by creating barriers to personal interest, prohibiting conflict of interest is logically fundamental to codes at every level of government (see Exhibit 8.3 and Chapter Three). Beyond this, little uniformity appears across jurisdictions.

The COGEL and the National Municipal League generally restrict conflict to the financial or economic. Often conflicts include personal issues (such as dating or sexual relationships), family issues (for example, nepotism), and even friendship (contracts, procurements). They are all treated under the title "financial interests," but getting a boyfriend or spouse a job seems to significantly stretch the typical understanding of financial interest.

In 2003, the OECD adopted an even broader perspective in its guidelines on conflicts of interest in the public sector for all of its member countries. Representatives for all of Western Europe, the United States, Canada, Mexico, Australia, Japan, and New Zealand agreed to abide by these standards. This agreement defines a *conflict of interest* as a "conflict between the public duty and the private interests of a public official, in which the public official has private capacity interests which could improperly influence the performance of their official duties and responsibilities."

The OECD (2003, p. 16) emphasizes the need to focus on four core principles when developing rules and strategies to prevent conflicts of interest:

1. Serving the Public Interest
2. Supporting Transparency and Scrutiny

3. Promoting Individual Responsibility and Personal Example
4. Engendering an Organisational Culture which is intolerant of conflicts of interest

Other definitions may include nepotism, soliciting sexual favors from subordinates, and releases of confidential information. More expansive formulations extend conflict to "social and political relationships and transactions which may compromise or *give the appearance* of compromising their [public servants'] objectivity, independence or honesty" (Josephson Institute, 1990, p. vii, emphasis added).

Many public officials rail against the concept of the *appearance* of conflicts of interest as either unfair or impossible to determine. Yet in reality, an appearance of a conflict of interest can do as much harm as an actual conflict of interest and has been enforced in courts of law. An official of the U.S. Department of Housing and Urban Development (HUD) was accused of being a slumlord and was fired by the agency. A federal court in the 1980s upheld the dismissal, despite the official's defense that he bought the properties to fix them up, because even the appearance of an official of HUD as a slumlord undermined the confidence of citizens in the impartiality of the government (Stark, 1997; see "Appearance of Impropriety" later in this chapter). Russell Williams correctly points out that conflicts of interest have been the most intractable challenge to an independent civil service since it was conceived in the late nineteenth century. Laws have been enacted, as well as administrative regulations, but any situation in which a public servant seems to place "self-interest ahead of public interest" is fraught with peril (Williams, 2002, unpaginated).

Financial Disclosure

A conventional way of encouraging compliance with conflict-of-interest prohibitions, financial disclosure is "the linchpin of government ethics laws" (Weimer, 1990, p. 2). Disclosure encourages employees' attention to conflict prohibitions and potential, uses scrutiny mechanisms for prevention and enforcement, and allows for corrective action against violations. One state ethics commission's executive director noted that "filers are reminded of what their financial interests are and of the need to avoid affecting them by their official acts" (Lewis, 1986, p. 17). At the first Global Forum Against Corruption (with participants from ninety countries; see Resource A) in 1999, U.S. Supreme Court Justice Stephen Breyer commented that as much as he hated filling out the required annual financial disclosure form, it was the single best way he knew to remind him of his ethical obligations and vulnerabilities.

Although disclosure does symbolize a commitment to fundamental standards, its utility as an enforcement mechanism indicates that someone has to read, verify, investigate, and act on the reports. Common Cause (1989b, p. 40) argues that filing alone is "not enough. To be effective, financial disclosure must be public." Common Cause's position (p. 8) is clear-cut: "In short, public disclosure forces the law to be taken seriously."

With the majority of states requiring some type of financial disclosure and federal service featuring two types, the many variations on the specifics come as no surprise. Numerous states require local officials to file. Sample forms, often readily available from local and neighboring ethics agencies and on-line, are provocative reading and are sometimes eye-openers for transition teams and new recruits.

Different administrative positions may have different disclosure requirements, keyed to salary or discretionary authority. For example, federal public disclosure is much more detailed than confidential reporting. In Pennsylvania, state, county, and local elected and appointed officials and public employees must file a disclosure with the state. New York State's Ethics in Government Act of 1987 requires employees who earn less than a specified salary or hold "nonpolicymaking" positions to submit a limited disclosure form.

Information subject to disclosure varies from specific dollar amounts to narrow or broad categories of either dollar amounts or holdings. For example, the disclosure system for the executive branch of the federal government has two distinct programs: (1) public disclosure and (2) confidential disclosure. Public disclosure is required of the most senior executive branch officials (political, civil service, and military) and requires identification of values in seven different dollar ranges. The confidential program requires only identification of assets, income, financial transactions, liabilities such as personal and bank loans, gifts from nonfamily sources, and reimbursements for travel and other activities. Disclosure is usually limited to immediate family and dependents, and neither states nor the federal government require reporting beyond this traditional circle of personal relationships (Weimer, 1990, p. 10; Freel, 2003). Definitions in model statutes from the National Municipal League, Common Cause, and COGEL are broader, to some extent allowing for mixed, blended, and unorthodox domestic arrangements.

There is no strong empirical evidence that the prospect of financial disclosure has led people to avoid or resign from public service, but the allegation has been part of the discussion for some time (Neely, 1984). Although careful crafting is needed to balance privacy and disclosure, burden and benefit (and later the evident contraction of public servants' privacy is discussed), the balance overall tips toward disclosure. "Virtually all state courts have upheld the constitutionality of financial disclosure" (Weimer, 1990, p. 15).

Appearance of Impropriety

The "appearance" standard is central to the federal approach. The media often apply it, irrespective of a jurisdiction's formal principles; appearance is not a universally adopted and legally enforceable norm. COGEL's draft model statute adopts it, as do many professional codes, including the American Bar Association's well-known Canon 9. Common Cause's and the National Institute of Municipal Law Officers' codes do not. Los Angeles, Chicago, and Buffalo expressly require avoiding the appearance of impropriety.

The irony is that an appearance of impropriety can be as damaging as an actual conflict of interest. Appearances potentially undermine the confidence of citizens in democratic institutions. Many public servants, as well as elected officials, will argue that such standards are unfair. Former California Senator Alan Cranston, who was reprimanded in the savings-and-loan scandals of the 1980s, claimed that no one knew what was in his heart, and he was the only one who could judge his actions. Taking exception to this, Dennis Thompson notes, "Because appearances are often the only window that citizens have on official conduct, rejecting the appearance standard is tantamount to denying democratic accountability" (Thompson, 1993, p. 376).

Avoiding the appearance of unethical conduct is a codified standard in many jurisdictions, including half of the states, as shown in Exhibit 8.3. The standard is written into the federal code for executive branch employees (Executive Order 12764, issued in 1989). Nonetheless, definitional lapses make a legally enforceable appearance standard problematic at best. Given the variations in legal provisions and state practices, the most definitive conclusion is that the jury is still out on appearance as an *enforceable* standard suitable for public service codes. However, the "appearance standard is still grounded in political values and is an expression of democratic accountability. The basis of appearance is the notion that civic employees are servants of the public, and therefore must do everything in their power to assure citizens that government officials are working for the public good" (Gilman, 2002, p. 19).

EXHIBIT 8.3. STATE ETHICS STANDARDS, 2003.

State	Commission	Appearance of Impropriety	Whistle-Blowing	Bribery	Conflict of Interest
Alabama	Yes	Yes	No	Yes	Yes
Alaska	Yes	Yes	No	No	Yes
Arkansas	Yes	No	No	Yes	Yes
Arizona	Yes	No	No	No	Yes
California	Yes	Yes	No	Yes	Yes
Colorado	Yes	Yes	No	No	Yes
Connecticut	Yes	No	No	Yes	Yes
Delaware	Yes	Yes	No	No	Yes
Florida	Yes	No	Yes	Yes	Yes
Georgia	Yes	Yes	No	Yes	Yes
Hawaii	Yes	No	No	No	Yes

State	Commission	Appearance of Impropriety	Whistle-Blowing	Bribery	Conflict of Interest
Idaho	Yes	No	No	Yes	Yes
Illinois	Yes	No	No	Yes	Yes
Indiana	Yes	No	No	Yes	Yes
Iowa	Yes	Yes	No	No	Yes
Kansas	Yes	Yes	No	Yes	Yes
Kentucky	Yes	Yes	No	No	Yes
Louisiana	Yes	Yes	Yes	Yes	Yes
Maine	Yes	Yes	No	No	No
Maryland	Yes	No	No	Yes	Yes
Massachusetts	Yes	Yes	No	Yes	Yes
Michigan	Yes	No	No	Yes	Yes
Minnesota	Yes	Yes	No	Yes	Yes
Mississippi	Yes	Yes	No	Yes	Yes
Missouri	Yes	No	No	No	Yes
Montana	Yes	Yes	No	Yes	Yes
Nebraska	Yes	No	No	No	No
New Hampshire	Yes	Yes	No	No	Yes
Nevada	Yes	Yes	No	Yes	Yes
New Jersey	Yes	Yes	No	No	Yes
New Mexico	Yes	No	No	No	No
New York	Yes	Yes	No	Yes	Yes
North Carolina	Yes	No	No	No	No
North Dakota[1]	No	No	No	No	No
Ohio	Yes	Yes	No	Yes	Yes
Oklahoma	Yes	No	No	No	Yes
Oregon[1]	No	No	No	No	Yes
Pennsylvania	Yes	No	No	Yes	Yes
Rhode Island	Yes	Yes	No	No	Yes
South Carolina	Yes	No	No	Yes	Yes
South Dakota[1]	No	No	No	No	No
Tennessee	Yes	No	Yes	No	Yes
Texas	Yes	No	No	No	Yes
Utah[1]	No	Yes	No	Yes	Yes
Vermont	Yes	Yes	No	No	Yes
Virginia	Yes	Yes	No	Yes	Yes
Washington	Yes	Yes	No	Yes	Yes
West Virginia	Yes	No	No	Yes	Yes
Wisconsin	Yes	Yes	No	No	Yes
Wyoming	Yes	No	No	Yes	Yes
District of Columbia	Yes	Yes	No	Yes	Yes

Note: [1] No ethics commission found on-line. Cited provisions for Utah are in general ethics code.

Data were gleaned from an Internet search conducted in February, 2003, of standards of conduct only; they exclude criminal statutes and specialized codes such as those for judges or teachers.

Revolving Door

More and more state governments prohibit the lobbying of former agencies on matters in which the official or employee was personally and substantially involved.

> Such restrictions must be defined narrowly so as not to discourage highly qualified professionals from entering government service, infringe on the constitutional rights of present state officials, or prevent the flow of communication and understanding between the public and private sector (Weimer, 1990, p. 2).

The complexity of the federal "revolving-door" statute (18 U.S.C. 207) is such that the OGE spent more than a decade promulgating regulations. Employees leaving federal service must distinguish between regulations on seeking and negotiating employment and on post-employment. A senior OGE administrator explained in May 2004 that most agencies require senior officials to have exit briefings on ethics, and ethics offices spend more and more time counseling *former* federal officials.

From the public's point of view, eliminating the revolving-door problem should be clear-cut. The U.S. political system encourages people to both enter and leave government with the idea that this encourages cross-fertilization and participation. Therefore, the problem is not the revolving door as such but individuals taking illicit advantage of their public positions when they leave the government. The question really is, How do we restrict this activity without preventing people from earning a living after they leave public service?

Other Common Elements

Other common provisions place permanent bans on disclosing privileged information or information not generally available to the public. Other elements may include an ethical commitment to the following: not discriminating on the basis of race, gender, disability, and more; limiting the acceptance of gifts (even from relatives and friends); avoiding preferential treatment to individuals or organizations; not making unauthorized commitments on behalf of the government; limiting outside employment; and protecting and preserving government resources. Standards may extend to off-duty activities undertaken in a nonofficial capacity, as suggested in Exhibit 8.4. Finally, many codes stipulate an obligation to report ethical misconduct to appropriate authorities.

Value of Ethics Training

One of the keys to a successful ethics program is effective, regular communication and training, which is needed to clarify expectations and provide guidance. Effective training must go beyond simply repeating rules. Public managers must have a sense of

EXHIBIT 8.4. ETHICS, DUTY, AND FREEDOM OF SPEECH.

Should a citizen who serves as a member of a municipal planning commission speak out publicly against a developer planning a subdivision before the planning commission has deliberated on the matter? Here's the case. You decide.

> In a letter to the editor in the local newspaper, Planning Commissioner Jones urged the local school board to oppose a planned subdivision that, in his opinion, would result in significant and uncompensated costs to the school district and the community at large. The developer complained to the mayor that Commissioner Jones should be removed from the planning commission inasmuch as he had demonstrated that he was no longer unbiased and impartial with regard to the situation. The mayor agreed, stating that Commissioner Jones should let the facts sway his opinion, not personal judgment.
>
> Commissioner Jones responded by saying that he did not sign the letter as a member of the planning commission. Rather, he had signed it as a citizen and was merely exercising his opinion as granted by the First Amendment of the Constitution.

Did citizen/Commissioner Jones cross over the ethical line? Or was his behavior above reproach?

Reprinted with revision by permission of the American Society for Public Administration. Anonymous author. Originally published in *PA Times,* "Ethics Moment" column, edited by Don Menzel, Sept. 2002. Internet [http://www3.niu.edu/~tp0dcm1/aspa/ethicsec/moments/moments.htm].

the rules but also need a solid understanding of the principles underlying them. It is one thing to memorize the rule that one cannot accept a gift worth over $20, but it is quite another to understand the principle of not using public office for private gain.

How does one effectively train public administrators in ethical behavior? Because most government ethics programs have been created without input from the public administration community and ethicists and designed to meet the mandated mission, the programs typically emphasize compliance and "training to the rule." By contrast, Leigh Grosenick (1995–96) argues for a values- or principle-based approach, with compliance-based elements tied to fundamental principles and, therefore, more likely to be remembered in an actual ethical crisis. Others may argue for some combination (Knouse and Giacalone, 1996).

Ethics training is not a once-in-a-lifetime inoculation. It is perishable. People forget, change jobs, get promoted, and face different ethics challenges. And regulations and laws change. For these reasons, regular ethics training is a key systemic component. In responding to this dynamic, many ethics programs have moved beyond the classroom or on-line training (for example, Maryland) to a variety of innovative approaches. Among these are plays or vignettes, with agency officials as the actors. Creative video games or simulations are also used in training, such as the U.S. Department of Justice's Quandaries game (see Resource B). The Web site of the Comprehensive Ethics Training Compendium [http://www.aspanet.org/ethicscommunity/compendium] is a useful resource.

Unfortunately, very little has been done to evaluate the training's impact. For the most part, programs start from the assumption that training works by osmosis, that is, simply by exposure to ideas. When evaluation is done, it generally focuses on the quality of instruction and materials. Little or nothing is available to answer questions about whether agency training of civil servants results in a better understanding of their ethical obligations or even the ethics rules. More important, the field has yet to assess the gold standard of ethics training: Does it have an impact on behavior? In a review of the literature on best practices in the public and private sectors, we have found no attempt to answer this basic empirical question.

A survey of the perceptions of graduates of four master's of public administration programs suggests that ethics courses in MPA programs influence behavior. Good ethics courses provide students with an awareness of ethics issues they might confront, as well as cultivate an attitude of ethical obligation in pursuing a career in public service (Menzel, 1997). This research is obviously limited because it only deals with perception without trying to correlate aggregate data. Admittedly, developing the latter is challenging, but it will be essential to evaluating the outcomes of ethics programs.

In a 1999 study of graduates from thirteen top-ranking schools of public policy and administration, *maintaining ethical standards* ranks first among the skills considered important for success in government. When queried about the importance at each level of maintaining ethical standards, 81 percent of respondents said it is the most important characteristic at the federal level. Similarly, 75 percent said it is the most important characteristic at the state level; at the local level, 84 percent expressed the same sentiment. In the private and nonprofit sectors, 81 percent said it is the most important skill in the private sector, while 89 percent of respondents said it is the most important skill in the nonprofit sector. Graduates also responded that they felt the biggest mismatch between what they were taught and what skills they considered they needed for success was in learning how to maintain ethical standards (Light, 1999, p. 100, Table 4–1; Resource A).

Another perception-based measure of training's effect on behavior is the reduced pressure to commit misconduct in organizations with the essential elements of an ethics program. ERC's study (2003a) suggests a relationship between more comprehensive ethics programs and lower amounts of perceived pressure to commit misconduct among employees in large business organizations (more than five hundred employees). Respondents reported a decrease in pressure if the employer had all four elements: (1) written ethics standards, (2) ethics training, (3) a dedicated ethics office, and (4) means or mechanisms to report misconduct. If one had only written standards, then almost one in four (23 percent) employees felt pressure to commit misconduct. If all four elements were in place, the perceived pressure dropped to 7 percent (Ethics Resource Center, 2003a, p. 37). The study also notes a strong relationship between empirically identifiable behaviors by leaders and supervisors and a significant reduction in pressure to commit misconduct.

Coming Attractions

In the evolutionary, adaptive system described earlier, today's innovation gives us a glimpse of tomorrow's standard practice. One development is the use of forward, multiyear, protected funding in several jurisdictions to insulate the ethics commission from political pressure, executive or legislative retaliation, and budgetary vagaries. Another emerging practice is seeking and sometimes getting direct subpoena powers for ethics commissions. An area to watch in the states is inclusive coverage of all jurisdictions and all branches of government statewide. Post-employment restrictions and treatment of part-time, contractual, and volunteer government officials and employees are volatile issues in which developments only hint at an emerging consensus.

There are signs of other things to come. Consider the wisdom of shaping financial disclosure to contemporary lifestyles and responsibilities associated with dual-career couples, blended families, adult guardianships, adult children living in a household, and life partners. In addition, the Internet has created the challenge of how to account for and correctly report activities, such as day trading. The increase in number, status, and influence of legislative staff members in state governments suggests that extending or adopting code provisions may mark a future phase. In states such as Connecticut and Minnesota, the state code is a term and condition of employment by virtue of its incorporation into union contracts.

Two areas of growth at the state level are in lobbying registration and regulating the ethics of local jurisdictions. The registration of lobbyists can present a problem for civil servants, as well as those in the nonprofit sector. For civil servants in a number of states, care must be taken in terms of interactions with lobbyists, even (especially?) those who are old friends. Knowing *who* is registered is the civil servants' obligation in many states. Then, too, civil servants unintentionally can become lobbyists when, for example, they are elected president of their homeowners associations. For nonprofits seeking state funds or access, it is very easy to slip into the role of "lobbyist," as defined by state laws. Arguably, Wisconsin has the most aggressive state legislation in this area (see http://www.state/wi/us/SiteMap.htm).

More and more states are setting ethics standards for local officials, whether elected, appointed, or in civil service. These standards often are in addition to ethics codes at the county, city, village, or town level. Ironically, in an attempt to create minimum standards throughout the state, legislatures have often created a multilayered system that may be both confusing and poorly administered. Overly complex and poorly administered ethics systems often send the message that ethics is trivial in that state and that programs are designed less for substance than for window dressing.

The *event horizon* for ethics programs will be how to deal with contractors. Although the number of government employees has declined somewhat over the past decade, there has been a very large increase in the number of contractors working for government agencies. The emphasis on privatizing government functions and contracting out will have a significant impact on the effectiveness of ethics programs, as the case, "The Contract," suggests in Chapter Four. It is now common to have government employees working with contractors or overseeing contract compliance. The government employee is covered by a host of rules, and generally there are ethics rules governing contractors. Yet problems are being reported by inspectors general at the federal and state level (President's Council on Integrity and Efficiency, 2002), and effective ethics programs will have to address this issue.

State agendas by and large overlook the way in which individual privacy conflicts with the public's right to know. In principle, this is a concern even if only the flawless or fearless participate. Examples of intrusion and confidentiality issues include polygraph and integrity tests and medical and insurance records. If the goal is to recruit the best (not the perfect) people into public service, then working with the media, professional associations, public interest groups, and statutory safeguards could help protect administrators' privacy in some carefully selected realms such as medical records, health insurance claims, intimate family relations, and other matters traditionally private and functionally irrelevant to job performance.

Yet the reality is that the media and public interest groups often find legitimate reasons to challenge a public servant's privacy with the public's right to know. This may result from the group's frustration about an administration's policy agenda. As one ethics official pointed out, "If they can't get you on policy grounds, they will try to get you on ethics." For this reason, a commission or agency with effective authority can act to protect privacy rights, as well as the public's right to know, if it is viewed as an independent third party in making decisions.

Model statutes are visions of the future to the extent that they are influential. Common Cause played a critical role in the early 1990s in California, West Virginia, and Massachusetts. Core elements in its model statute for state government include prohibitions on the abuse of office for personal gain and on conflicts of interest; standards of conduct to prevent and avoid abuse; personal financial disclosure for candidates and high-level officials, and a strong, independent commission with investigatory and civil enforcement powers. Common Cause's classic contribution, *A Model Ethics Law for State Government* (1989a), covers detailed disclosure, prohibitions against conflicts and procedures to avoid and prevent them, post-employment restrictions, a strong ethics commission, and investigatory procedures that ensure due process.

Current Practices in the Cities

Standardization is no more characteristic of local than of state practices; the authority behind codes and standards varies. By way of illustration, Chicago's ethics code was issued by Mayor Harold Washington by executive order in 1986 and passed by the city council in 1987. (The unanimous council vote of 49 to 0 conceals the earlier struggles.) Provisions also vary and run the gamut from tolerant to stringent (as in Los Angeles, for example). The 1990 draft code of the National Institute of Municipal Law Officers—a set of model guidelines intended to be used by municipal attorneys when they draft municipal codes—limited prohibited interests to "direct or indirect pecuniary or material benefit." Further, it requires disclosure of financial or personal interest in proposed municipal legislation and forbids "special consideration, treatment or advantage to any citizen beyond that which is available to every other citizen" (National Institute of Municipal Law Officers, 1990, pp. 3, 5–6). In 1990, this formulation was considered stringent. By 2003, the renamed International Municipal Law Association's municipal model ethics code section had grown to incorporate forty-four subsections and fifty-four pages. The section on conflicts of interest had become far more complex and was supplemented with a seven-page section on definitions necessary to interpret most of the guidance (see Exhibit 8.5.).

Relying on responses from only a small fraction of the hundreds of local ethics programs in the United States, the COGEL survey provides the most up-to-date data available on local ethics programs in the United States (Freel, 2003). The results show that local ethics programs vary (as do state programs). Often there are independent programs as well for police, fire, and education. In Los Angeles the political leadership appoints ethics commissioners for five-year terms (p. 36), while up the coast in Oakland three commissioners are appointed by the mayor and the other four by the commission as a whole (p. 40). The city of Jacksonville has broad financial disclosure requirements and detailed gifts rules (p. 65), and Honolulu has detailed revolving-door requirements and requires training for 2,500 "council members, managers, supervisors and board and commission members" (p. 89). The Ethics Commission for Montgomery County, Maryland, has a full-time administrator and uses interactive electronic financial disclosure statements (p. 147). Its close neighbor, the Ethics Commission of Anne Arundel County, Maryland, limits one political party to four of the seven seats and provides detailed guidance on the types of gifts that can be accepted by public employees (p. 142).

Although municipal ethics commissions or boards vary widely in terms of structure and authorities, there are common themes: they are structured to have representatives

EXHIBIT 8.5. EXCERPT FROM A MODEL MUNICIPAL CODE.

Section 9–107 (b): "No public servant shall accept or receive, directly or indirectly, from any person, including one whose identity is unknown to the public servant, any personal benefit under circumstances in which it can reasonably be inferred that the benefit is intended to influence the public servant in the performance or nonperformance of any official duty or as a reward for any official action of the public servant."

Source: International Municipal Law Association, 2003, p. 9–1.12.

of the community; they invariably have a code; and they are responsible for interpreting rules and giving findings. Two decades ago, it would have been difficult to find more than a handful of ethics programs at the municipal level. Within the next few years, it will be difficult to find many major municipalities that do not have such a system in place.

Is statewide uniformity emerging as accepted practice for local ethics systems? Some states blanket all officials and employees with specified standards of conduct. The observations made earlier in this chapter about borrowing from other jurisdictions should not be mistaken for arguments in support of uniformity (and Chapter Ten proposes adapting rules to particular administrative realities rather than touting them as universal remedies).

The trade-off is obvious: the logic and simplicity of statewide uniformity *versus* a local code tailored to local needs and conventions. National professional associations have discovered that variable community standards can be a sticky issue. Differences in size and complexity add other dimensions such as the size of the talent pool, readily observable and widely known behavior, and family or political connections to local businesses receiving municipal contracts, sometimes complicated by local contracting requirements. The case concluding Chapter Four—"The Contract"—illustrates one variant on this theme.

Localities are treated differently in different states and in different model statutes. Common Cause endorsed uniform standards many years ago, but the National Municipal League did not include local jurisdictions in its 1979 model statute. Passing the 1987 Ethics in Government Act, New York's state legislature defined conflicts of interest and required each jurisdiction, from counties to school districts, to adopt its own code. A glance at the New York Web site (www.nysethics.com) shows that the majority of cities and many counties have created ethics boards. On the other coast, California's conflict-of-interest code designates certain state, county, and city officials, along with state and local employees who are required to file annual statements of economic interest. City officials include mayors, council members, city managers, chief administrative officers, planning commissioners, and city attorneys.

The Massachusetts State Ethics Commission ("the primary civil enforcement agency") reports that the state's conflict-of-interest law

> has regulated the conduct of public officials and employees in the Bay State since 1963. The law limits what public employees may do on the job, what they may do after hours or "on the side," and what they may do after they leave public service and return to the private sector. It also sets the standards of conduct required of all state, county, and municipal employees in Massachusetts, articulating the premise that public employees owe undivided loyalty to the government they serve, and must act in the public interest rather than for private gain (Massachusetts, 1989, p. 2).

In 2003, the Massachusetts State Ethics Commission provided 400 written opinions and provided telephone advice to more than 3,300 individuals. "The Commission reviewed 1,037 complaints in FY 2003, issued 239 private educational letters and one public educational letter, initiated two public hearings, participated in a total of 14 hearings, four of which went to trial" (Freel, 2003, p. 161). The majority of cases resulting in criminal or civil penalties involved municipal employees.

Federal Offices and Standards

Conflict-of-interest prohibitions are central to federal standards of conduct. Ranging from affirmative ideals to unequivocal restrictions and on to the criminal code, these standards include the more positive, prescriptive Code of Ethics for Government Service (P.L. 96–303) enacted in 1980; detailed proscriptions administratively adopted by executive orders; OGE and agency regulations; and criminal conflict-of-interest statutes in 18 U.S.C. 201–209.

Federal conflict-of-interest statutes date from the Civil War, but the principle can be traced formally to 1789 when an Act to Establish the Treasury Department (I Stat. 12, 1789) created the very first domestic federal agency and prohibited conflict of interest (and promised a financial reward for whistle-blowers). Section 8 of the act states that "no person appointed to any office instituted by this act shall directly or indirectly be concerned or interested in carrying on the business of trade or commerce." The many federal statutes were first codified in 1962 and, except for post-employment provisions, have not been amended substantially since then. The general prohibition on conflict of interest is found in 18 U.S.C. Section 208. The Ethics Reform Act of November 30, 1989, revised this section by adding civil prosecution and injunctions to criminal prosecution.

Broader and more stringent standards have been adopted administratively. There are the executive orders, including Lyndon Johnson's 11222 (1965) and George H. W. Bush's 12674 (1989) and 12731 (1990), with the latter adding limits on outside earned income. Issuing supplementary rules and procedures, the OGE promulgates implementing regulations jointly with agencies. These reckon with agency particulars, including organic act limitations, statutory gift acceptance authority, procurement, human subject research, or other functional specialties. Executive Order 12731, Section 301(a), directs agency heads to augment the OGE regulations with "regulations of special applicability to the particular functions and activities of that agency."

U.S. Office of Government Ethics

The OGE was initially created in the federal Office of Personnel Management by the Ethics in Government Act of 1978, then given separate agency status a decade later. The 1988 reauthorization act defines the OGE's mission as "overall direction of executive branch policies relating to preventing conflicts of interest on the part of officers and employees of any executive agency." A small agency with a budget to match, the OGE is vulnerable as a discretionary domestic component of the federal budget.

Since 1989, the executive order in force has required the OGE to promulgate regulations establishing a "single, comprehensive and clear set of executive branch standards of conduct" (Executive Order 12674 specifies that they be "objective, reasonable, and enforceable"). The seriousness of this charge is shown in the OGE's swift response; it published interim regulations in the *Federal Register* (Jan. 18, 1990) to standardize rules and correct deficiencies in agency ethics programs. The OGE's tasks extend beyond regulatory authority to include financial disclosure, education and training, guidance and interpretation (U.S. Office of Government Ethics, 1990b), enforcement, and evaluation of conflict-of-interest laws. Its regulatory reach touches every executive employee in federal service (including the uniformed military) and every agency.

Compliance and the Ethics Industry

Although compliance may appear to be a growth industry in the nation's capital, the evidence for that is contradictory. Agency budgets belie the growth prediction. Executive Order 12674 states that agencies should have separate budget line items when "practical," and the 1990 order repeats the directive. Unfortunately, the U.S. Office of Management and Budget has decreed that this is impractical, and no federal agency has tried to exercise this authority since 1991.

Staffing is another story. In 1990, in ninety-nine agencies that account for almost five million employees, there were only 125 full-time-equivalent (FTE) employees working in the ethics function, but thousands were involved part-time (U.S. Office of Government Ethics, 1990a, p. 22). An OGE official calculates that by March 2003, these numbers had increased to 500 full-time employees working in ethics and almost 8,000 part-time employees.

Some staff members are Designated Agency Ethics Officers (DAEOs) who are responsible for the advisory aspects relating to federal standards. The DAEO's "primary duties are to provide training and counseling to agency employees on conflict of interest matters and to review financial disclosure statements" (General Accounting Office, 1987, p. 7). (Congress purposely separated the advisory from the enforcement function for fear that a merger would deter employees from asking advice.) The inspectors general in every major federal agency do investigations and audits when wrongdoing is suspected. Whistle-blowers are protected by the Office of Special Counsel. Prosecution is handled by regional U.S. Attorneys, unless politically charged issues shunt prosecution to the Public Integrity Section of the Department of Justice. Administrative actions, from time off without pay to dismissal, are handled by an agency's

General Counsel, with some oversight by the Merit System Protections Board. Add to this, special oversight activities such as procurement, special internal agency committees, the General Accounting Office, and congressional committee hearings.

Whether in a growth phase or holding pattern, compliance already ranks as big business in the executive branch. With administrative and criminal standards and numerous agencies and offices involved in oversight, reporting, investigation, prosecution, and other activities, the overlap and complexity is impressive, even for Washington.

The compliance clamor is at a predictably high decibel level. Over the past several years, the OGE has discovered that it is difficult to break out of a compliance mode and shift to a more advisory and counseling stance through guidebooks and media. (See the list of pamphlets and resources available at http://www.usoge.gov.) The most influential stakeholders are attorneys in OGE, the executive branch, and Congress who are trained to think and write in a highly technical manner. Unfortunately, the most important stakeholders—federal employees—are not necessarily well served by the fixation on compliance and insistence on detail and legalese. For example, two of the key concepts to federal ethics regulation are "particular matter" and "specific party." Neither of these is defined easily, and the definitional task is made even more daunting for federal employees by the refinements in dozens of the more than one thousand informal advisory opinions OGE has published since 1979.

Enforcement

The many investigatory authorities further complicate the ethics aspect of life in federal service. The General Accounting Office (1987) summarized the following three general routes to enforcement, meaning investigation of alleged violations of conflict-of-interest standards.

Agency enforcement: "The investigation . . . is primarily the responsibility of the Inspectors General. Also, allegations the DAEOs receive . . . are to be forwarded to the IG. The IG investigations may result in the case being referred to the Department of Justice for further investigation and possible prosecution or forwarded to others within the agency for possible administrative action (e.g., a reprimand or dismissal in cases involving current employees)" (General Accounting Office, 1987, p. 7). No uniform, formal referral process has developed in federal agencies (Office of Government Ethics, 1990a, pp. 23–24), and cases may be referred to one of the ninety-four U.S. attorneys' offices (General Accounting Office, 1987, pp. 8–9).

Prosecutorial enforcement: "The process by which the Public Integrity Section [of the Justice Department] and the U.S. Attorney's Office investigate and prosecute a conflict of interest case is . . . the same as any other criminal investigation or prosecution.

Cases that are prosecuted . . . are sometimes resolved by a finding or admission of guilt under other criminal statutes, such as those prohibiting false or fraudulent claims (18 U.S.C. 287), false or fraudulent statements (18 U.S.C. 1001), and perjury (18 U.S.C. 1621–1623). [T]he final test of protective merit in a conflict of interest case is the likelihood of obtaining a felony conviction" (General Accounting Office, 1987, pp. 10–11).

Agency administrative actions: Disciplinary actions for violations of noncriminal standards include termination, suspension, restitution, reassignment, reprimand, admonishment, recusal, and divestiture. Taking administrative action does not preclude criminal sanctions, and IGs review each action. "The IGs said they commonly refer cases that are declined by justice to the employee's bureau-level supervisor for administrative action" (General Accounting Office, 1987, p. 12). In 1989, about one-quarter of the over two thousand adverse actions on standards violations dealt with misuse of government vehicles and other property, while less than 2 percent related to conflicting financial interest and less than 3 percent to conflicting outside action (U.S. Office of Government Ethics, 1990a, p. 27).

Financial Disclosure

The Monitoring and Compliance Division of the OGE collects and reviews (in coordination with the home agency) approximately 1,000 of the most senior officials who file the public Executive Personnel Financial Disclosure Report, the SF 278. Another 20,000 or so disclosures are filed and reviewed in agencies for all senior officials, who file disclosure forms when they enter government service annually and when they leave federal service. The U.S. Senate usually does not hold a hearing to consent to a prospective nominee until the OGE reviews his or her disclosure form, agreements are made to eliminate all problems, and the director of OGE certifies the form. OGE must then ensure compliance with ethics agreements usually within ninety days of the person's taking office. This drives an impressive transition-period workload for the unit, which reviews something on the order of 1,000 disclosures during a presidential transition. In 1999, one of the last years of the Clinton administration, OGE reviewed 271 nominees and certified them to the Senate (U.S. Office of Government Ethics, 2000, p. 7).

The approximately five thousand annual filers of public disclosures include the president and vice president, and officers and employees who are members of the Senior Executive Service. High-level political, managerial, supervisory, and policy positions and the entire career Senior Executive Service file disclosures are available for public review. Others are military ranks at pay grade 0–7 or above (general officers), administrative law judges, most inspectors general, employees designated by the

OGE, selected senior postal service officers and the OGE's director, and agency DAEOs. The almost perfect compliance rate remains relatively constant.

Initiated by executive order in 1965, confidential disclosure is required from more than 200,000 employees each year. While the number of federal employees has decreased over the past decade, the number of confidential filers has increased as a percentage of the federal workforce. The driving force behind this is the contracting out of federal functions. This requires larger numbers of procurement and contracting officers, who generally file confidential disclosure statements. In March 2003, a senior OGE official noted that the number of confidential disclosure filers reached a peak of 270,000 in 2000. (The confidential statements do not require dollar amounts but otherwise have the same categories as the public disclosure system.) The confidential reports may lead to actions such as divestiture, disqualification, reassignment, letters, waivers, or warnings.

Managing the Code

An effective code demands a developmental process. It starts with a conflict-of-interest prohibition, defines what else is imperative in the community, moves on to enforcement, and finally shifts to more subtle aspects of implementation, such as training and before-the-fact advice. From beginning to end, the process is more like individualized programming for a broad application than buying off-the-shelf software for a particular task. (Managers who have survived the installation of a new computer system may appreciate the analogy.)

Ready-made standards and model provisions possibly suit more populous or complex jurisdictions. For smaller jurisdictions, some specific concerns include the need for and reasonableness of the appearance-of-impropriety prohibition, detailed public financial disclosure as a meaningful way of implementing conflict-of-interest prohibitions, nepotism and dual-employment restrictions, and investment limitations. And this list could go on. Taking size and diversity into account would contribute sensible and tenable standards and also acknowledge the variety that characterizes American public organizations and governmental structures.

> Codes of conduct should be crafted from a rich empirical base, understandable in the climate of the particular agency, making sense to those to whom they apply—down-to-earth, realistic. They should not appear as commandments from on high, generalized statements of good intentions, [or] lofty aspirations incapable of specific human responses. They need to be fashioned out of the everyday work life, become integral parts of staff development activities; a support to effective performance, not a burden. The goal is to underscore that standards of honesty go hand in hand with those of efficiency and competence (Robert C. Wood, quoted in Cox, 1988, p. 10).

Even with a code and a nonpartisan commission in place, most of the work remains to integrate the code's standards into the agency's way of doing business, its culture, and its style. Codes do make a difference, but only if they are well managed. In a recent survey with more than 60,000 respondents, the ERC (2003c) found that

> perceived pressure among employees to violate ethics standards is often symptomatic of deeper organizational problems and related risks. When pressures to violate standards are present, they generally reflect two main employee beliefs: (1) bosses and/or organizations require such behavior and or (2) they will be viewed negatively or suffer related job consequences if they don't give in to this pressure. Both of these beliefs reflect problems within the work environment such as ineffective ethical supervision and leadership. Although it is natural for organizations to push their employees toward greater productivity, leaders and supervisors must also be clear that such improvements cannot come at the expense of the organization's ethical standards.

In addition to executive example and leadership, serious implementation throughout the agency is vital. For a code to be operative, fair, and meaningful, it must be related to the organization's management and incentives. Ideally, the code should speak directly to the public manager, as shown in Exhibit 8.2. These concerns translate into the five general guidelines for managing the agency's code, as specified in the exhibit.

Ethics for Nonprofits

A variety of scandals, heightened public scrutiny, the threat of increased regulation and oversight, and the realization of the need for donor confidence fuel the move among nonprofits toward clearly articulated and broadly understood standards of conduct. The American Red Cross adopted detailed additional ethics standards as a result of the issues described in Chapter Three; the U.S. Olympic Committee's experience is laid out in Chapter Ten. The United Way of America developed a strong ethics regime because of a scandal in the 1990s. From the local Little League team and Boy Scouts to the county orchestra and local hospital, nonprofit organizations face issues with significant ethical content. Part of the response is to adopt codes of conduct and develop ethics programs.

But what kind of code? How detailed? How legalistic? And for what purpose—encouraging ethical behavior, preserving funding, avoiding increased regulation, or some combination? The answer to this last question speaks to another: Who is the audience—donors, general public, legislative leaders? How are nonprofits to make standards clear and understandable, give before-the-fact advice, and go about enforcement?

Nonprofit organizations confront many of the same problems that government agencies do. However, the majority are small organizations without the staff or resources to create effective ethics codes and full-blown programs on their own. The INDEPENDENT SECTOR is one of several professional organizations that help nonprofits build ethics codes and transparency systems. The consensus for nonprofits today is that standards of conduct are needed; they are the right thing to do; and, in many cases, professionally mandated and legally required. (See Resource B for other resources.)

Need for Well-Designed Programs

With standards of conduct at every level of government in the United States, there are wide variations on what codes state, how they are implemented, how they are communicated, and how they are enforced. From an administrative point of view, the effectiveness of the code is directly related to the institutions that are responsible for it. Many codes in the United States serve little more purpose than as wallpaper; others are dynamic, living frameworks essential to the mission of the agency. Since the first edition of this book, the number and complexity of these systems has grown exponentially.

It is important to recognize that a good ethics system is not a substitute for a good ethics code. The latter should be clear and should express the fundamental values of public service. It should provide more than "don'ts" by providing a clear vision of the value and purpose of public service.

It is also important to admit that a good code is no substitute for a good system. When ethics programs are implemented poorly, they may do more damage than good. Public employees may see the rules and principles as trivial and irrelevant. Well-designed and well-managed programs provide an ethical foundation that keeps public servants out of trouble and reinforces citizens' faith in their governmental institutions.

Case: Private Gain or Public Victim?

The Law Enforcement Oath of Honor of the International Association of Chiefs of Police (undated) states, "On my honor, I will never betray my badge, my integrity, my character, or the public trust. I will always have the courage to hold myself and others accountable for our actions. I will always uphold the constitution, my community, and the agency I serve." According to the Montgomery County Police Department (undated), Charles A. Moose is a member.

In the fall of 2002, an unknown sniper or snipers terrorized the Washington D.C. area, randomly killing people no matter their age, race, or gender. A person was killed mowing the lawn, a child shot on the way to school, a bus driver gunned down in the door of his bus, a woman shot through the head as she put packages in the trunk of her car, and an elderly man shot dead as he pumped gas into his car. The investigations drew in police from two states, over a dozen counties, the District of Columbia, and several federal police authorities. After the first week, police officials determined that they had to co-ordinate their own activities and needed a single voice to speak for the investigation. This would help squelch rumors and implement a strategy to use the media to help track down leads and provide accurate information. The decision was made to make Montgomery County Police Chief Charles A. Moose the spokesperson for the investigation. His calm persona and professionalism captured the national media, and Chief Moose became a common feature on national and international television for more than a month.

Chief Moose was hailed for his steady hand with the media and the public; he was viewed as the one individual responsible for coordinating the massive and successful law enforcement effort. John Lee Malvo and John Allen Mohammed were captured in the early morning of October 24, 2002, after remarkable police work that linked events in the states of Washington and Alabama to the horror that was occurring in the D.C. area. The men were accused of killing ten people and critically injuring three others, and were subsequently tried and found guilty.

Moose signed a deal with Dutton Publishing Company of New York in January 2003 to write a book about the manhunt. The chief also received more than $4,000 for an open movie contract about his experiences. Moose said money was a motivating factor in the decision to sign the deals. "If it helps me and my family with the law school bills my wife has . . . it's my good fortune" (Mosk, 2003c, B1). The chief negotiated the book and movie deals before he sought permission from his supervisor or from the ethics commission for any of the outside employment work he had pursued (and for which he was compensated), as required by law and specifically referenced in his employment agreement.

Montgomery County ethics officials soon began questioning whether it was appropriate for the nationally known lawman to profit personally from the investigation he helped lead. The ethics commission met on March 3 to hear Moose's requests for outside employment, including a possible waiver from stringent ethics laws that restrict county employees from profiting from their public work. The panel also was asked to consider whether it was proper for Moose to sell his story to a Hollywood television production company and to launch a consulting firm with his wife to market the chief's skills as a motivational speaker and his expertise in team-building, crisis management, and conflict resolution. The chief described the book as a "once-in-a-lifetime" chance to taste the rewards of fame.

The commission scheduled another meeting to decide the issues. According to the commission's chairperson, Elizabeth K. Kellar (2004), "All of this would have been kept confidential (required by law), except for Chief Moose's decision to talk about it with the media."

Hired after the chief requested a waiver, the chief's attorney argued that forbidding people to write books raises serious constitutional issues, and public officials do not give up the right to free speech when they enter public service. In addition, hearing about Chief Moose's experience would provide a real public benefit. The attorney also argued that the ethics rules were designed to prevent bribery or undue influence over legislation, which is not the case with Moose's book.

With the limelight comes opportunity, as well as the spotlight of increased public scrutiny. Capitalizing on new-found fame "'can easily overwhelm a person,' said Vivian Weil, head of the Illinois Institute of Technology's Center for the Study of Ethics in the Professions. 'You can understand someone being unsettled by it and even failing to pass it by the ethics board,' Weil said. 'To have clouded judgment—you can easily imagine that'" (Associated Press, 2003, unpaginated). According to John Kleinig, director of the Institute for Criminal Justice Ethics, Chief Moose is not the first police chief to write books on major crimes or their memoirs. "But that can lead to conflicts of interest. Those can include too much outside work that distracts a chief from his police job, a book or speech that reveals confidential information, or the appearance that a chief is cashing in on a tragedy. . . . He must be aware that others have had problems and that he could find himself in a bit of difficulty. . . . It's probably in his interest that it is reviewed." Kleinig notes, "It's like the guy who wins the lottery and suddenly finds he's the subject of enormous amounts of attention and pressures" (Associated Press, 2003).

The powerful, popular, and elected Montgomery County Executive, Doug Duncan, weighed in on behalf of permitting Moose to write his book. Duncan vowed to ask the county council to grant the chief a special exemption from the ethics rules, should the commission attempt to derail his book. Duncan argued that, if Chief Moose were turned down, he would only resign and find a job elsewhere. Duncan urged the members to grant Moose a waiver so that the county could retain this exemplary public servant.

On March 20, just before Moose was called to active duty in the Air National Guard, the five-member ethics commission issued a six-page ruling arguing that Moose's for-profit ventures would violate "bedrock principles" of county ethics law. The commission ruled:

> It is not in the best interest of the County to allow its employees to "trade on" their government activities for private gain in such a direct and immediate fashion. Such conduct leads citizens to question whether public employees are discharging their duties in the public interest or in furtherance of some private interest. This diminishes citizens' faith in their public servants and erodes their trust in [c]ounty government.

In the commission members' view, "These principles are at the core of the prohibition against using the prestige of one's office for private gain." The ruling added that neither Moose nor Duncan, who had asked the commission to make an exception for the chief, "has convinced the commission that this situation is a good platform to begin waiving those principles." A waiver now "could lead to undesirable behavior" in the future, the panel said, such as employees "jockeying for position" during high-profile incidents in hopes of winning fame and fortune.

His attorney protested the "flawed" decision and said he was astonished. "They concede that the county executive has decided that this is in the best interest of the county. But these five unelected members of this commission say, 'No, we know better'" (Mosk, 2003b, B1).

In late April, in a significant turnaround from its past positions, the *Washington Post*'s editors argued that in this balancing test they would come down on "the side of more speech in this case." But, they continued, he should not be allowed to write for the "wrong reasons," namely his poor salary as compared to other police chiefs. This created a double standard when it came to other police officers on the force. The solution, according to the newspaper's editors, was for the commission to "reexamine its earlier ruling barring police officers from accepting honorariums to speak about the sniper case." In October 2003, the *Washington Post* printed five long excerpts from Moose's book.

Charles Moose resigned as Chief of the Montgomery County Police on June 18, 2003, rather than comply with the ethics commission's ruling. The settlement agreement that he negotiated with Montgomery County when he resigned required that he return movie compensation to the county that he had accepted prior to seeking permission or a waiver and that he dismiss his lawsuit against the commission. The commission agreed that (absent any breach of confidentiality) it would not take any action to restrain Moose's book, movie, or speaking opportunities after he resigned.

◆ ◆ ◆

Discussion Questions

1. Most public codes forbid using public office for private gain. Is this the core problem here? What do you consider in arriving at your answer?

2. Should the value of free speech override ethics rules for public officials? Why? There is a long history of government employees' freedom of speech being restricted for reasons of "compelling government interest." Federal employees' participation in partisan activities has been restricted since 1939 under the Federal Hatch Act (5 U.S.C. §§ 7321–7326), amended to expand employees' rights in 1993. See the U.S. Office of Special Council at http://www.osc.gov. For some

important court cases on limitations and liberties of government employees, see *Wild v. United States Dep't of Housing & Urban Dev.*, 692 F.2d 1129, 1132–34 (7th Cir. 1982) and *Van Ee v. EPA*, 202 F.3d 296 (D.C. Cir. 2000).

3. Did Chief Moose do anything unethical by pursuing the book and movie contracts before seeking a waiver of the county's standards? Why?

4. Did Chief Moose do anything unethical by seeking a waiver of the county's standards? Why?

5. Did Chief Moose do anything unethical by resigning in order to fulfill the book contract? Why?

6. As a member of the ethics commission, would you have granted Chief Moose a waiver? Why?

CHAPTER NINE

BROADENING THE HORIZON

What can professional public managers learn from the global movement in public service ethics? Even a quick peek at the international scene might seem irrelevant to public managers busy with pressing problems close at home. Yet ethics systems and expectations are driven not only by internal domestic pressures but by external factors as well. A glance at colleagues in other administrative settings may help us better understand and appreciate our own. We can learn a lot about what is on our own horizon and what is bound to fail and fade away. Common problems may yield to new and innovative solutions if they are viewed from beyond a strictly parochial perspective. A look around at the global context is an efficient way to push back boundaries and a useful way to trigger the moral imagination.

Ethical challenges confront managers in public service around the globe, as the exhibits in this chapter, ground-breaking publications (such as Organization for Economic Co-operation and Development, 2000b), and the chronology in Resource A show. Whatever the categories on a roster of other nations and other cultures— high or low on corruption scales, developed or transitional, presidential and parliamentary democracies or authoritarian regimes, market- or non-market-based economies, large or small by size or population—we have this much in common.[1] Whether this fact is reassuring or of concern depends on one's worldview, but surely in today's interdependent world, this worldview must extend beyond national borders.

We also share ethical challenges with our predecessors, as Resource A indicates. Ethical issues have haunted democracies throughout history. This was certainly true for the ancient Athenian democracy and the Roman republic. It was also true for countries such as revolutionary France and, about a century later, Victorian Great Britain. The United States faced ethical issues from its very beginning, including George Washington's first administration (Gilman, 1995).

It is not that democracies are more prone to or accepting of corruption than any other form of government. Rather, democracies are more transparent, with more institutions gathering and independently reporting information. Dictatorships, authoritarian regimes, and nonconstitutional monarchies may be corrupt, but much is concealed, and unpleasant things may happen to those who tell about them.

Because the challenges are often wrapped up in government scandals but the responses may vary, it is important to distinguish anticorruption efforts from integrity programs. These are often linked, yet they begin from very different premises. Relying on prosecution, investigations, and audits, anticorruption systems begin with the assumption that corruption is caused by immoral individuals in government, with the bad apples in a good system, if you will (Huberts, 2003). Logically then, systems of this sort are designed to punish and so deter administrators by fear of punishment. However, integrity systems are preventative and assume that the vast majority of public administrators want to do the right thing if they have effective guidance and a clear set of values to emulate. Today, most developed democracies rely on both.

Globally, democratic and many other societies recognize that there must be an institutional fabric to protect and promote the integrity of governmental systems. Unfortunately, ethics processes in most countries have developed in an incremental and fragmented fashion. One agency may adopt a code of conduct, or a small proportion of the public workforce may be in merit-based personnel systems. The United States, for example, reacted to the Watergate scandal, in part, by creating the OGE in 1978.

Over the past quarter of a century, many countries throughout the world have begun to create administrative structures to anticipate and prevent ethical lapses (see Resource B). Governments as diverse as those in Great Britain, Hong Kong, Norway, and South Africa have developed ethics programs that are as robust as they are different. The international and multinational organizations advocating ethics programs as part of government reform include the United Nations, Organization of American States, Organization for Economic Co-operation and Development, the World Bank, the Inter-American Development Bank, the Asian Development Bank, the Organization for Security and Cooperation in Europe, the European Union and the Council of Europe, among others. Nongovernmental organizations such as Transparency International (TI) participate as well. They share in common the argument that effective anticorruption systems are critical for democratic development (Seligson, 2001) and reform and that their systems' success requires dynamic prevention elements, or integrity programs. The U.N.'s Anti-Corruption Convention, adopted by the General Assembly in October 2003, speaks of "the principles of proper management of public affairs and public property, fairness, responsibility and equality before the law and the need to safeguard integrity and to foster a culture of rejection of corruption."

Why has ethics in public service become an international movement, and why so recently? First, many public leaders and senior managers realized that the piecemeal, reactive approach was not effective. Second, many multinational organizations responsible for grants and loans learned that the lack of integrity was reducing their effectiveness. To illustrate, in the 1990s the World Bank reversed its policy of not meddling in recipients' internal affairs and refocused on corruption as a major inhibitor of development around the world. Others concur: "Fair and reliable public services inspire public trust and create a favorable environment for businesses, thus contributing to well-functioning markets and economic growth" (Organization for Economic Co-operation and Development, 2000a, p. 1). Third, many countries' leaders realize that punishment without prevention is not enough. No matter how effective law enforcement is, the publicity around corrupt officials undermines citizens' confidence in their governments. Increasing global interdependencies, technological advances, management reform, and other factors also spurred the movement on (Cooper and Yoder, 2002, pp. 334–335, 345).

First Efforts: National Initiatives

With the creation of the Office of Government Ethics in 1978, the United States stepped forward as one of the leaders in institutionalizing ethics systems in the public sector. This legislation did not come easily. For almost a century, the United States had a potpourri of overlapping laws and regulations, with no clear enforcement mechanisms.[2] At the same time, the U.S. House and Senate created ethics committees to oversee members' activities.

Almost simultaneously, Hong Kong created the Independent Commission Against Corruption (ICAC), with major prevention activities and so much power that it has been called the fourth branch of government. When unification occurred with China in 1997, the government decided to maintain the ICAC because of its recognized success in promoting integrity and combating corruption. During the same period, the state of New South Wales in Australia was creating a commission to deal with both corruption and integrity.

Canada and Great Britain soon followed, each with models very different from both the U.S. model and each other. Canada's prime minister created the Office of the Ethics Counsellor to provide advice and counsel to cabinet officials, while maintaining general ethics guidance for the public service through the Treasury Board and the Public Service Integrity Office. The British, by contrast, created the Committee on Standards of Public Life, with the responsibility to provide general guidance on ethics policy to the government and civil service of Great Britain.

By the mid-1990s, many countries had some type of ethics institution. The list includes those mentioned earlier, as well as Argentina, South Africa, New Zealand, Uganda, the Philippines, Norway, Lithuania, Namibia, Chile, France, and others. It is obvious that their power and their success vary widely, and there have been obvious failures. Nonetheless, almost all have some sort of code of conduct, transparency system, accountability program, training, and advisory power. Yet each has distinctive elements. For example, New Zealand has an office in the public service commission, but Uganda has an independent head. Chile emphasizes the transparency of procurements and contracts; South Africa emphasizes financial disclosure for senior ministers. In Norway, ethics is one of the standards for promotion to a senior position in public service; in Lithuania, it is one of the standards for being hired in the first place. The U.S. Code of Conduct for federal officials is more than seventy pages long; Great Britain relies on the seven general principles shown in Exhibit 9.1.

EXHIBIT 9.1. GREAT BRITAIN'S SEVEN PRINCIPLES OF PUBLIC LIFE, 2001.

The Committee has set out "Seven Principles of Public Life" which it believes should apply to all in the public service. These are:

Selflessness
Holders of public office should act solely in terms of the public interest. They should not do so in order to gain financial or other benefits for themselves, their family or their friends.

Integrity
Holders of public office should not place themselves under any financial or other obligation to outside individuals or organisations that might seek to influence them in the performance of their official duties.

Objectivity
In carrying out public business, including making public appointments, awarding contracts, or recommending individuals for rewards and benefits, holders of public office should make choices on merit.

Accountability
Holders of public office are accountable for their decisions and actions to the public and must submit themselves to whatever scrutiny is appropriate to their office.

Openness
Holders of public office should be as open as possible about all the decisions and actions that they take. They should give reasons for their decisions and restrict information only when the wider public interest clearly demands.

Honesty
Holders of public office have a duty to declare any private interests relating to their public duties and to take steps to resolve any conflicts arising in a way that protects the public interest.

Leadership
Holders of public office should promote and support these principles by leadership and example.

Source: Great Britain's Committee on Standards in Public Life, established Oct. 1994 [http://www.public-standards.gov.uk].

First Efforts: Multinational Organizations

The chronology in Resource A testifies to the fact that a number of major efforts have been undertaken at the global level since the mid-1990s. "The central thrusts of the international efforts . . . appear to be accountability, regulatory structures, and monitoring processes to prevent corruption and provide 'transparency'" (Cooper and Yoder, 2002, p. 344). In 1996, the Organization of American States (OAS) promulgated the first multinational anticorruption treaty that explicitly requires effective ethics measures. In Article III, titled "Preventative Measures," the member states commit, among other things, to standards of conduct, ethics systems, transparency systems, training, and whistle-blower protection (see Exhibit 9.2). Although the OAS has made some progress, including establishing a standing committee to evaluate the effectiveness of these programs, there is still considerable effort required to ensure that every country in the Americas meets these standards.

In the mid-1990s, the OECD began researching the kinds of ethics programs institutionalized in different countries and determining which of these were best practices for the public service. The result is some of the best comparative research available on the how and why of effective ethics programs. In 1997, it created its first *Ethics Checklist* for the public service. Designed as a benchmarking effort for member and nonmember countries, this was the first systematic attempt to look at program effectiveness (see Exhibit 9.3).

These two efforts created momentum for a variety of regional agreements in Africa, Asia, and Eastern Europe. The OECD engaged in several major analytical exercises to better understand how ethics programs fit into modern public management; with the publication of *Trust in Government* in 2000, the OECD completed the most detailed analysis to date (Organization for Economic Co-operation and Development, 2000b). The United States sponsored the first ministerial conference with specific focus on ethics in public service. This was followed by a commitment to meet biennially; in 2001 it was in The Hague and in 2003 in Seoul, South Korea (see Resource A).

Many other regional forums are taking anticorruption and integrity systems seriously. The Organization for Security and Cooperation in Europe, the Stability Pact, the Council of Europe, along with regional organizations in Asia, Africa, and the Middle East, are appreciating the benefits of strong ethical foundations in public service and exploring how to create and then maintain them.

Unfortunately, except for the OAS, very little has been done to measure program effectiveness. It is still too soon to say definitively what is working and what is not.

One driver that might spur advances in this area is the Corruption Perceptions Index, initiated in 1995 by TI (which was founded in 1993 by a former senior officer at the World Bank). With a powerful influence on many anticorruption fronts, the

EXHIBIT 9.2. ARTICLE III OF THE INTER-AMERICAN CONVENTION AGAINST CORRUPTION.

[T]he States Parties agree to consider the applicability of measures within their own institutional systems to create, maintain and strengthen:

1. Standards of conduct for the correct, honorable, and proper fulfillment of public functions. These standards shall be intended to prevent conflicts of interest and mandate the proper conservation and use of resources entrusted to government officials in the performance of their functions. These standards shall also establish measures and systems requiring government officials to report to appropriate authorities acts of corruption in the performance of public functions. Such measures should help preserve the public's confidence in the integrity of public servants and government processes.
2. Mechanisms to enforce these standards of conduct.
3. Instruction to government personnel to ensure proper understanding of their responsibilities and the ethical rules governing their activities.
4. Systems for registering the income, assets and liabilities of persons who perform public functions in certain posts as specified by law and, where appropriate, for making such registrations public.
5. Systems of government hiring and procurement of goods and services that assure the openness, equity and efficiency of such systems.
6. Government revenue collection and control systems that deter corruption.
7. Laws that deny favorable tax treatment for any individual or corporation for expenditures made in violation of the anticorruption laws of the States Parties.
8. Systems for protecting public servants and private citizens who, in good faith, report acts of corruption, including protection of their identities, in accordance with their Constitutions and the basic principles of their domestic legal systems.
9. Oversight bodies with a view to implementing modern mechanisms for preventing, detecting, punishing and eradicating corrupt acts.
10. Deterrents to the bribery of domestic and foreign government officials, such as mechanisms to ensure that publicly held companies and other types of associations maintain books and records which, in reasonable detail, accurately reflect the acquisition and disposition of assets, and have sufficient internal accounting controls to enable their officers to detect corrupt acts.
11. Mechanisms to encourage participation by civil society and nongovernmental organizations in efforts to prevent corruption.
12. The study of further preventive measures that take into account the relationship between equitable compensation and probity in public service.

Source: Adopted by the General Assembly of the Organization of American States in 1996. OAS [http://www.oas.org/juridico/english/followup.htm].

response to rankings has caused parliamentary governments to fall and leaders to resign. The index is a composite of surveys on perceived levels of corruption among politicians and public officials in 133 countries (Internet Center for Corruption Research, 2003; Resource B). Although criticized for false precision and other flaws,

EXHIBIT 9.3. OECD'S ETHICS CHECKLIST.

Are the basic principles and standards clear?

1. What are the basic ethical values for public officials?
2. In what ways do political leaders demonstrate visible and strong commitment?
3. How do the public officials know what ethical standards are expected of them?
4. What guidance is available to help public officials apply these standards?

How is an ethical culture fostered?

5. In what ways can senior managers demonstrate leadership in ethical conduct?
6. How do the public service employment conditions encourage ethical behavior?
7. Is advice available to public officials on resolving ethical tensions and problems?
8. How are the basic ethical values communicated to public servants?

[Are] there adequate oversight and accountability?

9. What accountability mechanisms are in place within agencies, at service-wide level and exter-nal to the public service?
10. Who is responsible for overall co-ordination, oversight and promotion of ethics in the public sector?
11. How clear are the rules and procedures for public officials to expose actual or suspected wrong-doing within the public sector? What are the procedures and sanctions . . . for wrongdoing?
12. What constitutional, administrative, civil service and/or criminal regulations are available for disciplinary action against public servants?
13. Are investigation and prosecution mechanisms sufficiently independent and adequately resourced?

Is the public well informed?

14. How can citizens be empowered for effective public scrutiny?

Source: Organization for Economic Co-operation and Development, "Ethics Checklist." Paris: Organization for Economic Co-operation and Development, Nov. 1997. Reproduced by per-mission of the OECD.

it is seen by some as the most innovative initiative against corruption in the past hun-dred years. TI, with chapters in many countries around the world, continues to be a leader in the fight against corruption.

In late 2003, the U.N. Anti-Corruption Convention was signed in Merida, Mexico. It tied together the various international agreements that included ethics pro-grams into a global compact. This agreement has the potential to profoundly affect the public and private sectors throughout the world.

Development of Consensus

One of the first international conferences solely devoted to public service ethics was held in Washington, D.C., in 1994. The more than one hundred conference delegates from fifty-three countries focused on both programmatic and normative concerns.

Among the many common threads was concern about the impact of scandals on public support for democracy. Governments must go beyond managing official behavior to being transparent enough to assure citizens that their government is operating in the public interest (Gilman and Lewis, 1996).

The delegates advocated action to enhance integrity in public service rather than simply design systems to catch and punish wrongdoers. The consensus was that governments were better able to empower public servants to do the right thing by emphasizing core values. As one delegate put it, "[P]reventative medicine always is preferable to surgery."

This gathering would become a springboard for ensuing international, multinational, national, and corporate initiatives in public service ethics. "From its usual idiosyncratic, nation-specific treatment, administrative ethics was converted into a concern to be addressed cooperatively, in part on the international level and in part with business participation" (Gilman and Lewis, 1996, p. 523). In other words, globalization, which is often associated with private enterprise, is material to ethics and ethics programs in the public sector.

One important commonality is the core prohibition against conflict of interest. The OECD defines it as a "conflict between the public duty and private interests of a public official, in which the public official has private-capacity interests which could improperly influence the performance of their official duties and responsibilities" (Organization for Economic Co-operation and Development, 2004). Also developments in the contemporary public sector present new challenges, to which Exhibit 9.4 speaks.

A second important commonality is that, although privacy issues represent a growing arena for concern and debate in many countries, the tilt is toward contraction when public servants are involved. In the United States and elsewhere, the use of public financial disclosure is an obvious example of the public interest trumping the value of public servants' privacy. Disclosure systems are growing worldwide (Organization for Economic Co-operation and Development, 2000b) and operate today in countries as diverse as Argentina, South Africa, and Slovakia; some systems such as the Canadian are confidential and not public.

A third point in common is the emphasis on transparency, referring to the general openness of government. From procurement to contracting, from hiring personnel to major policy decisions, the push for increased government transparency is designed to reduce impropriety and its appearance and increase citizen access and confidence in government. One legal example of this is the U.S. Freedom of Information Act. Because governmental use and regulation of the Internet and governments' protocols for such use are an example of the intersection of the issues of privacy, transparency, freedom of speech, and citizen access to information and services, developments in this arena bear watching (Negin, 2003; Bhatnagar, 2003). The very nature of the Internet dictates an approach relying on international and public-private collaboration.

EXHIBIT 9.4. OECD ON CONFLICT OF INTEREST, 2004.

What is conflict of interest? "Conflict of interest arises from the fact that public officials have to make decisions while accomplishing their official duties that may also affect their private interests. . . . Private interests that may generate a direct personal benefit to public officials have traditionally included financial interests, gifts and relationships. But business interests, secondary employment and affiliations are increasingly becoming an issue because of increased collaboration with the private sector."

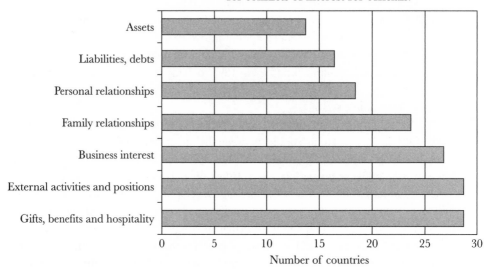

Which activities and situations are identified as holding potential for conflicts of interest for officials?

Number of countries

Key Recommendations for Managing Conflict of Interest
1. *Identify relevant conflict-of-interest situations*
2. *Establish procedures to identify, manage and resolve conflict-of-interest situations*
   • Set clear rules on what is expected of public officials in dealing with conflict-of-interest situations that enable managers to find proper resolution and management.
3. *Demonstrate leadership commitment*
   • Managers should take responsibility for the effective application of their conflict-of-interest policy, by deciding in individual cases and monitoring and evaluating the effectiveness of the policy.
4. *Create a partnership with employees: awareness, anticipation and prevention*
   • Ensure wide publication and understanding of the conflict-of-interest policy.
   • Review 'at-risk' areas for potential conflict-of-interest situations.
   • Identify preventive measures that deal with emergent conflict situations.
   • Develop an open organisational culture where dealing with conflict-of-interest matters can be freely raised and discussed.

5. Enforce the conflict-of-interest policy
- Provide procedures for establishing a conflict-of-interest offence, and proportional consequences for non-compliance with conflict-of-interest policy including disciplinary sanctions.
- Develop monitoring mechanisms to detect breaches of policy and take into account any gain or benefit that resulted from the conflict.
- Co-ordinate prevention and enforcement measures and integrate them into a coherent institutional framework.

6. Initiate a new partnership with the business and non-profit sectors
- Involve the business and non-profit sectors in elaborating and implementing the conflict-of-interest policy for public officials.
- Anticipate potential conflict-of-interest situations when public organisations involve persons representing businesses and the non-profit sector.
- Include safeguards against potential conflict-of-interest situations.

Source: Organization for Economic Co-operation and Development, "Managing Conflict of Interest in the Public Service," draft policy brief. Paris: Organization for Economic Co-operation and Development, June 2004. Reproduced by permission of the OECD.

Contrary to popular wisdom, professional public managers around the globe share some core values that are associated with their role and training rather than with cultural particulars: "There are fundamental values—treated at a higher level of abstraction—that are closely associated with democracy, market economy, and professional bureaucracy" (Gilman and Lewis, 1996, p. 518; see Chapter One and Exhibit 9.5 on South Africa). Although it would be foolish to deny that cultural specifics are operative and important, it is counterfactual to deny that shared ethical standards are developing on a global scale. International compacts from at least 1864 and the adoption of the first Geneva Convention through the U.N.'s Anti-Corruption Convention signed in 2003 (and beyond, no doubt) have spurred this development. So have international professional contacts; note that the *eleventh* International Anti-Corruption Conference (IACC) met in Seoul, Korea, in 2003 (see Resource A). "These various regional and global declarations, agreements, and organizations can be understood as elements in a process of socially constructing a new international reality" (Cooper and Yoder, 2002, p. 347). Surely the Internet is pushing in this same direction.

Among the values identified as central to developing global standards are honesty, trust, and stability (Cooper and Yoder, 2002, pp. 346–347). There is evidence of a worldwide rejection of official bribery (Gilman and Lewis, 1996). Professionalism is another value often cited, as in the mission statement of South Africa's Public Service Commission shown in Exhibit 9.5. These standards give rise to the duty for public managers to pursue the public interest (see Chapter Three). In its recommendation

EXHIBIT 9.5. SOUTH AFRICA'S PUBLIC SERVICE COMMISSION.

VISION

The Public Service Commission is an independent and impartial body created by the Constitution to enhance excellence in governance within the Public Service by promoting a professional and ethical environment and adding value to a public administration that is accountable, equitable, efficient, effective, corrupt-free and responsive to needs of the people of South Africa.

MISSION

The Commission aims to promote the constitutionally enshrined democratic principles and values in the Public Service by investigating, monitoring, evaluating, communicating and reporting on the public administration; through research processes it will ensure the promoting of excellence in governance and the delivery of affordable and sustainable quality services.

Source: Public Service Commission of South Africa [http://www.psc.gov.za].

for managing conflict of interest, the OECD declares, "Serving the public interest is the fundamental mission of governments and public institutions. Citizens expect individual public officials to perform their duties with integrity, in a fair and unbiased way" (Organization for Economic Co-operation and Development, 2003, p. 2). According to its homepage, "The OECD groups 30 member countries sharing a commitment to democratic government and the market economy. With active relationships with some 70 other countries, NGOs [nongovernmental organizations] and civil society, it has a global reach" (emphasis in original deleted).

A Multinational View at the Citizen Level

There are relevant empirical findings at a citizen level, as well as at the institutional and professional level:

The World Values Survey [WVS] is a worldwide investigation of sociocultural and political change. It is conducted by a network of social scientists at leading universities all around world. The survey is performed on nationally representative samples in almost 80 societies on all six inhabited continents. A total of four waves have been carried since 1981 allowing accurate comparative analysis (WVS [http://www.worldvaluessurvey.org], Introduction).

According to findings from the WVS, backing for democracy is associated negatively with citizens' justification of corruption" (Inglehart, 2000; see http://wvs.isr.umich.edu/index.shtml).

An index of *corruption permissiveness* based on the WVS captures "the extent to which individuals tend to justify certain practices that can be considered corrupt" (Moreno, 2002, p. 3). "Corruption permissiveness is, in particular, strongly and negatively correlated with support for democracy and with interpersonal trust, both of them being important components of a democratic political culture" (p. 2). "[C]ountries that have higher levels of corruption permissiveness in the WVS tend to be those with less corruption in the CPI" (p. 5), meaning TI's Corruption Perceptions Index (Moreno, 2002, pp. 1–5).

Some analysts see a shift in individuals' values taking place. In their view, socioeconomic development, cultural change, and democratization—with the "common theme of broadening human choice"—constitute a coherent syndrome of social change" (Welzel, Inglehart, and Klingemann, p. 1). Clustering WVS findings along the two dimensions of *self-expression values* against *survival values* and *secular-rational values* against *traditional values*, they identify similarities and differences and suggest a developmental trajectory.

> [M]ost theories of value change converge in the notion that traditional-deferential orientations, that subordinate the individual to the community, tend to give way to growing emphasis on autonomous human choice and individual self-expression. . . . We characterize this process as a shift from survival values to self-expression values. . . . Overall, high (or low) levels of individual resources, self-expression values and effective democracy tend to go together" (Welzel, Inglehart, and Klingemann, pp. 1–2).

Among the principal values in most current Western ethical perspectives, "[a]utonomy is often thought to be a paradigmatic value in personal ethics. Being autonomous means being true to our own principles and acting in a way which we have chosen or which we endorse" (May, Collins-Chobanian, and Wong, 1998, p. 9). It is related to self-respect and makes demands on society. "For autonomy to be maintained and maximized in a population it is crucial that social institutions be designed to minimize interference with life choices of individuals" (May, Collins-Chobanian, and Wong, 1998, p. 9).

Many non-Western ethical perspectives focus on the community and its well-being and view the individual primarily in relationship to the community (May, Collins-Chobanian, and Wong, 1998, pp. 10–13). A life is lived within a "fabric of relationships" in some traditional African, Confucian, and Buddhist perspectives. These differ in, for example, their orientation to worldly attachments to people and things and their passivity or acceptance *versus* political activism. "Like Hindu perspectives, Islamic ethics is highly activist and interventionist," with "highly partialist" rules for ethical conduct depending upon gender and religious affiliation (May, Collins-Chobanian, and Wong, 1998, p. 12; see also An-Na'im, 1998).

A stress on autonomy—a value associated with Western ethics—raises the specter of cultural bias, just as the denial of any possibility of shared values slips into another sort of preconception or bias. Cultural relativism "denies that any independent moral facts exist outside of a society . . . [but argues] that all moral beliefs are proper or improper in relation to a society's customs" (Terkel and Duval, 1999, p. 58, capitalization omitted). In response to the view that "no moral judgment can do more than reflect the customs of the society in which it is made" (Singer, 1979, p. 5), Peter Singer (1979, pp. 5, 11) declares,

> Ethics takes a universal point of view. This does not mean that a particular ethical judgment must be universally applicable. Circumstances alter causes. . . . What this does mean is that in making ethics judgments we go beyond our own likes and dislikes. . . . [E]thics requires us to go beyond "I" and "you" to the universal law, the universalizable judgment, the standpoint of the impartial spectator or ideal observers.

This argument underlies the expansive reach in Exhibit 7.1. A global perspective supports the manager's rejection of moral relativism and encourages open-minded leadership, even vision.

On the basis of the developments described here and the research findings associated with the World Values Survey (WVS) and Kohlberg's theory discussed in Chapter Five, we are suggesting neither an inevitable convergence or conversion to values associated with Western cultures nor an inescapable chasm separating different peoples. What we are suggesting is that political (democracy), social (urbanization and interdependency), and economic (income level) variables are in play, as are roles and culture.

One final point on values may be especially important for public managers to consider. There is evidence that human happiness is linked to economic development in a strong *curvilinear* way, meaning that income matters less to perceived happiness at lower and higher income levels. "Among advanced industrial societies, there is practically no relationship between income level and subjective well being" (Inglehart, 1999, p. 3; see also Cummins, 1995).

> Modern industrial society was made possible by two key institutions: the mass production assembly line and bureaucratic organizations. These institutions made it possible to process huge numbers of products and huge numbers of people using centrally controlled standardized routines. They were highly effective, but they sharply reduced individual autonomy, which takes on an increasingly high priority in advanced industrial societies. As a result, hierarchical, centrally controlled bureaucratic institutions are becoming less acceptable in postmodern society (Inglehart, 1999, p. 9).

It seems that there is something more to life once it gets well beyond subsistence. The data show this, and the citizens know it. Logically, if public managers aim at increasing perceived well-being in the community, then overall citizen satisfaction and government effectiveness are best defined and measured in terms broader than tax rates and cost-benefit ratios. Note, too, that for public service, individual autonomy entails citizen empowerment.

Perhaps this discussion of the normative and structural currents and commonalities is an example of the idea: *Think global, act local.* But this analysis suggests that possibly more important is the question, What do *you* think?

◆ ◆ ◆

The global movement shows fragmented, incremental development as the dominant pattern of institutionalization and the pervasive understanding that effective anti-corruption systems are critical for democratic development and managerial maturity. Also widespread is the recognition that the success of an ethics system requires dynamic prevention elements, which generally translates into integrity programs. The commonalities in these programs suggest that, globally, professionals in public service share in common some core values that are associated with their role and training rather than with cultural particulars. Among these values are honesty, transparency, and professionalism. These standards give rise to the duty for public managers to pursue the public interest, to which the evident pattern of the contraction of public servants' privacy is related. Among the relevant empirical findings at a citizen level are a relationship between democratic attitudes and tolerance of corruption, a curvilinear relationship between income and subjective well-being, and a high value placed on individual autonomy in postmodern societies.

◆ ◆ ◆

Discussion Questions

1. Does culture have an impact on what public servants consider ethical? Should it?
2. Do you think that the multilateral agreements show that there are issues of ethics in public management that cut across cultural lines? Are there shared concepts and values you see as particularly valuable to managing public sector organizations?
3. In this global context, what do you think is the relationship between the ethics of public servants, corruption, and citizen confidence in governmental institutions?
4. How are differences in economic condition and political system related to the incidence and perception of corruption?

5. Given the efforts over millenia and around the globe (see Resource A) to curb corruption and bolster citizen confidence in government, why do these problems persist?

◆ ◆ ◆

Notes

1. Although empirical evidence supports an association between level of development and level of corruption, it also shows high levels of corruption in both rich and poorer countries (Internet Center for Corruption Research, 2003).
2. The first proposal for resolving this confusion came from a U.S. Senate subcommittee under the leadership of Senator Paul Douglas (U.S. Senate, 1951).

CHAPTER TEN

BUILDING AN ETHICAL AGENCY

M oving inside the organization, this final chapter focuses on organizational interaction and routine agency operations that set the organization's ethical tone.
Here we spotlight the supervisory function as a central managerial responsibility and
advocate structuring operations and procedures to support and promote ethical behavior. Setting positive expectations through day-to-day functions contributes to an
open, positive, and ongoing conversation about the right thing to do and the right way
to do it. Laying out objections lets managers set them aside—the venture is possible,
desirable, and banks on prudential management.

The chapter examines ethical challenges facing supervisors and itemizes feasible
agency interventions through which managers daily build ethical concerns directly
into routine and expected conduct. An ethics impact statement integrates ethics
soundly and methodically into agency procedures and decisions, and agency audit
and risk-assessment tools contribute to the building of an ethical agency. Case studies in agency settings animate several of this book's main themes.

Shaping Ethics and the Boss

In a host of ways, including modeling, the manager shapes ethical conduct and the ethical agency. Supervising employee time is an ongoing stress point and demands special
care. Workforce diversity, alternate recruitment channels, mixed administrative settings,

and collaborative relationships, as illustrated by the procurement function, figure prominently among today's challenges.

Public managers are doers and deciders; that is the crux of their job. Bayard L. Catron once remarked, "Ethics is first, foremost, and finally about conduct." The upshot is that a passion for action is preferred over personal introspection, and this necessarily means dealing with other people. *A public manager's primary ethical concern is behavior toward other people.*

Service recipients or clients are especially important *others* today because of the surge in social services, the injection of equity and compassion by the new public administration, and the responsiveness-as-marketing concerns associated with entrepreneurial public management. (The dictum of customer service neglects the dependency, vulnerability, and civics aspects of many public services.) Recognizing users' dependency on public services, a focus on clients as external, direct stakeholders is a beneficial development. In effect, it repudiates the petty tyrant exercising government authority, the small-minded bureaucrat so aptly described by Dostoyevsky (n.d., pp. 108–109) in nineteenth-century Russia.

> I was a spiteful civil servant. I was rude and took pleasure in being rude. Mind you, I never accepted any bribes, so that I had at least to find something to compensate myself for that. Whenever people used to come to my office on some business, I snarled at them and felt as pleased as Punch when I succeeded in making one of them really unhappy. I nearly always did succeed. They were mostly a timid lot: what else can you expect people who come to a government office to be? . . . All I did, as a matter of fact, was to indulge in a little innocent fun at the expense of . . . the people who came to my office on business, for actually I never could become a spiteful man.

(Note how he divorces the office from the person and rationalizes his behavior.)

An emphasis on clients is all to the good, but not to the exclusion of all others. Dependency and vulnerability—factors that affect ethical responsibility—touch subordinates with a heavy hand. Because agency managers and employees are direct stakeholders in agency actions and operations, supervision's ethical aspects must be core concerns. Moreover, omitting ethics from the supervisory relationship implies endorsing market exchange as the sole basis of human relations in public agencies. Given the hours spent on the job and maintaining professional proficiency, few managers would be willing to make this argument. Nor would they want to live with the consequences.

Ethical Modeling

By way of illustration, step into the shoes of the manager to whom the arrogant entrepreneur reports in Exhibit 10.1. Is relaxed oversight justified? What does bending or ignoring the rules communicate to other employees? Why? And what does it say

EXHIBIT 10.1. ARROGANCE IN THE PUBLIC INTEREST.

The chosen setting is sanitized as a government agency somewhere far, far away. It enjoyed non-appropriated revenue streams such as charges and fees and grants. These resources were generated and managed by an entrepreneurial manager of high national and international stature for his work. He worked hard—long hours, creative leadership, high energy—and sustained an impressive track record of major successes. He brought a lot to the agency in terms of both resources and reputation, and his superiors usually left him alone to go to it. Oversight was half-hearted; accounting and personnel controls were relaxed; and agency policies weakly enforced. It just didn't pay to get in this guy's way.

Now the state manager himself was chaffing under restrictions and rules—the infamous paperwork of government bureaucracy. Especially irksome were the procurement and subcontracting rules that led to higher costs and delays. So he established personal accounts into which he placed revenues from fees and grants. No one knew how much went though these accounts, but one thing was for sure: he never used the money for personal purposes.

When the arrangements were disclosed, the organization was seriously embarrassed; the manager's sub-unit lay in ruins; and the fate of the public manager and his career testifies to the fact that self-destruction is an ugly thing. Success leads to relaxed reins in an organization and to an individual's growing sense of self-importance. What we see here is lust for power, empire building, and arrogance. What happened here is a classic tale of virtue and vice. (Remember the old-fashioned virtue of humility?) As arrogance developed, with organizational support, the manager began to believe quite sincerely that the rules did not apply to him and that everything he was doing was for the good of the agency. The result, again with agency sanction, was that accountability was nullified and the public interest defined by one person.

Source: Excerpted and reprinted by permission of *International Journal of Organization Theory and Behavior.* C. W. Lewis, "Mini-Symposium on Public Service Ethics: Introduction." *International Journal of Organization Theory and Behavior,* 2003a, *6*(3), 403–404.

about the agency? Thinking this through requires appraising two supervisors—yourself and your boss—as well as subordinates.

Proposals about the ethical aspects of the supervisory function touch on managers' *and* subordinates' behavior and, for that very reason, breed wariness in some minds. Doubts induce special care for the ethical dimensions of hierarchical relationships. A manager's treatment of subordinates sets the tone for the organization and models appropriate behavior to subordinates.

Public managers generally understand and accept this responsibility and know how both formal procedures and informal personal contact help meet it. Formerly responsible for a $100 billion budget, a former undersecretary of defense for acquisition explained to a business audience:

> Often, the informal rules of acceptable behavior of an organization's culture are more influential in governing behavior than the formal rules. . . . Ethics is an important element of an organization's culture. Therefore, ethics is the responsibility of

management, and is a matter of leadership . . . the leadership of an organization must *be,* and must *be seen,* as personally and professionally committed to good ethics. They [managers] must demonstrate through their actions that they will not tolerate unethical behavior by anyone with whom they do business (Betti, 1990, p. 12).

In this vein, Peter Drucker (1989, pp. 229–230) tells us, "Every enterprise requires commitment to common goals and shared values. Without such commitment there is no enterprise, there is only a mob. Management's first job is to think through, set, and exemplify those objectives, values, and goals."

Most of us learned how to deal with complex pressures and ethical dilemmas from our bosses in a modern version of apprenticeship called *modeling* or, if conscious and direct, *mentoring.* Social learning theory tells us that learning is fostered through observation and by the example of those who control rewards and deal out penalties. Ethical modeling is an ancient notion that is more cosmopolitan than American, or even Western, public administration. An illustration from Buddhism (Bukkyo Dendo, Kyokai, 1987, pp. 468–469) strikes a familiar chord:

> If an important minister of state neglects his duties, works for his own profit or accepts bribes, it will cause a rapid decay of public morals. Under such circumstances, faithful ministers will retire from public service, wise men will keep silent from fear of complications, and only flatterers will hold government positions, and they will use their political power to enrich themselves with no thought for the sufferings of the people.

Workforce Diversity

When it comes to dealing with other people in the office, old, automatic responses may no longer be as reliable as they once were. Disabled workers, the foreign-educated, single parents supporting a family, adult children caring for aging parents, and workers with nontraditional lifestyles all make the office a much more complicated place than it was when the boss-as-model learned on the job.

Today's catchphrase is *cultural diversity*—a descriptive term, because the workforce is changing, employee relationships are changing. Some behaviors may need rethinking; others may call for full-scale remodeling. For example, public organizations are compelled to reject discrimination and sexual harassment on ethical grounds. Another behavior that warrants censure is sexual assault, in response to which the Air Force Academy adopted a policy by which "a complaint will automatically prompt a formal criminal investigation but victims will no longer have the option of remaining anonymous" and announced it "will not tolerate discrimination, harassment, intimidation or assault of any kind!" (Schemo, 2003, unpaginated).

There are many other examples of changing relationships and behaviors. When the ICMA's code was originally adopted in 1924, city management was much simpler: no assistants, county administrators, consultants, women, or minorities (Tranter, 1987). Today these people are part of the team, along with private-sector collaborators and dual-career couples with investment interests and personal lifestyles that raise questions and entail commitments different from those of the profession's formative years. Fondly recalled, the "good old days" conjure up simplicity, not equity.

The new faces, new cultures, and new customs and norms are adding fresh dimensions to employee relations and novel ethical issues. "Even now, the average manager may think: 'To be fair, I should assume everyone is the same and treat them that way'" (Solomon, 1990, p. BI). That response begs the question. It is not bigotry or biased treatment—both are intolerable in public service—but more subtly demeaning behavior, stereotypical thinking and treatment, inadvertent slights, and misunderstandings.

Both personal idiosyncrasy and cultural variation in habits, mores, values, and even body language complicate the manager's job. What motivates the employee? How does the manager build trust in the office? Does eye contact signal trustworthiness or belligerence? Is an informal chat before the meeting gets down to business an inexcusable waste of time or a team-building tactic?

Loosely paraphrasing Lawrence D. (Larry) Fisher, director of Oklahoma's Human Relations Development Department (personal communication, August 20, 1990), an Oklahoma story evokes the ethical dimensions of workforce diversity: "At an agency meeting, a junior manager overhears a bigoted remark told by a Kiowa colleague about a Comanche. Should the manager say something?" Before answering, it is useful to think through three additional questions.

1. Does either speaking up or keeping silent define professional behavior? Ethical behavior?
2. As you respond, do you visualize the junior manager as Native American or Caucasian? Do you visualize the Kiowa as the manager's supervisor, peer, or subordinate?
3. Does a public manager's ethnic identity determine appropriate behavior?

Answers to the first question may be moderated by seniority, reporting lines, context, professional roles, and other considerations. But there is a significant distance between *should* and *would*. The concepts are distinguished by courage, prudence, responsibility, and other matters. Is only the *how* and *when* affected by these considerations, or is the obligation affected also? (Chapter Six's tools for assessing responsibility may be of help here.)

The second question raises the specter of bias or prejudice affecting the reasoning. Was it truly impartial? An emphatic no to the third question emphasizes professional commitment to impartiality, even—or especially—in the face of ethnic, age, sex, or other personal characteristics. The answers to the three questions may stimulate rethinking of the initial problem. Once again, *should* the manager say something?

New York State (Department of Civil Service, 1990, p. 4) responded to diversity with a "strategic workforce planning initiative," which offers the following perspective:

> Diversity has grown from purely a social agenda of enlightened government to include pragmatic concerns related to business viability for all employers, private or public. The very productivity that the state will need could be threatened by counterproductive workplace tensions if workers are unprepared to deal with cultural differences. Clearly, managers and supervisors will need greater skills in working with a multicultural and increasingly diverse workforce.

Mistakenly, and apparently bowing to the ethical neutrality argument (see Chapter Four), the New York plan (p. 70) argues that "this is not a social or moral issue, but rather a pragmatic one."

No one can predict for sure where diversity is taking public service, except to say that the workforce will be different and the workplace probably so. In preparation, we turn to the ethical dimensions of employee time as an everyday area of control, awkward bloopers, outright abuse, and chronic misunderstanding. This issue taps many ethical aspects of interpersonal relations in the office, including those that directly affect every manager.

The Problem of Time Abuse

Misuse of working hours and workers is a commonplace and costly problem posing serious ethical issues. It may constitute the rather simple appropriation of public property for personal gain or unauthorized use, which can be seen variously as intangible theft or conflict of interest. When the misuse stems from an unscrupulous supervisor's directive, the problem is abuse of office. Then too, the problem may be linked to carelessness or incompetence on the part of the employee or supervisor. All told, these behaviors are contrary to ethical standards in public service.

Time abuse is different from *lost time*, which refers to all time paid but not worked, whatever the reason, including legitimate reasons. In this regard, how many employees understand that vacation time may be devoted to personal purposes but that the employee is still on the payroll and still a public servant? It is up to the manager to explain that the ethical obligations binding on public employees still operate and that this is not the time for conflicting or unauthorized moonlighting. Authorized outside employment usually presents no problem, as long as it does not interfere with job performance, generate conflicts of interest, or appear improper.

A quick calculation in any agency reveals the serious financial implication of time abuse. With 21.5 million civilian employees in government alone, the aggregate and cumulative potential loss is striking. Time is money in government, too.

More broadly speaking, the productive use of working hours for public purposes is hardly a paltry matter. Payroll and benefits account for 75 percent or more of spending in many jurisdictions or agencies. As a big-ticket item for the organization *and the worker,* employee time and its ethical dimensions call for discriminating reasoning by supervisory staff. Even so, abusive supervisors and greedy, ill-advised, or wrong-thinking employees, abetted by careless supervision, perpetuate time abuse.

The federal government takes the straightforward position that personal use of working hours and government workers, like other resources or assets, is contrary to standards of conduct. Many states similarly prohibit personal use of working hours by statute, personnel rule, or legal opinion. The model ethics legislation for states and localities drafted in 1990 under the auspices of the Council on Governmental Ethics Laws, states, "A public official or employee shall not use public funds, *time, personnel,* facilities, or equipment for the official or employee's private gain or that of another unless the use is authorized by law" (Feigenbaum, Larsen, and Reynolds, 1990, Sec. 210; emphasis added). The last phrase is designed to allow for economic development ventures and the like that join state resources to private activities.

More knotty supervisor-subordinate interactions on both agency and personal time cause ethical problems in any office. Federal standards extend to superiors' requests to work *after hours,* as the OGE (1990a, pp. 833–834) spells out:

> While one normally thinks of [f]ederal property as being things, it also includes the time of federal employees while on government duty. Therefore, one employee cannot ask another employee to provide services in furtherance of purely personal projects while on official duty. And, if a supervisor asks someone he supervises to provide free personal services to the supervisor on non-official duty, the supervisor is requesting a gift from that employee which is prohibited by statute.

Less regulated environments tend to confine the ban to working hours (as implied in the case, "A Matter of Convenience," at the end of Chapter Five). With respect to working hours only, the Josephson Institute took a different tack by shifting responsibility so that it is the subordinate's responsibility to say no. This posture allows that, although the superior is obligated to the subordinate, obligations flow in the other direction, too. According to the Josephson Institute (1990, p. 8) guidelines, "Public employees should refuse to perform improper personal tasks on government time."

This advice strikes head-on against *team player* loyalties and an employee's economic dependence on the organization and is plumbed in Exhibit 10.2. These are matters of courage. Civil rights activist and author (*I Know Why the Caged Bird Sings*)

EXHIBIT 10.2. JUST SAY NO.

A technician employed by the city (population 100,000) complained to the city manager, to the corporation counsel, and later that same day, to a local television station that her supervisor had ordered her several times to do private jobs on city time and with city equipment. Once she was asked to install city equipment at a private site on her own time and felt she had to cooperate or "face the music."

After the investigators sifted through work orders, purchase orders, time cards, invoices, and the records of several local vendors, it looked as if charges soon would be brought against the supervisor and several other employees. The investigator who led the police inquiry reported no information implicating high officials outside the one office.

1. What are the ethical issues as distinct from legal or practical ones in this case?
     For the employee?
     For the supervisor?
2. Is the employee hiding behind her supervisor in order to escape responsibility? (See Chapter Four.)
3. Is the obligation to protect public time and property a license for suspicion?
     Is it a subordinate's ethical obligation to second-guess the boss?
     Does this disrupt the office?
4. Should the technician, who admits to illegal activity, be rewarded for blowing the whistle?
5. Does the technician appear to have answered the questions in Exhibit 7.5, and with what results?
6. Loyalty often is identified as an ethical value. What does loyalty mean in this case?
     Loyalty to whom and for what?
     Is loyalty simply an appeal to personal bonds and sentiment, or does it rightfully exert an ethical claim in public service?
     How does loyalty affect accountability?
7. How does this case compare with "A Matter of Convenience" in Chapter Five and what different issues affect your reasoning?

Maya Angelou says, "Courage is the most important virtue . . . because without courage you can't have other virtues" (Fuchs, 1989, p. 13). Ethics is about doing the right thing; it is not always easy. Fiduciary responsibility to the public and the ethical principle that calls for taking personal responsibility support the Josephson Institute's posture.

Clarification of Work Norms

A new recruit may not even be aware of the ethical—never mind the managerial or legal—aspects of a directive or of norms different from those of other work environments. Although cross-recruiting can be a positive, constructive, even creative step, it also builds in some trouble spots. From the dollar-a-year or on-loan executive to the transplanted military officer, volunteer, or part-time worker, the potential is there for confusion, casual misunderstanding, or undiscerned conflicts of interest. Potential problems bid selectivity, followed by precautionary exposure to public service obligations and agency expectations.

A manager's task is to clarify agency work norms when the new employee crosses over from, for example, a military to a civilian post. Although some evidence suggests potential problems in recruiting from the private sector, values such as telling the truth and avoiding conflicting claims obviously are not all that different in the world of private business. Although the pressures may be similar, in public service, where company time is public property, the moral compass points to the *unacceptability of* appropriating public property for personal use.

The business compass may point in a different direction, that is, toward organizational loyalty, stamina, grit, and a can-do approach to getting the job done. Some differences turn on the degree of private ownership. For example, although nepotism is contrary to public service standards, a parent hiring a child to work in a family-owned business is accepted, even expected.

The competition among values and interests that crop up in current debates over family leave, flex time, job sharing, rehiring retirees, and other recent innovations are results of organizational change. Of course, dogmatic insistence on certain working hours to the exclusion of number of hours worked, productivity, or competing demands in an employee's life may induce reactive rigidity such as clock watching, lackadaisical performance, and anxiety. It certainly tends to sacrifice compassion as an ethical value and stresses the organization as the preeminent, if not exclusive, stakeholder.

Need for a Team Ethic

Despite innovation and experimentation, many organizations that tend toward the private on the continuum depicted in Figure I.1 play down the team spirit that characterizes so much of public service. The term *team* evokes close association, a network of affiliation, kinship of goals, and mutual supports, dependency, and dependability. It is only when a "we-they" line is drawn around the agency and public employees forget that the *we* extends to the public that the team ethic undercuts public service ethics.

Public service may be performed by a team, but the team is not an exclusive club. In response to cross-recruiting, managers can smooth the transition and build an effective, ethical team. For starters, managers can preach public service reality. The challenge is to help new members join and then succeed by letting them in on the house rules.

Managers are called upon to proselytize and inspire, advocate and model, hearten and reward; training, supervision, controls, and incentives are marshaled. This is the time for straight talk, repeated talk, backed up by right action. Cross-recruiting is also a prime time for introducing the fusion route described in the Introduction.

The Challenge for Nonprofits and Volunteers

Managing employees and volunteers with different skills, backgrounds, and lifestyles is a special challenge in nonprofit organizations. As the public service workforce is diversifying, so are the type of agency and mode of organization. The scope and functions of the nonprofit or independent sector have grown remarkably over the past several decades and are today both broad and pioneering (see Resource B). The nonprofit umbrella covers many different career paths and opportunities in diverse fields. Nonprofits vary by size, revenues and financing modes, and mission. Some are local, some are national, and many speak for budgets and staffs that dwarf local governments. Some operate with a board of directors and function like a business, but without shareholders or owners.

Many nonprofits rely heavily on volunteers, who are often treated as unpaid staff. Many of them, retirees and others, are new to public service, its demands, and its ethical standards. Misguided compassion, however well meaning, can bring an agency to its knees and a community service to a standstill.

With one foot in the business camp and the other in public service, a nonprofit manager needs both eyes focused straight ahead. This means moving ethical modeling and public service expectations to the top of the manager's agenda. The reactive alternative risks letting scandal force a response.

Collaborative Relationships as a Source of Problems

Given different work norms, relationships and interactions get even stickier when we venture outside the pyramidal agency and into the indirect, sometimes convoluted ways we have of doing the public's business. Not everyone involved in decision making or service delivery nowadays fits neatly in a superior-subordinate relationship with a defined role in a hierarchical office. This is a source of many ethical problems that face public servants and more-or-less-public agencies of all sorts.

Complicating matters are network relationships and matrix-type organizations marked by flat or variable authority structures and collegial relationships. Intersectoral, international, intergovernmental, and inter-jurisdictional arrangements complicate matters further. Parties to proxy, third-party, or indirect administration use loans, grants, and contracts and, like associates in public-private partnerships, share no common chief in the weblike administrative environment.

Collaborative relationships, by definition, share no single command structure, organizational culture, or compulsory or even habitual behavioral standards (Goodsell, 2004). When public opinion and participation are added to the complexity, ambiguity, and blurred accountability, we clearly see the "new" administration Woodrow Wilson ([1887] 1987, p. 12) described more than a century ago: "There is scarcely a single duty of government which was once simple which is not now complex; government once had but a few masters; it now has scores of masters."

In a collaborative setting, where misunderstandings and foul-ups are predictable, it is helpful to put ethical standards and expectations up-front. What do we expect from special government employees such as temporary advisers, expert consultants, or corporate, academic, church, or other members of blue ribbon commissions? Do they know the prevailing ethical norms? Legal requirements? Is a briefing prudent or patronizing? Is financial disclosure advisable?

Does it matter whether decision makers are unpaid volunteers or part-time rather than full-time employees? Evidence for the seriousness of the question lies in their large number and important functions. Many state and local commissions, including land-use, ethics, and other commissions, rely on volunteer appointees, and millions of state and local government employees work on a part-time basis. Different jurisdictions respond to the issues differently. Some are more restrictive for full-time, paid employees.

Buying In

In the present climate, contact and communication with contractors and suppliers are especially sensitive. Much of the effort in this arena is confined to legal compliance rather than the integrity aspect of administrative ethics. (The case ending Chapter Four illustrates what can happen when there is a misunderstanding of public service obligations imposed by a contractual relationship with government.)

Contracting and procurement pose special problems and temptations inside government and out. The team's composition shifts; its objectives are shared only partially, and its coherence is marginal at best. Relationships are fluid and temporary; alliances and allegiances may change. In this atmosphere, tough and open talk, mutual responsibilities agreed to in advance, laid-out ethical expectations, and leveraged ethics programs are among the best ways to reduce risk and sponsor ethical behavior. This method gets all participants to buy in.

Propelled by scandal and public concern, the U.S. Department of Defense (DOD) took the lead in the procurement function. A commission appointed by President Reagan in 1985 reported that relying on government regulations alone is ineffectual, and major defense contractors responded with the Defense Industry Initiative on Business Ethics and Conduct [DII, at http://www.dii.org], whose signatory companies are pledged "to adopt and implement a set of principles of business ethics and conduct that acknowledge and express their federal-procurement-related corporate responsibilities to the Department of Defense, as well as to the public, the Government, and to each other."

Procurement fraud has been with us since the beginning of the republic. The very first congressional investigation—a 1792 inquiry into an Indian victory over troops serving under Major General Arthur St. Clair—was an eighteenth-century version of a defense procurement scandal. "Blame for the disaster was placed on the War Department, particularly the quartermaster and supply contractors, who were accused of mismanagement, neglect and delay" (*Congressional Quarterly*, 1974, p. 15).

Historically, scandals often provoke a statutory response. In 1863, Civil War scandals led to passage of the "forerunner of the principal conflict of interest law in the federal government—18 U.S.C. Section 208" (Maskell, 1989, p. 1). Nonetheless, some behavior seems to resist change, perhaps because the "market price" for it is so persuasive.

New and usually more stringent procurement rules are very productive if the gauge is "amount of legislation." Over and above objections to more bureaucratic paperwork, arguments against tightened standards of conduct are strong: unfair constraints on using professional expertise; dissuading experts from temporary career moves, and unwise, hermetically sealed boundaries between the public and private sectors. However, practical experience counters with a strong case on behalf of unique procurement taboos.

As risks multiply, so do administrative costs associated with reducing them. In a collaborative arena, relationships tend to be temporary and fluid, and to efficiently deliver a single good or service. Under these conditions, production-oriented managers may resist putting time and energy into *ethics*, of all things, when the relationship is designed single-mindedly on a market basis: get the job done. Unless a manager is willing to do the public's business on a buyer-beware basis, this rejection leaves us with armies of contract compliance officers and lawyers poring over detailed contract specifications in a suspicion-charged atmosphere.

Supplementary Tactic

As a supplementary approach, a manager can invest in a standard game plan to build trust, improve communication, and reduce risk. In summary, an experienced coach can call for a half-dozen plays:

1. Assert ethical values and behavioral expectations at the beginning of a project or relationship.
2. Articulate government or public ethical standards and their applicability to project operations and colleagues.
3. Notify and inform partners and collaborators covered by government or public service standards.
4. Support self-governance by private sector and nonprofit participants.
5. Prepare all parties for full disclosure and accountability.
6. Broadcast the principle of inexcusable ignorance; familiarity with public service's ethical standards is the responsibility of all parties.

The need is not merely to level the playing field but to insure we play in the same ballpark. Similar challenges and their related risks prompted President Kennedy to propose the first codification of federal conflict-of-interest legislation (some dating to Civil War scandals). In a message to Congress on April 27, 1961, he argued as follows:

> This need to tap America's human resources for public purposes has blurred the distinctions between public and private life. It has led to a constant flow of people in and out of business, academic life and government. It has required us to contract with private institutions and call upon part-time consultants for important public work. It has resulted in a rapid rate of turnover among career government employees. And, as a result, it has gravely multiplied the risk of conflicts of interest while seriously complicating the problem of maintaining ethical standards.

Developing an Ethical Agency

An agency is an abstraction, a legal authority, and a set of relationships. It does not really have moral obligations. These are reserved for individuals. Asserting an agency's moral responsibility actually symbolizes ethical responsibilities imposed on its members by the agency's officers, management, statutory authority, and functional mission. No matter how broad an ethics mandate is, its effectiveness—and the responsibility for it—turns on individual responsibility.

A critical item on the public service agenda is building ethical organizations. This is a symbol, too—a shorthand way of speaking about forging administrative relations, systems, processes, procedures, and standards that fortify the ethical individual, bolster ethical reasoning, nourish ethical dialogue, and inject ethical concerns into routine operations—admittedly, a tall order. Yet an ethical organization is the core of what we understand public service to be in democracies (Denhardt, 1993, chapter 6).

Most likely, agencies will go the route of fusion, described in the Introduction, by taking both the compliance and integrity roads to this goal. Stopping short, at compliance only, can be detrimental (Gilman, 2004b; Joseph, 2001); neither route has worked satisfactorily by itself. Decades ago, a report of the congressional General Accounting Office (1981, p. 1) advised, "Agencies need to develop programs that aggressively implement standards of employee conduct and actively promote ethical behavior."

If we agree on the goal and route, there still remains the question of the best vehicle: How can we move the item off the agenda and into office operations? Abstract answers include linking personal and public ethics through organizational practices and procedures, promoting an organizational framework to buttress ethical integrity and responsibility, supporting ethical practitioners, and sustaining ethical reasoning and behavior within public agencies. These are really skeletal goals that beg to be fleshed out with concrete proposals for action. This chapter offers proposals in three categories: (1) agency operations, (2) a model ethics audit and risk-assessment strategies, and (3) an ethics impact statement.

Other agencies, jurisdictions, and business practices are rich sources of tested ideas. The resulting ethics agenda draws on a mix of actual practices, as well as our experience and imagination. The ASPA, the Association for Applied and Practical Ethics, the Brookings Institution, and others, have sponsored dozens of public service ethics conferences. The U.S. OGE and, for state and local ethics programs, the COGEL, have annual meetings with hundreds of representatives in attendance. In addition, major international meetings focusing on ethical agencies have been sponsored by the OAS, OECD, and the World Bank. These meetings disseminate up-to-date thinking on how to develop, institute, refine, and maintain vigorous ethical agencies. The topics vary from effective institutional policies to organizational practices, from leadership models to analytical tools, and from effective training to meaningful ethics codes.

Some of this material is available through journals such as *Public Integrity* and the *Public Administration Review;* other work is available on-line. The latter include PUMA (the Public Management Group) of the Organization for Economic Co-operation and Development on ethics and anticorruption (www.oecd.org), the World Bank Institute or the Poverty Reduction and Economic Management (Governance and Public Sector Reform Section, www1.worldbank.org/prem) and, on international standards for evaluating effective ethics programs within countries, the OAS (http://www.oas.org).

Systematically Improving Conduct

A very first step is usually to formulate a written policy, often as an adopted code; some of the items listed here are part of managing the code (examined in Chapter Eight). "Although no organization can prevent isolated incidents of unethical conduct, much can be done to systematically improve ethical conduct" (Berman, 2002, unpaginated). Experiences with codes and with public and corporate ethics programs flag stable, ongoing attention, which works better than piecemeal or fitful approaches. This entails an *ethics program with leadership at the center.*

> Many studies support that top leaders are examples of moral conduct for others in organizations. When top leaders are seen to espouse the highest values of virtue, and are strong advocates that these values are adopted by others and incorporated into decisions and organizational systems (such as human resource management), then ethical conduct is readily promoted (Berman, 2002, unpaginated).

Senior managers' reputations and behavior, plus their commitment to the agency's ethics program, are vital to its success. Most leaders believe that simply being *a good person* is enough. A variety of studies suggest otherwise (Trevino, Hartman, and Brown, 2003; Office of Government Ethics, 2000, p. 10). Although rarely as cheap as the old adage would have us believe, talk is important. Officers' and managers' participation in programs and signing off on communications, from office memos and house newsletters to budgets and news releases, do play a role.

But talking commitment is not enough. Public employees are sensitive to the flow of real resources—an expressive nonverbal cue in any organization. Staff time and real dollars that go for training, incentives, performance, and the ethical aspects of agency policies and practices will be used by agency staff members to meter the authenticity of the talk and the priority of public service ethics in the agency. By way of illustration, consider the ethical content of SOPs incorporating service priorities and distribution rules, as shown in Exhibit 10.3. By way of clarification, what do you think is the more meaningful communication: fine words at a staff meeting or disregarded negligence and padded budget estimates? Why would colleagues and employees think otherwise?

EXHIBIT 10.3. HARDLY NEUTRAL.

A social service agency staffs evenings for three hourly appointment slots, each covered by two providers as accreditation dictates. Like many such agencies, it has a waiting list filled on a first-come, first-served basis (much like the first-in, first-out [FIFO] inventory system). But this inventory of people and problems is highly modified by apparent urgency, client convenience, providers' availability and capability, and service eligibility based on catchments, age, and income. The choice: who is to be denied immediate help because the agency can't meet all needs.

A judgment call on urgency is made by the referring institution or school, physician, parent, custodian or guardian, and so on, with the intention of acting quickly to minimize harm to the prospective client (who may very well not be fully responsible for his or her own actions). An agency worker also assesses urgency and seriousness of need during an initial intake or screening. Once the need is evaluated, consideration turns to client demand for particular time slots and types of service in conjunction with normal working hours of agency staff and professional standards of care.

The final factor in setting service priorities is potential effectiveness; resources are too scarce to waste. Is the problem of recent origin or of chronic duration? Acute, urgent need with positive prospects of treatment or meaningful intervention in an agency setting get preference over those on the waiting list. Without these extraordinary factors, clients at the head of the list get the next available time slot.

- What ethical concerns does the SOPs raise?
- Which, if any, agency SOPs do you reject on ethical grounds, and why?
- What is neglected by the agency that you believe should play a role in service provision? Why?

Ethics can be built into daily routine and expected conduct. Ethical reasoning can be made (1) creditworthy, (2) recognized, and (3) routinely expected. How? (Let us omit individualized tools for decision making such as the ethics responsibility statement in Exhibit 6.5.) A baker's dozen of feasible techniques can contribute to making ethics a standard dimension of management, decision making, and agency operations; these intervention techniques are laid out in Exhibit 10.4. The list converts into a training tool when we ask ourselves to identify items most effective in our own office, items least effective in our own office, items we intend to bring back to the office, and items we would like our supervisor to introduce.

These proposals load another set of duties on the human resource functions but, as a state personnel manager quipped about ethics-based tasks, "Why not? We handle everything that people care about, even parking. Especially parking."

The ethics agenda lands on *every* manager's desk, and earnest attention is a tough, constant demand. That managers teach subordinates by doing is hardly a trailblazing idea, but it needs to be extended directly to the ethical aspects of behavior in the agency. More than modeling is needed, however. Any one person and any number of people in the agency can play in this game. At every level and in every type of unit, there is something to be done to improve the ethical climate. The whole team can and should participate. It is the manager's job to see that they do. Ethics is not a spectator sport.

EXHIBIT 10.4. INTERVENTION TECHNIQUES FOR INTEGRATING ETHICS INTO AGENCY OPERATIONS.

1. Do both compliance and integrity training and counseling.
2. Give briefings on common ethical problems on the job for new hires.
3. Give termination briefings on potential postemployment problems.
4. Designate senior manager(s) for integrity issues, separate from compliance/investigative unit.
5. Require annual sign-off on prospective commitment and compliance.
6. Attend to ethical values and character in recruitment.
7. Integrate ethical performance into promotional exams and annual reviews; link ethical behavior to incentives.
8. Publicize positive, noteworthy role models.
9. Raise ethical concerns at meetings and through regular communication channels.
10. Train middle managers to recognize and commend subordinates' statements about ethical concerns.
11. Review management practices and administrative routines at every level and in every type of unit in the organization.
12. Get the whole team—all employees, all levels, all units—to participate; ethics is not a spectator sport.
13. Give earnest attention to ethical treatment of subordinates, clients, and others.

There is no doubt that effective ethics programs can alter institutional life. In fact, they must if they are to be effective. Many governments are creating independent ethics offices with reporting responsibilities to the head of the agency. For example, the Ethics in Government Act of 1978 (as amended) requires every agency head in the executive branch of the federal government to appoint a DAEO (as described in Chapter Eight). With responsibilities mandated by regulation, the DAEOs' independence is protected by OGE's regular evaluation of their program.

Surely, integrity-based, positive ethics can be integrated into an agency's operations. The widespread institutionalization of the merit principle over the past century shows that we *can* transform the way we do everyday business. It may be a slow, frustrating process, and there is much to learn. Woodrow Wilson ([1887] 1987, p. 16) warned over a century ago, "In government, as in virtue, the hardest of hard things is to make progress."

Countering Objections

Wilson also noted in a less frequently cited quote, "We go on criticizing when we ought to be creating" ([1887] 1987, p. 16). All new ideas ignite derivative problems, and an ethics agenda is no exception. For instance, West Virginia, "trying to recover both morally and financially from the loss of over $200 million through the mismanagement of state investment funds" (Hall, 1989, p. 20), pronounced itself the thirty-sixth state to create an independent ethics commission. The speaker of the West Virginia House of Delegates and cosponsor of the state's 1989 Ethics Act reviewed objections to the legislation. His arguments (Chambers, 1989, p. v) are relevant to objections to administrative ventures.

> "You can't legislate morality" was a common refrain for those who questioned the need for comprehensive ethics legislation. The bureaucracy of ethics regulations . . . seemed to outweigh any benefits. To some, an ethics law was merely window dressing, unlikely to change how real public officials act except to complicate being one. Inertia, rather than opposition, presented the greatest difficulty.

There are five major objections to agency action: (1) it substitutes ritual for responsibility; (2) ethical behavior is seen as an exception, not the rule; (3) red tape is generated; (4) some people object to behavior modification, and (5) there is the double-edged threat of vigilante ethics. Because we can lay the objections aside only by meeting them, let us take each one in turn.

Ritual Substituted for Responsibility The first objection views ritualistic compliance as a poor but likely proxy for ethics. It is valid as far as it goes, but it does not go far enough. Institutional mechanisms do endanger the broader goal by threatening to substitute formalistic compliance for ethical responsibility. But must they? Can we accommodate new concerns in administrative routines without trivializing fundamental principles? The answer is, "Of course." That is what responsive, innovative public management is all about.

Ethical Behavior Seen as Exception The second objection is keyed to defining ethical behavior as the exception, not the rule, by rewarding managers for ethical behavior. Some managers, noses wrinkled in distaste, resist linking ethical behavior to professional rewards or financial incentives. Unless we are willing to ignore ethics altogether, this objection undercuts the former by leaving no alternative except to make ethical behavior routine and an ordinary habit in daily operations.

Red Tape Generated The third objection hoists the red flag of red tape—a symbol of excessive bureaucratic routine derived from the banding once tied around legal papers and official documents in England. Regulations and procedures should be instrumental in the achievement of objectives, not valued for their own sake, and few public practitioners are particularly fond of rules and paperwork. The compliance side of the equation is heavily weighted toward red tape, but it also makes ethics programs less timely, less effective, and ultimately less relevant. Former Health and Human Services Secretary Donna Shalala argues that an ethical organization requires

> [a] culture to support those behaviors, and doesn't punish people for taking an action you want them to take. Structures or systems need to be in place to make employees feel comfortable expressing their views . . . raising difficult issues . . . questioning authority . . . or pushing back when necessary (Shalala, 2004, unpaginated).

A balance between compliance and values is needed for an effective agency ethics program. This attitude does not preclude necessary or desired rules and procedures; it takes account of assistance, guidance, values, and principles.

Federal employees already enjoy detailed standards and full-blown ethics programs with a heavy compliance slant. The OGE conducted the first executive branch ethics survey of employees in 2000. The vast majority of federal employees reported that they were aware of their ethics program and had a clear understanding of its objectives (U.S. Office of Government Ethics, 2000, p. 7). Further, those who had filed financial disclosure forms and supervisors reported significantly higher awareness of the scope and purpose of the ethics program. More than 25 percent of the respondents had asked for ethics advice in the past five years (p. 30). Employees viewed the ethics program quite positively. Those with more frequent ethics training had "significantly more positive perceptions of an ethical culture and employee behavior," and the more familiar employees were with the overall ethics program, the more likely that they would view themselves working in an ethical culture (U.S. Office of Government Ethics, pp. 8, 42). The study (p. 44, Exhibit 44) finds a profound relationship between certain "ethical factors" (defined as including executive leadership, rewarding ethical behavior, unethical behavior punished) and outcomes (unethical behavior observed, employees seek ethics advice, okay to deliver bad news).

Federal, state, and local managers undoubtedly and pragmatically would resist intricate, paper-laden, and immoderate proposals. Three rules of thumb let us respond to the need without adding unduly to the administrative burden. First, ethics dos, like ethics don'ts, should be as few as necessary and as simple as possible to do the job. Second, instead of force-feeding prototypical packages or universal remedies, ethics programs are best tailored to the administrative realities in different jurisdictions and agencies. Despite structural and substantive similarities, program design and implementation best address agency-specific issues. The third rule of thumb identifies the internal, direct clients of agency interventions as the ethical managers and employees who want to do the right thing. (These guidelines explain why the ethics impact statement proposed later in the chapter follows the contours of the simpler, shorter environmental assessment instead of the more rigorous environmental impact statement.)

Objection to Behavior Modification The fourth objection is to modifying behavior. It can be raised against all work routines and rules, including laws and standards of conduct. Yes, they modify behavior; that is what they are for. Yes, some people will spend a great deal of time figuring a way around them, and some will *have to do that* in order to do their job. A case in point is how performance is adapted to its measure; recall the old urban legend about sanitation workers watering down garbage because their productivity was measured by tonnage.

Then again, other people will ignore the spirit in favor of rigid application, as a case from Philadelphia reveals. This is the city portrayed as "corrupt and contented" at the turn of the century by muckraker Lincoln Steffens ([1904] 1982). Philadelphia's extensive ethics code dates to 1963. A decision once issued by its commission prohibited municipal employees from being foster parents (who were defined as "contracted agents with the city") because full-time employment meant that they could not receive additional government payments (Potamianos, 1990).

Cases throughout this book suggest that these problems are endemic. An annual sign-off can address them explicitly by targeting *next year's* performance and *future* commitment; it allows everyone a good-faith promise instead of ensuring a few pointless lies.

The upshot of the most carefully crafted ethics program may not be entirely what the public manager would want. Human imagination being what it is, some perverse behavior is predictable. Yet if we reject proposals until perfection is guaranteed, in effect, we reject all change.

Fear of Vigilante Ethics The fifth and final objection to agency action sees these proposals as a modern version of that sword hanging over Damocles. The threat is double-edged. One edge cuts into productivity: more shackles on the manager are a menace to effective public service. We have faced and overcome this problem before. In the nineteenth-century American bureaucracy, "agencies organized to avoid evil became that much less able to do good" (Nelson, 1982, p. 763).

The other edge is at our neck: the potential for harassment and coercion in an abstract sphere about which people disagree (Garvey, 1993). For this and other reasons, procedural protections are crucial to an agency's ethics program (described in Chapter Eight). Proposals that bear on personnel generally, but especially on recruitment and promotion, provoke legitimate concern about Fourth Amendment rights and the court-protected right of privacy. The backlash against polygraphs, reference and credit checks, urinalyses, and blood tests invites nightmarish visions about the probable response to public agencies' use of so-called integrity tests (honesty screening). A variety of protections for government employees has eroded in the past thirty years, including legal immunity.

However, certain programs such as financial disclosure, broadly criticized when they were proposed in the 1970s, today are accepted widely. Finding for the federal government's right to demand financial disclosure, the court's decision in *Duplantier* v. *United States* argued that an individual's privacy as a government employee is trumped by the public's right to know. In 1989, the Supreme Court upheld drug testing for government employees who operate hazardous equipment or carry weapons; later that year, the court ruled that mandatory drug testing without prior labor union approval is permitted for rail and airlines employees.

Some ideas sound good in theory but in practice are negative, obsessed with compliance, and even demoralizing. Do these threats bid managers to hold out for no risk and then do nothing? Or can managers go ahead and rely on an ancient virtue to minimize risk?

Need for Prudence

Managers can and should move ahead, with prudence. The success of an agency's ethics agenda turns on its managers' prudence, in the age-old meaning of wisdom and caring for the community and general good. It demands the rejection of its modern corruption into personal expediency or self-interest.

In the *Nicomachean Ethics* (Book VI), Aristotle associates *practical wisdom* with the statesman who is concerned with right action; others, solely concerned with right thinking, may indulge in purely abstract wisdom. Edmund Burke and others have argued that "although principles are necessary, they are not enough. They must be applied to concrete reality by a type of practical reasoning which Burke called prudence" (Canavan, 1963, p. 606). Prudence tempers the impeccable with the practical in order to pursue the ideal, not simply substitute the doable. Recall that pragmatism is built into the initial decision-making model in Chapter Two.

Public managers are, by and large, creative, judicious, and capable of conceiving of positive, nonthreatening ways of incorporating ethics into agency procedures. In annual reviews, for example, the criterion could be self-defined by having the employee respond to the question, What do you do to contribute to the ethical operations or practices in this agency? A contractual format is suitable for an annual sign-off on prospective code commitment and compliance. Both illustrate the practical importance of both trust and oath giving (Chapters One and Two), along with personal commitment. Considering the volume of paper crossing a manager's desk, flagging important communication becomes an art.

A city manager offers a word of advice for prudent managers with first-rate ethics programs. Expect mistakes. "It then becomes important to deal with them quickly and openly. An analysis and discussion with staff on why the ethical impropriety occurred and how to prevent such an occurrence in the future is essential" (Bonczek, 1990, p. 7).

Rules of Thumb

Rules of thumb for the prudent manager are culled from this and earlier chapters and listed here as general guidelines for ready reference. They speak to managers' decisions about both ethical issues and ethics in the agency (see Exhibit 10.5). Serving public managers best when combined with the fundamentals shown in Exhibit 6.2, these rules of thumb give purpose and direction to ethical action in the agency and to agency intervention techniques.

A Proposed Ethics Impact Statement and Process

The ethics impact statement (EthIS) we propose provides for a decision-making process that integrates several analytic methods and tools laid out in this book. Figure 10.1 charts the steps in this process. Formally adopted (and adapted), it procedurally secures a role for ethical analysis in agency deliberations, particularly over policies and regulations. Another application is critiquing potent SOPs in the agency, such as in Exhibit 10.3. An individual manager can apply the process informally to work through the wrenching dilemma that seems an inevitable part of public service. The design is deliberately slanted toward process rather than outcome because *the objective is to integrate systematically ethical analysis into decision making.* The goal is to amplify managers' thinking, not usurp it.

EXHIBIT 10.5. RULES OF THUMB.

The "rule of thumb" derives from English common law that permitted the head of household to beat the spouse using a stick with a diameter no larger than the thumb. (Gender references in the original formulation are removed to meet contemporary standards.)

1. Danger! Justifying an action in the name of a greater good or higher authority, instead of taking action for the sake of that purpose (Chapter One).
2. Disobedience is preferred to illegality; refuse an illegal directive (Chapter Two).
3. Public position may not be used for dissent as a citizen (Chapter Two).
4. Ethical public service rejects naïveté and cynicism and opts for hard-headed optimism (Chapter Two).
5. Beware of those who wrap themselves in the common good or confidently assert future interests (Chapter Three).
6. Respect for future generations is a test for the public interest (Chapter Three).
7. Empathy is another test of commitment to the public interest (Chapter Three).
8. Use of office for personal gain for oneself or others is unethical (Chapter Three).
9. Individual responsibility is by no means identical to sole responsibility (Chapter Four).
10. A public manager's first task is fixing the problem and only secondarily fixing the blame (Chapter Four).
11. We cannot hide behind our boss or our desk to escape responsibility (Chapter Four).
12. We cannot hide behind our subordinates (Chapter Four).
13. We cannot hide behind our ignorance (Chapter Four).
14. Ethical neutrality strips the humanity from managers and service recipients; dehumanizing the victims denies the ethical element (Chapter Four).
15. The obligation for *informed* ethical reasoning falls on the individual public manager accommodation (Chapter Five).
16. Ethical judgment is best when it is self-applied (Chapter Five).
17. Ethical public service demands that public servants touch base with all ethical perspectives (Chapter Five).
18. In public service, the search is for compatibility and balance, reconciliation and accommodation (Chapter Five).
19. Impartial open-mindedness is the first-order test of genuine empathy in public service (Chapter Five).
20. The impartial public manager is ethically driven, not ethically empty (Chapter Five).
21. Danger! Militant claims to moral superiority (Chapter Five).
22. A typical starting point for ethical decision making is accepting the minimum prescription: avoid doing harm (Chapter Six).
23. Public service's posture of avoiding harm leads to an obligation to correct direct or indirect problems we create (Chapter Six).
24. Anticipate follow-through by inquiring, "Can I live with this?" (Chapter Six).
25. Apply the acid test of prospective publicity and ask what kind of person would do this and whether you want to be and be known as that kind of person (Chapter Six).
26. Future generations are the most dependent stakeholders of all, and public officials are their only institutional trustee (Chapter Six).
27. Ethical managers exercise reasonable selectivity among responsibilities and choose their battles in a principled way (Chapter Seven).
28. The willingness to listen is a component of ethical decision making (Chapter Seven).

29. Where to draw the line? The more unethical one judges a behavior, the less likely one will practice it or tolerate others' doing it (Chapter Seven).
30. Ethics is not a toggle switch. Ethical managers exercise reasonable selectivity among responsibilities (Chapter Six) and choose their battles in a principled way (Chapter Seven).
31. Danger! The slippery slope and losing the capacity to make moral judgments or act on them (Chapter Seven).
32. Ethical managers and employees are the internal, direct clients of agency intervention (Chapter Eight).
33. Many employees look to ethics rules as a basic moral compass, but everyone should understand that rules are only the beginning of ethical responsibility (Chapter Eight).
34. A public manager's primary ethical concern is behavior toward other people (Chapter Ten).
35. In a diversifying workforce, some behaviors need rethinking; others need full-scale remodeling (Chapter Ten).
36. In a collaborative setting, put ethical issues and standards on the table, right up front (Chapter Ten).
37. Ethics dos, like ethics don'ts, should be as few as necessary and as simple as possible to do the job (Chapter Ten).
38. Tailor operations to specific administrative realities (Chapter Ten).
39. A responsible manager seeks to minimize opportunities and temptation and encourage integrity, both individual and institutional (Chapter Ten).
40. Your rule of thumb: _____

An EthIS or similar framework can help add ethical analysis to the decision maker's formidable inventory, customarily amassed through years of cultivating new skills and mastering new techniques. Take inventory for a moment. Counting in dollars? Use cost-benefit analysis. Accounting for nonquantifiable factors? Turn to cost-effectiveness analysis. Pull out a standardized format for fiscal notes when proposed legislation calls for cost estimates. Develop performance and productivity measures. Apply evaluation techniques and statistical analysis. Attack the project with program evaluation and review techniques (PERT). Today public managers must puzzle over scenarios worked up on a spreadsheet or scrutinize once-novel variables in environmental impact statements, risk assessments, and comparable-worth analyses. The point is, in order to assist decision making and improve decisions, each analytic skill adds new techniques, technical tools, and some new vocabulary. Responsible for specialized knowledge that keeps accumulating, public managers, in effect, sign up for lifelong learning.

Ethical analysis is no different. It makes comparable intellectual demands. Like the other items in the inventory, it is sound only when used soundly. An EthIS must be properly applied, at the right time, in carefully selected situations. Perhaps there is one major difference: it cannot be farmed out to paid consultants or outside authorities. (Expert advice and external assistance are appropriate in the fact-finding and analytic stages.) The process is dynamic, consultative, participatory, and cooperative (versus adversarial). But it is not perfunctory. Ethics involves individual responsibility for moral

FIGURE 10.1. ETHICS IMPACT STATEMENT AND PROCESS.

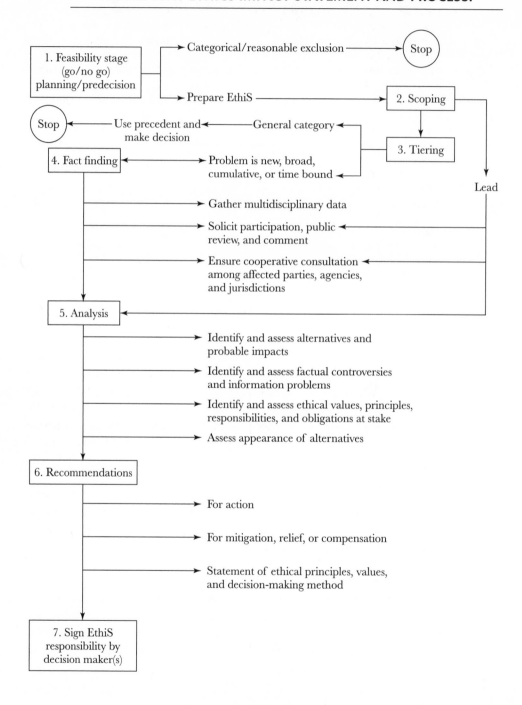

judgments and choices. The last step in the process, signing the EthIS, is not a hollow symbol; it is a critical component of the seven-step process. Ethics responsibilities cannot be delegated, bought, or temporarily rented.

For efficiency's sake and to minimize the administrative burden and paperwork, the EthIS is patterned after the environmental impact assessment. It is a shorter, simpler, streamlined version of a formal environmental impact statement. The acronym EthIS distinguishes the process from its environmental kin, developed by the Council on Environmental Quality in 1987. Situated in the Executive Office of the President, the council issued regulations for implementing the National Environmental Policy Act—the underlying charter for environmental protection nationally. Many recommendations that follow are adaptations of these regulations (40 CFR 1500–1508).

Step 1: Determining Feasibility

Timing Because the objective is ethical action, not after-the-fact justification, the EthIS process begins in planning, when a proposal's initial feasibility is appraised and before a decision is made.

Exclusion Answers to Rion's questions in Chapter Six—Why is this bothering me? and Is it my problem?—when asked at the agency level, may mean that no ethics impact statement is needed. Proposals with no significant ethical facets, either individually or cumulatively, may be excluded categorically. Note, however, that an ethical dimension permeates all significant decisions. Because ethics for public managers is linked to behavior, proposed agency actions that will not practically be affected by EthIS (for example, a legal mandate) or emergency responses in which delay constitutes a decision (crisis management) may be reasonably excluded. Yet an EthIS on otherwise reasonably excluded actions may yield ideas for corrective action or statutory change (activating the inventive resolution from Chapter Six).

Step 2: Scoping

A decision to prepare an EthIS initiates scoping: "an early and open process for determining the scope of issues to be addressed and for identifying the significant issues related to a proposed action" (40 CFR 1501.7). *Scope* refers to "the range of actions, alternatives, and impacts to be considered" (1508.25). A pilot diagnosis exercises selectivity again and sets boundaries. That can be accomplished by asking Rion's question—"What is the ethical concern?—and responding in terms of Cooper's formulation of obligation as responsibility *for* and accountability as responsibility *to*. The diagnosis is used to identify and eliminate insignificant elements. Relevant criteria in scoping include severity of effects, controversy and uncertainties, and gravity of values and principles at stake.

At this point, a *lead* senior manager is designated, appropriate staff members are assigned, and a reporting date is set. A team may include a low-level line manager for purposes of responsibility and effectiveness. "The person performing the task is in an ideal position to assess the outcomes of the action in terms of human impact" (Denhardt, 1988, p. 147).

Step 3: Tiering

The lead manager satisfies a core value in public service—efficiency—by forestalling repetition. Where appropriate, the manager folds the proposal into an umbrella category keyed to general ethical (as opposed to legal or pragmatic) criteria and makes the decision by using precedent and logic. This potential shortcut also checks for consistency. The EthIS process proceeds only with new, broad, or cumulative factors or when a review is suitable. Note that past decisions may be time-bound. As a check on obsolescence, the manager can consider revisiting dated decisions.

Step 4: Fact Finding

Many decision-making models begin with getting the facts, getting them all, and getting them straight. Realistically, there are informational limits that are best set by preliminary stakeholder analysis (see Chapter Seven). However, inexcusable ignorance scuttles the whole EthIS process (Exhibit 4.4 poses general but critical questions about information). It is imperative to identify legal obligations and mandates; Chapter Four raises three questions about the legal context so critical to public service.

Because a wide sweep in fact finding helps minimize bias, error, and omission in the analytic stage, the process calls for multidisciplinary data. An inclusive sweep covers four categories of information about facts and values: objective, subjective, quantitative, and qualitative. Expert opinion and advice are solicited at this step and the next. Preliminary stakeholder analysis is crucial to designing meaningful participation and consultation.

At some point, too much information complicates matters instead of clarifying them. "[A]rriving at ethical decisions requires a greater tolerance for ambiguity than does arriving at decisions based on empirical evidence alone" (Denhardt, 1988, p. 120). When to stop collecting facts and to proceed to the next step is a decision critical to the process.

Step 5: Analyzing

The EthIS team selects an ethical analytic framework at this stage (criteria underlying selection are discussed in Chapter Six). A truly momentous issue or having no team consensus calls for the application of either several frameworks or one framework that combines different ethical perspectives (see the checklist in Exhibit 6.1). Possible analytic techniques include one or more of the following: identifying values or principles at risk (Figure 1.1 and Exhibit 1.6); assessing and ranking responsibilities by rigor, perhaps using the tools discussed in Chapter Six; and using the stakeholder diagnostic presented in Exhibit 7.1. Note that information standards in Exhibit 4.4 entail disclosure of all major opinions, points of controversy, and incomplete or unavailable information.

In this stage, substance is assessed and so is appearance. The latter's separate entry in Figure 10.1 symbolizes its eminence in public service, not its analytic isolation from the assessment of alternatives and probable effects.

Step 6: Making Recommendations

Once obligations, effects, principles, and values have been sorted out and selected in Step 5, the EthIS now recommends an action or decision. The go/no-go decision model in Chapter Two honors legal and pragmatic boundaries in ethical decision making. In a true dilemma, the fundamental obligation to serve the public interest implies reconciliation where possible (see Chapters Three and Five). As a result, the team successively corrects and modifies proposals. In this context, a rigorous obligation to avoid doing harm implies that the team's goal is to minimize harm and reduce any adverse impact on values, principles, or stakeholders (see Chapter Six). The end result is that the decision maker (or makers) identifies the public interest by proposing an action, discloses the decision-making method, and recommends action triggered by the proposal that he or she considers obligatory.

As for the document, its general style and overall format are best when concise rather than wordy and in clear prose—plain language that is comprehensible to the general public.

Step 7: Taking Responsibility

The importance of taking responsibility for a decision has already been discussed in Chapters Four and Six. The format for the ethics responsibility statement to be signed by the EthIS team members and the agency head can be adapted from the model statement shown in Exhibit 6.6 or a similar declaration. A simple statement might read, "I certify that the attached policy, regulation, or procedure is recommended after due consideration of its ethical dimensions."

There remain, of course, the implementation and evaluation processes once the decision is made.

Pros and Cons of Ethics Impact Statements

The EthIS and similar instruments promise advantages not too different from evaluation assessments (Wholey, 1983, p. 103; Fischer, 1995, pp. 27–41). The list is tempting: assist in setting priorities and realistic objectives, identify early on the problems and needed corrections in policy or regulation, pinpoint unsettled issues and unanticipated effects for legislative proposals or executive decision, and inform decision makers and the public.

As an *action-forcing device,* an ethics impact statement can contribute to resolving disputes quickly and fairly, which is one of the stated goals of environmental impact statements (40 CFR 1501.1[c]). The EthIS process, like its parent model, has the paradoxical potential for accomplishing just the opposite. As a *disclosure instrument,* it could freeze action by increasing political opposition over newly clarified controversies and stakes. Even with subdued enthusiasm, one can still admit that an ethics impact statement reserves a role and formalizes a process for ethical analysis. At minimum, it is an advocacy device and learning tool for ethical reasoning and ethical decision making in the agency.

Other Useful Tools

More modest, usually noninstitutional, frameworks for probing public policy's ethical aspects have been and are now being developed for those "unperceived angles and forgotten dimensions" (Fischer, 1983, p. 32). Recently, the OECD began a massive evaluation of assessment strategies of ethics programs around the world (Gilman, 2004). Managers may prefer to insert an examination of the normative elements of operating procedures, policy, and other decisions into evaluation techniques already in place.

Conducting Agency Ethics Audits

The agenda outlined in this chapter is double-pronged. A jurisdiction's or agency's ethics program realistically cannot be divorced from compliance issues. Legally enforceable standards and controls play an important part in establishing a fair, productive, and supportive workplace. Complying with agency procedures and obeying rules *are* important. But an agency's ethics program need not and should not focus exclusively on the adequacy of and compliance with internal controls and legal prohibitions. It can also target ethical reasoning and behavior and their role in the organization by expanding workaday priorities to managers' receptivity to ethical considerations and the scope for ethical deliberation in the agency. The aim is to move on both fronts, in line with the fusion route discussed in the Introduction.

Before we agree on what needs to be done, it makes sense to evaluate current practice, problems, and potential. A practical, accessible tool is necessary for assessing the agency as an ethical environment. Model ethics assessment tools designed to profile the agency's strengths and deficiencies and produce an action agenda are available on-line from the ERC, INDEPENDENT SECTOR, OECD, and others (see Resource B, Exhibit 9.3, and Berman, 2002). They function somewhat like an audit manual in less regulated jurisdictions and more informal agencies. The word *model is* aimed at encouraging adaptation to each agency's peculiarities.

The OGE's Agency Ethics Program Questionnaire is another useful resource. Federal agencies are required by the 1978 Ethics in Government Act, as amended, to submit an annual report to OGE on their ethics programs. Given the federal executive branch's elaborate standards of conduct, formal ethics offices and systems, and control mechanisms and audit procedures, other assessment or audit tools the model audit necessarily serve in federal offices as a diagnostic tool or vulnerability checklist.

An audit absorbs managers' time and energy, along with staff resources. Even allowing that any operation can be improved, no manager can do it all, all at once. Some realistic selectivity is needed. A quick overview can give a reading on urgency and criticality, which can be done using the mapping diagnostic in Figure 1.6. A serious mismatch between preference and practice could move the full-fledged assessment to a high priority on a manager's agenda.

A cautionary note is in order here. At a hearing on Housing and Urban Development a U.S. senator asked, "What's the thermometer that you inject into an agency to get an immediate readout of the health of that agency?" The then-chairman of the President's Council on Integrity and Efficiency answered, "Well, unfortunately, I don't think the level of the technology is at the level of the thermometer. It's more the hand to the brow that maybe your mother did to establish whether or not you have a fever. So it's not a perfect instrument" (U.S. Senate, 1990).

Assessing Job Risk

Job vulnerability assessment is a related method limited to identifying potential snags or staff that needs special assistance. A form of risk assessment, it concentrates on compliance, detection, and enforcement. For fraud or other abuses, "[a]n initial step is learning to recognize indicators of the presence of fraud or of the potential for it" (U.S. Department of Defense, 1984, preface).

The GAO analyzed fraud cases from 1976 to 1979 and found that federal employees were responsible for 29 percent of the attributable cases (General Accounting Office, 1981, p. 1). Using a Delphi technique to pool expert judgments and statistical techniques to analyze responses, the GAO identified fifty-two factors affecting relative job exposure. The GAO's method is not meant to predict the behavior of individual incumbents but to play the odds on certain jobs. It rests on a proportional relationship between problems and opportunities, all else held constant (p. 10). For example, the position of food inspector ranked high on relative vulnerability among the jobs selected for evaluation. A poor "integrity record" (reported misconduct) or reputation did not appear to influence rankings in a test evaluation; the second-highest exposure was awarded another position with "an excellent integrity record" (p. 11).

Isolation and discretion are defining characteristics for the food inspector's job. If the manager's objective is to minimize temptation and opportunity among line employees assigned off-site discretionary leverage, then the implication of the GAO's study is that preventive action (subject to position count and budget constraints) calls for teaming employees and rotating frequently among partners and sites.

Assuming that ingenuity outpaces detection, analysis necessarily lags behind novel abuses. This is true, for example, in the area of information technology and security, procurement, and more (President's Council on Integrity and Efficiency, 2003, p. 21).

If one suspects that white-collar crime is especially ingenious and therefore undetected to some degree, then the fact that recurring abuses are pedestrian comes as no surprise. Some traditions are honored, even in the face of vigorous enforcement efforts. Typical patterns and related examples include police selling protection; case fixing; contract bid rigging and kickbacks; regulatory crimes involving building and utility inspectors, licensing, and land use; judicial conflicts of interest; election crimes, including ballot and campaign finance fraud; narcotics-related abuses, such as firearms violations, and graft of all kinds.

Dealing with Temptation

Some local governments prove that America is still the land of opportunity. No stranger to corruption, cities provoked the reform movement of the Progressive Era at the turn of the century and its literary genre, muckraking. Old-time, big-city machine politics is associated with corruption for good reason. George W. Plunkitt of New York's former Tammany machine bestowed upon us the standard specimen of conflict of interest:

> Everybody is talkin' these days about Tammany men growin' rich on graft, but nobody thinks of drawin' the distinction between honest graft and dishonest graft. There's all the distinction in the world between the two. There's an honest graft, and I'm an example of how it works. I might sum up the whole thing by sayin': "I seen my opportunities and I took 'em" (quoted in Riordan, 1974, p. 7).

In his celebrated autobiography, Lincoln Steffens wrote of corruption in Los Angeles's early days. Seemingly foreseeing the contemporary scene, Steffens argued that "society really offers a prize for evil-doing: money, position, power." He concluded that the fault lies not so much with Adam, Eve, or even the serpent. "Now I come and I am trying to show you that it was, it is the apple" ([1931] 1974, p. 289).

Big-city government is big business, and that offers a chance for big but ill-begotten prizes. (Just think of the opportunities in economic development alone.) From the business front, Laura Nash (1990, p. 3) prescribes "facing up to fallibility. When you couple the undeniable pervasiveness of human fallibility with the age-old temptations of money and power, the need for a deliberate exploration of the moral challenges of management becomes clear."

Responsible managers try to reduce temptation through routine procedures and controls. Concerned with creating a supportive environment for compliance but also for ethical behavior, *a manager seeks to minimize opportunities and temptations and to encourage integrity, both personal and institutional.* This managerial responsibility of prevention applies to government no less than to nonprofit or other components of public service. High-risk, vulnerable areas identified with incipient problems can be targeted for preventive action across dozens of federal agencies.

The many steps along the Introduction's fusion road to a supportive ethical environment partly follow a paper trail. As Paul Appleby (1951, p. 169) rightfully pointed out, "The bureaucratic substructure and its red tape often provide the bulwark of agency conscience." Although *bureaucracy* has become a much-maligned word, in many ways *good* public management is an essential foundation of modern democracies. While modeling ethical behavior in public service and mentoring newer recruits to the agency, senior professional public managers often also find themselves in the awkward position of managing "up"—and managing "out," that is, tutoring those with whom the agency has working or collaborative relationships and others who exercise oversight over the agency.

Many newly appointed political officials are unaware of the ethical demands of their jobs because they mistakenly assume that ethical standards are the same in all environments. Legislators as well as recruits from the private sector may find out the hard way that this is not true. They may learn this lesson not because they are unethical but because no one has communicated to them the special values and norms of the public sector and the public's expectations that these will be met scrupulously. This chapter identifies critical tools that can be used to focus the ethical use of power in public agencies. It also provides some ways of understanding how good ethics regimes can help public servants do the right thing the right way. Those who exercise political power may be tempted to confuse ends and means by thinking, for example, "So what if we short-cut the procurement process, as long as the project comes in on time?" The result not only can damage their careers or land them in jail but it can have a profound effect on the agency: budget cuts, weakened morale, difficulty in hiring new staff, or immobility that translates into failing to meet critical policy objectives.

As guardians of the ethical integrity of their organizations, professional public managers breathe life into ideas such as "accountability" and "responsiveness" by facilitating the political agenda and policy initiatives of duly elected leaders. This is part of what it means to be *good* public servants. And another part? Grasping their moral compass, holding firm to personal integrity, and nourishing the ethical agency.

Case: Fair Play or Foul at the U.S. Olympic Committee?

The *Olympic Athletes' Oath* (dating to Antwerp Games, 1920): "In the name of all competitors, I promise that we shall take part in these Olympic Games, respecting and abiding by the rules that govern them, in the true spirit of sportsmanship, for the glory of sport and the honor of our teams."

The *Olympic Creed* (recited by host country's judge): "The most important thing in the Olympic games is not to win but to take part, just as the most important thing in life is not the triumph, but the struggle. The essential thing is not to have conquered, but to have fought well."

The worldwide Olympic movement, begun in the late nineteenth century, embodies the ideals of fair and open competition as well as cultural understanding. The declared mission of its recognized U.S. agency—the United States Olympic Committee (USOC)—is to promote the Olympic ideal, support sports, and inspire Americans. Yet in 2003, the USOC was embroiled in an extraordinary ethics controversy that led to the removal or resignation of several of its officials and a reorganization all but directed by a U.S. Senate committee.

The USOC is a nonprofit agency relying on volunteers and donations and, like many such organizations, has a somewhat cumbersome governance structure. (See sources on nonprofits in Resource B, Part 8.) Its board, made up of more than a hundred volunteers and run by an executive committee, elects a volunteer president and hires a chief executive officer to manage the professional staff. By 2001, the organization had had three CEOs in two years. The first resigned under an ethics cloud. The second was forced to resign shortly after taking the position when it was discovered that she had lied on her résumé.

In 2000, the board had created an ethics officer position and hired an experienced corporate ethics officer, Pat Rogers, to take the job. To support Rogers in his role, a group of ethics luminaries (including a former chief of staff to the president of the United States, the former head of the federal Office of Government Ethics, and the executive director of the Ethics Officers Association) were appointed to the USOC's Ethics Oversight Committee. Everything seemed to be in place to build a solid ethical foundation for the USOC.

After an extensive search, the board selected a new CEO who had a corporate background, Lloyd Ward. Among his major responsibilities was stewardship of the millions of dollars that the USOC received from private donations and the government; this money would be supplemented significantly by the upcoming winter games in Salt Lake City. Generally, Ward was to move the USOC out of the negative spotlight that had been turned on the organization during the past several years.

The precipitating event was a letter of introduction on behalf of a friend to senior officials in the Dominican Republic, a potential host of the Pan Am Games. Ward introduced his childhood friend, whose company he urged the Dominicans select to provide back-up electrical services for the games, and indicated that he deemed this choice necessary before confirming the selection of the Dominican Republic as host. In the subsequent investigation, it was discovered that the friend's company was new and that he had no experience in providing these services.

In a subsequent conversation with these officials, the friend offered a kickback if his company was selected. The Dominican officials refused and ordered him out of their office. He did not know that they had recorded the entire conversation. The tape was sent to the USOC's president and was later released to the press and the Department of Justice for a potential violation of the Foreign Corrupt Practices Act.[1] Although the USOC's president vigorously denied releasing information, the executive committee ultimately forced her to resign. At the same time, Rogers was asked to investigate the allegations and report to the Ethics Oversight Committee.

There was concern among some on the ethics committee that an investigation would further tarnish the USOC's reputation. Much of the committee's internal deliberations focused on the question of how to *balance* a report that, at the same time, voiced members' concerns. Over Rogers's objection, the committee resolved to focus on the appearance of a conflict of interest.

According to informed sources, the executive committee of the USOC invited all ethics committee members to attend a meeting. However, before this could occur, the ethics committee chairman, via conference call, had the ethics committee by majority vote commit to the following: (1) no one would attend the meeting, (2) no one would respond to any questions, and (3) no one would make any recommendations. Given this, the executive committee voted to accept the report and take no action. As a result, Rogers, three members of the ethics committee, and one member of the executive committee resigned. Subsequently, the ethics committee chairman stated that Rogers seemed "out to get" Ward—no matter what—and vehemently denied Rogers's countercharge that the chairman's directions to him was "make this go away."

This resulted in considerable congressional interest because the federal government had given millions of dollars in cash and in-kind donations to the USOC, which had been incorporated by an act of Congress in 1950. There were several unsuccessful attempts by the executive committee to head off congressional involvement by announcing "major changes" and "internal reorganization." By that time, Senators Ben Nighthorse Campbell (R-Colorado), John McCain (R-Arizona), and Ted Stevens (R-Alaska) had entered the fray by arguing that the USOC was involved in a cover-up and illicit activities. They held hearings where the senior USOC leadership looked at least inept, if not corrupt. On March 1, 2003, CEO Lloyd Ward resigned. After additional accusations of misuse of funds and improper activities by Ward, the Senate forced the resignations of the USOC's chief financial officer and chief operating officer. The U.S. Senate appointed a commission to make recommendations on how to reorganize the USOC, and may dictate a new governance structure through legislation.

◆ ◆ ◆

Discussion Questions

1. What are the ethics principles and values involved here?
2. The USOC seemed to be doing the "right thing" by putting in place a new CEO, an ethics officer, and an ethics committee. Where did it go wrong? Or did it?
3. Was there anything wrong with Ward (the CEO) providing a letter of introduction? Did he do anything improper? What criteria do you use here?
4. Did the CEO's friend do anything improper? Would your answer be different to question 3 if the friend's company had had experience in this area?
5. Did the Ethics Oversight Committee operate effectively? What standards should be applied in evaluating its performance?
6. Was the issue for the committee in fact striking a balance between confronting ethics breaches and doing damage to the organization? If you were sitting on the 9ethics committee, how would you frame the problem, and why?
7. Should Congress weigh in so heavily in reorganizing what is, after all, a nonprofit organization? Why? Does operating in a political environment change the ethical principles and values at play?
8. Is a prominent nonprofit organization such as the USOC obliged to serve the public interest? To maintain impartiality? And to *appear* to do both? Why?

◆ ◆ ◆

Note

1. The U.S. Foreign Corrupt Practices Act of 1977 prohibits U.S. companies from bribing foreign officials for business purposes and includes substantial criminal penalties for firms and individuals. For details, see www.lectlaw.com/files/bur21.htm.

The Job Ahead

A few indelible words summarize the many values, diverse responsibilities, and anticipated trajectory of ethical public service. The preamble to the U.S. Constitution states, "We the people of the United States, in order to form a more perfect Union, establish justice, insure domestic tranquility, provide for the common defense, promote the general welfare, and secure the blessings of liberty to ourselves and our posterity, do ordain and establish this Constitution for the United States of America."

It is a testament to the wisdom of those who founded this republic that public servants swear an oath to uphold the Constitution, not to their boss, to the government, or even the mayor or president. And it is clear from the preamble that their responsibility is to the people, now and in the future.

Those same writers of the Constitution also understood the threat to liberty of unrestrained public power. "A dependence on the people is, no doubt, the primary control on the government; but experience has taught mankind the necessity of auxiliary precautions" (Federalist no. 51).

For that reason, Juvenal's renowned question from the second century, *Quis custodiet ipsos custodes?* or "Who guards the guardians?" is a permanent fixture in American public service. The question begets innumerable answers: oversight and watchdog agencies, internal controls, grand juries and congressional investigations, the courts, criminal statutes, and enforced standards of conduct. Yet rules and regulations alone are inadequate guarantees of ethical behavior.

Institutions are important to public integrity, but the character of public servants is critical. Excellent public service and good government rely first and foremost on good people with the character, vision, and courage to do the right thing. Drawing on their skills at moral reasoning (Chapter Six) and their devotion to the public interest (Chapter Three), public managers have an ethical responsibility to help define what the right thing is. T. S. Eliot warns us in *Murder in the Cathedral*, "The last temptation is the greatest treason: To do the right deed for the wrong reason." We also must beware of doing the right thing the wrong way and of confounding ends and means.

By oath, office, and profession, public managers voluntarily commit themselves to thoughtful, ethical action. President Theodore Roosevelt summed up the point that technical expertise alone is not up to the task: "To educate a man in mind, and not in morals, is to educate a menace to society."

Good counsel advises us to consent to a lifelong commitment and to anticipate change as experience and cognitive development move us to different places, different spaces (as Chapter Five explains). In this spirit, and to stress the inspirational role of mentor, model, or exemplar (the journal *Public Integrity* publishes a feature on exemplars) in order that we accept the role for ourselves, we offer Exhibit A.1.

To help set the stage, we turn to an age-old practice in ethics: telling a parable. This little story is about a new public manager. On his first day on the job, the new manager discovered on his desk three envelopes, left by the manager he was replacing. She had numbered the envelopes 1, 2, and 3 and marked each: "Advice. Open only in case of crisis."

The new manager faced his first crisis about six months later. The public was furious over the proposed tax increase. He opened the first envelope to read: "Call a press conference and blame me." He decided to follow her advice.

Within a year, the next crisis arose. This one was over the site of a low-security correctional facility. He opened the second envelope: "Blame chance events beyond your control." Again, he followed her advice.

When the third crisis came along, the manager opened the third and last envelope. Her advice: "Resign, and prepare three envelopes."

This little scenario emphasizes taking responsibility and shows that it cannot—and should not—be avoided in ethics or in public service.

Ethics in public service is a perpetual responsibility to implement and comply with the law, to serve the public interest, to avoid doing harm, to hold the future in stewardship, and to accommodate clashing definitions of what is right and important in public life.

The job ahead is no more and no less. From here we meet the ethics challenge in public service in the twenty-first century.

EXHIBIT A.1. VALUES AND VISION FOR
THE TWENTY-FIRST CENTURY.

To avoid losing sight of ethical values and principles even under crisis but especially in the press of humdrum routines, identify long-term guidelines for yourself. Using about a half-dozen virtues you prize, write yourself a memorandum describing yourself as you are now and the kind of person you wish to be after the next election or promotion.

To: My future self
From: Myself, a person of moral character
Subject: Personal integrity

Focal virtues I want to

Retain	Gain

The central principles and duties I want to guide my official actions include

I want to be like and be known as someone like (select role model and explain choice)

_____

_____

_____

For inspiration, write yourself a two- or three-sentence vision statement reflecting these statements. What will propel you to the office and drive your best efforts?

Print your name and the date five years from now on an envelope. Put this inside and seal.
Open on date indicated and re-examine your memorandum.

RESOURCE A

Chronology of Theoretical and Applied Ethics in Public Service (Work in Process)[1]

A people without history
Is not redeemed from time, for history is a pattern
Of timeless moments.

T. S. ELIOT, NOBEL LAUREATE (*FOUR QUARTERS,* "LITTLE GIDDING")

Key to Entry Classifications

Publications other than works of philosophy [A]
Corruption [C]
Human rights [H]
International or multinational initiative or agreement [I]
Laws and codes [L]
Media [M]
Philosophy [P]
Religion [R]

c. 19th century B.C.	Life of Abraham, biblical patriarch, whose halt (credited to divine intervention) to the sacrifice of his son Isaac teaches prohibition against human sacrifice. [R] [H]
18th century B.C.	Collection of laws and edicts of Hammurabi, King of Babylonia, as earliest complete known legal code; known as the Code of Hammurabi; sets forth in cuneiform legal procedure and penalties for unjust accusations, false testimony, judicial injustice, and other rules with the goals of "stable government and good rule" and that "the strong may not oppress the weak." [H] [L]

13th century B.C.	Prescriptions and proscriptions collectively known as the Ten Commandments (two biblical versions, in *Exodus* 20:1–17 and *Deuteronomy* 5:6–21); date to the Israelites' exodus from slavery during the reign of Egyptian Pharaoh Ramses II (19th dynasty); include prohibitions against idolatry, profanity, murder, theft, adultery, false witness, and covetousness; exodus led by Moses—Hebrew prophet and lawgiver. [R] [L]
c. 1200 B.C.	Introduction of Hinduism into ancient India; *dharma* refers to religious and moral precepts governing personal and social behavior and supports hierarchical (caste) social system based on *karma,* which determines status in cycle of reincarnation. [R]
c. 604–521 B.C.	Purported life of Chinese philosopher Lao-tze (Old Master), credited with authoring the *Tao Te Chin* (Classic of the Way of Virtue) and founding Taoism (The Way), which stresses acceptance and harmony with universe ("Be still like a mountain and flow like a great river"), development of virtue (notably the *Three Jewels* of compassion, moderation, and humility); China's state religion in 440–1911; whether actual historical figure is contested. [R]
563–483 B.C.	Life of Siddhartha Gautama, later called Buddha (Enlightened One), founder of Buddhism, whose core teachings include *Four Noble Truths* about suffering and the nature of human existence; *Noble Eightfold Path* (e.g., right thought, intent, action, contemplation); individual accountability through *karma* or intention for acts, their consequences, and operation of moral law; ultimate goal of *nirvana,* associated with compassion and equanimity. [R]
c. 551–479 B.C.	Life of Confucius, Chinese philosopher during Chou dynasty; teacher, magistrate, and provincial justice commissioner; teachings stress devotion to classical learning, parents, and rulers' moral excellence; disciples compile his philosophy that emphasizes virtues (e.g., being humane) and propriety. [R]
c. 500 B.C.	*Principles of Art of War,* attributed to Chinese General Sun Tzu; includes "All warfare is based on deception" (chapter 1), preference for strategy over battle, and recognition of costs of war. [A]

c. 496–406 B.C.   Life of Sophocles, author of *Antigone,* classic statement of difference and possible conflict between ethics and law. [P]

c. 460–377 B.C.   Life of Greek physician Hippocrates, formulater of Hippocratic Oath—a statement of physicians' professional and moral duties, including patient confidentiality; "Into whatever houses I enter, I will go into them for the benefit of the sick, and will abstain from every voluntary act of mischief and corruption." [L]

c. 410–399 B.C.   Codification of Athenian law. [L]

c. 399 B.C.   Sentencing of philosopher and teacher Socrates, found guilty of charges of impiety and guiding Athenian youth to filial irreverence, to die by drinking poison hemlock. [P]

c. 428–347 B.C.   Life of Plato, Greek philosopher, whose dialogues, including *The Republic, The Statesman,* and *The Laws,* address political questions of good government, right conduct, and justice. [P]

384–322 B.C.   Life of Aristotle, Greek philosopher, founder of formal study of logic, and author of *Nicomachean Ethics* and *Politics,* which argues that a political life develops the practical virtues, that proper goal of law is human welfare, and moderation is a virtue (golden mean). [P]

335–263 B.C.   Life of Zeno of Citium, founder of Stoicism, which argues all faculties in a unified soul are rational and passions are errors of judgment; influence on Plato. [P]

c. 0   Sermon on the Mount: collection of Jesus' religious and moral teachings (the Holy Bible, Matthew 5–7); includes mercy, peace, righteousness, forgiveness, and love. [R]

354–430   Life of Augustine, theologian and author of *The City of God,* argues that political authority restrains wickedness rather than promotes virtue. [P] [R]

570–632   Life of Mohammed (or Muhammad), to whom Muslims believe the holy book of Islam, the *Qur'an* (Koran), was revealed; teachings of moral, ethical, legal, and social conduct, submission to God, and individual responsibility for moral life and accountability at final judgment. [R]

1135–1204   Life of Rabbi Moses ben Maimon (Latin, *Maimonides;* referred to by acronym *Rambam*), born in Spain, court physician in Egypt, author of Jewish legal commentary

	and code; major philosophical work, *The Guide for the Perplexed*, combines Aristotelian philosophy with Jewish theory of law and ethical conduct. [P] [R]
1215	Signing of Magna Carta (Great Charter) by King John at Runnymede under threat of civil war; a source of basic principles in English law, including Clause 39, which prohibits arrest and imprisonment "except by the lawful judgment of his peers or by the law of the land." Clause 40 prohibits bribery: "To no one will we sell, to no one will we refuse or delay right or justice"; annulled by papal bull after two months but reissued in modified form in 1217 and 1225; underwent minor changes in 1297. [L]
1224–1274	Life of Thomas Aquinas, Dominican priest, theologian, teacher, author of *Summa Contra Gentiles* and *Summa Theologiae;* strongly influenced by Aristotle, whom he reintroduces to Western thought; provides systematic treatment of what evolves into "just war" theory. [P] [R]
1469–1527	Life of Niccolo Machiavelli, Florentine during Italian Renaissance, government official and author of *Discourses on Titus Livy* and *The Prince*, his best-known work, which offers largely secular perspective on political rule. [P]
1651	Publication of *Leviathan,* by Thomas Hobbes (1588–1679), English philosopher and royalist supporter who used reason (rather than authority) to argue on behalf of absolute sovereignty and drew on the concept of *social contract* among self-interested human beings. [P]
1620	Signing of the Mayflower Compact, which pledges to adopt laws for the public good ("most meete and convenient for the Generall Good of the Colonie"). [L]
1670	Publication of *Theologico-Political Treatise,* major work of political philosophy endorsing democracy by Baruch Spinoza (1632–1677), author of the posthumously published *Ethics.* [P]
1689	Publication of *Two Treatises of Government* and other works by John Locke (1632–1704), English political philosopher associated with moral and political individualism and distinction between private and public realms, the latter to secure peace and security for private pursuits in civil society based on voluntary consent. [P]

1712–1778	Life of Jean-Jacques Rousseau, who writes that "Man is born free, and everywhere in chains" (*Social Contract*) and argues that civil and political obligations cannot be based on natural law but rather through social contract, without which human beings are neither free nor moral; critical of John Locke and inspiration for Immanuel Kant. [P]
1734	Acquittal of John Peter Zengler, editor and printer of *New York Weekly Journal*, on charge of seditious libel; popularly credited with establishing freedom of the press in U.S. [M]
1739	Publication of *A Treatise of Human Nature* by David Hume (1711–1776), Scottish philosopher and historian, author of *The History of England* (vol. 1, 1754); provides critique of moral rationalism. [P]
1759	Publication of *The Theory of Moral Sentiments* by Scottish philosopher, teacher, and government official, Adam Smith (1723–1790), which draws on the notions of empathy, impartial spectator, and moral imagination that would heavily influence subsequent political philosophy and ethics; Smith's *An Inquiry into the Nature and Causes of the Wealth of Nations* (1776) argues on behalf of liberal, commercial society and complementary virtue, liberty, and prosperity. [P]
1773	Thomas Jefferson's writing of the Virginia Act for Establishing Religious Freedom, first legislation positing freedom of conscience as fundamental right; passed by Virginia State Legislature in 1785. [H] [L]
1776	Signing of the Declaration of Independence on July 4; this explanation for revolution is a formal statement of core values of nascent American political system. [L]
1784	Publication of the first successful daily newspaper, *Pennsylvania Packet & General Advertiser*, sets stage for media's watchdog role. [M]
1785	Publication of *Groundwork for the Metaphysics of Morals* by Prussian moral and political philosopher of European Enlightenment, Immanuel Kant, who espouses republican government, peace through international organization and law, unconditional human freedom and dignity, and deontological principle of categorical imperative; author of *Critique of Pure Reason* (1781), *Critique of Practical Reason* (1788), *Critique of Judgment* (1790), and other works. [P]

1787	Convening of the U.S. Constitutional Convention in Philadelphia. [L]
1787–1789	Publication of *The Federalist Papers,* supporting ratification of new U.S. Constitution (antifederalist counterarguments included); Federalist 51 argues for "necessity of auxiliary precautions" ("If men were angels, no government would be necessary"); 57 states, "The aim of every political constitution is, or ought to be, first to obtain for rulers men who possess most wisdom to discern, and most virtue to pursue, the common good of the society; and in the next place, to take the most effectual precautions for keeping them virtuous whilst they continue to hold their public trust." [L]
1789	Publication of *An Introduction to the Principles of Morals and Legislation* ("The Public Good ought to be the object of the legislator; General Utility ought to be the foundation of his reasonings") by Jeremy Bentham (1748–1832), English philosopher espousing utilitarian principle by which actions are judged by their effects on community members' happiness. [P]
1789	Establishment of U.S. Treasury Department as first domestic federal agency, with prohibition against conflict of interest and financial reward for whistle-blowers. [L]
1790	Signing, by Benjamin Franklin (1707–1790), as president of the Pennsylvania Abolition Society, a petition to U.S. Congress urging abolition of slavery and slave trade; suggests that virtues and ethics must be practiced, not just learned by rote. [H]
1791	Ratification, on December 15, of the Bill of Rights—ten original amendments to the U.S. Constitution. [L] [H]
1791	Accusation of Henry Knox, U.S. Secretary of War, of illegal land speculation in Maine to cover his wife's gambling debts. [C]
1792	Conduct of first congressional investigation: an inquiry into an Indian victory over federal troops. [C]
1798	Dismissal by U.S. Secretary of State Timothy Pickering of two clerks in passport office for accepting illegal gratuities. [C]

1804	Establishment of Haiti, first independent, black republic, after successful slave revolt in French colony. [H]
1807	Abolishment by British Parliament of slave trade after years of political action associated with evangelical William Wilberforce and Society of Friends (Quakers). [H]
1813–1855	Life of Søren Kierkegaard, Danish philosopher, first self-labeled existentialist; critiqued conventional morality and Christianity; focused on individualism, the personal, and subjectivity, as opposed to liberal conception of rationality and choice. [P]
1817	Initiation of two congressional investigations of President James Monroe. [C]
1818–1883	Life of Karl Marx, Prussian philosopher and social critic, strongly influenced by Hegel and Ludwig Feuerbach; espoused concept of alienation and dialectic progression of history based on class struggle (materialism), and advocated future communal ownership of means of production. [P]
1820	Banning of slavery, through Missouri Compromise, west of Mississippi River and north of 36°30' latitude, except in Missouri. [H]
1821	Publication of *Philosophy of Right* by Georg Wilhelm Friedrich Hegel (1770–1831), which espouses view that individual is subordinate to the state ("state in and by itself is the ethical whole") and sees history as progress; associated with dialectic and moral relativism. [P]
1827	Imprisonment of Dr. Tobias Watkins, first senior U.S. federal official imprisoned for embezzlement. [C]
1827	Absconding of Samuel Swartwout, Collector of Customs for New York City, to England with more than 5 percent of U.S. Treasury. [C]
1829	Issue, by U.S. Postmaster General Amos Kendall, of first Code of Conduct for federal employees. [L]
1833	Passage, by British Parliament, of the Slavery Abolition Act freeing all slaves in British Empire. [H] [L]
1837	Founding of the Aborigines' Protection Society in Great Britain; in 1909 merges with the Anti-Slavery Society, a public charity self-identified as the world's oldest continuing international human rights organization. [H]

1838	Forcing of Cherokee Native Americans to move to Oklahoma, along the "Trail of Tears." [H]
1839	Formation of British and Foreign Anti-Slavery Society (now Anti-Slavery International), dedicated to abolishing slavery worldwide. [H]
1845	Publication of autobiography by Frederick Douglass (c. 1817–1895), escaped slave, participant in Underground Railroad, advocate of slaves' right of rebellion and fugitive slaves' right of resistance; important to abolitionist and suffrage movements, Equal Rights Party's vice-presidential candidate in 1872; later U.S. minister to Haiti. [H]
1848	Publication of the *Communist Manifesto,* first published fruit of collaboration between Karl Marx and Friedrich Engels and declaration of socialist (later, Communist) doctrine, which ends with celebrated utopian vision of end to exploitation: "The proletarians have nothing to lose but their chains . . . workers of all countries, unite!" [P]
1848	Launch of women's rights movement in U.S. when Lucretia Mott and Elizabeth Cady Stanton, abolitionists and suffragists, call first women's rights convention at Seneca Falls, New York; declaration modeled after U.S. Declaration of Independence pronounces, "We hold these truths to be self-evident: that all men and women are created equal." [H]
1861	Publication of *Utilitarianism* by John Stuart Mill (1806–1873), English philosopher strongly influenced by utilitarianism of his father, James Mill, and Jeremy Bentham; adds qualitative differences to utilitarian calculus of hedonistic pleasures, with mental and spiritual pleasures rated superior ("Better to be a human being dissatisfied than a pig satisfied"); reformer as political activist and early advocate of women's suffrage and social reform. [P]
1863	Initiation of humanitarian movement now known as Red Cross by Henri Dunant and other Swiss; established initially as International Committee for Relief to the Wounded. [H]
1863	Declaration, on January 1, by President Abraham Lincoln, that all slaves residing in territory in rebellion against Union are to be freed. [H] [L]

1863	Passage of forerunner of the principal federal conflict-of-interest law, 18 U.S.C. Section 208 after Civil War scandals. [C] [L]
1864	Adoption by twelve governments of the first Geneva Convention to protect the war-wounded. [H] [I]
1864	Issue of General Order 212, which provides two-year jail sentence and $10,000 fine for public officials who represent private parties back to U.S. government, including Representatives and Senators. [C] [L]
1865	Deliverance, on Mar. 4, by President Lincoln of his Second Inaugural Address, a model of reconciliation: "with malice toward none; with charity for all; with firmness in the right . . . to bind up the nation's wounds." [H]
1868	Impeachment of President Andrew Johnson, first president impeached by House of Representatives, on grounds of alleged violations of the Tenure of Office Act; by one vote, Senate fails to convict. [C]
1868	Ratification of Fourteenth Amendment to U.S. Constitution; prohibits states from denying or abridging citizens' rights and requires states to grant all persons equal protection and due process. [H] [L]
1871	Petition sent to Congress, signed by Susan B. Anthony, Elizabeth Cady Stanton, and other suffragists, on behalf of voting rights for women. [H]
1883	Passage of Pendleton Act in effort to end spoils system and institute merit-based federal civil service. [C] [L]
1878	Founding of American Bar Association in August by 100 lawyers from 21 states; begins the U.S. legal profession; ethics standards, Model Rules of Professional Conduct first adopted in August 1983 and amended in 1987, 1989, 1990, 1991, 1992, 1993, 1994, 1995, 1997, 1998, 2000, and 2002. [L]
1883	Publication of *Thus Spake Zarathustra* by Friedrich Wilhelm Nietzsche (1844–1900), German philosopher, associated with existentialism espousing individualism and choice and opposing the 19th-century liberal concept of rationality; argues that traditional values represented by Christianity are weakening ("God is dead") and on

behalf of concept of superior or *overman*, later imported in vulgar usage into Nazi doctrine. [P]

1887   Publication of Woodrow Wilson's "The Study of Administration" in *Political Science Quarterly*; often cited as "founding" academic study of public administration, the article mentions neither ethics nor morals but does speak of duty; author becomes 28th U.S. president (1913–1921). [A]

1891   First publication, *On Aphasia*, by Sigmund Freud (1856–1939, Austrian), founder of psychoanalysis, who revolutionizes understanding of personality with its unconscious mental processes, including repression and resistance, and profoundly influences intellectual developments in ethics and many other fields. [A]

1900   Ratification of Geneva Convention, which protects belligerents, casualties, and prisoners of war in order "to serve . . . the interests of humanity and the ever increasing requirements of civilization." [H] [I]

1901   Beginning of Nobel Peace Prize by first annual awarding of Nobel Prize for achievements in physics, chemistry, medicine, literature and peace, as established in will of Alfred Nobel, inventor of dynamite (1866), and extended to economics in 1968 by the Bank of Sweden; Henri Dunant and Frederic Passy share first prize (http://www.nobel.no). [H]

1903   Publication of *The Souls of Black Folk* by W.E.B. Du Bois (1868–1963), founding officer of the National Association for the Advancement of Colored People, whose sociological and historical work focuses on duality of African American identity and who opposes Booker T. Washington's political strategy of conciliation for African Americans. [H]

1909   Founding of the National Association for the Advancement of Colored People (NAACP), whose legal challenges to segregation and discrimination play an important role in the development of U.S. human rights. [H]

1910   Passage of first U.S. comprehensive but weak campaign finance reform, Federal Corrupt Practices Act; revised in 1925 and replaced in 1971. [L]

1915	Beginning of genocide of Armenians by Ottoman Empire; lasts until 1923 and results in death of estimated 1.5 million people and many refugees. [H]
1919	Founding in Paris by five national societies in Britain, France, Italy, Japan, and United States of International Federation of Red Cross and Red Crescent Societies; 178 recognized societies today. [H] [I]
1920	Ratification of Nineteenth Amendment to the U.S. Constitution; grants women right to vote. [H] [I]
1921	Publication of first article on intelligence by Jean Piaget (1896–1980), Swiss cognitive psychologist whose groundbreaking work on children's intelligence and moral development influenced Lawrence Kohlberg. [A]
1924	Adoption of first ethics code by the International City/County Managers Association, which was founded in 1914 to promote professional local government management worldwide; amended in 1998. [L]
1922–1923	Years of the Teapot Dome scandal during the administration of U.S. President Warren G. Harding; involves secret leasing of naval oil reserve lands to private companies; becomes symbol of government graft and corruption. [C]
1927	Publication of *Being and Time* by Martin Heidegger (1889–1976), German philosopher, influenced by Kierkegaard and Nietzsche; associated with existentialism (which he later rejected); influenced Michel Foucault, author of *An Introduction to Metaphysics* (1953). [P]
1933	Extension of government help through President Franklin D. Roosevelt's New Deal to people hurt by the Great Depression; launched U.S. welfare state. [H] [L]
1935	Announcement of Nuremberg Race Laws at Congress of the National Socialist Workers' Party (NAZI), convened in Nuremburg, Germany, in September; laws include (1) the Law for the Protection of German Blood and German Honor, prohibiting intermarriage and extra-marital intercourse between Jews and Germans and the employment of German woman under age 45 in Jewish households, and (2) the Reich Citizenship Law,

	which deprives Jews of German citizenship and invidiously distinguishes between *Reich citizens* and *nationals*; these laws formalize and legalize heretofore unofficial Nazi oppression. [H] [L]
1935	Beginning of debate between Carl Friedrich and Herman Finer on the utility of internal versus external political-bureaucratic controls for ensuring ethical administrative behavior. [A]
1938	Enactment of Italy's government, under Mussolini, of anti-Semitic racial laws and regulations outlawing mixed marriages, expelling Jews from universities and ownership of certain property. [H]
1938	*Kristallnacht* or "Night of Broken Glass": November 9, pogroms in the Third Reich see murder of dozens of Jews, burning of synagogues, desecration of cemeteries, and wrecking and looting of Jewish businesses, hospitals, schools, and homes, while police and fire brigades stand by. [H]
1938	Adoption of first ethics code for public finance profession by Government Finance Officers Association, founded in 1906 as Municipal Finance Officers Association as professional association of state-provincial and local finance officers in U.S. and Canada; in 1989 approves revision that is still in force. [L]
1939	Passage of The Hatch Act, which restricts the political activity of federal executive branch employees and state and local government employees whose work is touched by federal funds; less restrictive amendments passed in 1993; U.S. Office of Special Counsel has jurisdiction. [C] [L]
1942	Wannassee Conference in January in Berlin; Rheinhard Heydrich (in charge of organizing extermination of European Jews), Adolph Eichmann (director of deportations to death camps), and 15 Nazi bureaucrats plan and organize the *Final Solution*, meaning annihilation of estimated 11 million Jews in Europe and Soviet Union. [H]
1945	First use of atom bomb in war, by U.S., on Hiroshima, Japan, on August 6. [H]
1945	Second use of atom bomb in war, by U.S., on Nagasaki, Japan, on August 9. [H]

1945	End of World War II with the surrender of Germany and Japan. [H] [I]
1945–1946	Conduct of year-long Nuremberg Trials (International Military Tribunal, including judges from Great Britain, France, U.S., and U.S.S.R.), of 24 major Nazi war criminals; establishes that obeying orders is in no way a justification for inhumane behavior. [H] [I]
1948	Adoption, on December 10, by the General Assembly of the United Nations, of the Universal Declaration of Human Rights, which proclaims the right to life, liberty, and security of person; prohibits slavery and more. [H] [I]
1948	Assassination of Mohandas Karamchand Gandhi (revered as sage, Mahatma; born 1869), seen as a spiritual ascetic; developed philosophy and techniques of nonviolence (*satyagraha*, derived from Hinduism), civil disobedience, and passive resistance (noncooperation) in political struggle and evolved into international symbol of same; leader in struggles for civil and political rights for Indians in South Africa (1893–1914) and India's independence from Great Britain (granted in 1947); opponent of the caste system and untouchability and advocate of Hindu-Muslim concord. [H]
1948	Enactment of apartheid laws in South Africa that institutionalize racial discrimination and segregation; ensuing laws systematize apartheid (*Afrikaans* for apartness). [H]
1949	Signing, in August, of four Geneva Conventions, supplemented by two protocols in June 1977. [H] [I]
1949	Publication of *A Sand County Almanac* by Aldo Leopold, U.S. forester, scientist, and conservationist who helped popularize link between ecology and ethics: "That land is a community is the basic concept of ecology, but that land is to be loved and respected is an extension of ethics." [A]
1950	Passage of Population Registration Act requiring that all South Africans be classified into racial categories of white, black (African or Bantu), or colored (mixed decent); category of "Asian" later added; government's Department of Home Affairs responsible for classifying citizenry. [H]

1950–1951	Investigations by the Kefauver Commission (headed by Senator Estes Kefauver), a crime-investigating committee, reveal that organized crime still operates in U.S. [C]
1951	Hearings chaired by U.S. Senator Paul Douglas of Illinois; corruption charges are presented against Rural Recovery Administration, Internal Revenue Service, and the Department of Justice. [C]
1954	Prohibition of racial discrimination in schools enacted into law; on May 17, the 1896 *Plessy v. Ferguson* decision overturned by U.S. Supreme Court; racial segregation in public schools prohibited in Brown *v.* Board of Education of Topeka, Kansas, *as a violation of* the U.S. Constitution; Thurgood Marshall argues for NAACP that fourteenth amendment's *equal protection clause* prohibits "separate but equal" facilities. [H] [I]
1955	Refusal by Rosa Louise Parks, a member of the local branch of the NAACP, to relinquish her seat on a bus in Montgomery, Alabama; she is arrested and fined for her personal defiance of *de jure* racial segregation; her act leads to the 1956 bus boycott; in 1992 her autobiography is published; in 1996 she is awarded the U.S. government's highest civilian honor, the Presidential Medal of Freedom, and in 1999 receives the Congressional Gold Medal. [H]
1956	Adoption by U.N. of Supplementary Convention on the Abolition of Slavery. [H] [I]
1958	Adoption by Congress, in July, of 10-point "Code of Ethics for Government Service for all federal officeholders and employees, whom the code exhorts to (1) "Put loyalty to the highest moral principles and to country above loyalty to [g]overnment, persons, party, or department and (10) be "ever conscious that public office is a public trust." [L]
1961	Publication of *The History of Madness in the Classical Age* by Michel Foucault (1926–1984), French psychologist, historian, and philosopher; closely associated with postmodernism, whose work inverts Kantian epistemology, arguing scientific objectivity and rationality are artifacts and conventional; sees "man" as epistemological concept and explicitly treats ethical issues in studies of Greek and

	Roman sexuality (The Use of Pleasure and The Care of the Self, 1984); author of *The Order of Things* (1966), *The Archaeology of Knowledge* (1969). [P]
1961	Call issued for international campaign on behalf of "prisoners of conscience" by Peter Benenson and British newspaper, *Observer;* launch of Amnesty International, a global advocacy organization for human rights; recipient of Nobel Peace Prize in 1977 and United Nations Human Rights Award in 1978. [H] [I]
1962	Execution of Adolph Eichmann (born 1906), head of Gestapo's Department of Jewish Affairs in 1941–1945 and director of deportations to death camps, after being kidnapped by agents of Israel's Mossad in Argentina; tried in Israel in 1961; found guilty of crimes against the Jewish people, crimes against humanity, and war crimes; defense of "just obeying orders" is rejected. [H]
1962	Codification of U.S. federal conflict-of-interest statutes (18 U.S.C. Section 208). [C] [L]
1962	Publication of *The Structural Transformation of the Public Sphere* by Jurgen Habermas (b. 1929), German sociologist and philosopher, associated with Frankfurt School of critical theory, concept of "public sphere," discourse theory of deliberative democracy, and critique of positivism that opens way for using critical social theory for political consciousness and activism; author of *The Theory of Communicative Action* (vol. 1, 1984; vol. 2, 1989). [P]
1963	Launch, in April, of Martin Luther King Jr.'s (1929–1968) crusade for nonviolent resistance to unjust laws; ordained as a Baptist minister and doctor of theology, a leader of the U.S. civil rights movement, and an international symbol of nonviolent resistance and racial justice, sets out arguments for moral responsibility to disobey unjust laws (civil disobedience) in *Letter from Birmingham City Jail*; gains national prominence as a leader of 1956 bus boycott in Montgomery, Alabama; founds, in 1957, the Southern Christian Leadership Conference (dedicated to nonviolent protest); stirring appeal to Christian morals and American ideals in the speech, "I Have a Dream," delivered in August 1963; passage of the 1964 Civil Rights Act traced, in part, to

his letter and speech; wins the Nobel Peace Prize in 1964; assassination in Memphis in April 1968 provokes riots in more than 100 U.S. cities; Congress designates national holiday in his honor in 1983. [H]

1964	Enactment of Civil Rights Act, which prohibits discrimination in voting and jobs in U.S. [H] [L]
1965	Passage of Voting Rights Act, which prohibits race, color, or previous condition from affecting right to vote and requires uniform standards for voting qualifications in U.S. [H] [L]
1965	Issue of Executive Order 11222 by President Lyndon B. Johnson; code of conduct for executive branch links public confidence and trust to integrity of public officials in conduct of official duties. [L]
1967	Appointment of Thurgood Marshall (1908–1993), chief counsel for the NAACP Legal Defense and Education Fund, renowned for arguing *Brown v. Board of Education* of Topeka, Kansas in 1954, as first African American justice on the U.S. Supreme Court. [H]
1970	Passage of Racketeer Influenced and Corrupt Organizations Act (RICO), part of U.S. Organized Crime Control Act, which grants law enforcement broad power to fight organized crime; subsequently evolves broad applications. [C] [L]
1971	Publication of *A Theory of Justice* by American political philosopher John Rawls (1921–2002), whose work, in tradition of classic liberalism, draws on Jean Jacques Rousseau's "social contract" theory and Immanuel Kant's deontological perspective; argues that principles of justice can be justified only if free and rational persons, from behind a veil of ignorance (unaware of their place in society), would choose such principles to govern the basic structure of society; basic principles of Rawl's *justice as fairness* formulation are (1) individual has right to broadest liberty compatible with same for others, and (2) inequalities in wealth and power are just only when they can be reasonably expected to advantage those who are worst off; poses *veil of ignorance* to safeguard distributive justice in decision making; provides philosophical basis for social equity in the New Public Administration. [P]

1972	Beginning of the Watergate scandal on June 17, when five men are arrested while trying to bug the offices of the Democratic National Committee at the Watergate hotel and office complex. [C]
1973	Resignation, on October 10, of Vice President Spiro Theodore Agnew; plea of "no contest" to single charge of failing to report income received in 1967 brings a $10,000 fine and three years of probation; Representative Gerald R. Ford assumes vice presidency under 25th amendment to U.S. Constitution (passed February 10, 1967) that defines presidential succession. [C]
1974	Resignation, on August 8, of Richard M. Nixon, first U.S. president to resign after House Judiciary Committee approves three articles of impeachment based on evidence gleaned in congressional Watergate investigations; Vice President Gerald Ford is sworn in as president. [C]
1974	Issue of pardon by President Ford, on September 8, of former President Nixon; Nixon accepts an unconditional pardon for all federal crimes that Nixon "committed or may have committed or taken part in" while in office. [C]
1974	Release of model ethics law by Common Cause, founded in 1970 by John Gardner; overhauled in 1989. [L]
1974	Passage of California's Political Reform Act, which requires every government agency—local and state—to adopt a Conflict of Interest Code; approved by referendum in 1990, Proposition 112 adds the Ethics in Government Act and the Post-Government Employment Restrictions Act to the 1974 act. [L]
1974	Publication of *Anarchy, State, and Utopia* by American political philosopher Robert Nozick (1938–2002), libertarian advocate of minimal state and individual rights (including "floor of equality") and opponent of liberalism's using state to pursue distributive justice; argues state's intrusion on individual choice coercively infringes on liberty; challenges liberalism associated with John Rawls. [P]
1974	Creation of Hong Kong's Independent Commission against Corruption, in response to pervasive bribery (e.g., "backdoor route" and "tea money"); adopts a triple focus on investigation, prevention, and education; then

	develops Hong Kong Ethics Development Center (business ethics) and ICAC Moral Education Web. [C]
1976	Publication of initial Norwegian version of *Ecology, Community, and Lifestyle* by Arne Naess, Norwegian philosopher, environmental activist, and founder of the *Deep Ecology* movement, which accords nonhuman life or nature value independent of human utility and extends ethical consideration to all life. [P]
1977	Passage of U.S. Foreign Corrupt Practices Act that prohibits U.S. companies from bribing foreign officials for business purposes and includes substantial criminal penalties for firms and individuals. [C] [L]
1977	Ethics Resource Center founded.
1977	Death of Stephen Biko (born 1946), Bantu intellectual and political activist; among founders of South African Students' Organization in 1968 and its first president; inspiration to student movements central to 1976 uprisings; expelled from medical school and movement limited (banned and restricted); arrested at roadblock and subsequent death from brutal treatment in detention draws international condemnation; author of famous statement of hope: "In time, we shall be in a position to bestow on South Africa the greatest possible gift: a more human face." [H]
1977	Initiation of Sullivan Principles by Reverend Leon Sullivan, member of board of directors of General Motors, large employer in South Africa; aimed at persuading U.S. companies to treat South African employees like U.S. counterparts; uses economic pressure to undermine apartheid and advance human rights and justice. [H] [C]
1978	Passage of Ethics in Government Act (Pub. L. 95–521, 92 Stat. 1824–1867), which establishes Office of Government Ethics to prevent and resolve executive employees' conflicts of interest and promote impartiality and integrity. [L]
1978	Passage of Independent Counsel Law, originally enacted as Title VI of the Ethics in Government Act of 1978; provides for court-appointed independent counsels (originally, special prosecutors) to investigate criminal allegations against high government officials. [C] [L]

1978	U.S. Congress passes the Civil Service Reform Act of 1978, establishing the Office of Special Counsel to protect whistle-blowers from retaliation for reporting waste, fraud, and abuse; first office ever created for this express purpose. [L]
1978	Publication of Aristotle's *De Motu Animalium* (1978) by Martha Nussbaum (born 1947), U.S. feminist philosopher in tradition of liberalism and individualism; associated with feminist critique of liberalism; author of *Sex and Social Justice* (1999). [P]
1979	Delivery of speech (his *malaise* speech) by President Jimmy Carter describing a crisis of America's spirit and a lack of confidence in America's purpose and its future; his approval ratings decline as result of public's response.
1980	U.S. Congress passes unanimously and president signs the federal ethics code (P.L. 96–303), with mandatory posting in every federal building; code developed by Ethics Resource Center. [L]
1981	Publication of Lawrence Kohlberg's *The Philosophy of Moral Development: Moral Stages and the Idea of Justice*, an influential work of developmental psychology that details moral reasoning at various stages of cognitive development. [A]
1981	Adoption of ethical principles by American Society for Public Administration (founded in 1939); its first code is adopted in 1984 and revised in 1994. [C]
1982	Publication of *In a Different Voice* by Carol Gilligan; influences study of women's moral development and offers critical response to justice perspective associated with Kant, Rawls, and Kohlberg; critique developed by Martha Nussbaum, Susan Okin, and others; inspires development of "ethics of care" based on relationships, contrasted with "ethics of justice" based on rights and principles. [A]
1983	Convening of first International Anti-Corruption Conference (IACC) in Washington D.C. as mechanism for information exchange and networking among anticorruption law enforcement agencies; meets biennially hereafter. [C] [I]

1984	Publication of *Caring: A Feminine Approach to Ethics and Moral Education* by educator Nel Noddings, proponent of caring as basis for moral action and relationships rather than principles as basis for moral development; inspiration for perspective termed ethic of care. [A]
1984	Adoption by New Jersey of American Bar Association's Model Rules of Professional Conduct; first state to do so. [L]
1985	Appointment by President Ronald Reagan of the Packard Commission (in response to defense industry scandal, "Ill Wind"); recognizes limits of federal regulation and recommends corporate self-governance that evolves in 1986 into Defense Industry Initiative on Business Ethics and Conduct. [C] [L]
1985	Formation of first business ethics office at General Dynamics by Ethics Resource Center. [L]
1986	Endorsement by Canada's Institute of Public Administration of its *Statement of Principles Regarding the Conduct of Public Employees.* [L]
1987	Tower Report on Iran-Contra issued in November, authored by Special Review Board appointed by President Ronald Reagan and headed by Senator John Tower of Texas; points to president's management style as factor contributing to wrongdoings. [A]
1988	Memorandum issued from director of U.S. Office of Government Ethics, Judge Frank Nebeker, on the investigation of Attorney General Edwin Meese III, stating that "simply avoiding criminal conduct is not the mark of public service." [L]
1988	Use of chemical weapons against Kurdish village, Halabja, by Iraqi regime under Saddam Hussein, killing thousands. [H]
1989	International outcry provoked by bloody army crackdown on student "democracy" protesters in Beijing's Tiananmen Square, People's Republic of China, in June; picture of one person halting tank column comes to symbolize what an individual can accomplish in pursuit of freedom. [H]

1989	Separation of U.S. Office of Government Ethics from Office of Personnel Management; becomes a separate agency under Office of Government Ethics Reauthorization Act. [L]
1989	Issue of Executive Order 12674, by President George H. W. Bush, on standards of conduct for federal executive branch employees. [L]
1989	Enactment of Whistle Blower Protection Act; simplifies whistle-blowers' proof of retaliation by their agencies and gives whistle-blowers increased procedural protections, guarantees of confidentiality, and right to appeal to Merit Systems Protection Board. [L]
1989	Issue of report, *To Serve with Honor,* by President's Commission on Federal Ethics Law. [A]
1989	Issue of Executive Order 12674, by President George H. W. Bush, which adds limits on outside earned income to standards of conduct for federal executive branch employees. [L]
1990	Announcement by signatories of Defense Industry Initiative on Business Ethics and Conduct (based on findings of President Reagan's blue ribbon commission appointed in 1985) that they obligate themselves to monitor their compliance with federal procurement laws and voluntarily disclose violations and corrective actions; group accounts for about half of all U.S. Defense Department's contract funds. [C] [L]
1990	Establishment of Center for Public Integrity that forms the International Consortium of Investigative Journalists in 1997 to support "watchdog journalism in the public interest." [M]
1991	Announcement of repeal of last remaining apartheid laws by South African Prime Minister F. W. de Klerk. [H]
1991	Fines raised for white-collar crimes by U.S. Sentencing Guidelines for Organizations; fines reduced if "effective program for preventing and detecting" wrongdoing is in place and company cooperates with investigation. [C] [L]
1991	Media report navy's mishandling of sexual assault scandal, called Tailhook. [C] [H]

1992	Publication of *Reinventing Government* by David Osborne and Ted Gaebler, which popularizes entrepreneurial management that is oriented to customers and performance—in government; neither "ethics" nor "morality" is listed in index. [A]
1992	Formal Establishment by Executive Order 12805, in May, of President's Council on Integrity and Efficiency as coordinating body for Inspectors General and Executive Council on Integrity and Efficiency to foster integrity, economy, and effectiveness. [L]
1992	Founding of Ethics Officer Association for managers of ethics and compliance programs in business and nonprofit agencies in U.S. and other countries, as cross-industry network to supplement DII (1990). [L] [I]
1993	Launch of fight against global corruption by Transparency International, a nongovernmental organization. [L] [I]
1993	Establishment of first U.N. special tribunal, International Criminal Tribunal for Yugoslavia, to prosecute war crimes and genocide; former Yugoslav President Slobodan Milosevic is among defendants. [H] [I]
1994	Establishment of Canada's Office of Ethics Counsellor, with responsibility for the conflict-of-interest and post-employment code for public officials and lobbyists' registration and code. [L]
1994	Establishment of Great Britain's Committee on Standards in Public Life. [L]
1994	Increase in efforts by Office of Government Ethics to participate in foreign governments' anticorruption efforts after Conference on Ethics in Government organized by Office of Government Ethics in cooperation with U.S. Information Agency, at request of federal foreign policy-making agencies. [C] [I]
1994	Launch of investigation by independent counsel Kenneth W. Starr of alleged financial improprieties in Whitewater land deal in Arkansas by President William Jefferson Clinton and First Lady Hillary Rodham Clinton. [C]

1994	Inauguration, in May, of Nelson Rolihlahla Mandela (born 1918) as president of South Africa; a leader of the struggle against apartheid and of African National Congress (formed in 1912 and outlawed in 1960); serves until June 1999; statement at the opening of the Rivonia Trial before Pretoria Supreme Court in April 1964 concludes, "I have fought against white domination, and I have fought against black domination. I have cherished the ideal of a democratic and free society in which all persons live together in harmony and with equal opportunities;" in June 1964, he and seven co-defendants found guilty and sentenced to life imprisonment; released in February 1990; received Nobel Peace Prize in 1993. [H]
1994	Establishment of U.N.'s second special international criminal tribunal to prosecute those responsible for war crimes and genocide, primarily against Tutsis, in Rwanda; other tribunals follow. [H] [I]
1995	Massacre of more than 7,000 Muslim men during war in Bosnia by Bosnian Serbs; Srebrenica known as worst war crime in Europe since World War II. [H]
1995	Authorization of establishment of the Truth and Reconciliation Commission; South Africa's Promotion of National Unity and Reconciliation Act, No. 34, based on the final clause of the Interim Constitution of 1993, confronts events under apartheid, including human rights violations on all sides of the conflict. [H]
1995	Proposal by Economic and Social Council of the United Nations to Draft International Code of Conduct for Public Office Holders. [L] [I]
1995	Publication of Model Ethics Law by Council on Governmental Ethics Laws; council formally established in 1978, consisting of executives of federal and state ethics agencies; by 2003, identifies ethics programs in 43 U.S. states, 11 major U.S. cities, and all Canadian provinces. [L]
1995	Passage, in December, of Lobbying Disclosure Act, requiring registration with House and Senate by individuals making lobbying contact with specified government officials and employees. [C] [L]

1996	Debut of *Public Integrity*, an annual publication that becomes a quarterly journal in 1997. [A]
1996	World Bank, pinpointing corruption as the single greatest obstacle to development, is publicly committed by its president to fighting corruption at World Bank-International Monetary Fund meeting; adopts anticorruption strategy in 1997. [C] [I]
1996	Adoption, in March, by General Assembly of the Organization of American States, of Inter-American Convention Against Corruption; convention becomes effective in March 1997. [C] [I]
1996	The Republic of South Africa establishes the Registrar of Assets for the Parliament. This office investigates ethical issues involving parliamentarians and publishes their annual financial disclosure statements on the Internet. [C]
1997	Release by International Monetary Fund, with 184 member countries, of *Guidance Note* on good governance to implement its commitment to combating corruption. [C] [I]
1997	Adoption of anticorruption strategy and action program in Lima, Peru, by Eighth International Conference against Corruption Issues, 93 countries participating; Lima Declaration states that corruption "erodes the moral fabric of every society." [C] [I]
1997	Creation of Ethics Section of American Society for Public Administration; first officers elected in 1998.
1998	Adoption of Recommendation on Improving Ethical Conduct in the Public Service, by Organization for Economic Co-operation and Development, with 35 signatory countries; its Programme on Public Management and Governance (PUMA) based on its Principles for Managing Ethics in the Public Service: "Although governments have different cultural, political, and administrative environments, they often confront similar ethical challenges, and the responses in their ethics management show common characteristics." [C] [I]
1998	Release of report by Independent Counsel Kenneth W. Starr September 10; report of investigation of President Clinton's actions with respect to perjury and obstruction of justice. [A]

1998	Impeachment, on December 19, of President Clinton, second U.S. president to be impeached by U.S. House of Representatives.
1998	Establishment of the International Criminal Court, with jurisdiction to prosecute genocide, war crimes, and crimes against humanity and based in The Hague; court established by the Rome Statute and adopted by 120 countries participating in United Nations Conference; first permanent, treaty-based international criminal court. [H] [I]
1998	Publication of *Three Seductive Ideas* by Jerome Kagan, the developmental psychologist who refutes fallacies such as "infant determinism" and argues on behalf of humans' capacity for change and growth and that humans are motivated by a biologically based concern for right and wrong and empathy. [A]
1999	Declaration issued, by first Global Forum on Fighting Corruption, in February: "we emerge persuaded that corruption is not inevitable" (Declaration on Safeguarding Integrity among Justice and Security Officials); hosted by U.S. Vice President Al Gore and with participants from 90 countries; further, "Corruption, dishonesty and unethical behavior among public officials represent serious threats to the basic principles and values of government, undermining public confidence in democracy and threatening to erode the rule of law" (Guiding Principles). [C] [I]
1999	United Nations Department of Economic and Social Affairs' Division for Public Economics and Public Administration launches project to assist African governments in enhancing ethics policies and anticorruption programs in their public services. [C] [I]
1999	Activation, in February, of Convention on Combating Bribery of Foreign Public Officials in International Business Transactions of the Organization for Economic Cooperation and Development. [C] [I]
1999	Resignation of twenty-member executive committee of European Commission, in March, over allegations of pervasive, chronic corruption in the bureaucracy it oversees. [C] [I]

1999	Issue of Durban Commitment on Corruption; with participants from 135 countries meeting in Durban and opened by South Africa's President H. D. Thabo Mbeki, the Ninth International Anti-Corruption Conference (IACC) declares "one of the most debilitating legacies of the twentieth century." [C] [I]
1999	Creation of the Organization for Economic Co-operation and Development's on-line ethics information center. [I]
1999	Initiation of global compact; U.N. Secretary General Kofi Annan and Leon Sullivan (Sullivan Principles, 1977) initiate global compact based on Sullivan Principles of Corporate Social Responsibility and advocate corporate support of human rights, just treatment of labor, and environmental responsibility. [H] [I]
2000	Issue, in January, of the Declaration of the Stockholm International Forum on the Holocaust; states that the "Holocaust (*Shoah*) fundamentally challenged the foundations of civilization" and that the "unprecedented character of the Holocaust will always hold universal meaning." [H] [L]
2000	Adoption, in July, of International Monetary Fund's code of conduct for members of its executive board. [L] [I]
2000	Issue of Organization for Economic Cooperation and Development's "Trust in Government: Ethics Measures in OECD Countries." [C] [I]
2000	End of Starr's investigation, September 20; after six years of investigation costing more than $50 million, Starr concludes that there is insufficient evidence to charge President and Mrs. Clinton with criminal wrongdoing in the Whitewater case. [C]
2001	Admission by President Clinton, in January, under an agreement with Independent Counsel Robert Ray, that prior to leaving office he knowingly gave misleading testimony about Monica Lewinsky; accepts suspension of his license to practice law, a fine, and any claim to repayment of his legal fees in return for termination of Whitewater investigation and freedom from criminal prosecution. [C]

2001	Issue of declaration, Defeating Corruption Through Integrity, Transparency and Accountability; at The Hague, Netherlands, Second Global Forum on Fighting Corruption, hosted by Dutch government and cosponsored by U.S. [C] [I]
2001	Signing of USA PATRIOT Act (P.L. 107–56) into law on October 26 and later Homeland Security Act of 2002 (H.R. 5005); acts reorganize many parts of U.S. federal government; legislation follows the September 11 act of international terrorism in which four hijacked airplanes kill thousands at three sites, including the World Trade Center in New York City, the Pentagon, and Shankesville, Pennsylvania. [H] [L]
2001	Collapse of Enron, an energy-trading firm; bankruptcy is declared in December, draining billions of dollars from creditors, shareholders, and employee pension plans; report of the Permanent Subcommittee on Investigations finds that members of Enron's board of directors failed in their fiduciary responsibility. [C]
2002	Publication of John M. Doris's *Lack of Character: Personality and Moral Behavior,* in which empirical studies support "situationalism" and refute moral character as basis of ethical behavior. [A]
2002	Finding of guilt, by Texas jury, of audit firm of Arthur Andersen, on charges of obstruction of justice for destroying documents during Security and Exchange Commission's investigation of Enron. [C]
2002	Signing into law, in July, of corporate responsibility legislation (Sarbanes-Oxley Act of 2002); provides tougher penalties for fraud and holds executives personally responsible for their corporate financial statements; follows in response to numerous accounting scandals that led to bankruptcy filings of Enron, WorldCom, and Global Crossing. [L]
2002	Meeting of the First United Nations Interagency Anti-Corruption Coordination in Vienna, Austria. [C] [I]
2002	Seizure, by U.S. Naval Academy in Annapolis, of nearly 100 student computers suspected of storing downloaded music and movies in violation of copyright law. [C]

2002   Ratification of International Criminal Court (1998); its statute enters into force. [H] [I]

2003   Looting in April of Iraq's National Museum of Antiquities, allegedly by mob and professional thieves during U.S. military action in Iraq; outcry from international community often articulated in terms of "duty to preserve history and art for future generations"; by June it is learned that the damage and theft, while severe, are far less serious than initially reported. [H] [I]

2003   Provision by U.S. Air Force of first official accounting (resulting from a congressional probe) of reports of sexual assaults at Colorado Springs service academy; policy for handling such charges revamped in June. [C] [L]

2003   Enactment of U.S. federal law, Health Insurance Portability and Accountability Act (HIPAA, passed in 1996), with aim of ensuring privacy, security, and confidentiality of patients' medical records. [L]

2003   Meeting of Third Global Forum on Fighting Corruption and Safeguarding Integrity in Seoul, Korea. [C] [I]

2003   Meeting of Eleventh International Anti-Corruption Conference (IACC) in Seoul, Korea. [C] [I]

2003   Issue of Organization for Economic Co-operation and Development's (OECD) Recommendation on Guidelines for Managing Conflict of Interest in the Public Service: "Serving the public interest is the fundamental mission of governments and public institutions." [C] [I]

2003   Release of Peru's government-appointed Truth and Reconciliation Commission report on atrocities committed in 1980–2000 during fighting by government forces, Shining Path guerrillas, peasant militias, and others. [H]

2003   Acceptance of Nobel Peace Prize by Shirin Ebadi, Iran's first female judge, activist in opposition to oppression of women. [H]

2003   Signing of U.N.'s Anti-Corruption Convention in Merida, Mexico. [C] [I]

◆ ◆ ◆

Note

1. Readers are encouraged to suggest additional entries, especially on developments outside the United States. The U.S. and contemporary tilt reflects this book's dominant audience and, necessarily, the authors' own interests and limitations.

   Criteria for selection include historical and contemporary relevance (as innovative, enduring, or otherwise core contribution) to the development of theory and practice in ethics; the number of adherents or cultures affected, and strong association with a particular moral perspective. Key topics include corruption, human rights, international and multinational initiative or agreement, laws and codes, media developments, philosophic and religious contributions, and empirical works and other publications of special note.

   Special thanks are extended to Chris Guiletti, graduate student at the University of Connecticut, for his research assistance, and colleagues Bayard L. Catron, James Heichelbech, and Morton J. Tenzer for their comments and suggestions on numerous entries.

RESOURCE B

Selected Internet Resources

Print and Electronic Journals, Newsletters, and News Media Links

Public Administration Review — http://www.aspanet.org/publications/par/index2.html

Public Integrity (American Society for Public Administration's Ethics Section) — http://www.publicintegrity.org

Ethics & Justice — http://www.members.tripod.com/~s_hayes/

Ethics Today, newsletter of Ethics Section of American Society for Public Administration — http://www.unpan.org/namerica-aspa-ethics.asp

Federal Ethics Report and *Ethics in Government Reporter* (CCH Washington Service Bureau) — http://secnet.cch.com

Global Virtue Ethics Review — http://www.govt.ucsd.edu/newjour/g1/msg02415.html

The Journal of Ethics via Society for Ethics — http://www.rohan.sdsu.edu/faculty/corlett.se.html

Journal of Power and Ethics	http://www.spaef.com/JPE_PUB/index.html
State Capitals Newsletters	http://www.statecapitals.com
States News	http://www.statesnews.org
CNN	http://www.cnn.com and search via key words (e.g., integrity, corruption)
BBC	http://news.bbc.co.uk and search via key words
The New York Times	http://www.nytimes.com and search via key words
The Straits Times, Singapore	http://straitstimes.asia1.com.sg
The Washington Post	http://www.washingtonpost.com

Professional Associations and Standards of Conduct

American Bar Association Standing Committee on Professionalism	http://www.abanet.org
American Society for Public Administration	http://www.aspanet.org
American Society for Public Administration (ethics section via ASPA homepage)	http://www3.niu.edu/~tp0dcm1/aspa/ethicsec/index.htm
American Society for Public Administration (compendium of resources)	http://www.aspanet.org/ethicscommunity/compendium/
Association of Inspectors General via homepage	http://www.lib.jjay.cuny.edu/ig/front11.htm
Council on Governmental Ethics Laws	http://www.cogel.org
Ethics Officer Association (for corporate and nonprofit ethics and compliance programs)	http://www.eoa.org
International Association of Chiefs of Police	http://www.theiacp.org

National Association of State Budget Officers	http://www.nasbo.org (see module 12 of the training program for Standards of Professional Conduct)
International City/County Management Association	http://www.icma.org/abouticma/ ethics/index.cfm
National Association of State Budget Officers Guidelines for Common Ethics Questions	http://www1.icma.org/main/ bc.asp?bcid=40thsid=1+ssid2=24
International Personnel Management Association	http://www.ipma-hr.org

Public Interest, Research, and Academic Organizations and Institutes

Internet Center for Corruption Research	http://wwwuser.gwdg.de/~uwvw/ corruption.index.html
Association for Practical and Professional Ethics	http://php.ucs.indiana.edu/ ~appe.home.html
Australian Association for Professional & Applied Ethics	http://www.arts.unsw.edu.au.aapae
Center for Business Ethics, Bentley College	http://ecampus.bentley.edu/dept/ cbe/
Center for Business Ethics (links to external resources)	http://ecampus.bentley.edu/dept/ cbe/resources/ethicsorgs_ domestic.html
Center for Public Integrity	http://www.publicintegrity.org/ dtaweb/home.asp
Center for Responsive Politics	http://www.crp.org
Center for the Study of Ethics in the Professions	http://www.iit.edu/~csep
Common Cause	http://www.commoncause.org
Council of State Governments	http://www.csg.org
Ethics on the World Wide Web (with extensive links)	http://commfaculty.fullerton.edu/ lester/ethics/ethics_list.html
Ethics Resource Center	http://www.ethics.org

Ethics Resource Center (links)	http://www.ethics.org/resources/links.cfm
Institute for Business & Professional Ethics (extensive links)	http://www.depaul.edu/ethics/
Institute for Global Ethics	www.globalethics.org
Institute for Global Ethics weekly newsletter	http://www.globalethics.org/newsline/members/index.tmpl
Institute for the Study of Applied and Professional Ethics	http://www.dartmouth.edu/artsci/ethics-inst.html
National Conference of State Legislatures	http://www.ncsl.org
Pew Center for the States	http://www.stateline.org
Society for Ethics	http://www.rphan.sdsu.edu/faculty/corlett/se.html
Transparency International, U.S. chapter	http://www.transparency-usa.org
University of South Queensland, Australia	http://www.usq.edu.au/dvc/ETHICS

Codes of Conduct

Illinois Institute of Technology Center for the Study of Ethics in the Professions: Codes of Ethics Online Project	http://www.iit.edu/departments/csep/PublicWWW/codes/
Online Ethics Center for Engineering and Science, with links to codes and case materials	http://www.cwru.edu.affil/wwwethics
Common Cause, *A Model Ethics Law for State Government* (1989) via homepage	http://www.commoncause.org/states/elaw_intro.htm

Council on Governmental
Ethics Laws, *A Model Law for
Campaign Finance, Ethics, and Lobbying
Regulation,* July, 1990 Proposed
Draft for Adoption, edited by
E. D. Feigenbaum, J. L. Larsen,
and B. J. Reynolds (1990)

http://www.cogel.org

INDEPENDENT SECTOR's
compendium

http://www.independentsector.org/
issues/accountability/standards.html

U.S. Government and Related Sites: Federal

Office of Government Ethics

http://www.usoge.gov

Office of Government Ethics
Resource Library (including
executive orders, statutes,
opinions, forms, and other resources)
via homepage

http://www.usoge.gov/usoge006.html

Department of Agriculture,
Office of Ethics

http://www.usda.gov/ethics

Department of Defense,
Standards of Conduct Office

http://www.defenselink.mil/dodgc/
defense_ethtics/main.html

Department of Interior, Ethics Office

http://www.ios.doi.gov/ethics/
ethics.html

Office of Special Counsel (Hatch Act)

http://www.osc.gov

Department of Justice,
Office of Legal Counsel

http://www.usdoj.gov.olc.htm

National Archives and Records
Administration, General Counsel Staff

http://www.nara.gov/gc/ethics/
ethics.html

House Committee on Standards
of Official Conduct

http://www.house.gov/ethics

Senate Ethics Committee

http://www.ethics.senate.gov

U.S. Government and Related Sites: State

Council on Governmental Ethics Laws	http://www.cogel.gov
Council on Governmental Ethics Laws (full text state statutes and legislation on the Internet)	http://www.prairienet.org/ ~scruffy/f.htm
Legal Information Institute, Cornell Law School	http://www.law.cornell.edu/ statutes.html
PIPER Resources: State and Local Government on the Net	http://www.piperinfo.com/state/ inde.cfm
Connecticut State Ethics Commission	http://www.ethics.state.ct/us/
Florida Commission on Ethics	http://www.ethics.state.fl.us
Georgia State Ethics Commission	http://www.ethics.state.ga.us
Hawaii State Ethics Commission	http://www.state.hi.us/ethics
Illinois Board of Ethics	http://www.ethics.state.il.us
Indiana State Ethics Commission	http://www.state.in.us/ethics
Iowa Ethics and Campaign Disclosure Board	http://www.ethics.state.ia.us
Kansas Governmental Ethics Commission	http://www.ethics.state.ka.us
Kentucky Legislative Ethics Commission	http://www.ethics.state.ky.us
Louisiana Board of Ethics	http://www.ethics.state.la.us
Maine Commission on Governmental Ethics and Election Practices	http://www.ethics.state.me.us
Maryland State Ethics Commission	http://www.ethics.state.md.us
Massachusetts State Ethics Commission	http://www.ethics.state.ma.us
Missouri Ethics Commission	http://www.ethics.state.mo.us
New York State Ethics Commission	http://www.ethics.state.ny.us
Ohio Ethics Commission	http://www.ethics.state.oh.us/ ethicshome.html
Oklahoma Ethics Commission	http://www.state.ok.us/~ethics
Pennsylvania Ethics Commission	http://www.state.pa.us
Rhode Island Ethics Commission	http://www.ethics.state.ri.us
South Carolina State Ethics Commission	http://www.state.sc.us/ethics

Texas Ethics Commission	http://www.ethics.state.tx.us
University of Houston's Texas Ethics Reporter (with opinions and links)	http://www.lawlib.uh.edu/ethics
Washington State Executive Ethics Board	http:/www.wa.gov/ethics
West Virginia Ethics Commission	http://www.wvethicscommission.org
Wisconsin Ethics Board	http://ethics.state.wi.us

U.S. Government and Related Sites: Local (Suggestive)

Chicago Board of Ethics	http://www.ci.chi.il.us/ethics/ overnew.html
King County (WA) Board of Ethics	http://www.metrokc.gov/ethics
Los Angeles City Ethics Commission	http://www.cityofla.org/ETH
San Francisco Ethics Commission	http://www.ci.sf.ca.us/ethics/info.htm
Seattle Ethics & Elections Commission	http://www.ci.seattle.wa.us/ethics

General U.S. Government Resources

FirstGov	http://www.firstgov.gov
Govspot	http://www.govspot.com
Government Printing Office (GPOAccess)	http://www.access.gpo.gov/su_docs
Library of Congress resource links	http://lcweb.loc.gov/rr/news/ extgovd.html

International and Multinational Sites

Business for Social Responsibility's Global Business Responsibility Resource Center	http://www.bsr.org/resourcecenter
Business Ethics and Stakeholder Relations Program (Canada)	http://www.cdp-hrc.uottawa.ca/ globalization/busethics/busmain.html
Canada, Office of the Ethics Counsellor	http://strategis.ic.gc.ca/SSG/ oe00001e.html

European Business Ethics Network (EBEN)—with links	http://www.eben.org
European Commission	http://europa.eu.int
European Commission (codes of conduct)	http://europa.eu.int/comm/ codesofconduct/index_en.htm
Inter-American Development Bank	http://www.iadb.org
International Monetary Fund	http://www.imf.org
Latin American Centre for Development Administration, anticorruption and ethics network	http://www.isop.ucla.edu.lac
Organization of American States	http://www.oas.org
Organization of American States (anticorruption efforts, including model laws and Inter-American Conventional against Corruption)	http://www.oas.org/juridico/ english/followup.htm
Organization for Economic Co-operation and Development's Anti-Corruption Unit	http://www.oecd.org/topic/ 0,2686,en_2649_37447_1_1_1_1_ 37447,00.html
Anti-Corruption Resources	http://www1.oecd.org/daf/ nocorruptionweb/
Ethics and Corruption in the Public Sector	http://www.oecd.org/about/ 0,2337,en_2649_37447_1_1_1_1_ 37447,00.html
Ethics and Corruption in the Public Sector and Principles for Managing Ethics in the Public Service	http://www.oecd.org/searchResult/ 0,2665,en_2649_37447_1_1_1_1_ 37447,00.html
Transparency International: Coalition Against Corruption in International Business Transactions	http://www.transparency.org
TI's Corruption Perception Index at Internet Center for Corruption Research	http://wwwuser.gwdg.de/~uwvw/ corruption.cpi_2003.html
Global Corruption Report	http://www.globalcorruptionreport. org/
United Nations	http://www.un.org
United Nations Global Compact	http://www.unglobalcompact.org/ Portal/Default.asp

United Nations Online Network in Public Administration and Finance (UNPAN)

http://www.unpan.org/index.asp, especially the on-line centers and on accountability and transparency http://www.unpan.org/ corethemes-transparency.asp

U.N. Governance Project

http://www.un.org/partners/ civil_society/calendar/c-gov.htm

U.N. Governance Project (anti-corruption links)

http://www.undcp.org/unodc/en/ corruption_links.html

U.S. Agency for International Development (USAID) (anti-corruption program and resources)

http://www.usaid.gov/democracy/ anticorruption

U.S. Agency for International Development (more resources)

http://www.usaid.gov/democracy/ anticorruption/resources.html

U.S. Office of Government Ethics on international developments

http://www.usoge.gov/internat.htm

World Bank's Anti-Corruption Knowledge Resource Center

http://www.worldbank.org/ publicsector/anticorrupt

Public Opinion Sites on Values and/or Confidence in Government

Inter-University Consortium for Social and Political Research (University of Michigan), which includes the General Social Survey (National Science Foundation), ICPSR

http://www.icpsr.umich.edu

Opinion series since 1972 on whether, on important values, Americans are divided or united; go to homepage, then codebook and variable united

http://www.icpsr.umich.edu/ codebook/united.

and confidence in government

http://www.icpsr.umich.edu/ codebook.htm

On-Line Survey Research/ Public Opinion Centers: A Worldwide Listing (University of Kansas)

http://www.ukans.edu/cwis/units/ com2/po/index/html

Pew Research Center for the People and the Press	http://www.people-press.org
its values update	http://www.peoplepress.org/dataarchive.htm
and report, *Deconstructing Distrust*	http://www.people-press.org.trustrpt.htm
National Election Studies (NES, University of Michigan)	http://www.umich.edu/~nes
its trust in government index	http://www.umich.edu/~nes/nesguide/toptable/tab5a_5.htm
and graph	http://www.umich.edu/~nes/nesguide/graphs/g5a_5_1.htm
University of Michigan, World Values Survey	http://wvs.isr.umich.edu/index.shtml
National Opinion Research Center (NORC, University of Chicago)	http://www.norc.uchicago.edu
Roper Center for Public Opinion Research (University of Connecticut)	http://www.ropercenter.uconn.edu
The Washington Post 1998 series on morals and values in the U.S.	http://www.washingtonpost.com/wp-srv/politics/polls/vault/vault.htm
and its guide to public opinion data on the Internet from nonpartisan sources via homepage	http://www.washingtonpost,com/wp-srv/politics/polls/datadir.htm]

Nonprofit Sites

INDEPENDENT SECTOR at	www.independentsector.org/
including its model code for nonprofits	http://www.independentsector.org/members/code_main.html
and compendium of standards and codes	http://www.independentsector.org/issues/accountability/standards.html
BBB Wise Giving Alliance	http://www.give.org/standards/newcbbbstds.asp
Georgia Center for Nonprofits	www.gcn.org/ethics.html

Maryland Association of Nonprofit Organizations	http://www.mdnonprofit.org,
including its ethics standards	http://www.mdnonprofit.org/ethicbook.htm
Evergreen State Society's Internet Nonprofit Center	http://www.nonprofits.org/
Association of Fundraising Professionals	http://www.afpnet.org/ethics
Pennsylvania Association of Nonprofit Organizations	http://www.pano.org/standards/standardscode.php
Urban Institute's Center on Nonprofits and Philanthropy	http://www.urban.org/content/PolicyCenters/Nonprofitsand Philanthropy/Overview.htm
Leader to Leader Institute (formerly Peter F. Drucker Foundation for Nonprofit Management)	http://www.pfdf.org
Nonprofit Quarterly	http://www.nonprofitquarterly.org
Nonprofit Sector Research Fund, projects and findings on accountability and evaluation	http://www.nonprofitresearch.org
Brookings Institution, numerous publications on nonprofit management	http://www.brook.edu

Ethics Cases, Scenarios, and Games

U.S. Office of Government Ethics resources and links	http://www.usoge.gov/pages/comp_web_trng/comp_web_trng.html
"Ethics Moment" column in *PA Times*, newsletter of American Society for Public Administration	http://www.aspanet.org/patimes/
Federal Standards of Conduct (U.S. Office of Government Ethics)	http://www.lexrex.com/interative.eg/main.html
Games and scenarios (BellSouth)	http://www.ethics.bellsouth.com/briefcases.htm
Harvard Business School Publishing's management case studies, including government contract compliance	http://www.hbsp.harvard.edu/products/cases/index.html

Journalism (*Washington Post*)	http://www.washingtonpost.com/wp-srv/local/longterm/tours/newseum/ethics/front.htm
Quandaries (U.S. Department of Justice on standards of conduct)	http://www.usdoj.gov/jmd/ethics
Scenarios and explanation of federal standards (U.S. Department of Agriculture)	http://www.usda.gov/ethics/training/index.htm
New York City's Conflicts of Interest Board, On-Line Ethics Quiz	http://www.nyc.gov/html/conflicts/html/quiz/quiz01.shtml

Note: This catalogue is necessarily limited; a search conducted on December 14, 2003 for the keyword *ethics* drew more than 4.2 million hits! The sites here illustrate available resources in broad categories and/or reflect the authors' primary research interests and audiences. All sites are in English. It may be necessary to search from a homepage to arrive at the desired destination. Useful key words for searching international, media, and other sites include *ethics, morals, morality, integrity, transparency, accountability, fraud, corruption,* and *bribes*. All these sites were accessed last on September 21–22, 2004, and since have been updated individually.

RESOURCE C

Tools for Making Ethical Decisions

Ten tools for decision making are compiled here for ready reference. As their titles indicate, they are oriented toward action. We argue in Chapter One that ethics is about decisive action that is rooted in moral values and publicly defensible in terms of moral principles, right results, or both. These tools are designed to assist the public manager in ethical decision making.

Tool 1: Assess Roles Using Role Diagnosis

Begin by assessing the roles you play and the seriousness of competing ethical claims. A role defines the capacity in which one is acting and the behavior befitting it. No simplistic trump, please; although there may be strong reasons for opting for one role over another, they need not be ethical reasons.

FIGURE 1.4. ROLE DIAGNOSIS.

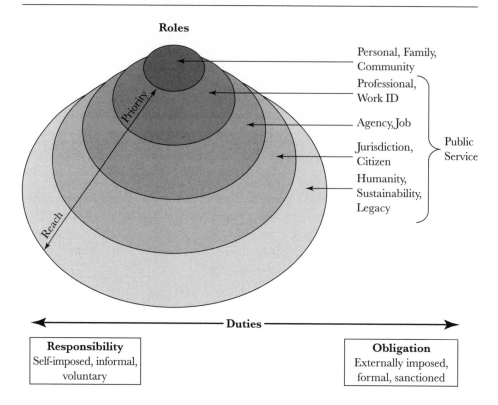

- Begin by assessing the roles you play and the seriousness of competing ethical claims. A role defines the capacity in which one is acting and the behavior befitting it.
- No simplistic trump, please; while there may be strong reasons for opting for one role over another, they need not be ethical reasons.

Graphic courtesy of Brian Baird, doctoral student in engineering at the University of Connecticut and research assistant in the Connecticut Center for Economic Analysis.

Tool 2: Use Go/No-Go Decision Model

FIGURE 2.2. GO/NO-GO DECISION MODEL.

Three judgment calls on immediate action:
1. Is it legal?
2. Is it ethical?
3. Is it effective?

	Ethical	Unethical
Illegal	*no action**	*no action*
Legal and Ineffective	*no action†*	*no action*
Legal and Effective	*action*	*no action*

* Pursue change in law? † Innovative redesign?

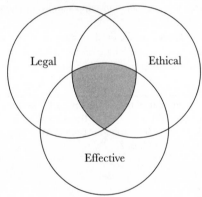

***Take immediate action
only at the intersection.***
(Proportions do not depict number
or scope of activities or decisions
each arena represents.)

Tool 3: Pursue the Public Interest

EXHIBIT 3.1. PURSUE THE PUBLIC INTEREST.

Step 1. Touch Four Bases in Sequence . . . Dismiss None

1. ***Democracy:*** delegate, agent
   How? Listen and respond, balance competing popular preferences
   Values: responsiveness, receptiveness,
   Tools: cost/benefit analysis, public opinion polls

2. ***Mutuality:*** statesman, trustee/steward
   How? Create and define community, use moral imagination and dialogue
   Values: inclusion, ethics, impartiality, civic virtue
   Tools: analysis of constitution, mission statement, regime and professional values

3. ***Sustainability:*** steward, sustainer
   How? Preserve, protect, anticipate
   Values: empathy, benevolence

4. ***Legacy:*** steward, custodian, legator
   How? Preserve, transmit, educate, cherish
   Values: empathy, benevolence

Step 2. Reflect on Four Principles

- **Trustee Principle**—Protect future generations' interests.
- **Sustainability Principle**—Secure future generations' opportunity for comparable quality of life.
- **Chain of Obligation Principle**—Provide for the needs of current and coming generations and give near-term concrete risks priority over long-term hypothetical risks.
- **Precautionary Principle**—Absent compelling need, avoid imposing risk of irreversible harm or catastrophe.

Step 1 is adapted from C. W. Lewis, "In Pursuit of the Public Interest," delivered at the 2004 Ethics Forum, national conference of the Ethics Section of the American Society for Public Administration, Portland, Oregon, March 27, 2004; the four principles in Step 2 are from the National Academy of Public Administration, 1997, p. 7.

Tool 4: Rank Responsibilities

EXHIBIT 6.3. RANK RESPONSIBILITIES.

When you must make a trade-off, think about this:

Given the very real prospect of having to exceed legal authority, budget, energy, credibility, and more, what do you do when you can't do it all?

The lower the claim on the list that follows, the more appropriate is a *principled no:*

Avoid harm, the most stringent and the negative obligation
Remedy or relief for problems we provoke
Affirmative help for problems others cause
Voluntary charity, the least stringent, doing good works

Tool 5: Use Threshold Test

EXHIBIT 6.4. USE THRESHOLD TEST.

If you're dealing with problems others cause, consider this:

A *principled yes* emerges from considering as many factors as possible. The four listed are the most pertinent.

1. Vulnerability: potential injury, risk to affected party
2. Proximity: know or should know, access, authority, competence, span of control
3. Capability: can help without excessive risk, danger, liability
4. Dependency: no place else to turn, weak or needy with few options or advocates, and low probability of alternative remedies or services

Tool 6: Audit Decisions Against Four Standards

EXHIBIT 3.8. AUDIT DECISIONS AGAINST FOUR STANDARDS.

☑ The mirror test for integrity asks,
"What kind of person do I admire and want to be?"

☑ The publicity test for accountability asks,
"Am I willing to read about this in the newspaper? Tell my family?"

☑ The visceral test for implementation and authenticity asks,
"Am I willing and likely to follow through? Can I live with this?"

☑ The signature test symbolizes personal responsibility and asks,
"Do I take public responsibility for this recommendation, analysis, or decision?"

Signed _____

Date _____

Tool 7: Creatively Lead

EXHIBIT 7.2. CREATIVELY LEAD.

Redefine the problem to satisfy as many ethical values and principles as possible. Instead of stopping at doing as little harm as possible (the usual minimum duty), a public manager with moral imagination seeks to reconcile and execute four time-honored ethical principles and harmonize duties and values:

1. *Reciprocity* signals respect for human dignity and rights and to avoid doing harm; the Golden Rule is a familiar example.
2. *Reversibility* (or empathy) calls for seeing oneself as subject or victim, trading places, or walking in someone else's shoes.
3. *Utility* (or net good results, however defined) urges concern for the number of people affected and how deeply, in both the long and short term.
4. *Universality and consistency* block arbitrary, haphazard, or unscrupulous behavior in favor of impartiality, fairness, and predictability.

Tool 8: Use Stakeholder Diagnostic

EXHIBIT 7.1. STAKEHOLDER DIAGNOSTIC.

Category (check one)

☐ Internal

☐ External and direct

☐ External and indirect

Description of Stake

_____

_____

_____

Step 1. Score each factor.

       High = 3

       Medium = 2

       Low = 1

       None = 0

    The higher the score, the less acceptable the decision for that stakeholder.

Factors	*Score*
Dependency on agency—inaccessible alternative services	_____
Dependency—improbable relief or remedy from harm/injury	_____
Vulnerability to decision—likelihood or risk of potential harm/injury	_____
Vulnerability—gravity (*versus* triviality) of effect	_____
Scope—broad policy impact (*versus* negligible)	_____
Risk to fundamental ethical value, duty, or principle	_____

                                            Add column for total score:

Step 2.

Repeat the scoring for each of the stakeholders to allow comparisons among them.

Next, add all stakeholders' scores together for a measure of the overall potential.

    A decision that causes severe permanent harm or injury receives a high score.

Step 3. *Action*

A high score across the board should prompt managers to reject the proposal outright

    (#1, below).

A high score for some stakeholders coupled with a low score for others may prompt managers to

    recommend alternatives or targeted relief (#2, below).

1. Manager recommends obligatory action or relief?   ☐ Yes   ☐ No

2. Score triggers manager's considering alternative action or relief?   ☐ Yes   ☐ No

Tool 9: Seek Inclusion

FIGURE 7.1. EXPANSIVE REACH OF PUBLIC SERVICE.

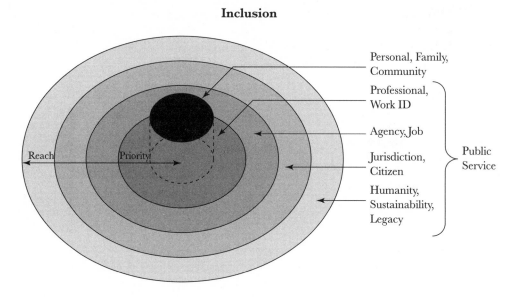

Graphic courtesy of Brian Baird, doctoral student in engineering at the University of Connecticut and research assistant in the Connecticut Center for Economic Analysis.

Tool 10: Before You Blow

EXHIBIT 7.4. BEFORE YOU BLOW.

Given the high risk and no guarantee of effectiveness, when should a loyal team player, with strong organization ties, break ranks? Whistle-blowing is suitable only after

> Facts are verified.
> The soul is searched.
> Organizational channels are exhausted.

Before reaching for the whistle, ask

1. Is the violation serious enough to warrant the risk to self and to the organization?
2. Are you prepared for this action to become known and for heroism to mutate into betrayal?
3. Are you sure of your facts? Are you sure you are right?
4. Are you sure that superiors or colleagues are not trying to correct the situation?
5. Is your motive purely in the public interest?
6. Are you ready to accept the consequences if you are wrong?

Six *yes* answers signal ethical leaders to do the right thing.

REFERENCES

ABC News/*Washington Post* Poll. National adult telephone survey, Oct. 9–13, 2003. Data provided by The Roper Center for Public Opinion Research, University of Connecticut.

Ackerman, F., and Heinzerling, L. "Pricing the Priceless: Cost-Benefit Analysis of Environmental Protection." *University of Pennsylvania Law Review,* 2002, *150*(5), 1553–1584.

Adams, G. B., and Balfour, D. L. *Unmasking Administrative Evil.* Thousand Oaks, Calif.: Sage, 1998.

Alabama Supreme Court. Order No. 03–01. 2003. Internet [http://news.findlaw.com/wp/docs/religion/glsthmre82103alsc.pdf] (accessed Aug. 31, 2003).

Allison, G. T. "Public and Private Management: Are They Fundamentally Alike in All Unimportant Respects?" In J. M. Shafritz and A. C. Hyde (eds.), *Classics of Public Administration.* (2nd ed.) Chicago: Dorsey Press, 1987, pp. 510–529. Originally published in *Proceedings for the Public Management Research Conference,* Nov. 19–20, 1979. Washington, D.C.: Office of Personnel Management, OPM Document 127-53-1, Feb. 1980, pp. 27–38.

Alt, P. M., and Weinstein, M. "Human Subjects Research, U.S. Public Policy." In J. Rabin (ed.), *Encyclopedia of Public Administration and Public Policy.* New York: Marcel Dekker, 2003. Internet [http://marceldekker.com] (accessed Apr. 26, 2004).

American Bar Association. *Model Code of Professional Responsibility and Code of Judicial Conduct.* Chicago: National Center for Professional Responsibility and the American Bar Association, 1980.

American Red Cross. "Red Cross Announces Major Changes in Liberty Fund." Press Release, Nov. 14, 2001. Internet [http://www.redcross.org/press/disaster/ds_pr/011114fundpressconf.html] (accessed Aug. 31, 2003).

American Red Cross. "Frequently Asked Questions." 2002a. Internet [http://www.redcross.org/sys/search/faqnew.asp#13] (accessed July 3, 2003).

American Red Cross. "KPMG Issues Unqualified Opinion on Liberty Disaster Relief Fund as of June 30, 2002." 2002b. Internet [http://www.redcross.org/press/disaster/ds_pr/021126kpmgaudit.html] (accessed Aug. 31, 2003).

American Society for Public Administration. *Ethics Resource Notebook.* Developed for ethics conference sponsored by the American Society for Public Administration, Washington, D.C., Nov. 12–15, 1989.

Anechiarico, F., and Jacobs, J. *The Pursuit of Absolute Integrity: How Corruption Control Makes Government Ineffective.* Chicago: University of Chicago Press, 1996.

An-Na'im, A. A. "Islam, Islamic Law and the Dilemma of Cultural Legitimacy for Universal Human Rights." In L. May, S. Collins-Chobanian, and K. Wong (eds.), *Applied Ethics: A Multicultural Approach.* (2nd ed.) Englewood Cliffs, N.J.: Prentice Hall, 1998.

Appleby, P. H. "Government Is Different." In J. M. Shafritz and A. C. Hyde (eds.), *Classics of Public Administration.* (2nd ed.) Chicago: Dorsey Press, 1987. (Originally published in *Big Democracy,* New York: Knopf, 1945.)

Arendt, H. *Eichmann in Jerusalem: A Report on the Banality of Evil.* (rev. ed.) New York: Penguin, 1964.

Arthur Andersen. "Executive Branch Employee Ethics Survey 2000." Report prepared for the U.S. Office of Government Ethics, Washington D.C., 2000.

Associated Press. "Commandments and Courts, Justices May Be Asked to Resolve Debate Over Monuments." *Washington Post,* Nov. 24, 2002. Internet [http://www.washingtonpost.com] (accessed Nov. 24, 2003).

Associated Press. "Charles Moose Faces Ethics Probe." CNN, Mar. 3, 2003. Internet [http://www.cnn.com] (accessed Mar. 8, 2003).

Associated Press. "USOC Task Forces want to Change Board." *New York Times,* Mar. 17, 2003, p. A1.

Bailey, S. K. "Ethics and the Public Service." *Public Administration Review,* 1964, *24,* 234–243.

Barna Research Group. National adult survey, July, 1993. Data provided by The Roper Center for Public Opinion Research, University of Connecticut.

Barnard, C. *The Functions of the Executive.* Cambridge, Mass.: Harvard University Press, 1938.

Barrett, D. "Deadline for 9-11 Compensation Passes." *Washington Post,* Dec. 23, 2003 [washingtonpost.com] (accessed Dec. 23, 2003).

Barringer, F. "Changing Times Turn Tables on a 'Saint' of the Stalin Era." *New York Times,* Mar. 21, 1988, pp. A1, A7.

Barringer, F. "Judge Voids New Rule Allowing Snowmobiles in Yellowstone." *New York Times,* Dec. 17, 2003. Internet [http://www.nytimes.com] (accessed Dec. 17, 2003).

Barry, D. "A New Account of Sept. 11 Loss, with 40 Fewer Souls to Mourn." *New York Times,* Oct. 29, 2003. Internet [http://www.nytimes.com] (accessed Oct. 29, 2003).

Behn, R. B. *Rethinking Democratic Accountability.* Washington, D.C.: Brookings Institution, 2001.

Belkin, L. "Just Money." *New York Times,* 2002, Sec. 6, p. 92.

Bell, D., and Kristol, I. "What is the Public Interest?" *Public Interest,* 1965, *1.* Internet [http://www.thepublicinterest.com] (accessed Dec. 17, 2003).

Berger, J. "In School Bureaucracy, Despair at the System." *New York Times,* Feb. 5, 1990, pp. A1, B2.

Berman, E. M. "Ethics in Organizations, Implementation of." In J. Rabin (ed.), *Encyclopedia of Public Administration and Public Policy.* New York: Marcel Dekker, 2002. Internet [http://marceldekker.com] (accessed Apr. 26, 2004).

Better Business Bureau. "Donor Expectations Survey: Executive Summary." 2001. Internet [http://www.give.org/news/survey1.asp] (accessed July 3, 2003).

Better Business Bureau. "Charity Report: American Red Cross. BBB Wise Giving Alliance." Aug. 2002. Internet [http://give.org/reports/arc.asp] (accessed June 12, 2003). Subsequently replaced by an updated BBB opinion based on changes the Red Cross made.

Better Business Bureau. "American Red Cross, Evaluative Conclusions." 2003a. Internet [http://give.org/reports/arc.asp] (accessed Aug. 31, 2003).

Better Business Bureau. "BBB Wise Giving Alliance Standards for Charity Accountability." 2003b. Internet [http://www.give.org/standards/index.asp] (accessed July 3, 2003).

Betti, J. A. Remarks to Best Practices Forum, Defense Industry Initiative on Business Ethics and Conduct. Washington, D.C., June 7, 1990. (Duplicated.)

Bhatnagar, S. "E-Government and Access to Information." In *Global Corruption Report 2003*. Berlin: Transparency International, 2003 [gcr@transparency.org] (accessed Sept. 5, 2003).

Bogdanos, Col. M. "On the Trail of the Iraq Museum's Treasures." *Wall Street Journal*, Sept. 18, 2003, p. D6.

Bok, S. *Lying. Moral Choice in Public and Private Life.* New York: Vintage Books, 1978.

Boling, T. E., and Dempsey, J. "Ethical Dilemmas in Government: Designing an Organizational Response." *Public Personnel Management Journal*, 1981, *10*, 11–19.

Bonczek, S. J. "Clean Up with Ethics Code, Dedicated Leadership." *City & State*, Aug. 27, 1990, *7*.

Booth, W., and Guggliotta, G. "Red Cross to Clarify How Money Is Spent," June 5, 2002, A9.

Booth, W., and Guggliotta, G. "All Along, Most Iraqi Relics Were 'Safe and Sound.'" *Washington Post*, June 9, 2003. Internet [http://www.washingtonpost.com] (accessed June 9, 2003).

Booth, W., and Sanchez, R. "A New 'Shadow' Over the LAPD." *Washington Post*, Sept. 25, 1999. Internet [http://www.washingtonpost.com] (accessed Sept. 25, 1999).

Boren, J. H. Testimony given to the Subcommittee on Investigations and Oversight of the Committee on Public Works, U.S. House of Representatives, June 22, 1971.

Bovens, M. *The Quest for Responsibility, Accountability and Citizenship in Complex Organisations.* Cambridge: Cambridge University Press, 1998.

Bowman, J. S. "Whistle-Blowing in the Public Service: An Overview of the Issues." *Review of Public Personnel Administration*, 1980, *1*, 15–28.

Bowman, J. S. "The Management of Ethics: Codes of Conduct in Organizations." *Public Personnel Management Journal*, 1981, *10*, 59–66.

Bowman, J. S. "Virtue Ethics." In J. Rabin (ed.), *Encyclopedia of Public Administration and Public Policy*. 2003. Internet [http://marceldekker.com] (accessed Apr. 7, 2004).

Bowman, J. S., and Williams, R. L. "Ethics in Government: From a Winter of Despair to a Spring of Hope." *Public Administration Review*, 1997, *57*(6), 517–526.

Branigan, T. "Backlog of Whistleblower Cases Growing, Agency Report Says." *Washington Post*, July 21, 2003, p. A04. Internet [http://www.washingtonpost.com] (accessed July 21, 2003).

Branigin, W. "Army General Says Abuse Caused by Faulty Leadership." *Washington Post*, May 11, 2004. Internet [http://www.washingtonpost.com] (accessed May 11, 2004).

Brown, M. T. *Working Ethics: Strategies for Decision Making and Organizational Responsibility.* San Francisco: Jossey-Bass, 1990.

Brownlow Committee. "Report of the President's Committee on Administrative Management." In J. M. Shafritz and A. C. Hyde (eds.), *Classics of Public Administration.* (2nd ed.) Chicago: Dorsey Press, 1987, pp. 90–95. (Originally published 1937.)

Bukkyo Dendo, Kyokai. *The Teaching of Buddha.* (509th rev. ed.) Tokyo: Toppan Printing Co., 1987.

Burns, A. I. "Combatting Public Corruption." *Investigators Journal,* 1987, 3, 4647.

Canavan, S. J. "Edmund Burke." In L. Strauss and J. Cropsey, (eds.), *History of Political Philosophy.* Chicago: Rand McNally, 1963, pp. 601–620.

Cannon, L. "One Bad Cop." *New York Times,* Oct. 1, 2000, magazine section. Internet [http://www. nytimes.com] (accessed Oct. 1, 2000).

Cantor Fitzgerald's Submission to the Special Master. Sept. 12, 2002. Internet[http://www. cantorusa.com/vcf/DOJsubmission.pdf][http://www.cantorusa] (accessed Sept. 12, 2003).

Carter, J. *Why Not the Best?* New York: Bantam Books, 1976.

Catron, B. L. "Principles and Strategies for Intergenerational Equity, Balancing Risks, Costs and Benefits Fairly across Generations." Paper presented at the National Academy of Public Administration, Washington D.C., 1994.

Catron, B. L. "For Future Generations . . . Stewardship/Trusteeship and Ecological Sensibility." Unpublished electronic manuscript (unpaginated and undated).

Chambers, R. "Introduction." In R. T. Hall, *The West Virginia Governmental Ethics Act: Text and Commentary.* Charleston, W.Va.: Mountain State Press, 1989.

Chambliss, W. J. *On the Take.* (2nd ed.) Bloomington: Indiana University Press, 1988.

Chandler, R. C. "A Guide to Ethics for Public Servants." In J. L. Perry (ed.), *Handbook of Public Administration.* San Francisco: Jossey-Bass, 1989a.

Chandler, R. C. "Moral Grandeur." Remarks to ethics conference sponsored by the American Society for Public Administration, Washington, D.C., Nov. 12–15, 1989b.

Chen, D. W. "Victims' Kin Fund Fault with Overseer of 9/11 Fund." *New York Times,* Nov. 13, 2002a.

Chen, D. W. "Worst-Hit Firm Faults Fairness of Sept. 11 Aid." *New York Times,* Sept. 17, 2002b. Internet [http://www.nytimes.com] (accessed Sept. 17, 2002). Internet [http://www.nytimes.com] (accessed Nov. 13, 2002).

Chen, D. W. "A Slow, Deliberate Process of Weighing 9/11 Awards." *New York Times,* Jan. 18, 2003, Internet [http://www.nytimes.com] (accessed Jan. 18, 2003).

Chicago Metro Ethics Coalition. "Ethics in Government: The Chicago Experience." Chicago: AMOCO, 1989.

City of Oklahoma City. "Alfred P. Murrah Federal Building Bombing, April 19, 1995, Final Report." Stillwater, Okla.: Fire Protection Publications, 1996.

"City Must Comply with New State Ethics Law." *Quincy Herald-Whig,* Mar. 29, 2004. As quoted on the COGEL Web site's news summary. Internet [www.stateandfed.com/ weekly_updates/email0405.htm] (accessed Mar. 29, 2004).

Clark, J. "Chemical/Biological Information and Checklist." Memorandum written in capacity as Emergency Planning Coordinator of Oklahoma City's Police Department. June 4, 1998.

Cockburn, A. "Beat the Devil." *Nation,* Mar. 26, 1988, 402–440.

Cohen, S., and Eimicke, W. "Is Public Entrepreneurship Ethical?" *Public Integrity Annuals,* Lexington, Ky.: Council of State Governments, 1996.

Columbia Accident Investigation Board. Synopsis of Report, Aug. 26, 2003. Internet [http://history.nasa.gov/columbia/Troxell/Columbia%20Web%20Site/CAIB/ CAIB%20Synopsis.htm] (accessed Apr. 19, 2004).

Common Cause. *A Model Ethics Law for State Government.* Washington, D.C.: Common Cause, Jan. 1989a.

Common Cause. *Conflict of Interest Legislation in the States*. Washington, D.C.: Common Cause, Sept. 1989b.

Commonwealth of Massachusetts. *Annual Report of the State Ethics Commission*. Boston: State Ethics Commission, 1989.

Congressional Quarterly. "Watergate: Chronology of a Crisis," Vols. 1 and 2. Washington, D.C.: Congressional Quarterly, 1974.

Cooper, T. L. "Hierarchy, Virtue, and the Practice of Public Administration." *Public Administration Review*, 1987, *47*, 320–328.

Cooper, T. L. *The Responsible Administrator: An Approach to Ethics for the Administrative Role*. (3rd ed.) San Francisco: Jossey-Bass, 1990, 1998.

Cooper, T. L. "The Emergence of Administrative Ethics as a Field of Study in the United States." In T. L. Cooper (ed.), *Handbook of Administrative Ethics*. (2nd ed.) New York: Marcel Dekker, 2001.

Cooper, T. L., and Yoder, D. E. "Public Management Ethics Standards in a Transnational World." *Public Integrity*, 2002, *4*(4), 333–352.

"Council Ethics Policy Proposed." *Wilmington Star News*, Feb. 17, 2003, p. B1.

Cowan Commission. Option reports prepared for the Commission to Draft a Code of Ethics for Los Angeles City Government. Los Angeles: Cowan Commission, Oct. 1989.

Cox, A. Testimony given at hearings before the Subcommittee on Oversight of Government Management of the Committee on Governmental Affairs, U.S. Senate, Apr. 12–13, 1988. Washington, D.C.: U.S. Government Printing Office, 1988.

Crisp, R. "Well-Being." In E. N. Zalta (ed.), The Stanford Encyclopedia of Philosophy, *Summer 2003*. Internet [http://plato.stanford.edu/archives/sum2003/entries/well-being] (accessed Apr. 4, 2004).

Culhane, J. G. "Sandbags Full of Money, Victim Compensation after 9/11." *Dissent* [http://www.dissentmagazine.org]. Oct. 12, 2003, unpaginated (accessed Oct. 12, 2003).

Cummins, R. A. "On the Trail of the Gold Standard for Subjective Well-Being." *Social Indicators Research*, 1995, *35*, 179–200.

Defense Industry Initiative on Business Ethics and Conduct. 1989 Annual Report to the Public and the Defense Industry. Washington, D.C.: Defense Industry Initiative on Business Ethics and Conduct, Feb. 1990.

Deming, W. E. *Out of the Crisis*. Cambridge, Mass.: MIT Center for Advanced Engineering Study, 1986.

Denhardt, J. V., and Denhardt, R. B. *The New Public Service*. Armonk, N.Y.: M. E. Sharpe, 2003.

Denhardt, K. G. *The Ethics of Public Service, Resolving Moral Dilemmas in Public Organizations: Contributions in Political Science*, no. 195. Westport, Conn.: Greenwood Press, 1988.

Denhardt, K. G. "The Management of Ideals: A Political Perspective on Ethics." *Public Administration Review*, 1989, *49*, 187–193.

Denhardt, R. B. *The Pursuit of Significance: Strategies for Managerial Success in Public Organizations*. Belmont, Calif.: Wadsworth, 1993.

Dobel, J. P. "Integrity in the Public Service." *Public Administration Review*, 1990, *50*, 354–366.

Dobel, J. P. *Public Integrity*. Baltimore, Md.: Johns Hopkins University Press, 1999.

Dobel, J. P. "Can Public Leaders Have Friends?" *Public Integrity*, 2001, *3*(2), 145–158.

Douglas, M., and Wildavsky, A. *Risk and Culture*. Berkeley: University of California Press, 1982.

Downs, A. *Inside Bureaucracy*. Boston: Little, Brown, 1967.

Drucker, P. F. "What Is 'Business Ethics'?" *Public Interest*, 1981, *63*, 18–36.

Drucker, P. F. *The New Realities*. New York: Harper Collins, 1989.

Duplantier, et. al. v. United States, U.S.C.A., 5th Circuit, 606 F.2d 654, Nov. 19, 1979.

Egan, T. "In West, a Showdown Over Rules on Grazing." *New York Times*, Aug. 19, 1990, pp. Al, A20.

Ethics Resource Center. "2003 National Business Ethics Survey; How Employees View Ethics in their Organizations." May 2003a. Internet [http://ethics.org/nbes2003/2003nbes_summary.html] (accessed June 15, 2004).

Ethics Resource Center. *How to Write a Workable Company Code*. Washington, D.C.: Ethics Resource Center, 2003b.

Ethics Resource Center. *Report to the Office of Government Ethics of Puerto Rico: 2003 Employee Ethics Survey*. Washington, D.C.: Ethics Resource Center, 2003c.

"Fact File: Attitudes and Characteristics of This Year's Freshmen." Survey by American Council on Education and Higher Education Research Institute at the University of California, Los Angeles. *Chronicle of Higher Education*, Jan. 24, 1990, pp. A33–A34.

Federal Inspector General. "A Progress Report to the President, Fiscal Year 2002." May 1, 2003. Internet [http://www.ignet.gov/randp/fy02apr.pdf] (accessed July 3, 2003).

Feigenbaum, E. D., Larsen, J. L., and Reynolds, B. J. (eds.). "A Model Law for Campaign Finance, Ethics, and Lobbying Regulation" (proposed draft for adoption). Lexington, Ky.: Council on Governmental Ethics Laws, 1990.

Fieser, J. "Internet Encyclopedia of Philosophy." Internet [http://www.utm.edu/research/iep] (accessed Aug. 31, 2003).

Fillo, M. "Protections Proposed for Ethics Agency." *Hartford Courant*, Dec. 2, 2003. Internet [http://www.ctnow.com] (accessed Dec. 2, 2003).

Fischer, F. *Evaluating Public Policy*. Chicago: Nelson-Hall Publishers, 1995.

Fischhoff, B., Lichtenstein, S., Slovic, P., Derby, S. L., and Keeney, R. L. *Acceptable Risk*. Cambridge: Cambridge University Press, 1981.

Frederickson, H. G. (ed). Symposium on Social Equity and Public Administration. *Public Administration Review*, 1974, *34*(1).

Frederickson, H. G. "Toward a New Public Administration." In J. M. Shafritz and A. C. Hyde (eds.), *Classics of Public Administration*. (2nd ed.) Chicago: Dorsey Press, 1987.

Frederickson, H. G. "Public Administration and Social Equity." *Public Administration Review*, 1990, *50*, 228–237.

Frederickson, H. G. "Can Public Officials Correctly Be Said to Have Obligations to Future Generations?" *Public Administration Review*, 1994, *54*(5), 457–464.

Frederickson, H. G., and Hart, D. K. "The Public Service and the Patriotism of Benevolence." *Public Administration Review*, 1985, *45*(5), 547–553.

Freel, D. "Ethics Update–2003." Paper presented at the Council of Government Ethics Laws Conference, Austin, Tex., Sept. 21, 2003.

French, P. A. *Ethics in Government*. Series in Occupational Ethics. Englewood Cliffs, N.J.: Prentice Hall, 1983.

Fuchs, L. "Maya Angelou." *Facing History and Ourselves News*, Winter 1989-1990, 12–13.

Gallup/CNN/*USA Today* Poll. National adult survey, April 1996. Data provided by The Roper Center for Public Opinion Research, University of Connecticut.

Gallup Organization. National polls, April 1990 through April 2004. Data provided by The Roper Center for Public Opinion Research, University of Connecticut. Internet [http://roperweb.ropercenter.uconn.edu] (accessed June 11, 2004).

Garment, S. *Scandal: The Culture of Mistrust in American Politics.* New York: Dell, 1992.

Garvey, G. *Facing the Bureaucracy: Living and Dying in a Public Agency.* San Francisco: Jossey-Bass, 1993.

Gawthrop, L. C. *Public Service and Democracy: Ethical Imperatives for the 21st Century.* New York: Chatham House of Seven Bridges Press, 1998.

General Accounting Office. *Framework for Assessing Job Vulnerability to Ethical Problems.* FPCD-82–2. Washington, D.C.: General Accounting Office, Nov. 4, 1981.

General Accounting Office. *Ethics Enforcement: Process by Which Conflict of Interest Allegations Are Investigated and Resolved.* GAO/GGD-87–83BR. Washington, D.C.: General Accounting Office, June 1987.

Gettleman, J. "Court Orders Alabama's Chief Justice Removed from the Bench." *New York Times,* Nov. 13, 2003. Internet [http://www.nytimes.com] (accessed Nov. 13, 2003).

Gillette, C. P., and Hopkins, T. D. "Federal Agency Valuations of Human Life: Report to the Administrative Conference of the United States." July 7, 1988. (Duplicated.)

Gilligan, C. *In a Different Voice.* Cambridge, Mass.: Harvard University Press, 1982.

Gilman, S. C. "Many Hands, Dirty Hands, and No Hands: Bringing Applied Ethics to Public Management." *Practicing Manager,* 1989, *9,* 20–26.

Gilman, S. C. "Presidential Ethics and the Ethics of the Presidency." *Ethics in American Public Service: The Annals of the American Academy of Political and Social Science,* 1995, *537,* 58–75.

Gilman, S. C. "Institutions of Integrity in the United States." In Organization for Economic Co-operation and Development (ed.), *Public Sector Transparency and Accountability: Making It Happen.* Paris: Organization for Economic Co-operation and Development, 2002.

Gilman, S. C. "Appearance of Impropriety." In J. Rabin (ed.), *Encyclopedia of Public Administration and Public Policy.* New York: Marcel Dekker, 2003. Internet [http://marceldekker.com] (accessed Apr. 26, 2004).

Gilman, S. C. "Assessment Strategies and Practices for Integrity and Anti-Corruption Measures in the Public Service." Address to Symposium on How to Assess Measures for Promoting Integrity and Preventing Corruption in the Public Service. Paris: OECD, Public Governance Committee, Sept. 9, 2004a.

Gilman, S. C. "Sentencing Guidelines: An Incentive for Organizational Ethics." *Government, Law and Policy Journal,* 2004b, *6*(1), 32–36.

Gilman, S. C., and Denhardt, K. "Extremism in Search of Virtue: Why Zero Gift Policies Don't Work." *Public Integrity,* 2002, *4*(1), 71–80.

Gilman, S. C., and Lewis, C. W. "Public Service Ethics: A Global Dialogue." *Public Administration Review,* 1996, *56*(6), 517–524.

Glaberson, W. "Lawyer Math in Sept. 11 Deaths Shows Varying Values for a Life." *New York Times.* Nov. 11, 2001. Internet [http://www.nytimes.com] (accessed Nov. 11, 2001).

Goldstein, A. "Official Says He Was Told To Withhold Medicare Data." *Washington Post,* Mar. 13, 2004, p. A01. Internet [http://www.washingtonpost.com] (accessed Mar. 13, 2004).

Goodpaster, K. E. "Some Avenues for Ethical Analysis in General Management." Harvard Business School Case 9–383–007. (rev. ed.) Boston: Harvard Business School Case Services, 1984.

Goodsell, C. T. "Public Administration and the Public Interest." In G. L. Wamsley, and others, *Refounding Public Administration.* Thousand Oaks, Calif.: Sage, 1990, 96–113.

Goodsell, C. T. *The Case for Bureaucracy: A Public Administration Polemic.* (4th ed.) Washington, D.C.: CQ Press, 2004.

Gormley, W. T., Jr., and Balla, S. J. *Bureaucracy and Democracy, Accountability and Performance.* Washington D.C.: CQ Press, 2004.

Graham, G. A. *Morality in American Politics.* New York: Random House, 1952.

Graham, G. A. "Ethical Guidelines for Public Administrators: Observations on Rules of the Game." *Public Administration Review,* 1974, *34,* 90–92.

Great Britain, Committee on Standards in Public Life. "Seven Principles of Public Life." June 2001. Internet. [http://www.public-standards.gov.uk] (accessed Mar. 14, 2004).

Green, D. P., Jacowitz, K. E., Kahneman, D., and McFadden, D. "Referendum Contingent Valuation, Anchoring, and Willingness to Pay for Public Goods." *Resources and Energy Economics,* 1998, *20*(2), 85–116.

Green, D. P., Kahneman, D., and Kunreuther, H. "How the Scope and Method of Public Funding Affect Willingness to Pay for Public Goods." *Public Opinion Quarterly,* 1994, *58*(1), 49–67.

Grosenick, L. "Federal Training Programs: Help or Hindrance?" *Public Manager,* 1995–96, *24*(4), 18–26.

Groudine, C. J., and Miller, J. L. "Nonprofit Board Culture and the Public Trust: Reconciling Rival Ideas." *Public Integrity,* 2002, *4*(2), 115–131.

"Groups Seek 2 Probes by House Ethics Panel." *Washington Post,* Mar. 3, 2004, p. A11.

Guy, M. *E. Ethical Decision Making in Everyday Work Situations.* Westport, Conn.: Quorum Books, 1990.

Hall, R. T. *The West Virginia Governmental Ethics Act: Text and Commentary.* Charleston W.Va.: Mountain State Press, 1989.

Hamilton, R. A. "Navy and Roman Catholic Doctor Struggle to Find Middle Ground. Prescribing Birth Control Is Against His Religious Beliefs." Feb. 16, 2004. *New London Day* [http://www.newlondonday.com] (accessed Feb. 16, 2004).

Hansen, J. *Oklahoma Rescue.* New York: Ballantine Books, 1995.

Hardin, G. "The Tragedy of the Commons." In G. Hardin, *Exploring New Ethics for Survival.* New York: Viking, 1972, 250–264. (Originally published in *Science,* 1968, *162,* 1243-1248.)

Harmon, M. M. "The Responsible Actor as 'Tortured Soul': The Case of Horatio Hornblower." In B. L. Catron and H. D. Kass (eds.), *Images and Identities in Public Administration.* Thousand Oaks, Calif.: Sage, 1990.

Harmon, M. M. *Responsibility as Paradox: A Critique of Rational Discourse on Government.* Thousand Oaks, Calif.: Sage, 1995.

Harris Poll. July 17–19, 1992. Data provided by The Roper Center for Public Opinion Research, University of Connecticut. Internet [http://roperweb.ropercenter.uconn.edu] (accessed June 11, 2004).

Hart, D. K. "Social Equity, Justice, and the Equitable Administrator." *Public Administration Review,* 1974, *34,* 3–11.

Heath, T. "Streamlining USOC Debated at Hearing." *Washington Post,* Mar. 20, 2003, p. D03.

Heclo, H. "Bureaucratic Dispositions." In D. L. Yarwood (ed.), *Public Administration, Politics and the People.* New York: Longman, 1987.

Heichelbech, J. R. "Deontology." *Encyclopedia of Public Administration and Public Policy.* 2003a. Internet [http://www.dekker.com] (accessed Jan. 29, 2004).

Heichelbech, J. R. "Teleology and Utilitarianism." *Encyclopedia of Public Administration and Public Policy.* 2003b. Internet [http://www.dekker.com] (accessed Jan. 29, 2004).

Heichelbech, J. R. "John Rawls." *Encyclopedia of Public Administration and Public Policy.* 2004. Internet.[http://www.dekker.com] (accessed June 16, 2004).

Henriques, D. B. "Concern Growing as Families Bypass 9/11 Victims' Fund." *New York Times*, Aug. 31, 2003. Internet [http://www.nytimes.com] (accessed Aug. 31, 2003).

Herring, P. *Public Administration and the Public Interest*. New York: McGraw-Hill, 1936.

Hirschkorn, P. "Poll: New Yorkers want 9/11 victims honored equally." CNN [http://www.cnn.com/2003/US/Northeast/09/10.wtc.memorial/index.html]. Sept. 11, 2003 (accessed Sept. 11, 2003).

Hirschmann, N. J. "Freedom, Recognition, and Obligation: A Feminist Approach to Political Theory." *American Political Science Review*, 1989, *83*, 1227–1244.

Hochschild, A. *King Leopold's Ghost, A Story of Greed, Terror, and Heroism in Colonial Africa*. Boston: Houghton Mifflin, 1998.

Hospers, J. "Rule Utilitarianism." In C. H. Sommers (ed.), *Right and Wrong: Basic Readings in Ethics*. Orlando: Harcourt Brace, 1986.

Hotz, R. L. "Butterfly on a Bullet." *Los Angeles Times*, Dec. 22, 2003. Internet [http://www.latimes.com] (accessed Dec. 22, 2003).

Huang Liu-Hung D. (C. Tucson, trans. and ed.). *A Complete Book Concerning Happiness and Benevolence: A Manual for Local Magistrates in Seventeenth-Century China*. University of Arizona Press, 1984.

Huberts, Leo W.J.C. "Global Ethics and Corruption." *Encyclopedia of Public Administration and Public Policy*. 2003. Internet [http://www.dekker.com] (accessed Mar. 14, 2004).

Hummel, R. P. *The Bureaucratic Experience*. (3rd ed.) New York: St. Martin's Press: 1987.

INDEPENDENT SECTOR. Survey of charitable giving after September 11th, 2001. Conducted by Withlin Worldwide [http://www.independentsector.org/PDFs/Sept11_giving.pdf/, Oct. 23, 2001 (accessed Jan. 4, 2004).

INDEPENDENT SECTOR. *The New Nonprofit Almanac & Desk Reference*. Washington, D.C., 2002. Internet [http://www.independentsector.org] (accessed June 9, 2004).

INDEPENDENT SECTOR. *Statement of Values and Code of Ethics for Nonprofit and Philanthropic Organizations*. 2004. Internet [http://www.independentsector.org/members/code_main.html](accessed Mar. 8, 2004).

Inglehart, R. "Globalization and Postmodern Values." *Washington Quarterly*, 2000, *23*(1), 215–228. Internet. [http://www.worldvaluessurvey.org/library/index.html] (accessed Sept. 5, 2003).

International Association of Chiefs of Police. Oath of Honor. Internet [http://www.theiacp.org/profassist/ethics/presentation_of_oath.htm] (accessed Feb. 29, 2004).

International Association of Chiefs of Police. Law Enforcement Code of Ethics. Internet [http://www.theiacp.org/documents/index.cfm?fuseaction=document&document_type_id=1&document_id=95] (accessed Feb. 29, 2004).

International City/County Management Association. Code of Ethics, as amended Sept. 2002. Internet [http://www2.icma.org] (accessed Feb. 29, 2004).

International Municipal Law Association, 2003. *Model Ordinances*, Chapter 9: Ethics, 2003, pp. 9–1.1–9–1.55.

Internet Center for Corruption Research. Press release on TI-Corruption Perceptions Index 2003. University of Passau and Transparency International, Oct. 7. 2003. Internet [http://wwwuser.gwdg.de/~uwvw/corruption.cpi_2003_press.html] (accessed Mar. 16, 2004).

Jehl, D. "Head of Inquiry on Iraq Abuses Now in Spotlight." *New York Times*, May 11, 2004. Internet [http://www.nytimes.com] (accessed May 11, 2004).

Jennings, B. "Too Much of a Good Thing?" *State Government*, 1989a, *62*, 173–175.

Jennings, B. "Ethics in Government: There Still Is Hope." Reprinted in *Ethics Resource Notebook*, developed for ethics conference sponsored by the American Society for Public Administration, Washington, D.C., Nov. 12–15, 1989, 23–29. Originally published in *World and I*, May 1989b.

Johnson, M. "A Filmmaker's Odyssey." *Facing History and Ourselves News*, Winter 1989–1990, 18–21.

Johnson, R. B. "The Patient Always Comes First." *New London Day*, Feb. 29, 2004. Internet [http://www.newlondonday.com] (accessed Feb. 29, 2004).

Johnston, D. C. "On Tax Day, I.R.S. Prepared to Fire Star Whistle-Blower." *New York Times*, Apr. 17, 1999. Internet [nytimes.com] (accessed Apr. 17, 1999).

Jos, P. H., Tompkins, M. E., and Hays, W. S. "In Praise of Difficult People: A Portrait of the Committed Whistleblower." *Public Administration Review*, 1989, *49*, 552–561.

Joseph, J. *Integrating Ethics and Compliance Programs: Next Steps for Successful Implementation and Change.* Washington, D.C.: Ethics Resource Center, 2001.

Josephson Institute. *Preserving the Public Trust: Principles of Public Service Ethics, Standards of Conduct & Guidelines for Government Decision Making.* Marina del Rey, Calif.: Josephson Institute for the Advancement of Ethics, Government Ethics Center, 1990.

Josephson, M. *Power, Politics, and Ethics: Ethical Obligations and Opportunities of Government Service.* (3rd ed.) Marina Del Rey, Calif.: Josephson Institute for the Advancement of Ethics, 1989.

Jotman, M. *George Washington's Expense Account.* New York: HarperCollins, 1988.

Kahneman, D., and Lovallo, D. "Timid Choices and Bold Forecasts: A Cognitive Perspective on Risk Taking." *Management Science*, 1993, *39*(1), 17–31.

Kahneman, D., Slovic, P., and Tversky, A. *Judgment under Uncertainty: Heuristics and Biases.* New York: Cambridge University Press, 1982.

Kahneman, D., and Tversky, A. "Prospect Theory: An Analysis of Decision under Risk." *Econometrica*, 1979, *47*(2), 363–391.

Kane, Parsons and Associates for *Parents Magazine*. National adult telephone survey, Jan. 15–31, 1989.

Kass, H. "Stewardship as a Fundamental Element in Images of Public Administration." In H. D. Kass and B. Catron (eds.), *Images and Identities in Public Administration.* Thousand Oaks, Calif.: Sage, 1990.

Katz, R. "Friendly Fire: The Mandatory Military Anthrax Vaccination Program." *Duke Law Journal*, 2001, *50*, 1835–1865. Internet [http://www.law.duke.edu/shell/cite.pl?50+Duke+L.J.+1835] (accessed June 14, 2004).

Keller, B. "Chernobyl Plant Being Mismanaged, Pravda Charges." *New York Times*, Apr. 25, 1988, pp. Al, A6.

Kernaghan, K., and Langford, J. W. *The Responsible Public Servant.* Halifax, Canada: Institute for Research on Public Policy and Institute of Public Administration of Canada, 1990.

Key, V. O., Jr. "The Lack of a Budgetary Theory." *American Political Science Review*, 1940, *34*, 1137–1140.

King, M. L., Jr. "Letter from Birmingham City Jail." Apr. 16, 1963. Philadelphia: American Friends Service Committee, May 1963.

Kleinig, J. *Valuing Life.* Princeton, N.J.: Princeton University Press, 1991.

Knight, M. (comp.). *Forever Changed.* Amherst, N.Y.: Prometheus Books, 1998.

Knouse, S., and Giacalone, R. "Six Components of Successful Ethics Training." *Business and Society Review*, 1996, *98*, 10–13.

Kolbert, E. "The Calculator: How Kenneth Feinberg Determines the Value of Three Thousand Lives." *New Yorker*, Nov. 25, 2002. Internet [http://www.newyorker.com/fact/content/?021125fa_fact] (accessed Sept. 13, 2003).

Kopel, D., and Blackmun, P. "Moose Bull, 'The D.C. Sniper' Police Chief's Version of History." *National Review Online*, Dec. 11, 2003. Internet [http://www.nationalreview.com/kopel/kopel-blackmun200312110800.asp] (accessed Jan. 20, 2003).

Kohlberg, L. "Stages of Moral Development as a Basis for Moral Education." In B. Munsey (ed.), *Moral Development, Moral Education, and Kohlberg*. Birmingham, Ala.: Religious Education Press, 1980.

Kohlberg, L. *The Philosophy of Moral Development, Moral Stages and the Idea of Justice*. Vol. 1. New York: HarperCollins, 1981.

Kurtz, H. "Why We Blew the HUD Story." *Washington Post*, Nov. 12, 1989, p. D5.

Lee, J. "Court Blocks Easing of E.P.A. Rules on Industrial Pollution." *New York Times*, Dec. 24, 2003. Internet. [http://www.nytimes.com] (accessed Dec. 24, 2003).

Lewis, C. W. *Scruples & Scandals: A Handbook on Public Service Ethics for State and Local Government Officials and Employees in Connecticut*. Storrs: Institutes of Public Service and Urban Research, University of Connecticut, 1986.

Lewis, C. W. "Power without Privilege." In R. T. Golembiewski and J. Rabin (eds.), *Public Budgeting and Finance*. (4th ed.) New York: Marcel Dekker, 1997.

Lewis, C. W. "Mini-Symposium on Public Service Ethics: Introduction." *International Journal of Organization Theory and Behavior*, 2003a, *6*(3), 403–404.

Lewis, C. W. "Ethics in Public Service." In J. Rabin, R. Munzenrider, and S. M. Bartell (eds.), *Principles and Practices of Public Administration*. New York: Marcel Dekker, 2003b.

Lewis, C. W., and Catron, B. L. "Professional Standards and Ethics." In J. L. Perry (ed.), *Handbook of Public Administration*. (2nd ed.) San Francisco, 1996.

Lewis, C. W., Tenzer, M. J., and Harrison, T. "The Heroic Response to Terror: The Case of Oklahoma City." *Public Personnel Management*, 1999, *28*(4), 617–635.

Lichtenberg, J. "What are Codes of Ethics For? In M. Coady and S. Bloch (eds.), *Codes of Ethics and the Professions*. Melbourne: Melbourne University Press, 1996.

Light, P. C. *The New Public Service*. Washington D.C.: Brookings Institution, 1999.

Light, P. C. Pathways to Nonprofit Excellence. Washington D.C.: Brookings Institution, 2002.

Lindblom, C. E. "The Science of 'Muddling Through.'" *Public Administration Review*, 1959, *19*, 79–88.

Linnerooth, J. "A Critique of Recent Modelling Efforts to Determine the Value of Human Life." Unpublished, duplicated manuscript. Austria: International Institute for Applied Analysis, 1975.

Lipset, S. M., and Schneider, M. *The Confidence Gap, Business, Labor, and Government in the Public Mind*. (rev. ed.) Baltimore, Md.: Johns Hopkins University Press, 1987.

Lipsky, M. *Street-Level Bureaucracy: Dilemmas of the Individual in Public Services*. New York: Basic Books, 1980.

Loewenstein, G. "Frames of Mind in Intertemporal Choice." *Management Science*, 1988, *34*(2), 200–214.

Loewenstein, G. "The Creative Destruction of Decision Research." *Journal of Consumer Research*, Dec. 2001, *28*, 499–505.

Mackenzie, G. C. *Scandal Proof: Do Ethics Laws Make Government Ethical?* Washington, D.C.: Brookings Institution, 2002.

Marini, F. (ed.). *Toward a New Public Administration: The Minnowbrook Perspective*. Scranton, Pa.: Chandler Press, 1971.

Marlowe, J. "Part of the Solution, or Cogs in the System? The Origins and Consequences of Trust in Public Administrators." *Public Integrity*, 2004, *7*(2), 5–25.

Maskell, J. H. "Ethics Laws and Regulation in the Federal Sector: Executive and Legislative Branches." Paper presented at ethics conference sponsored by the American Society for Public Administration, Washington, D.C., Nov. 12–15, 1989.

May, L., Collins-Chobanian, S., and Kai Wong, K. *Applied Ethics: A Multicultural Approach*. (2nd ed.) Englewood Cliffs, N.J.: Prentice Hall, 1998.

May, P. "FEMA's Role in Emergency Management: Examining Recent Experience." *Public Administration Review*, Jan. 1985, *45*, 46.

Menzel, D. C. "Teaching Ethics and Values in Public Administration: Are We Making a Difference?" *Public Administration Review*, 1997, *57*(3), 224–230.

Miale, F. R., and Selzer, M. *The Nuremberg Mind: The Psychology of the Nazi Leaders*. New York: Quadrangle, 1975.

Milgram, S. *Obedience to Authority: An Experimental View*. New York: HarperCollins, 1983.

Montgomery County Department of Police. "Career History of Charles Alexander Moose." Internet [http://www.montgomerycountymd.gov/mc/services/police/chiefbio.htm] (accessed Jan. 25, 2004).

Montgomery County Ethics Commission. "Advisory Opinion 03–011: Transcript, Mar. 3, 2003." Internet [http://www.montgomerycountymd.ws/MooseEthicsTranscript.PDF] (accessed Aug. 31, 2003).

Montgomery County Ethics Commission. Transcript of meeting to Consider Advisory Opinion 03–011: Transcript, Mar. 3, 2003. Internet [http://www.montgomerycountymd.ws/MooseEthicsTranscript.PDF] (accessed Aug. 31, 2003).

"Moral Dilemma." *Internet Encyclopedia of Philosophy*, 2001. Internet [http://www.utm.edu/research/iep/m/m-dilemm.htm] (accessed Aug. 8, 2003).

Moreno, A. "Corruption and Democracy: A Cultural Assessment." Sept. 2002. Internet [http://www.worldvaluessurvey.org/library/index.html] (accessed Sept. 5, 2003).

Morgan, D. F. "The Public Interest." *Handbook of Administrative Ethics*. (2nd ed.) New York: Marcel Dekker, 2001.

Morgan, P. W., and Reynolds, G. H. *The Appearance Of Impropriety: How the Ethics Wars Have Undermined American Government, Business, and Society*. New York: Free Press, 1997.

Morin, R., and Broder, D. S. "Americans' Moral Worries Test Reluctance to Judge." *Washington Post*, Sept. 11, 1998. Internet [washingtonpost.com] (accessed Oct. 30, 1998).

Morris, E. *Theodore Rex*. New York: Modern Library, 2001.

Mosk, M. "Moose Hires Law Firm Over Ethics: Chief Seeks Approval for Sniper Book Case." *Washington Post*, Mar. 14 2003a, p. B2.

Mosk, M. "Panel Forbids Moose's Book and Movie: Montgomery Chief Had Boss's Backing for Deals from Sniper Case." *Washington Post*, Mar. 21, 2003b, p. B1.

Mosk, M. "Moose Feared Losing His Job." *Washington Post*, May 23, 2003c, p. B1.

Moyers, B. *The Secret Government: The Constitution in Crisis*. Cabin John, Md.: Seven Locks Press, 1988.

Naess, A. *Ecology, Community and Lifestyle: Outline of an Ecosophy*. Boston: Cambridge University Press, 1989.

Nash, L. L. "Ethics without the Sermon." *Harvard Business Review*, 1981, *59*, 79–90.

Nash, L. L. *Good Intentions Aside: A Manager's Guide to Resolving Ethical Problems.* Boston, Mass.: Harvard Business School Press, 1990.

National Academy of Public Administration. *Deciding for the Future: Balancing Risks, Costs, and Benefits Fairly Across Generations.* A Report for the U.S. Department of Energy. Washington D.C.: National Academy of Public Administration, 1997.

National Institute of Municipal Law Officers. *NIMLO Model Ordinance on Code of Ethics.* Draft prepared by staff attorney J. C. Pinson, Washington, D.C.: National Institute of Municipal Law Officers, Mar. 1990.

National Park Service. "The National Park System: Caring for the American Legacy." 2001. Internet [http://www.nps.gov/legacy/mission.html] (accessed Dec. 17, 2003).

National Victim Assistance Academy. "Chapter 22." Dec. 2, 2002. Internet [http://www.ojp.gov/ovc/nvaa2002/Chapter22_9.html] (accessed Nov. 13, 2003).

NBC News/*Wall Street Journal* Poll. July 8–11, 1988. Data provided by The Roper Center for Public Opinion Research, University of Connecticut. Internet [http://roperweb.ropercenter.uconn.edu] (accessed June 11, 2004).

NBC News/*Wall Street Journal* Poll. Mar. 1–4, 2001. Data provided by The Roper Center for Public Opinion Research, University of Connecticut. Internet [http://roperweb.ropercenter.uconn.edu] (accessed June 11, 2004).

Neely, A. S., IV. "Ethics-in-Government Laws: Are They Too "Ethical"? *Studies in Legal Policy.* Washington, D.C.: American Enterprise Institute for Public Policy Research, 1984.

Negin, B. "Ethics and Information and Communication Technology." In J. Rabin (ed.), *Encyclopedia of Public Administration and Public Policy.* Marcel Dekker, Mar. 2004. Internet [http://www.marceldekker.com] (accessed Mar. 14, 2004).

Nelson, M. "A Short, Ironic History of American National Bureaucracy." *Journal of Politics,* 1982, *44,* 747–778.

"New Ethics Rule Sought." *Hartford Courant,* Feb. 23, 2004. As quoted on the COGEL Web site's news summary. Internet [http://www.stateandfed.com/weekly_updates/email0405.htm] (accessed Apr. 5, 2004).

New York State Department of Civil Service. *New York State Work Force Plan, 1990.* Albany, N.Y.: New York State Department of Civil Service, 1990.

Noddings, N. *Caring: A Feminine Approach to Ethics and Moral Education.* Berkeley, Calif.: University of California Press, 1984.

Nozick, R. *Anarchy, State, and Utopia.* New York: Basic Books, 1974.

Nussbaum, M., and Sen, A. (eds.). The Quality of Life. Oxford: Clarendon Press, 1993.

Ochs, H., and Whitford, A. B. "Milgram Experiments." In J. Rabin (ed.), *Encyclopedia of Public Administration and Public Policy.* New York: Marcel Dekker, 2004. Internet [http://marceldekker.com] (accessed Apr. 26, 2004).

Organization for Economic Co-operation and Development. Public Management Group. "Ethics Checklist." Paris: Organization for Economic Co-operation and Development, Nov. 1997.

Organization for Economic Co-operation and Development. "Building Public Trust, Ethics Measures in OECD Countries." Public Management Policy Brief no. 7. Paris: Organization for Economic Co-operation and Development, Sept. 2000a. Internet (accessed Mar. 14, 2004).

Organization for Economic Co-operation and Development. *Trust in Government: Ethics Measures in OECD Countries.* Paris: Organization for Economic Co-operation and Development, Sept. 2000b.

Organization for Economic Co-operation and Development. "Recommendation of the Council on OECD Guidelines for Managing Conflict of Interest in the Public Interest." Paris: Organization for Economic Co-operation and Development, 2003. Internet [http://www.oecd.org/dataoecd/60/43/1899427.pdf] (accessed Mar. 17, 2004).

Organization for Economic Co-operation and Development. Recommendation of the Council on OECD Guidelines for managing conflict of interest in the public service. Paris: Organization for Economic Co-operation and Development, June 2003. Internet [http://www.oecd.org/dataoecd/13/22/2957360.pdf] (accessed Sept. 5, 2003).

Organization for Economic Co-operation and Development. "Managing Conflict of Interest in the Public Service." Draft Policy Brief. Paris: Organization for Economic Co-operation and Development, June 2004.

Organization of American States (OAS), General Assembly. "Inter-American Convention against Corruption." 1996. Internet [http://www.oas.org/juridico/english/followup.htm] (accessed Mar. 14, 2004).

Osborne, D., and Gaebler, T. *Reinventing Government: How the Entrepreneurial Spirit is Transforming the Public Sector.* Reading, Mass.: Addison-Wesley, 1992.

Osiel, M. "Obeying Orders: Atrocity, Military Discipline, and the Law of War." *California Law Review,* 1998, *86,* 939. Internet [http://www.law.berkeley.edu/journals/clr/library/osiel01.html] (accessed June 14, 2004).

Parkinson, C. N. *Parkinson's Law and Other Studies in Administration.* Boston: Houghton Mifflin, 1957.

Patterson, B. H., Jr. *The Ring of Power: The White House Staff and Its Expanding Role in Government.* New York: Basic Books, 1988.

Peter, L. J., and Hull, R. H. *The Peter Principle.* New York: Morrow, 1969.

Peters, T. "Contrasting Public and Private Leadership: An Interview with Tom Peters." *State Government,* 1987, *60,* 241–244.

Pew Center for the People and the Press. "How Americans View Government: Deconstructing Distrust." 1998. Internet [http://people-press.org] (accessed Oct. 18, 1998).

Pianin, E. "Study Finds Net Gain from Pollution Rules, OMB overturns Past Findings on Benefits." *Washington Post,* Sept. 27, 2003. Internet [http://www.washingtonpost.com] (accessed Sept. 27, 2003).

Pitcaithley, D. T. "Philosophical Underpinnings of the National Park Idea." 2001. Internet [http://www.cr.nps.gov/history/hisnps/NPSThinking/underpinnings.htm] (accessed Dec. 17, 2003).

Plant, J. "Standards of Conduct." In J. Rabin (ed.), *Encyclopedia of Public Administration and Public Policy.* Marcel Dekker, 2003. Internet [http://marceldekker.com] (accessed Apr. 14, 2003).

Pollock-Byrne, J. M. *Ethics in Crime and Justice: Dilemmas and Decisions.* Pacific Grove, Calif.: Brooks/Cole, 1989.

"Popularity of Electronic Filing Saves State Resources." *The Ethics Report: A Publication of the NY State Ethics Commission,* Apr. 2004, p. 1.

Potamianos, P. "Codes of Ethics in Municipal Government: A Survey of Major Cities." Unpublished paper submitted to author's seminar on administrative ethics at the University of Connecticut, Spring 1990.

Powers, R. "To Obey or Not to Obey?" *About U.S. Military Newsletter.* 2004. Internet [http://usmilitary.about.com/cs/militarylaw1/a/obeyingorders.htm] (accessed June 14, 2004).

President's Commission on Federal Ethics Law Reform. *To Serve with Honor: Report and Recommendations to the President*. Washington, D.C.: U.S. Government Printing Office, 1989.

President's Council on Integrity and Efficiency. *A Progress Report to the President, Fiscal Year 2002*. Washington, D.C.: President's Council on Integrity and Efficiency, 2003.

Public Broadcasting Service, 2002. Compensation Victims. NewsHour Online, Feb. 6, 2002. Internet [http://www.pbs.org/newshour/bb/terrorism/jan-june02/victims_2-6.html] (accessed Dec. 12, 2003).

Quinnipiac University Poll, national registered voters, February 13–19, 2002. Data provided courtesy of The Roper Center for Public Opinion Research, University of Connecticut.

Raspberry, W. "Give the Candidates Amnesty." *Washington Post,* Oct. 9, 1987, p. A27.

Rawls, J. *Theory of Justice*. Cambridge, Mass.: Harvard University Press, 1971.

Recer, P. "Shuttle Probe Cites 'Missed Signals.'" Associated Press, May 14, 2003. Internet [http://www.msnbc.com/news/913529.asp?0sl=-13] (accessed May 13, 2003).

Rest, J. "Developmental Psychology and Value Education." In B. Munsey (ed.), *Moral Development, Moral Education, and Kohlberg*. Birmingham, Ala.: Religious Education Press, 1980.

Rest, J. *Moral Development*. New York: Praeger, 1986.

Rhoads, S. (ed.). *Valuing Life: Public Policy Dilemmas*. Boulder, Colo.: Westview Press, 1980.

Rice, D., and Dreilinger, C. "Rights and Wrongs of Ethics Training." *Training and Development Journal,* 1990, *44,* 103–108.

Richter, W. L. "Have Ethics Regulations Gone Too Far?" *PA Times,* July 21, 1989.

Richter, W. L., Burke, F., and Doig, J. W. (eds.). *Combatting Corruption, Encouraging Ethics: A Sourcebook for Public Service Ethics*. Washington, D.C.: American Society for Public Administration, 1990.

Rimer, S. "Bright, Eager and Willing to Cheat." *New York Times,* July 2, 2003, p. A18.

Rion, M. *The Responsible Manager. Practical Strategies for Ethical Decision Making*. West Hartford, Conn.: Resources for Ethics and Management, 1996. Originally published New York: HarperCollins, 1990.

Riordan, W. L. "Honest Graft." In J. A. Gardiner and D. J. Olson (eds.), *Theft of the City: Readings on Corruption in Urban America*. Bloomington: Indiana University Press, 1974.

Roberts, N. "Keeping Public Officials Accountable through Dialogue: Resolving the Accountability Paradox." *Public Administration Review,* 2002, *62*(6), 658–669.

Roberts, W. *Leadership Secrets of Attila the Hun*. New York: Warner Books, 1987.

Rohr, J. A. *Ethics for Bureaucrats: An Essay on Law and Values*. (2nd ed.) New York: Marcel Decker, 1989.

Rohr, J. A. "Law and Ethics." In J. Rabin (ed.), *Encyclopedia of Public Administration and Public Policy*. Marcel Dekker, Mar. 2003. Internet [http://marceldekker.com] (accessed Apr. 14, 2003).

Roig-Franzia, M. "Two Tablets May Renew a High Court Headache." *Washington Post,* Aug. 31, 2003. Internet [http://www.washingtonpost.com] (accessed Aug. 31, 2003).

Romzek, B. S., and Dubnick, M. J. "Accountability in the Public Sector: Lessons from the Challenger Tragedy." *Public Administration Review,* 1987, *47*(3), 227–238.

Rosenbaum, D. E. "Disaster Aid: The Mix of Mercy and Politics." *New York Times,* Nov. 1, 2003. Internet [http://www.nytimes.com] (accessed Nov. 1, 2003).

Rosenbloom, D. "The Constitution as a Basis for Public Administration." In P. Madsen and J. M. Shafritz (eds.), *Essentials of Government Ethics*. New York: Penguin Books, 1992.

Ross, J., and Myers, P. *We Will Never Forget*. Austin, Tex.: Eakin Press, 1996.

Ruch, W. A., and Newstrom, J. W. "How Unethical Are We?" *Supervisory Management*, 1975, *20*, 16–21.

Sakharov, A. "Foreword." In G. Medvedev (E. Rossiter, trans.), *The Truth About Chernobyl*. New York: Basic Books, 1991.

Saner, M. "Ethics Codes Revisited: A New Focus on Outcomes." Policy Brief no. 20. Ottawa, Canada: Institute on Governance, June 2004. Internet [http://www.iog.ca] (accessed June 30, 2004).

Schelling, T. C. "Economic Reasoning and the Ethics of Policy." *Public Interest*, 1981, *63*, 37–61.

Schemo, D. J. "Policy Shift on Handling Cases of Complaints at Air Force Academy." *New York Times,* June 7, 2003. Internet [nytimes.com] (accessed June 7, 2003).

Schön, D. A. *The Reflective Managers: How Professionals Think in Action*. New York: Basic Books, 1983.

Seidman, H., and Gilmour, R. *Politics, Position, and Power: From the Positive to the Regulatory State*. (4th ed.) New York: Oxford University Press, 1986.

Seligson, M. A. "Corruption and Democratization: What is to Be Done?" *Public Integrity*, 2001, *3*(3), 221–241.

Semple, K. "General Blames Command and Training Lapses for Prison Abuse." *New York Times*, May 11, 2004. Internet [http://www.nytimes.com] (accessed May 11, 2004).

Shabecoff, P. "Head of E.P.A. Bars Nazi Data in Study on Gas." *New York Times*, Mar. 23, 1988, pp. Al, A17.

Shalala, D. E. "The Buck Starts Here: Managing Large Organizations with Honesty and Integrity." Elliot Richardson Lecture delivered at the annual meeting of the American Society for Public Administration, Portland, Ore., Mar. 28, 2004. Internet [www.aspanet.org/about/history/RichardsonLecture.2004.pdf] (accessed June 29, 2004).

Shipley, A. "Campbell Cites Other USDOC Officials." *Washington Post*, Mar. 5, 2003, p. A3.

Shklar, J. N. *Ordinary Vices*. Cambridge, Mass.: Belknap Press of Harvard University Press, 1984.

Shogren, J. F., and Stamland, T. "Skill and the Value of Life." *Journal of Political Economy*, 2002, *110*(5), 1168–1173.

Shrader-Frechetter, K. "Risk." *Routledge Encyclopedia of Philosophy: Version 1.0*. 1998. Internet [http://www.rep.routledge.com] (accessed Mar. 10, 2003).

Simon, H. *Administrative Behavior*. New York: Macmillan, 1947.

Singer, P. *Practical Ethics*. Cambridge: Cambridge University Press, 1979.

Smart, J.J.C. "Utilitarianism." In C. H. Sommers (ed.), *Right and Wrong: Basic Readings in Ethics*. Orlando: Harcourt Brace, 1986.

Society of Professional Journalists. "Code of Ethics, revised 1996." Internet [http://www.spj.org/ethics_code.asp] (accessed Apr. 19, 2004).

Solomon, D. "Life after Whistle-Blowing." *New York Times,* June 6, 2004, magazine section. Internet [http://www.nytimes.com] (accessed June 6, 2004).

Solomon, J. "As Cultural Diversity of Workers Grows, Experts Urge Appreciation of Differences." *Wall Street Journal*, Sept. 12, 1990, pp. BI, B13.

Sprinthall, R., and Sprinthall, R. C. "Value and Moral Development." *Easier Said Than Done*, 1988, *1*, 16–22.

Stark, A. "The Appearance of Official Impropriety and the Concept of Political Crime." *Ethics*, Jan. 1995, *105*, 326–351.

Stark, A. "Beyond Quid Pro Quo: What Is Wrong With Private Gain From Public Office." *American Political Science Review*, 1997, *91*(1), 108–120.

Stark, A. *Conflict of Interest in American Public Life.* Cambridge, Mass.: Harvard University Press, 2000.

Steffens, L. "Los Angeles and the Apple." In J. A. Gardiner and D. J. Olson (eds.), *Theft of the City: Readings on Corruption in Urban America.* Bloomington: Indiana University Press, 1974. (Originally published in *The Autobiography of Lincoln Steffens.* San Diego, Calif.: Harcourt Brace Jovanovich, 1931.)

Steffens, L. "Philadelphia: Corrupt and Contented." In W. Murin (ed.), *Classics of Urban Politics and Administration.* Oak Park, Ill.: Moore, 1982. (Originally published in *The Shame of the Cities.* New York: Hill & Wang, 1904.)

Stein, H. (ed.). "The Glovis-Ballinger Dispute." In *Public Administration and Policy Development: A Case Book.* The Inter-University Case Program. Orlando: Harcourt Brace, 1952.

Stewart, D. W. "Managing Competing Claims: An Ethical Framework for Human Resource Decision Making." *Public Administration Review,* 1984, *44,* 14–22.

Stewart, D. W., Sprinthall, N. W., and Shafer, D. M. "Moral Development in Public Administration." In T. L. Cooper (ed.), *Handbook of Administrative Ethics.* (2nd ed.) New York: Marcel Dekker, 2001.

Stillman, R. J., II (ed.). *Public Administration: Concepts and Cases.* (3rd ed.) Boston: Houghton Mifflin, 1984.

Summers, H. G. "Introduction." In L. J. Matthews and D. E. Brown (eds.), *The Parameters of Military Ethics.* Washington, D.C.: Pergamon-Brassey's-International Defense Publishers, 1989.

Sumner, W. *Welfare, Happiness, and Ethics.* Oxford: Clarendon Press, 1996.

"Supervisors Plan to Aid S.F. Official." *San Francisco Chronicle,* Mar. 30, 2004. As quoted on the COGEL Web site's news summary. Internet [http://www.stateandfed.com/weekly_updates/email0405.htm] (accessed Apr. 5, 2004).

Swisher, L. L., Rizzo, A., and Marley, M. A. "Moral Reasoning among Public Administrators." *Public Integrity,* 2002, *3*(1), 53–68.

Taylor, F. G. "A Matter of One Man's Faith, Sub Base Physician Files Complaint against Navy after Clash over His Birth Control Views." *Hartford Courant,* Jan. 25, 2004. Internet [http://www.ctnow.com] (accessed Jan. 25, 2004).

Tedesco, M., and Harris, J. "Civil Disobedience." In J. Rabin (ed.), *Encyclopedia of Public Administration and Public Policy.* 2002. Internet [http://www.dekker.com] (accessed Apr. 14, 2004).

Terkel, S. N. "Reflections on a Course in Ethics." *Harper's,* Oct. 1973, 11–18.

Terkel, S. N., and Duval, R. S. (eds.). *Encyclopedia of Ethics.* New York: Facts on File, 1999.

Thompson, D. F. "Moral Responsibility of Public Officials: The Problem of Many Hands." *American Political Science Review,* 1980, *74,* 905–916.

Thompson, D. F. "The Private Lives of Public Officials." In J. L. Fleishman, L. Liebman, and M. H. Moore (eds.), *Public Duties: The Moral Obligations of Government Officials.* Cambridge, Mass.: Harvard University Press, 1981.

Thompson, D. F. "The Possibility of Administrative Ethics." *Public Administration Review,* 1985, *45,* 555–561.

Thompson, D. F. "Mediated Political Corruption: The Case of the Keating Five." *American Political Science Review,* 1993, *87*(2), 369–381.

Time/CNN/Harris Interactive Poll. July 10–11, 2002. Data provided by The Roper Center for Public Opinion Research, University of Connecticut.

Tong, R. *Ethics in Policy Analysis.* Series in Occupational Ethics. Englewood Cliffs, N.J.: Prentice Hall, 1986.

Transparency International. *Global Corruption Report 2004.* 2004. Internet [http://www.globalcorruptionreport.org] (accessed Apr. 7, 2004).

Tranter, R.A.F. "Ethical Problems Today." *Public Management,* 1987, *69,* 25.

Trevino, L., Hartman, L., and Brown, M. "A Qualitative Investigation of Perceived Executive Ethical Leadership: Perceptions from Inside and Outside the Executive Suite." *Human Relations,* 2003, *1,* 5–38.

Tuohy, L. "Public Information vs. Personal Privacy." *Hartford Courant,* Dec. 21, 1993, C1, 13.

United Nations. "Secretary General Urges Full Enforcement of New Merida Convention, Seen as Major Victory in Struggle against Corruption." Press Release SG/SM/9065, L/T/4376, SOC/CP/274. Sept. 12, 2004. Internet [http://www.un.org/News/Press/docs/2003/sgsm9065.doc.htm] (accessed Apr. 7, 2004).

United Nations Online Network in Public Administration and Finance (UNPAN). *UNPAN Newsletter,* Feb. 2004, *2*(1). Internet [http://unpan1.un.org/intradoc/groups/public/documents/un-other/unpan014576.html] (accessed Apr. 7, 2004).

U.S. Bureau of the Census. *Statistical Abstract of the United States.* 2003. Internet [http://www.census.gov/prod/www/statistical-abstract-03.html] (accessed June 8, 2004).

U.S. Bureau of Labor Statistics. "Labor Statistics." Internet [http://data.bls.gov/servlet/SurveyOutputServlet] (data extracted June 8, 2004].

U.S. Department of Defense. Office of the Inspector General. *Indicators of Fraud in Department of Defense Procurement.* Washington, D.C.: U.S. Department of Defense, June 1, 1984.

U.S. Department of Justice. Announcement of Interim Final Rule for VCF. Dec. 20, 2001. Internet [http://www.usdoj.gov/victimcompensation/pressdec20.htm] (accessed Aug. 8, 2003).

U.S. Department of Justice. Victims Compensation Fund, Interim Final Rule. Dec. 21, 2001. Internet [http://www.usdoj.gov/victimsCompensation/victimcompfedreg.pdf] (accessed Sept. 13, 2003).

U.S. House of Representatives. "Abuses, Favoritism, and Mismanagement in HUD Programs" (Pt. 1). Hearings before the Employment and Housing Subcommittee of the Committee on Government Operations, May 8–June 16, 1989. Washington, D.C.: U.S. Government Printing Office, 1990.

U.S. Military Academy. Associates, Department of Behavioral Sciences and Leadership. *Leadership in Organizations.* (3rd ed.) West Point, N.Y.: United States Military Academy, 1985.

U.S. Office of Government Ethics. *First Biennial Report to Congress.* Washington, D.C.: U.S. Office of Government Ethics, Mar. 1990a.

U.S. Office of Government Ethics. *The Informal Advisory Letters and Memoranda and Formal Opinions of the United States Office of Government Ethics, 1979–1988.* Washington, D.C.: U.S. Government Printing Office, 1990b.

U.S. Office of Government Ethics. *Annual Performance Report, FY1999.* Washington, D.C.: U.S. Office of Government Ethics, Mar. 2000.

U.S. Office of Government Ethics. Letter to a designated agency ethics official, informal advisory opinion 02 x 9, Oct. 30, 2002. Internet [http://www.usoge.gov] (accessed Apr. 5, 2004).

U.S. Olympic Committee. "Documents on Governance and Ethics." Internet [http://www.olympic-usa.org] (accessed Sept. 1, 2003).

U.S. Senate. Committee on Labor and Public Welfare. *Report of the Subcommittee on Labor and Public Welfare on Ethical Standards in Government.* 82d Cong., 1st Sess., 1951.

U.S. Senate. "Abuses in the Section 8 Moderate Rehabilitation Program." Hearings before the Committee on Banking, Housing, and Urban Affairs, May 17–Oct. 31, 1989. Washington, D.C.: U.S. Government Printing Office, 1990.

U.S. Senate Select Committee on Ethics. *Revising the Senate Code of Official Conduct Pursuant to Senate Resolution 109.* 96th Congress, 2nd sess., Nov. 1980.

Usher, D. "The Value of Life for Decision Making in the Public Sector." *Social Philosophy & Policy,* 1985, *2*(2), 168–191.

van Natta, D., Jr. "Questioning Terror Suspects in a Dark and Surreal World." *New York Times,* Mar. 9, 2003. Internet [http://www.nytimes.com] (accessed Mar. 9, 2003).

Vela, S. "Major Who Refused Vaccine Leaves Service." *Cincinnati Enquirer,* Mar. 31, 2000. Internet [http://enquirer.com/editions/2000/03/31/loc_major_who_refused.html] (accessed June 14, 2004).

Viscusi, W. K. "Value of Risks to Life and Health." *Journal of Economic Literature,* 1993, *31*(4), 1912–1946.

Volcker Commission. *Leadership for America: Rebuilding the Public Service.* Report of the National Commission on the Public Service. Washington, D.C.: National Commission on the Public Service, 1989. (Commission copy.)

Waldo, D. *The Enterprise of Public Administration.* Novato, Calif.: Chandler 8C Sharp, 1981.

Wall Street Journal. Survey of 1,000 corporate executives, Apr. 6, 1988, p. 27.

Walzer, M. "Political Action: The Problem of Dirty Hands." *Philosophy and Public Affairs,* 1973, *2,* 160–180.

Wamsley, G. L., and others. *Refounding Public Administration.* Thousand Oaks, Calif.: Sage, 1990.

Warren, K. F. "Administrative Discretion." In J. Rabin (ed.), *Encyclopedia of Public Administration and Public Policy.* Marcel Dekker, Mar. 2003. Internet [http://marceldekker.com] (accessed Apr. 14, 2003).

Washington Post. "Red Cross's 9/11 Fund Questioned: Better Business Bureau Wants to See if Account Meets Standards," Feb. 17, 2002a, p. A7.

Washington Post. "Red Cross to Clarify How money is Spent," June 5, 2002b, p. A9.

Washington Post/Henry J. Kaiser Family Foundation/Harvard University Value Study. July 29–Aug. 18, 1998. *Washington Post,* Oct. 4, 1998. Internet [http://www.washingtonpost.com] (accessed Oct. 30, 1998).

Waugh, W. L., Jr., and Hy, R. J. "Introduction to Emergency Management." In W. L. Waugh, Jr., and R. J. Hy (eds.), *Handbook of Emergency Management.* Westport, Conn.: Greenwood Press, 1990.

Weale, A. "Public Interest." In *Routledge Encyclopedia of Philosophy,* Version 1.0. Internet [http://www.rep.routledge.com] (accessed Mar. 10, 2003).

Weimer, L. Memorandum on ethics codes, Alaska State Legislature. May 2, 1990.

Welzel, C., Inglehart, R., and Klingemann, H-D. "Human Development as a Theory of Social Change: A Cross-Cultural Perspective." Undated. Internet [http://wvs.isr.umich.edu/papers/KRISEJPR.pdf] (accessed Mar. 14, 2004).

Wenker, Lt. Col. K. H. "Morality and Military Obedience." *Air University Review,* July-Aug. 1981. Internet [http://www.airpower.maxwell.af.mil/airchronicles/aureview/1981/jul-aug/wenker.htm] (accessed June 14, 2004).

Werhane, P. H. *Moral Imagination and Management Decision-Making.* Oxford: Oxford University Press, 1999.

White, L. D. *The Jacksonians: A Study in Administrative History, 1829–1861.* New York: Macmillan, 1954.

White, R. D., Jr. "Public Ethics, Moral Development, and the Enduring Legacy of Lawrence Kohlberg: Implications for Public Officials." *Public Integrity,* 1999, *1*(2), 121–134.

White, R. D., Jr. "Moral Development Theory." In J. Rabin (ed.), *Encyclopedia of Public Administration and Public Policy.* 2003. Internet [http://marceldekker.com] (accessed Apr. 14, 2004).

Wholey, J. S. *Evaluation and Effective Public Management.* Foundations of Public Management Series. Boston: Little, Brown, 1983.

"Who's Who on County Ethics Commission." *Washington Post,* Mar. 13, 2003, pp. B1, B3.

Wildavsky, A. "What Is Permissible So That This People May Survive? Joseph the Administrator." The 1989 John Gaus Lecture. *PS: Political Science & Politics,* 1989, *22,* 779–788.

Williams, R. L. "Conflict of Interest." In J. Rabin (ed.), *Encyclopedia of Public Administration and Public Policy.* New York: Marcel Dekker, 2002. Internet [http://marceldekker.com] (accessed Apr. 14, 2004).

Wilson, J. Q. *Bureaucracy: What Government Agencies Do and Why They Do It.* New York: Basic Books, 1990.

Wilson, W. W. *Congressional Government: A Study in American Politics.* New York: World Publishing, 1956. (Originally published Boston: Houghton Mifflin, 1885.)

Wilson, W. W. "The Study of Administration." In J. M. Shafrtiz and A. C. Hyde (eds.), *Classics of Public Administration.* (2nd ed.) Chicago: Dorsey, 1987. (Originally published in *Political Science Quarterly,* 1887, *2,* 197–222.)

Wolf, C. "The Special Master's Spin." *Fix the Fund.* Updated Mar. 7, 2003a. Internet [http://www.fixthefund.org] (accessed Aug. 15, 2003).

Wolf, C. "Letter of Nov. 17, 2003 to Kenneth Feinberg," Nov. 2003b. Internet [http://www.fixtheFund.org/Submission-Letter-to-Feinberg.htm] (accessed Dec. 20, 2003).

World Values Survey. "Introduction." Internet [http://www.worldvaluessurvey.org] (accessed Feb. 23, 2004).

Young, J. R. "Students' Political Awareness Hits Highest Level in a Decade." *Chronicle of Higher Education,* Jan. 30, 2004, *50*(21), A30.

Zernike, K. "Only a Few Spoke Up on Abuse as Many Soldiers Stayed Silent." *New York Times,* May 22, 2004. Internet [http://www.nytimes.com] (accessed May 22, 2004).

Zimmerman, J. S. "Ethics in Local Government." *Management Information Service Report 8.* Washington, D.C.: International City Management Association, Aug. 1976.

NAME INDEX

SUBJECT INDEX

A

ABC News, 67

Aborigines' Protection Society, 278

Abortion, 67

Abu Ghraib prison abuses, 99–100

Abuse of office: incompetence as, 112–114; for personal dissent, 61–62, 63–64; for personal gain, 80–83; temptation of, 264–265; time abuse as, 240–242; vulnerability assessment for, 263–264

Academic organizations, 303–304

Accommodation, 136–138, 139

Accountability: controls and, 16, 32–33; as formal obligation, 32–33; individual responsibility and, 98–117; publicity test for, 93

Act to Establish the Treasury Department, 209

Act utilitarianism, 126, 127

Action guides, 148

Administrative actions, agency, 210–211, 212

Administrative law judges (ALJs), 189

Administrative Procedure Act, 58

Adulthood, 29

Africa: ethics programs in, 224, 296; regional agreements of, 224; traditional values of, 231

African National Congress, 294

Agencies: building ethical, 235–268; collaborative relationship issues of, 244–247; enforcement in, 210, 211; ethics audits for, 262–265; ethics impact statement (EthIS) and process for, 255, 257–262; ethics programs and systems for, 248–255; managers' role in, 235–236; objections to ethics systems in, 251–254; rules of thumb for, 255, 256–257; team ethic in, 243; techniques for integrating ethics into, 250; time abuse in, 240–242; work norms in, 242–243; workforce diversity in, 238–240. *See also* Rules and regulations, agency

Agency Ethics Program Questionnaire, 263

Alabama: ethics code of, 196, 200;

Supreme Court, 56–57

Alaska: ethics code of, 190, 200; land claims scandal in, 177

Altruism, 170

Ambiguity, 29; ethical reasoning and, 121, 125; personal integrity and, 36–37, 139; role-generated claims and, 35–36

American Bar Association, 85, 280; Canon 9 of, 199; Model Rules of Professional Conduct of, 192, 280, 291

American Board of Internal Medicine, 67

American Institute of Certified Public Accountants, 32

American Red Cross (ARC), 49, 93, 94, 214; fundraising ethics case study of, 93–97

American Revolution, 130, 174

American Society for Public Administration (ASPA), 17, 32–33, 125, 138, 191, 248, 290; ethics code and values of, 27, 37, 53, 86, 111, 112, 192, 290

Amnesty International, 286

Anarchy, State, and Utopia (Nozick), 288